MW01128397

Robert Morris's Folly

THE LEWIS WALPOLE SERIES

IN EIGHTEENTH-CENTURY CULTURE AND HISTORY

The Lewis Walpole Series, published by Yale University Press with the aid of the Annie Burr Lewis Fund, is dedicated to the culture and history of the long eighteenth century (from the Glorious Revolution to the accession of Queen Victoria). It welcomes work in a variety of fields, including literature and history, the visual arts, political philosophy, music, legal history, and the history of science. In addition to original scholarly work, the series publishes new editions and translations of writing from the period, as well as reprints of major books that are currently unavailable. Though the majority of books in the series will probably concentrate on Great Britain and the Continent, the range of our geographical interests is as wide as Horace Walpole's.

Published with assistance from the Annie Burr Lewis Fund.

Yale University Press books may be purchased in quantity for educational, business, or promotional use.
For information, please e-mail sales.press@yale.edu (U.S. office) or sales@yaleup.co.uk (U.K. office).

Set in Fournier type by Westchester Book Group.
Printed in the United States of America.

Library of Congress Cataloging-in-Publication Data
Smith, Ryan K.
Robert Morris's folly : the architectural and financial failures of an American founder /
Ryan K. Smith.
pages   cm—(The Lewis Walpole series in eighteenth-century culture and history)
Includes bibliographical references and index.
ISBN 978-0-300-19604-7 (hardback)
1. Morris, Robert, 1734–1806—Finance, Personal.   2. Morris, Robert, 1734–1806—Homes
and haunts—Pennsylvania—Philadelphia.   3. Founding Fathers of the United States—Finance,
Personal.   4. Founding Fathers of the United States—Homes and haunts—Pennsylvania—
Philadelphia.   I. Title.
E302.6.M8S58 2014
973.3092'2—dc23
[B]
2014003765

A catalogue record for this book is available from the British Library.

This paper meets the requirements of ANSI/NISO Z39.48–1992 (Permanence of Paper).

10 9 8 7 6 5 4 3 2 1

Robert Morris's Folly

The Architectural and Financial Failures of an American Founder

Ryan K. Smith

Yale

UNIVERSITY PRESS

NEW HAVEN AND LONDON

When follies are pointed out, and vanity ridiculed,
it may be very improving.

Mary Wollstonecraft (1787)

Contents

Robert Morris's Philadelphia

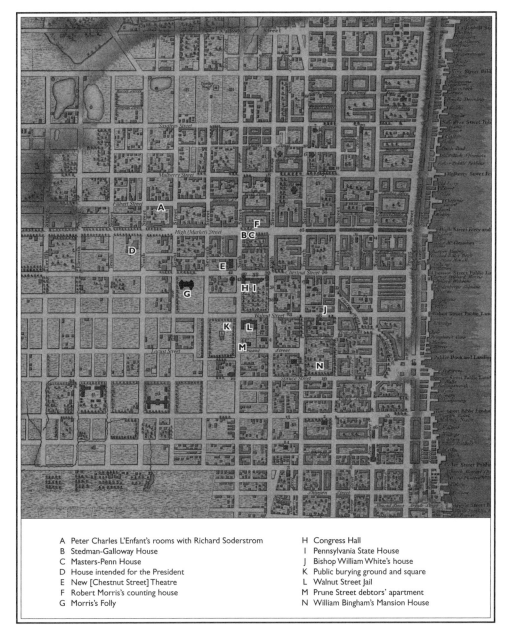

A Peter Charles L'Enfant's rooms with Richard Soderstrom
B Stedman-Galloway House
C Masters-Penn House
D House intended for the President
E New [Chestnut Street] Theatre
F Robert Morris's counting house
G Morris's Folly

H Congress Hall
I Pennsylvania State House
J Bishop William White's house
K Public burying ground and square
L Walnut Street Jail
M Prune Street debtors' apartment
N William Bingham's Mansion House

Philadelphia as it appeared at the turn of the nineteenth century; the city's eastern border—the Delaware River—is visible at right. (Detail of image from John Hills and John Cooke, *This Plan of the City of Philadelphia and it's [sic] Environs* . . . [Philadelphia: John Hills, 1797; London: John and Josiah Boydell, 1798]. Courtesy of the Library of Congress, Geography and Map Division. Customization by Bill Nelson.)

Robert Morris's Folly

Prologue

George Washington strode past the high wall along the street and headed for the barred doors of the building before him.

He had been in Philadelphia for nearly three weeks, having left Mount Vernon to again take command of the United States army. France and England were in the midst of a long war, and neither had accepted American attempts at neutrality. President John Adams knew his young nation could not afford a fight with either power. But as relations with France reached a crisis in 1798, he had called Washington out of his retirement, asking him to oversee the army as it prepared to defend against a rumored invasion.

Despite the clouds of war, Washington had enjoyed his return to the seat of the federal government. Each step of his journey north from Virginia had been accompanied by formal escorts, military exercises, salutes, and adoring crowds. Following his trumpeted arrival in Philadelphia on November 10, a procession of cavalry, infantry, and spectators had accompanied the old general to his lodgings, where, in the words of a newspaper editor, "he was saluted by the acclamations of the citizens who had collected once more to behold their Chief." Over the following weeks, Washington had attended feasts and celebrations thrown in his honor, and he had visited old friends and landmarks from his past.[1]

But on this late November day, the very day after he dined in the executive mansion with President Adams, he steeled himself for a different sort of reunion. He probably walked the few blocks from his boardinghouse to his destination in company with a commissioner or warden.

I

The general was going to visit the Walnut Street Jail, to take dinner with one of its inmates.

The jail's large, three-story façade was a familiar sight (fig. P.1). It stood across the street from Congress Hall and the memorable old Pennsylvania State House. In making their way toward the jail, Washington and his anxious escort bypassed its main entrance on Walnut Street to follow its wall around the side of the complex. After turning the final corner onto Prune Street, Washington faced his destination—a smaller, secure stone building known as the Prune Street debtors' apartment (figs. P.2 and P.3).

After treading up the narrow walk and gaining entry through the locked door, the visitors found a space more intimate than the larger jail but no less downcast. Inside, the air of a common room hung with the smells of beer, sweat, and tobacco smoke, amid the heat from a nearby stove. Benches along the walls were filled with the swaying forms of men and women.[2]

Figure P.1. Front entrance of the Walnut Street Jail as it appeared circa 1800. (William Russell Birch and W. Barker, *The City of Philadelphia, in the State of Pennsylvania, North America; as it Appeared in the Year 1800*, 2d ed. [(Philadelphia): W. Birch, 1804], plate 18. Courtesy of the Library Company of Philadelphia)

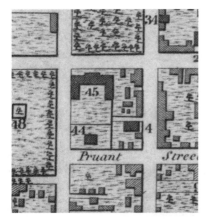

Figure P.2. Plan showing the Walnut Street Jail, with the main building (45) on the north and the Prune Street debtors' apartment (44) on the south. (Detail of image from John Hills and John Cooke, *This Plan of the City of Philadelphia and it's* [*sic*] *Environs* . . . [Philadelphia: John Hills, 1797; London: John and Josiah Boydell, 1798]. Courtesy of the Library of Congress, Geography and Map Division)

Figure P.3. The Prune Street debtors' apartment as it looked in 1798, as recalled by C[harles]. A. P[oulson], 1858. (Castner Scrapbooks, vol. 19, p. 36. Courtesy of the Free Library of Philadelphia)

Were these inmates quiet as they encountered Washington's recognizable face? Did they salute? Did they risk a hoot or a yell?

Certainly as solemn as he ever was, the former president followed the warden up to an inner chamber. Its door opened to reveal a whitewashed room furnished with a bed, some desks and chairs, two mirrors, and a borrowed table set for a formal meal. The man who stood to greet Washington was tall, though not as tall as his guest, and stout. His clothes were neat and adjusted with care. His thinning white hair was swept back and descended around the back of his neck. The man's jowls were thicker than when he and Washington first met. His grayish blue eyes surely displayed gratitude that the most revered man in the nation would come to see him here.[3]

That gratitude was doubly deserved. Washington risked not only his reputation in the visit, but also his life. Two weeks earlier, the prisoner had attested to a friend: "I have not been yet Honoured with the *visit,* there are People who think and tell others that it is unsafe to come here." Inmates and staff of the prison had been dying over the previous months, for Philadelphia had been roiled by a yellow fever epidemic during the summer. As the fever spread through the city, killing thousands of residents, the crowded prison was particularly hard-hit. In August, prisoners in the east wing rioted in order to flee the scene, seizing keys from a doctor and hoisting axes, iron bars, and other makeshift weapons until their uprising was put down by musket fire. Even into the cooler fall weather, prisoners continued to contract the gruesome disease. Doctors came to bleed and purge them in vain hopes of recovery, and as the buildings were aired and scrubbed and reorganized, Washington's "host" had been moved from one room to another. Until, in late November, he found himself face to face with his friend.[4]

The inmate was Robert Morris (fig. P.4). The two had known each other well for some twenty years, and despite Morris's recent, public failures he remained one of Washington's few intimate friends. They last dined together the previous year, at the final dinner Washington hosted as the nation's president. There, Morris raised his glass as a free man alongside other notables. His fortunes had taken a shocking turn since then.[5]

In his diary entry for November 27, 1798, Washington noted simply that he dined "in a family with Mr. Morris," suggesting that Morris's wife, Mary, and their grown daughter Maria—both of whom regularly attended Morris despite the risks and were close with the Washingtons—joined the small party.[6]

No record survives of what the group spoke about over their meal. But Morris and Washington had many issues from which to choose. Perhaps they recalled their most heroic times together. As a wealthy Philadelphia merchant, Robert Morris had played a key role in the American Revolution from the start. He served in Continental Congress and signed the Declaration of Independence. Washington befriended Morris in the midst of the latter's extraordinary efforts to supply and finance the troops, from the hungry,

Figure P.4. Portrait of Robert Morris by Bass Otis and Thomas Sully, 1824, based on a portrait by Gilbert Stuart, circa 1795. (Courtesy of the Historical Society of Pennsylvania)

frozen winter at Valley Forge in 1777 to the threatened mutinies over pay in 1781. Morris, with his extensive international fortune, had been able to secure funds through his own personal credit that the fledgling Continental government could not. Washington, exasperated by the states' inability or unwillingness to support his rabble army, came to view Morris as the sole force keeping his troops on the field. On one memorable occasion, when Washington called desperately for ammunition, Morris provided ninety tons of lead ballast from one of his own recently returned ships, to be made into musket cartridges. On another, Morris wheedled 144,000 livres of silver from the French commanders just in time to dispatch it to Washington's troops at the head of the Chesapeake, where his long-suffering men had refused to go any farther toward Yorktown without pay.[7]

Then too, the group may have reminisced about more pleasant social occasions during Washington's presidency. Both men had sat through the summer convention in 1787 when the new constitution was drafted, the Virginian living as a houseguest of the Morrises. Together they signed it (as Morris had likewise done for the Articles of Confederation preceding it), and they later celebrated its ratification. Upon Washington's election to the presidency, Morris took a position in the first Congress as senator from Pennsylvania, and the two families enjoyed the parties and visits that became so much a part of Washington's administration.

Most likely, Washington and the Morrises commiserated over recent events. Washington would have agonized with them over the sudden loss of the Morrises' grown son William a few weeks earlier to a "bilious" fever in Philadelphia during the epidemic. Morris lamented at the time, "His Value to his Family I never counted untill he was lost & now I see its magnitude & that it is irreparable." Earlier that summer, Washington had heard of the city's perils and extended what comfort he could from afar, writing the Morrises from Mount Vernon, "It is with extreme concern I hear that Philadelphia is again visited with the malignant fever. I hope neither you, nor Mrs Morris will remain in situations exposed to the Infection of it." He then offered to shelter the family: "If it were practicable, we should be very happy if She & Miss Morris & you along with them could remove to this place. Mrs W. & Miss C: unite in every good & friendly wish for you & them."[8]

At that time, Washington seems not to have heard of Morris's recent imprisonment, or perhaps he was being discreet. But as they all ate together, Washington would have shared in the sorrowful circumstances of Morris's disgrace. The speculations that were involved—mostly in land—were no different, though certainly more extensive, than hundreds of schemes embarked upon by others. While Washington and others had cautioned restraint, Morris himself had seen only limitless potential. He purchased millions upon millions of acres, from the Canadian border to Georgia, including western lands where counties had not yet been organized, as well as thousands of undeveloped lots in the new city of Washington. To Morris, the final outcome of such a gamble never seemed in doubt. The settlement and resale of these lands in the young republic—with its people overspreading the lands west of the Appalachians and its ports filling daily with European immigrants—promised wealth that beggared the imagination of even the richest man in America. But the republic proved more fractious than expected, and the French Revolution brought turmoil, leaving Morris in the humiliating position of having to flee the city and hide from his creditors, like a skulking thief. His subsequent arrest had been grim, although Morris bore up when the sheriff led him to debtors' prison in February 1798.

Rash speculation and the resulting debt had landed him in jail. And his failure had impoverished countless others in turn, threatening the entire economy. But another element in his downfall better captured the imaginations and the tongues of those outside the prison walls. It was the Folly, Morris's Folly, as the unfinished building was becoming known. This empty hulk stood only a few blocks from the Walnut Street Jail, commanding an otherwise undeveloped stretch between Seventh and Eighth streets on Chestnut Street. Morris had broken ground for it five years earlier, at the height of his power, and poured hundreds of thousands of dollars into its unique plan. It was intended to be his crowning achievement, a proud home where his family could reap the rewards of Morris's long labor and service.

Now it was a joke, a mocking allegory. When the architect Benjamin Henry Latrobe toured Philadelphia that April, just after Morris was imprisoned, he pronounced Morris's Folly a "monster. . . . [A]ll the proportions are bad, all the horizontal & perpendicular lines broken to pieces, & the whole mass giving the idea of the reign of Lewis XIII [sic] in France or James I in England." Latrobe concluded simply, "It is impossible to decide which of the two is the maddest, the architect, or his employer. Both of them have been ruined by it." Morris, owing millions of dollars to creditors for his land schemes, was seen as being ruined by a house.[9]

Fate further twisted the irony. While Morris spent his days in jail threatened by yellow fever, city authorities had moved an overflow of the "vagrant and untried criminals" from the prison to temporary quarters in that very Folly that had made him notorious—into the drawing rooms and dining rooms Morris had intended for his family. Soon, local citizens would assail it with their own hands, pulling chimneypieces, carvings, and other prizes out of its wreckage. Decades later, local journalists were still telling the house's story, explaining that "such a magnificent edifice . . . , which was intended to have all the characteristics of a palace, was looked upon as offensive to plain and simple people. Hence, as the building progressed it was the talk, the wonder, and on many tongues the censure, of the town."[10]

It was true that the building's architect shared a fate similar to that of Morris, dying impoverished and disgraced. The Folly was designed by Peter (Pierre) Charles L'Enfant, the much lauded, French-born engineer who had served on Washington's wartime staff. After L'Enfant's monumental vision for the federal city on the Potomac River went foul, he brought that same sensibility to Morris's residence. He foresaw a Parisian-inspired masterpiece, breaking Philadelphia's provincial mold with a sprawling plan, decorative sculptured marble, a mansard roof, and plasterwork from the hands of master craftsmen. And why not, on behalf of one of the first citizens of the republic? After all, Morris explained, his fate was one "brought on me by a desire to provide too amply for a family whose happiness is my greatest enjoyment."[11]

But to debate the point was useless. By November 1798, Morris found himself living out a cautionary tale for his young nation. On one level, it was a universal lesson on human pride and greed. But on another level, Morris's story demonstrated the new nation's precariousness. After a difficult war followed by a series of rough experiments in democracy, Americans in the 1790s were divided by region, torn by the French Revolution and British traditions, unsettled by new political parties, alarmed by Indian uprisings on the borderlands, and buffeted by all manner of epidemics, financial panics, revivals, and social reforms. In this atmosphere, citizens prized their developing ideals and worked to guard those ideals against perceived threats. Everything was a portent. L'Enfant's designs for Morris's unprecedented house sparked questions about how a grandiose French mansion—a *palace*—fit into Philadelphia's streetscape. In a nation established on republican principles, what did it mean for Morris and his family to presume to live in such a manner? Was this a stride forward in the development of American art, or something sinister?

Washington offered a differing example. Although he lived on a lavish estate, it nevertheless fit within the customs and expectations of the Virginia gentry. He had walked a fine line as president, holding something like an aristocratic court, but he still retained the people's affections as "Mr. President." And he understood the importance of the public renunciation of power. Twice he had endeared himself to Americans in impressive displays of restraint, the first time when he returned his sword and command to Congress at the conclusion of the Revolutionary War, and the second when he voluntarily withdrew from the presidency after two terms. Such restraint composed the fabric of their experimental new government. Civic virtue, the ability to value public interest over individual gain, was widely acknowledged as necessary for a self-governing republic to hold. These broader concerns would outlast the early republic and animate later generations, as big bankers, railroad barons, oil men, media kings, hoteliers, entertainers, and con artists sought to set themselves apart through extravagant individual visions that shook the social fabric. Morris's Folly, in light of Washington's deliberate example, set up the essential question: what do the very wealthiest Americans owe their fellow citizens?[12]

Washington and Morris remained friends, loyal to one another even in Morris's disgrace. In the prison room, each man toasted the other's health, and that of their families, with drink provided by Morris's scant resources. Washington would have repeated his invitation of hospitality to Mary and Maria, and then, when it was time, stood to leave. He turned from the cell, and then from the prison, leaving Morris to brood over the dark, unfinished palace that was to cap the career of America's most ambitious founder.

1. His Capital

He bumped along in his carriage all day until it came to rest at the darkened New Jersey wharf. The evening was cool and windy, and the river in front of him churned. The fires and snug lights of New York City houses glowed across the river through the fog, but in this weather the distance was just too far. Robert Morris remembered his wife's earlier words of caution, so he determined to prolong the journey one more day and risk "an uncomfortable night lodging" rather than risk his life crossing the waters.[1]

At least he had company. Earlier in the day, his carriage had overtaken his fellow senator from Pennsylvania, William Maclay, also traveling north to New York for the opening session of the first federal Congress under the new Constitution. Morris had then invited Maclay to ride with him for the rest of the trip. Maclay, a lawyer from the Susquehanna region, was a polite man, though moody and suspicious. Morris would have to make do with his conversation. Somewhere behind the two senators, Pennsylvania's four newly elected delegates to the House of Representatives followed on their own.[2]

Who could have foreseen this caravan? Less than two years earlier, in the summer of 1787, Morris had sat among an assortment of delegates in a tense, closed-door convention in Philadelphia as they haggled over a brash new plan to strengthen the national government. That fall, their proposed Constitution had faced severe, dogged criticism in the various states. But with that battle successfully behind them, on March 4, 1789, after a fitful night's rest on the waterfront, Morris, Maclay, and the rest of their party rose early, and, with the assistance of Morris's coachman, they boarded the first light's ferry and prepared to enter the seat of the new government to take up their elected roles.

Once ashore, the travelers stepped into a carnival of expectation. The day began with the roar of eleven cannons saluting the new government, one for each of the states that had already ratified the Constitution. Morris checked in with his host, William Constable, a local merchant and business partner, and then made his way through the busy streets to the senate chamber. Along the way, he noted that the cannon salute, the federal colors flapping from the tops of buildings, and the "ringing of Bells & crowds of People . . . gave the air of a grand festival." Such sights and their prospects stirred the fifty-five-year-old financier. This day, he noted, "no doubt will hereafter be celebrated as a new era in the annals of the world."[3]

Morris arrived at the federal building to find it a work of art. And despite his patriotic pleasure in the day, he wanted nothing better than to heave up this capitol-like contraption from its foundation and carry it back to his home state. In this he was not alone. The federal government's location—what we would call the nation's "capital"—remained a controversial subject. Seven years earlier, at the end of the Revolutionary War, a frustrated mob of soldiers demanding back pay had prompted Congress to flee its original station in Philadelphia, and the tenuous national government under the Articles of Confederation had flitted across the country, from Princeton to Annapolis, to Trenton, and then to New York City. The new Constitution addressed this tenuousness, and, in one measure intended to strengthen the government's position, it authorized Congress to create a special, independent federal district not exceeding ten square miles for its seat. The language did not specify a location; hence political wrangling began immediately for the district's placement, as well as for the location of the temporary capital while the district was being prepared. Citizens across the country, whether politician or not, were abuzz with what Morris and others termed this "question about residence."[4]

Morris wanted the residence fixed close to *his* home. He had a fine site in mind near his investment properties at the falls of the Delaware River opposite Trenton. Or perhaps the federal district should be placed just outside Philadelphia, near the village of Germantown, also close to his properties and influence. Whichever site was chosen, of course, Congress's temporary residence should be returned to Philadelphia in the meantime. Morris could argue numerous public benefits for such moves, but, like so many others involved in the debate, it was also apparent that he personally stood to gain.

Such moves would increase the prestige and demand for his own landhold-ings and bring all the contracts, jobs, and influence of the federal government into the embrace of his society. They would also keep him off the long, bumpy roads. His Pennsylvania colleagues shared his enthusiasm for removing the seat of government to their state, but even they disagreed among themselves regarding the preferred site. Senator Maclay refused to let go of the stubborn insistence that his own Susquehanna River would suit the country best. If they could reach no consensus, they would prove as useless to Pennsylvania as the Potomac, Baltimore, Wilmington, Trenton, or New York City men.[5]

For their part, the New Yorkers were making a serious bid to maintain their city as the temporary site. And the sumptuous federal building which Morris found this March morning was part of the strategy. Six months earlier, in preparation for the first presidential inauguration, city leaders had commis-sioned Major Peter Charles L'Enfant, a local resident at the time, to renovate their old City Hall for the federal government's use. L'Enfant understood the importance of the moment and the power of this stage set. He set to work at a furious pace with over two hundred laborers and transformed this drab build-ing at the corner of Wall and Nassau streets. His resulting "Federal Hall" ran at least $20,000 over budget, but it was spacious, luxuriously appointed, and striking in its blend of classical features and American symbolism (fig. 1.1). Morris took special note of the building, describing it as the "Fine Federal Edifice." He observed that "Major L'enfant has not finished his work," but "the room intended for the Senate" was ready. Standing in a chamber enclosed by crimson damask canopies and curtains, beneath a ceiling decorated with a sun and thirteen stars, Morris met seven other senators to open the minutes and promptly adjourn without a quorum. Later that day, Morris acknowl-edged that L'Enfant's lavish Federal Hall was being called "the Trap," while his fellow Pennsylvanian Frederick Muhlenberg soon added the hope that "however well contrived we shall find Room to get out of it."[6]

Weeks went by, and still there was no quorum, to the chagrin of Mor-ris and his pro-Constitution friends. Morris, away from his brood at home, passed the time with his grown son Thomas, who was in New York studying law. Once enough congressmen arrived for the electoral votes for president and vice president to be counted, Morris intended to return to Philadelphia and greet the sure victor on his journey north from Mount Vernon. Morris would help extend a proper welcome with other Pennsylvania dignitaries

Figure 1.1. "A view of the Federal Hall of the City of New York, as appeared in the year 1797; with the adjacent buildings thereto." The elegant new Federal Hall, standing amid New York City's colonial-era streets. (Lithograph by Henry R. Robinson [1847], based on "A View of Broad Street, Wall Street, and the City Hall," by John Joseph Holland, 1797. Courtesy of the Library of Congress, Prints and Photographs Division)

and then return to New York "in company with the General." But a new idea struck. Morris began pressuring the awaiting members of Congress to adjourn from New York as soon as the presidential votes were counted, and then immediately reconvene for good in Philadelphia as Washington arrived there. In the words of a representative from Virginia, "R. Morris says we may adjourn to that Place & meet the President, saving at least 3 Days by it: as no Business can be done here till he arrives." This controversial proposal— particularly shocking to the New Yorkers—met with little enthusiasm, and no motion to this effect was ultimately made. But Morris could wait a bit longer.[7]

The Senate finally convened and counted the votes on April 6, confirming that George Washington and John Adams had been elected president and vice president. Riders were immediately dispatched to Mount Vernon and Braintree with the news, while Morris sent a congratulatory letter to Washington, full of noble sentiments as well as his proposal to host the general overnight along his way. "I conclude that the unanimous voice of America is irresistable, and that you will soon set out on your journy," he wrote. "Mrs. Washington I hope, will accompany you, and as Philadelphia is in the route, Mrs. Morris joins me in the request that you will honour us with your company during your stay in that City." Further, "as the journy will be fatiguing, we hope you will make it a resting place of some days" before setting out to establish a household in New York City.[8]

Washington knew the financier well enough to understand his motivations. Still, he was tempted, though he had earlier decided not to accept any private accommodations on this momentous trip in order to avoid any appearance of favoritism. Thus Washington began his long ride, traveling without Martha, who would follow later, and on the morning of April 20 he passed out of the hands of his Delaware escorts into the mass of Pennsylvanians waiting for him at the state line. Over a rousing breakfast at Chester, he informed Morris that he would be lodging at the City Tavern. Morris satisfied himself by insisting upon hosting Martha and the family when they arrived. After breakfast, the procession entered Philadelphia for a day of parades, speeches, and fireworks, but Washington continued north the very next morning, finding a rapturous twenty-six-oar, four-part-harmony, thirteen-gun, mile-long welcome a few days later in New York on April 23.[9]

The following month, Mary Morris met Martha and her family outside Philadelphia on their journey north and brought the train to her town house amid the processions and throngs. After three days together, the two families set out for New York. Mary and Martha soon found their husbands waiting for them together at the Elizabeth Town docks, along with yet another celebratory public welcome for "Lady Washington."[10]

They would enjoy each other's company and the diversions of New York City until early July, when Mary Morris and daughter Maria returned home. By then, the formalities of opening the government had been completed, and Robert was engaged with several issues in Congress. There was an impost bill to provide federal revenue (Morris wanted a sizable, reliable income), a judiciary bill to organize the federal courts (Morris asked the opinions of his lawyer friends), a debate about official salaries (good pay was proper and necessary, he thought), and a series of proposed amendments to the Constitution (unimpressive to a federalist like Morris). He also bent Washington's ear on the subject of appointments to the judiciary, the executive branch, and other governmental positions.[11]

Behind it all, the residence question brewed. Would the northeasterners be able to hold New York as the temporary seat of government? Would the southerners be able to claim the permanent federal district? Could Pennsylvania play one group against the other for its own purposes? In May, a Massachusetts representative reported the plotting that had been ongoing for months: "The federal Hall is convenient & elegant far beyond my expectations. [E]very thing is done here to induce Congress to remain in this City, while Pensilvania Maryland and Virginia are holding up every alurement to call us away." A Pennsylvania representative murmured in June that "the people here presumptiously call their town the Capital, I don't suppose this folly will be suffered to last very long." In August, Peter Muhlenberg told a fellow Pennsylvanian that "the important question for removal from this place . . . is much agitated in private." As the issue moved toward its formal, public airing, members of Congress exchanged promises and threats across the city.[12]

Morris played an active role in the jockeying that summer. He brokered shifting deals with all numbers of other players in a confusing game of intrigue, despite the passions such a contest provoked in the delicate union. In the first week of September, the residence question finally opened on the floors of Congress. "This town has been much agitated for a week past upon the Questions of permanent & temporary residence," Morris wrote to his wife in early September. "I have not been a meer Spectator as you may easily suppose." On September 8, Morris brought up the delicate topic in conversation with Washington, whose resolute desire for a Potomac site was well known. It was not a good idea. Morris found him "very cautious in expressing himself, but I perceived that He is much dissatisfied with what is doing in this business and I think not a little angry at my agency in it." Morris supposed his own actions had "been represented to him as proceeding from interested motives but as I know my motives to be pure" and "as I believe that I am promoting the public interest, and faithfully discharging my Duty I shall go on let who will dislike or like it." In any case, Washington was hardly disinterested himself.[13]

Their friendship would survive, but it was further tested by Morris's ongoing labors for the residence. "I have been the prime mover in this affair," Morris boasted to another friend later in September. On the twenty-first, Morris stood up in the Senate to convey his state's official offer of the use of any publicly owned buildings in Philadelphia should Congress "incline to make choice of that city for the temporary residence of the Federal

Government." And the next day, when a bill promising to locate the permanent residence on the Susquehanna arrived in the Senate from the House, Morris moved to strike the mention of that location for another more to his liking. During heated deliberations two days later, he even suddenly told the Senate that Pennsylvania would give $100,000 for a settlement at Germantown. His appalled colleague Maclay responded by pointedly asking Morris before the entire Senate where he had gotten the authority to make such an offer. Morris, in the words of Maclay, "now came forward the Great Man & the Mercht. and pledged himself that if the State would not He would find the money." A prime mover indeed.[14]

But Morris's pockets were not deep enough that season. Morris was outmaneuvered at the last minute by the Virginians, led by James Madison, and, in a surprise move, by his own northeastern allies, who distrusted his promises to keep the temporary site in New York for a while longer and who were happy to postpone any decisions regarding the move. So the Pennsylvanians returned home in late September empty-handed. Their local press was not pleased with the results of Morris's parliamentary gamble, when the Susquehanna site had seemed within their grasp.[15]

In October, Senator William Grayson passed through Philadelphia on his way home to Virginia, and he spent a day with the frustrated financier. They met in the street, whereupon Morris characteristically invited Grayson to dinner. "I found him very much irritated with his dissapointment," Grayson reported to his colleague Madison. Morris indicated he had not given up the battle; he would pick up the bill in January at the start of the next session of Congress. From other sources, Grayson confirmed that the Pennsylvanians were still plotting, though discouraged and in disarray. One found "Morriss & Co. . . bewailing their misfortunes in as pathetic strains as ever Don Quixote & Sancho did." Madison himself met with the quixotic Morris in Philadelphia the following month and found him to have regained his poise, ready to start the dealing anew.[16]

Morris would find belated success. He did not get his wish to revisit the matter at the start of the next session in 1790; Madison and others blocked him on procedure. By then, the political landscape had changed—Washington's executive cabinet was in place, and Secretary of the Treasury Alexander Hamilton's newly introduced fiscal program entered the debate. From afar, Mary Morris, who had once told Robert, "You know that I am something of a Politician," followed this second round through her hus-

band's New York letters as eagerly as she had the first. As the struggle re-
commenced in May, Morris told her "You will readily conceive . . . that it is
not an easy matter to remove a Body of men composed as we are, and the
greater part of whom are not only contented but pleased with their situation." After a series of shadowy exchanges in June, involving Hamilton,
Madison, and Secretary of State Thomas Jefferson, among others, Philadelphia emerged as the temporary capital for ten years while the permanent site
for the district was to be laid out on the Potomac River. Morris, though not
entirely triumphant, still proved satisfied, and he wrote to Mary on July 2,
1790, to "congratulate you my Dearest Friend upon our Success." It would
at least keep him off the roads for the duration of time he wished to be a
senator. Others certainly played significant roles in the final outcome, but
Morris, leading the Pennsylvania contingent, had helped dislodge the temporary capital from New York City for Philadelphia. And who knew? Once
it was reestablished in the elegant Quaker city, perhaps it would be near
impossible to remove for the rough Potomac.[17]

Angry over their loss, New Yorkers blamed the person they felt most
responsible—Robert Morris. At least five different cartoons related to the
matter circulated on the streets that decisive summer, as the final removal
dealings became public knowledge. In one oversize print, Morris is the
central, larger-than-life figure shown walking in mid-stride toward Philadelphia with L'Enfant's Federal Hall, itself filled with tiny cheering congressmen, on his shoulder (fig. 1.2). The devil leads him on ("Come along, Bobby,"
the devil says) toward an enticing assemblage including a cross-dressed man
identified as Congress's "Pr[o]c[ures]s" and a Philadelphia prostitute ("here's
the Girls"). Behind Morris, citizens make disparaging remarks, while a
preacher offers to preach anywhere he is paid. The depiction of Federal Hall
itself is remarkably accurate, though Morris's own features are distorted.[18]

Other prints that summer employed different imagery but showed
Morris in the same role. In one cartoon, a giant Morris is shown leading the
way to Philadelphia while holding a money bag (fig. 1.3). He hoists a "Ladder of Preferment" up his back, its rungs filled with small, hat-waving congressmen ("Stick to it Bobby," one says). Morris pulls the minority members
along behind with strings tied to their noses ("What will they move to prolong our next session," asks one, with the reply from another, "The devil &
bobby will help them to something"). A final, particularly ominous cartoon
shows Morris at the helm of the ship *Constitution*, again following the devil's

Figure 1.2. Anonymous, Robert Morris moving Federal Hall to Philadelphia (1790). (Courtesy of the American Antiquarian Society)

lead. Morris's ship sails past New York, bound for the Potomac River by way of Philadelphia, yet with a waterfall before it in the river. This ship carries many huzza-ing representatives, but it also pulls a smaller, separate boat behind, which is filled with dissenting members who threaten to cut its tie cord (severing the union) before encountering the "danger" ahead. Such cartoons were discussed up and down the coast, in private letters and in newspapers, some of which contained poems or doggerel attacking Morris for his role in the removal. Newspaperman Philip Freneau published his widely circulated poem titled "The Removal" on August 10, 1790. Its second stanza read: "Such thankless usage much we fear'd / When Robert's coach stood ready geer'd, / And he, the foremost on the floor, / Sat pointing to the Quaker shore." Its concluding lines reversed Morris's Paulus Hook, New Jersey, ferry stop from a year and a half earlier: "This day the Federal Hall is clear'd, / To *Powles Hook* their barge is steer'd / Where Robert's coach stands ready geer'd." All these cartoons and verses attributed an Atlas-like power to his commanding figure.[19]

Morris acknowledged the abuse but remained sanguine. "The Yorkers are cunning and intrigueing," he wrote Mary. "They lay all the blame of

Figure 1.3. Y. Z. Sculp, "What think ye of C_o_n_ss now" / "View of C_o_n_ss on the road to Philadelphia" Robert Morris hauling Congress to Philadelphia, with a "Ladder of Preferment & the Majority" on his back and "the Manority" in tow (1790). (Courtesy of the Historical Society of Pennsylvania)

this measure on me, and abuse me most unmercifully, both in the Public Prints, private conversations, and even in the streets." "However," he con-cluded, "I don't mind all they can do, and if I carry the point, I will, like a good Christian, forgive them all." Morris, though a proud member of Phila-delphia's Christ Church, did not have a holier-than-thou personality. He was well aware of past sins; several of the newspaper attacks referred to him as "bawdy Bob"; and he never scrupled to miss a good meal, a play, or merry-making with friends. Rather, he was genial, a man who could roll with events and relish his moments of success. All of the attacks merely confirmed whom he thought himself to be: one of the new nation's foremost public fig-ures and patrons, "the Financier" who had saved the war effort while draw-ing occasional fire for his methods from "smaller" men.[20]

　　We might consider how the cartoons looked from Philadelphia. For that city's boosters, Morris was not in league with the devil, he was a conquering hero. His fellow Pennsylvanian in the House of Representatives, Henry Wynkoop, from Bucks County, exclaimed that credit for the removal "is due to our Senators." "Mr. Morris," he continued, "who is ridiculed, insulted & abused here, is entitled to the gratitude & Esteem of every man who regards the

Interest of Pennsylvania." True to the agreement, Congress reentered Philadelphia in December 1790, and Morris enjoyed the toasts of his town. Though
he had taken his blows, a newspaper reporting his recent activity hailed
him as a distinguished and "worthy citizen," who had offered many examples
of "real and substantial patriotism." He had carried away the capital after all.[21]

Morris had made a mark on his city since before the Revolution. Even New
York's hostile cartoonists knew his storied background. Born in Liverpool,
England, in 1734, he had arrived on American shores at the age of thirteen.
His father, the gregarious Robert Morris, Sr., had once been a nail maker but
later acquired a position with a Liverpool trading firm as a tobacco agent. He
and Morris's mother apparently never married. Robert Sr. left England
for his firm's station at Oxford, Maryland, a port on Chesapeake Bay, where
he had called for his son to join him once the boy was old enough for the trip.
Morris arrived from his voyage to find that his father had struck up a
common-law union with a local woman, who soon became pregnant. Morris
did not stay in Maryland for long; only a year later, in 1748, his father placed
him with a merchant friend in Philadelphia, Robert Greenway. Two years
after that, his father died suddenly, leaving Morris with a fair inheritance, a
bit of rudimentary schooling, and an insecure place in the bustling city.[22]
     But like the runaway Benjamin Franklin twenty years earlier, Morris
then began a rapid rise up Philadelphia's social ladder. The spark came when
Greenway secured for him an apprenticeship at the merchant firm of Charles
Willing, a successful operation run by a respected family, where Morris
learned the principles of accounting and trade. He quickly impressed his
wealthy employer. In short order, Willing promoted him from menial to
clerk, to work alongside Willing's own privileged son Thomas. Morris
achieved partner status with Thomas in 1754—at twenty-one years old—
and the firm that emerged, Willing, Morris, and Company, would last for
decades and transact more business than nearly any other in North America.
It sent its ships to Europe, the West Indies, and Africa, carrying out flour,
timber, tobacco, fish, and other products, and returning with molasses, spirits, tea, and sometimes slaves, or ceramics, cloth, furnishings, and other finished goods. Thomas Willing was composed and conservative (his friends
called him "Old Square Toes"); Morris was openhanded and took risks.
Each complemented the other's role in an enterprise that saw many competi-
tors lose cargoes, sales, and credit in any number of misfortunes.[23]

And as with Franklin, Morris's wealth, ingenuity, and new connections led the one-time outsider into prominence and politics. In 1765, with Parliament's passage of the Stamp Act, Morris helped direct Philadelphia's bristling response. He helped the city's Committee of Merchants establish a nonimportation agreement with other colonies and compel the local tax collector to abandon his orders to enforce the hated tax. The Stamp Act was repealed, but the imperial tensions did not die, and Morris continued to help mount protests to London's ongoing attempts to tax and discipline the colonies.[24]

In the midst of these struggles, in 1769, Morris reinforced his new status with his wedding. His bride, Mary White, was the daughter of Thomas White, an English emigrant himself who had acquired a considerable amount of property in Maryland and then moved as a widower to Philadelphia around 1745. There, White remarried, and the new couple had a son, William, who would grow to take the reins at Philadelphia's Christ Church as an Anglican minister and, later, as a bishop. William's younger sister Mary was born in April 1749, making her nineteen years old at her March 1769 wedding to the thirty-five-year-old Morris. No story survives of how the couple met, but it may have been at the city's regular dancing assembly, where Mary's brown hair and eyes drew public notice from other gentlemen. The social advantages of the marriage were clear for Morris, but the couple also formed a loving bond (Robert called her "my dear Molly"; she called him "my dearest Husband") that would stand the test of their marriage vows.[25]

As the colonial crisis with London worsened, Morris was elected in 1775 to Pennsylvania's state assembly. That same year, he was also among those chosen to represent Pennsylvania as delegates to the newly formed Continental Congress. On the issue of independence, his was a moderately conservative voice, like others from the Pennsylvania delegation. He insisted on a redress of colonial grievances, but he argued against the adoption of the Declaration of Independence in 1776, seeing it as premature and unnecessarily divisive among the Americans. His wife made no secret of her opposition to the measure. In a gesture symbolizing his mixed feelings on the issue, he absented himself from Congress's vote on the Declaration's adoption on July 4. Yet by August, when the final copy was ready for the fateful signatures, he signed it, joining those who pledged "our Lives, our Fortunes, and our sacred Honor" to the cause.[26]

Then came the harried but productive days upon which Morris and Washington could later reflect together with such satisfaction. He outlined his goals for service in a 1777 letter to a fellow Philadelphian, in tones that he would continue to ring into the 1790s. "For my own part," he stated, "I mean in all my conduct to promote the general Interests of America & lay outside local attachments except in such instances as they become a duty." He did not see his own mercantile activities as a conflict of interest with his public responsibilities. Further, he did not harbor any real desire for political power: "My inclination prompts me to decline a public station, but being called on I cannot gratify myself, when the consequence will be to deserve blame from the worthy part of those that are embarked with me in this cause & you may depend I will not spare my exertions to serve & [save] my Country." Morris soon became extensively involved in Congress's attempts to build its navy; to equip its army; to secure funding from the states and from foreign loans; to stabilize a currency; to enlist international allies; and to cohere as a national unit. By this time, Mary had sided entirely with the cause.[27]

In 1778, after three tumultuous years, Morris resigned from his position in Congress. He took a place in the Pennsylvania legislature for a few rounds as a leader of the conservative party challenging the radically democratic state constitution. Certain voices, including those of Thomas Paine, American diplomat Arthur Lee, and congressional delegate Henry Laurens, accused Morris of corruption—of enriching himself while he had acted for Congress. So Morris also defended himself against a subsequent congressional inquiry into his blurry public/private business dealings, which ended in his official vindication. And in 1780, he helped found the Bank of Pennsylvania with his partner, Thomas Willing, and others as a means to help supply the army.[28]

The lingering controversy surrounding his activities did not prevent Congress from returning to Morris in a particularly desperate hour. In February 1781, Congress unanimously voted him "Superintendent of Finance," a brand new, far-reaching executive position created to address the government's financial woes and effect a conclusion to the war. In his diary that month, Morris claimed that "this appointment was unsought, unsolicited, and dangerous to Accept of as it was evidently contrary to my private Interest," by which he meant his focus on his own business and domestic "enjoyments," as well as the position's inherent controversy. He clearly remembered the "unmerited abuse I had formerly received as the reward" for his previous services, and the congressional inquiry into his procurement dealings, which had "determined me against every public station." But he also saw the dire necessity for the work to be done, "or else to meet my Ruin in the common Wreck," so he prepared to take the position. He insisted on the right to continue his own carefully cultivated business affairs and the right to control personnel appointments in his office. Congress agreed to his conditions, and Morris began his duties in May. As the news circulated, numerous supporters wrote him letters of confidence tempered with dread for the future. Shortly thereafter, he also received charge of the duties of agent of marine, effectively heading the fledgling navy.[29]

It was true that upon his appointment, the situation was bleak. Continental notes were valued less than the cost to print them, and Congress could not meet even the interest charges on its debts. Generals from the field complained of naked, hungry soldiers and weighed the prospect of seizing private stores by force. To respond, Morris as superintendent found bread and clothing and drew heavily upon his private credit. More broadly, he undertook a centralizing program that involved founding a national Bank of North America, funding the government's debts, requisitioning payments from the states, attempting to regulate interstate commerce, and promoting American industries. He negotiated additional loans from Paris and Amsterdam. He outfitted and launched ships. He exchanged tobacco, rice, indigo, and other goods on behalf of Congress. He celebrated the difficult military victories as they came, and he managed the rocky transition to peacetime after the Treaty of Paris in 1783. When the soldiers' mutiny in Philadelphia led to Congress's flight, he soon reopened the Treasury office with his able assistant, Gouverneur Morris (of no relation), and the two continued to sign Morris's own personal paper notes ("Long Bobs" and "Short Bobs") for the soldiers' pay in arrears.[30]

Around this time, Morris commemorated his auspicious position as superintendent by commissioning a series of portraits of himself and of his family. Curiously, he commissioned the paintings from his recent, bitter enemy in state politics, the noted artist Charles Willson Peale. Again, the amiable Morris could "forgive them all." One of the resulting portraits showed Morris and Gouverneur Morris together as colleagues in the Office of Finance, situated behind a desk and its papers, with the portly Financier standing and giving the viewer a commanding stare (fig 1.4). He points to a paper on the desk, which reads, "A plan of Finance to restore public credit & for establishing a national Bank." Office files stand ready in the left corner.[31]

In another portrait, Peale depicted Morris's heavy frame seated alone in a red patterned armchair (fig. 1.5). Morris wears a blue suit with white shirt

Figure 1.4. Portrait of Gouverneur Morris and Robert Morris by Charles Willson Peale, 1783. (Courtesy of the Pennsylvania Academy of Fine Arts, Philadelphia. Bequest of Richard Ashhurst)

and stockings, and his hand holds a rolled document, perhaps the Bank of North America's charter. In the window just beyond stands a large, uniden-tified neoclassical building. It probably represented the Bank of England (recognizable to Peale and many American travelers and readers), a refer-ence to Morris's banking innovations for the country, and served as a visual metaphor for Morris's role in the nation's economic architecture. In any case, the building is elaborate, foreshadowing a destiny for Morris then only be-ginning to take shape.[32]

After long efforts in the face of the Articles of Confederation's con-straints as he acted as the most powerful minister in a powerless government, Morris finally resigned his position in frustration in November 1784. He left the government heavily in debt yet solvent and, unimaginably, with a small surplus in the Treasury. He then began the long process of settling his ac-counts, while concerns about his dealings were raised anew. Did Morris

Figure 1.5. Portrait of Robert Morris by Charles Willson Peale, from life, circa 1782. (Courtesy of Independence National Historical Park)

abuse his positions and his insider's knowledge to enrich himself and his firms? Or, did he use his own name as a necessary cover and then as a source of contacts and credit for the fledgling Congress? In either case, the results seem to have benefited both the war effort and his pocketbook. Accusations of war profiteering, of monopolizing flour while citizens clamored for bread, would haunt him the rest of his career. Yet so would his reputation as a

Herculean force. Even his enemies acknowledged this force; as late as 1801, President Thomas Jefferson lamented to James Madison that Morris was at that time imprisoned and disgraced, and therefore unable to serve in his administration as secretary of the navy. After Morris's resignation, his political legacy continued to ripple through the new nation. His centralizing efforts as superintendent of finance laid important groundwork for the constitutional convention and then the Federalist political party that developed around Alexander Hamilton in the 1790s.[33]

All this inflated the larger-than-life persona represented in the New York cartoons in 1790. At that point, Morris was not just a signer of the Declaration or a U.S. senator. He was more than a supremely wealthy financier, or even *the* Financier. Closer to the president than Vice President John Adams himself, Morris had reached that rarified realm of movers and doers, of "founders"—one who could carry out an impossible war, oversee the writing and rewriting of constitutions, and move capitals. But could he, or any of the other leaders, keep the national ship together, and afloat? And as voiced in the grumblings of cartoon bystanders ("D[amne]d dirty work," "The Public pay for this"), in what ways was he still obliged to the mass of ordinary, skeptical citizens?

In August 1790, Morris returned to Philadelphia and helped ready the city for the federal government's arrival. His first concern was to assist Washington in his search for the new executive office and residence. Like everyone, Morris had been distressed by the poor health the president had endured in New York, and he hoped that the change would do the old general good. He also intended to ensure that the relocated president settled into a firm Philadelphia foundation.[34]

Philadelphia was relatively new, founded just over one hundred years earlier, but it had no shortage of grand homes from which to choose. Its founder, the Quaker aristocrat William Penn, had envisioned a healthy, well-ordered town, and he had picked an advantageous site stretching between the banks of the Schuylkill and Delaware Rivers. Penn and his surveyors introduced a grid plan for the city's streets, with wide blocks, a central square, and four large parks. Penn promoted his city and colony throughout Europe; he offered religious tolerance; he made gestures of peace to the local Indians. The resulting flood of immigrants from England and western Europe quickly swelled the city's population to 2,500 by 1700. But the incomers did not settle evenly throughout Penn's grid. They jostled next to the busy port on the Delaware, at the city's eastern end, dividing and subdividing the spacious blocks, and only gradually spread westward. All this activity, along with the surrounding farms, brought great wealth to the city's Quaker elite and the rising merchant class represented by Morris and the Willings. By 1790, the Philadelphia area had grown to 43,000 residents, making it the most populous in the nation, filled with a cosmopolitan jumble of Africans, Indians, Germans, French, and Swedes alongside the English. A stock of substantial Georgian town houses survived from the colonial era, and newer, neoclassical mansions also fronted its paved streets. Expansive estates lined the waterways in the outlying suburbs, while narrow workers' homes and sheds packed into the city's rows and alleys.[35]

Morris owned many properties in the city and suburbs, but his main home was a large brick house on Market [High] Street between Fifth and Sixth streets (fig. 1.6). Built in the late 1760s by a wealthy widow, the building had seen a series of famous residents prior to the Morrises, including the acting governor of the colony and then, in the midst of war, the general of the British army during Philadelphia's occupation. Known as the Masters-Penn House, it had a four-bay façade, essentially the size of two contiguous row houses. The Morrises, their children, and about nine servants had moved into the house around 1782, after recent fire damage was repaired. They settled into its six bedrooms, four servant rooms, dining rooms, and other spaces distributed among three floors and a garret. Morris made significant changes to the outdoor areas. The grounds held a kitchen, a washhouse, and two coach and stable houses, in addition to walled yards and a garden. He purchased surrounding properties to consolidate the yards, converted the washhouse into a two-story bathhouse with running hot water, and, true to the family's passion for the table, added a hothouse, ice house, and smokehouse. The property was only a couple blocks' walk to the State House and government buildings.[36]

Washington knew the house well from his previous visits. In early September 1790, after leaving New York for Mount Vernon, he stayed with the Morrises in Philadelphia to explore his options for the residence. But upon arrival, he discovered that a committee assembled by the city to assist in the matter had already made a decision. The committee had reviewed several possibilities and determined that "no House was to be found in the City that would accommodate the President & his Family without additions or

Figure 1.6. The Masters-Penn house as it appeared around 1795. ("The Residence of Washington in High Street," by William L. Breton, circa 1825. Courtesy of the Historical Society of Pennsylvania)

alterations." Working closely with Morris, the committee had then decided that "the House of Robert Morris Esquire approached the nearest of any to what was desired & was capable of being rendred sufficiently commodious at the least Expence." Morris, in the committee's words, "politely agreed to give it," under certain rental conditions.[37]

First, the city would help break the lease of Morris's own tenant next door so that his family could move there. By inhabiting their own rental property—the Stedman-Galloway House, as it was known, at the corner of Sixth and Market Streets—the Morrises would be neighbors with the Washingtons (fig. 2.3). And the city agreed to pay for all upgrades to the two houses to suit the families. Of the arrangement, Morris considered "my having given up my house to accommodate the President" a "sacrifice," adding "I think there is no other man for whom I would have done it."[38]

Washington approved the committee's actions. "It is," he agreed, "the best *single House* in the City." But even with the extraordinary size of the Masters-Penn House, Washington found it "inadequate to the *commodious* accommodation of my family." After all, this would be his executive office; it would serve as the place of reception for diplomats and other callers; it would be the site of state dinner parties and levees; and it would house his attendants and slaves. In one memorable phrase, Washington observed that "there are good Stables, but for 12 Horses only." So Washington directed numerous changes, while keeping and swapping some of the Morrises' personal items, such as mirrors, lamps, and a clothes iron. Most notably, he ordered a two-story bow to be added to the rear of the main house, a newly fashionable touch that would enhance the state dining and drawing rooms. Washington remained sensitive to charges of favoritism inherent in the arrangement; after he had departed for Virginia two months before the government's reassembly, his secretary, Tobias Lear, informed him from New York City that "the people here appear pleased with the prospect of your being so well accommodated; and the circumstance of its being in Mr Morris' house does not seem to be noticed *here* in the manner which there was reason to think it might, from the idea that was formed of Mr Morris' agency in the removal of the Government." Morris also acknowledged this concern. The move "will have the effect of keeping me at a greater distance from him, although I shall live next door," he told a friend. "I have nothing to ask of him for myself. He cannot render me a service, and if I am seen much there it will create envy, jealousy, and malice, and I do not see why I should expose myself to be the object of such passions. I have suffered, most undeservedly, by them too often already." Washington also insisted on paying rent, as he had done in New York City, so as not to give the city any little leverage for retaining the permanent seat of government. After Washington pressed for a figure, Morris and the commissioners set the rent at £500 Pennsylvania currency annually.[39]

Washington left for Mount Vernon as Morris hired and oversaw a corps of carpenters and masons, directing them to his Stedman-Galloway House first. Tobias Lear arrived on the scene in mid-October and directed a hectic stream of correspondence to Washington in Virginia to keep the president posted on the latest developments, from the arrival of the furniture to the painting of the rooms. Mary Morris became ill in October and delayed the family's removal next door for about a week. But by November, she was back on her feet and active in the move, helping Lear decide how to arrange the Washingtons' furniture and which rooms the busy workmen, now in the Masters-Penn House, should try to finish first. On November 28, 1790, with the house mostly ready, Washington moved in with about thirty others: his family, staff, and servants. This number included about eight slaves from

Mount Vernon—a charged addition that would prove complicated under Pennsylvania's gradual abolition law.[40]

Members of Congress also began arriving in the city that month. As they settled into homes, boardinghouses, and taverns, they were followed by federal officials, foreign diplomats, land agents, printers, hairdressers, tailors, portrait painters, actors, rum sellers, and other interested parties. The Philadelphians launched their own offensive to keep Congress pleased, hoping to erase any lingering memories of the scene of the last residence in the city. Though the historic State House was not given over to Congress, the city refashioned the smaller, county court house next door as Congress Hall, with customized furniture, art, and other comforts along the lines of New York's Federal Hall. Social life in the city broke out into balls and elaborate dinners.[41]

With the business of carrying away capitals done, the government in Philadelphia turned to innumerable other concerns, including Treasury Secretary Hamilton's controversial finance plan. Yet by the end of 1790, Morris was no longer paying much attention to these workings of government. "I have no real attachment to public life," he said at the time, "although, from the share I have had in it, most people suppose otherwise." He rejected suggestions that he run for state governor, and he grew quiet in the Senate, dutifully handling his share of committee work. He had his mind and energies set on different—bigger—prizes, in the private realm. He knew the nation's challenges as well as anyone, but, as he had demonstrated since a teen, he also believed in his own ability to capitalize on them. He continued as a partner in his merchant activities, sending out ships across the seas. He sought to purchase large amounts of bank stock and debt certificates. He experimented with factories in Pennsylvania and New Jersey. More than anything, he bought up unsettled land and began promoting its resale through every contact he had. Regarded as one of the wealthiest men in the country, he sought to expand and enjoy his fruits. Perhaps he would build a suitable monument to these achievements.[42]

2. His Family

Mary Morris had several things on her mind. As a longtime member of the city's Dancing Assembly, she had a notion of what the evening's event would be like. She had chosen her dress, deciding among French and Chinese silk, and she and her servants had planned an elaborate arrangement for her long, graying hair (fig. 2.1). She knew that her husband, wearing a dark suit and stockings, would be in fine spirits, and that their carriage would likely leave for the festivities held nearby at Oeller's Hotel at around seven o'clock. The ball's main room would certainly be handsome, decorated with flowers and festoons and with a gallery for the musicians at one end. She also knew whom she would see that evening—all those familiar members' faces, no more, save for the carefully screened, politically important guests. And surely, as at so many other occasions, she would be seated at Mrs. Washington's right during supper.[1]

But there were things she did not know, and she would have lingered over these. With whom might she dance? What foods would be served? What toasts would be made?

Most important, what would the president's mood be? This night, February 21, 1792, marked the eve of Washington's sixtieth birthday. The Dancing Assembly had gone to particular lengths to prepare a special ball in his honor this year. Washington's birthday had been celebrated yearly since the Revolution by all classes of Americans, in parlors and taverns, in the streets and in military camps, as the British monarch's birthday had been. The Philadelphia Dancing Assembly could now host the man himself at its own function, in this auspicious year. Sixty was a notable age for the

Figure 2.1. Portrait of Mary White (Mrs. Robert) Morris by Charles Willson Peale, from life, circa 1782. This portrait was painted a decade earlier than the birthday ball, around the same time as that of Robert Morris (see figure 1.5). Mary is shown in elaborate headgear and cape, dress, and sash, with portrait miniatures on each wrist, probably of Robert and her father. (Courtesy of Independence National Historical Park)

beloved patriarch, and further, there was to be a presidential election in November, with Washington considering retirement and thereby stirring widespread alarm. Here was precisely the kind of moment Mary had envisioned while following her husband's earlier political efforts in New York.

He had once written her from his station there praying "not to part again during life for where you are there is my heart & happiness." Robert was now by her side, and they were both in a position to help their government and their country by pressing Washington to stay for another term.[2]

Mary also considered more local concerns. What would be the dress and demeanor of the younger women now attracting so much attention, such as Miss Anne Allen, Miss Sophia Chew, and particularly "the dazzling Mrs. Bingham"? In New York, a courtlike society had formed around the first president, composed of high officials, military officers, and the wealthiest city families, all lending the inner circles of the new government a decidedly aristocratic air. Indeed, later observers would name it the "Republican Court," those two words jarring together to suggest all its attendant contradictions and insecurities. At the president's executive residence, the mood had been formal yet restrained, but such restraint lifted at the many sumptuous private dinners and balls elsewhere. This "Republican Court" had reestablished itself in Philadelphia with the government's move, to the consternation of the city's Quaker establishment. And Anne Bingham, twenty-eight years old in 1792, had emerged as the premier hostess and vivant of the city's high society. She was the daughter of Robert Morris's partner, Thomas Willing, and the wife of Morris's exceedingly wealthy friend and associate, William Bingham. Abigail Adams was awed by the young Mrs. Bingham's charms, like so many of Philadelphia's visitors, effusing that "Mrs. Bingham has certainly given laws to the ladies here, in fashion and elegance." A few years earlier, upon the Binghams' return from a European honeymoon, a young Maryland girl had noted that Anne "blaz'd upon a large party at Mr. Morris's in a dress which eclips'd any that has yet been seen." Surely all eyes at the exclusive Dancing Assembly's ball would be looking to see her.[3]

It needled Mary, then forty-four, that Anne Bingham would be leaving for the ball from a house decidedly superior to her own. For the Binghams' mansion had attracted as much attention as Anne's blazing dress. The newlyweds had conceived the house during their grand tour of Europe in 1785, while admiring the Duke of Manchester's London residence. They obtained plans based on this house's design and sent them home to their builders, intending to eclipse any yet seen in Philadelphia. Construction began in their absence on their Third Street lot, which stretched across a third of the entire block, including the length of Spruce Street to Fourth Street. Two years later, the Binghams returned and moved into what awestruck Philadelphians simply called the "Mansion House." A three-story behemoth, it featured a flat front with five bays and two flanking wings. A low brick wall screened it from the street, from which it stood forty feet back, while a greenhouse, stables, and formal gardens adorned the rear lot. Inside, the Binghams stuffed the house with every sort of luxury they had found in Europe and beyond. A Polish visitor in the 1790s, Julian Niemcewicz, observed that inside, upon mounting a staircase of white marble, "One enters an immense room with a sculptured fireplace, painted ceiling, magnificent rug, curtains, armchairs, sofas in Gobelins of France. The dinner is brought on by a French cook; the servants are in livery, the food served in silver dishes, the dessert on Sevres porcelain." Niemcewicz also took note of Anne herself: "This mistress of the house is tall, beautiful, perfectly dressed and has copied, one could not want for better, the tone and carriage of a European lady." This was a high compliment, if a bit unsettling. Anne eagerly opened her house to the Republican Court, and from it she presided over a rich mix of politics and gaiety, modeled after the salons of Paris. Even George Washington was impressed, noting once that he dined there "in great Splender."[4]

All this dazzle and show had plenty of detractors. Preachers had warned against sinful luxury and pride from the first colonial settlements, and Philadelphia's Quaker community was particularly forceful in its attempts to foster a plain, frugal tone in its city, though Quaker influence had slipped some over the years. Further, a good portion of the emerging nation's myths heralded its frontier pragmatism and simplicity. Everyone could recite *Poor Richard's Almanack* advice. "Away then with your expensive Follies," Benjamin Franklin had instructed, for "*Pride breakfasted with Plenty, dined with Poverty, and supped with Infamy.*" Likewise, "homespun" cloth had become a powerful symbol during the Revolution. For contrast, American critics commonly ridiculed the hollow spectacle of European nobility, the foppery of landed, inherited wealth that rested on the backs of peasants. The fact that much American wealth was built on the backs of slaves and servants, that Americans tirelessly pursued the latest European fashions, and that courtly notions of gentility radiated ever outward into all classes of society did little to dampen the general criticism.[5]

By the late 1780s, these critiques had gained even greater urgency in the American experiment. A republic was seen as demanding a high moral character of its citizens in order to survive. How else would a new country hold without the control of a monarch? Virtue, the classical value, would replace fear in

binding citizens together. Through virtue, leaders would set aside private interests to work for the public good, while citizens would be able to form a just
basis for their leaders' authority. In 1782, one of Robert Morris's correspon-
dents explained this necessary quality as "a public and patriotick spirit reign-
ing in the breast of evry individual superseding all private considerations—it
was this spirit alone that carried several of the Græcian States and the Roman
Republic triumphantly through so many ages." A free republic, without permanent, settled leadership and power, offered new opportunities as well as new
dangers. Thus excessive, striving, vain luxury—perhaps of the sort beheld at
the Dancing Assembly—could undermine the fragile bonds of liberty. Americans would find ways to reconcile prosperity and the pursuit of self-interest
with their republican experiment, but there were ideal limits on luxury.[6]

The personal passions displayed in episodes like the struggle over the
nation's capital would seem to have given pause to adherents of republican virtue and simplicity. Anti-Federalists seized upon the issue in the wake of the
new Constitution. In 1789, Massachusetts politician James Warren responded
to the opening spectacle of Congress with the observation that "perhaps history cannot furnish an Instance when simplicity & frugal Manners have so
suddenly Changed to Pomp & Expensive parade & Republican habits & Sentiments Changed to Monarchical." But even high Federalists like John Adams,
William Bingham, and Robert Morris acknowledged the importance of these
concerns. Earlier, Morris had praised "Geneva, where as I am told, the Manners of the People are favorable to the Practice of Virtue, and being a republic,
I should suppose the Stile of living may partake of that Plainess, and simplicity,
best adapted to such Governments." William Bingham nodded along, as when
he praised English architecture for its "remarkable show of simplicity united
with elegance" even while instructing his father-in-law from afar not to circulate the plan he sent for his new mansion, "as it would only expose it to criticism." President Washington walked the tightrope of such concerns every day.
When he was moving into Morris's home, he made clear to his secretary, Tobias Lear, that the additions and alterations "ought to be done in a *plain* and
neat, not by any means in an extravagant style." That year, Washington also
explained to a friend that his wife's "wishes coincide with my own as to simplicity of dress, and every thing which can tend to support propriety of character without partaking of the follies of luxury and ostentation."[7]

But who was to judge the proper degree of "simplicity" and "propriety"? The balance was tricky. On one hand, for example, in 1791, a French

nobleman visiting Philadelphia found, to his smiling surprise, that a "small house, similar to those around it, was the palace of the President of the United States." It had "no guards, not even any men-servants," and a "young girl" opened the door to his knock. He "asked if the general was at home," and she promptly led him back "through one of those narrow corridors which serve as vestibules to English houses, and left me in a parlour, where she begged me to wait for the general." Was this the picture of a nation that could shoulder up to European powers on the world's stage? On the other hand, the ambitions of the Morrises and the Binghams made their countrymen uneasy. Despite William Bingham's caution, his mansion quickly drew the censure of numerous observers. Charles Bulfinch, a rising Boston architect visiting Philadelphia after a recent European tour, declared the Bingham House to be "in a stile which would be esteemed splendid even in the most luxurious part of Europe. Elegance of construction, white marble staircase, valuable paintings, the richest furniture and the utmost magnificence of decoration makes it a palace in my opinion far too rich for any man in this country." Bulfinch's words came from a man who would work for elite clients throughout his career, yet they made it clear that material elegance and beauty were expected to maintain proper limits in "this country." Though he and the French nobleman each used the term "palace" differently, both saw it as a charged metaphor. Here was the enviable dilemma of America's wealthy.[8]

The issue intruded on the Dancing Assembly's plans. City residents grumbled about its exclusivity, as when an eminent French émigré once reported that a representative of the organization refused him a guest ticket to attend the presidential birthday ball, telling him, "Since I was a *storekeeper* I could not aspire to this honor." And in 1793, as the Assembly geared up for the birthday ball again, "a subscriber" to Benjamin Franklin Bache's *General Advertiser* viciously attacked the event's continuation. "Will this *monarchical farce* ever have an end? Must freemen again be insulted with the *pageantry* of royalty?" The writer hinted that the participants had expectations of special favors from their "*sycophance*," while "the blood shed in opposition to a *King* is scarcely exhaled from our soil." The writer went so far as to suggest that Washington's personal role in the event contaminated "his countrymen with the follies of royal station" and sanctioned customs "like vapour, destructive of the electrical fluid of republicanism."[9]

An additional challenge had arisen as the Morrises readied themselves for the 1792 ball. That year, a rival "New Dancing Assembly" had formed and pointedly invited President Washington to its *own* celebratory function. This rival Assembly was composed of successful "tradesmen"—such as prosperous tailors, shoemakers, carriage makers, carpenters, and others—as well as lesser merchants and professionals shut out of the old Dancing Assembly. In early February, leaders of the New Dancing Assembly appealed to the old, requesting that the two Assemblies join together for the special sixtieth birthday ball. They were rebuffed, on the grounds that "the Rooms are not sufficiently large to accommodate the Personages & Company intended to be entertained." The two groups seem to have jockeyed for the same space, with the result that the old Assembly decided to celebrate the birthday on the eve thereof—Tuesday, February 21—and to "drink his Health and long Life in the morning." Meanwhile, the new Assembly scheduled their patriotic recognition of Washington's birthday for Wednesday, February 22, and the group invited the same slate of governors, congressmen, foreign ministers, and officials. City residents wondered at the challenge. Which would the president attend? Or perhaps he should attend neither?[10]

Washington resolved the standoff by attending both. On February 21, the original Dancing Assembly's event proved a success, with many honored guests and what the *Federal Gazette* and *Claypoole's Daily Advertiser* called "one of the most brilliant displays of beauty ever exhibited in this city." There were minuets, country dances, and cotillions. The party toasted the day, the United States, their hospitable and industrious land, the "Departed Sons of Liberty," the "Daughters of Columbia," and the president, among others. The following evening, after a day full of processions, presentations, and salutes to mark the birthday, the Washingtons and nearly the same guests of honor attended the New Dancing Assembly. There, the *Federal Gazette* found that "joy and satisfaction were strongly marked in every countenance," and many ladies "had in their head-dresses, wrought in gold letters, sentiments expressive of the general sensations of the evening." Again, they toasted the day, the United States, the president, and other common subjects. But they also toasted the "Nations in friendship with the United States," "the Rights of Man," and "the flame of Liberty which hath been lighted up in the Western World." These were pointed, partisan references to revolutionary France, which would not have been shared by the more pro-British, aristocratic, Federalist set in the old Assembly.[11]

Claypoole's Daily Advertiser attempted to conclude the whole affair on a note of tentative moderation: the two balls "were equally distinguished for elegance of manners and gentility of dress and deportment." And Washington "had equal pleasure in the festivity of every description of citizens." But darker shadows gathered; the correspondent ventured that as "a good republican," Washington "must look with extreme disapprobation on any arbitrary attempts to introduce ideas of fastidious distinctions of rank among them." The correspondent lamented:

> What a pity that at a time when the most fashionable nation of the universe [France] is producing so many instances of the abolition of titles and distinctions, some other people, so apt to take after them in dances and in the stile of dress and ornament, should be so slow at copying them, in these more valuable and necessary improvements of the social state. What a pity that in America such distinctions should be ever thought of—a country so young, and in which the claims of hereditary birth and honors are without a plea, and one of whose choicest blessings has hitherto been the equality of its citizens.

Washington had understood the danger. Indeed, "The President did wisely in counteracting the prejudices of any of our modern aristocrats, and in joining with his lady in all the popular amusements of respectable people." Thus *Claypoole's* singled out the contradictions embedded in the city's striving upper class. For members of this class, history was transforming their associations with France into a double-edged sword; on the one hand, elite French culture provided the Morrises and their set with their most fashionable and enjoyable dress, ornaments, and meals. On the other, the increasingly radical French Revolution challenged America's recently settled political order, and the display of French luxuries belied the equality of American citizens. Mary Morris could have justly observed that every pursuit, no matter how seemingly innocent, became swept up in political concerns.[12]

The Morrises navigated these waters with a steady focus on their large family. The couple doted on their children; they embraced them, in Robert's words, with the "warmest approbation which can flow from paternal affection." It was not always easy, though. Robert had brought his half-brother Thomas from Maryland, sixteen years his junior, into the marriage, and the Morrises treated him as a son. But Thomas was troubled and died in 1778 during an extended drinking and gambling binge in France during the war. Robert also came into the marriage having fathered an illegitimate daughter.

Mary (known as Polly) was born around 1763 to an unknown mother, and she apparently never lived with her father. Still, Morris recognized her and supported her financially, maintaining an interest in her affairs throughout his life. By 1792, Polly was married to Charles Croxall from Baltimore and lived with him and their children on one of her father's estates in western New Jersey. Mary Morris acknowledged the link, corresponding with Polly at times and forwarding gifts to her on Robert's behalf.[13]

Robert and Mary had seven children of their own, beginning with Robert, Jr., born in December 1769, ten months after their wedding. The next six came in rapid succession: Thomas, William, Esther (known as Hetty), Charles, Maria, and then Henry, their youngest. The family started in a respectable house on Front Street near the Delaware River, below Dock Street. Then, when Morris was offered the position of superintendent of finance in early 1781, they made preparations to move westward into the expanding city, closer to the governmental chambers. Morris found a property with a great deal of promise—the grand Masters-Penn House on Market Street, which would eventually become the presidential residence—and also bought two adjoining lots to further extend the grounds around the home. In 1782, Morris and his wife, then with six children plus servants, moved into their spacious new home on Market Street. Within a few months, Morris relocated the Office of Finance to the same block. He was then within an easy stroll from his own dining table to his new offices.[14]

Robert and Mary sent their two eldest sons, at ages twelve and ten, abroad for the formal education Morris himself had never received. Morris instructed their tutor to impress upon them, among other morals, the importance of financial economy "as a leading virtue." He elaborated that he would pay liberally for any proper expenses, but he did not expect them "to spend my Fortune" freely, for some expenses were "extravagant and improper, & extravagance leads to ruin not only of Fortune, but of good principles." To this grave instruction, the boys showed only mixed success. After six years of touring the continent and worrying their parents, the two returned in 1788 to take up roles in Morris's enterprises. By the evening of Washington's birthday in 1792, Thomas had finished his legal apprenticeship in New York City and was in the process of moving upstate as Morris's land agent. Robert, Jr., meanwhile, had returned to Europe, newly charged as one of Morris's sales agents.[15]

In contrast, the two middle sons, William and Charles, remained at home and attended the University of Pennsylvania. In 1792, Morris still paid the twenty-year-old William a weekly allowance as well as his subscription to the Dancing Assembly, as he knocked about the city at the end of his studies. His father apprehended that the young man displayed "strong symptoms of Indolence." Meanwhile, Charles remained at school. The Morrises' youngest son, Henry, was only eight years old in 1792, and he, too, was attending a local academy.[16]

The family's daughters, Hetty and Maria, were domestic and devoted, as seen in Maria's later visits to her father in prison. They received formal tutoring in the polite arts, with lessons in penmanship, the French language, history, dance, harpsichord, and the like. Once, in 1789, young Maria's "playfull disposition" so charmed one of her father's friends that the man named a brig after her. Hetty, on the other hand, did not share this disposition; indeed Mary worried that Hetty's "extrem reserve in Company" might "give an unfavorable opinion of her understanding." Still, Hetty "took her place" as a young lady in society at the age of sixteen in 1791. When she received a romantic disappointment around this time, her father consoled her with the hope that she would use the opportunity to gain wisdom from the experience and reflect upon "the vanity, folly & uncertainty of Human affections & pursuits." It was good advice.[17]

Mary, as seen in Peale's portrait, was a proud woman who relished her position. Though occasionally prone to infirmity—family letters describe her at times as suffering from a headache, a sprained ankle, arthritis, or a minor illness—she upheld a steady presence. She served as a partner in Morris's undertakings, offering her husband political advice, helping to cultivate his financial connections, directing their household, and overseeing their children's activities. She took particular pleasure in dress, ordering fine European hats, caps, clothes, lace, and flowers through traveling friends or her grown children. Closer to home, she regularly handled money and dealt directly with an assortment of shopkeepers and suppliers, paying for everything from linens to blankets to stays to gloves to tea. She also enjoyed theater and dance, from the formal Assembly occasions to more impromptu gatherings. "My children on Monday last was at a ball given by the little Miss Chews," she wrote to Robert in 1788. "I was there too invited by Mrs. Chew to see them & a vast Pleasure it is to see so large a Collection of lovely Children dance as well as they did." And yet she also had a seriousness and formality not shared by the younger generation at the Republican Court.[18]

Finally, the couple embraced Mary's other family connections. The Morrises mourned in December 1790, when the children's last remaining grandparent, Mary's mother, died in Philadelphia after a brief illness. The parentless Robert had felt the loss "as much as if she had been my own mother," he said at the time, and he observed that Mary, too, "grieves at the loss, but has too much sense and too much integrity of mind to make parade of grief." Esther White was buried in the family vault at Philadelphia's Christ Church, where Mary's brother, William White, served as bishop and the Morrises occupied a front pew. Robert had once voiced his summary view of the clan in a letter he wrote to an acquaintance in England shortly before the birth of their last child: "I have a Family that make me perfectly happy so far as it depends on them, a most Worthy Woman to my Wife and six good Children." Almost a decade later, in 1791, Mary echoed her husband's sentiments, writing to Gouverneur Morris, "You see me as I rea[l]ly am surrounded by an amiable and promiseing young family and one of the happiest of women." Here was a domestic setting they could indulge.[19]

Through all of their comings and goings, the Morrises earned a reputation for hospitality. Their private dinners, teas, card games, and music nurtured the same associations as those so publicly celebrated at the Dancing Assembly. They took great pleasure in such occasions, but they also understood the political importance of a shared meal, so perhaps the couple would not have been surprised at the barbs directed at the Assembly's function in 1792. The dinner table, the tea set, and the card room provided important venues through which they could demonstrate Robert's extensive credit, their access to prime goods, and their social position. Robert cultivated an air of confidence, since wealth begat wealth in the eyes of prospective associates, creditors, and clients. His hospitality undergirded his reputation as the wealthiest man in America, as all guests made comparisons with the hospitality found in the homes of friends and rivals. And the occasions aided Morris's governmental duties, by cementing relations among his allies and softening the rancor of opponents (fig. 2.2). Thus the Morrises paid close attention to their guests' countenances as well as to their own plates.[20]

Events at the Morrises' Market Street house during his tenure as superintendent of finance set an enviable tone that would continue into Washington's presidency. In 1781, the Marquis de Chastellux traveled through the area and judged that "his house is handsome, resembling perfectly the houses in London; he lives there without ostentation, but not without expense, for he spares nothing which can contribute to his happiness, and that of Mrs.

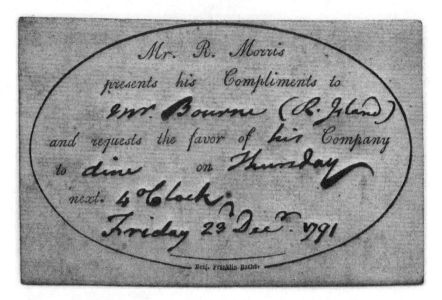

Figure 2.2. A printed dinner invitation card, from Robert Morris to Benjamin Bourne, member of Congress from Rhode Island, December 23, 1791. (Carson Collection, Box 54. Courtesy of the Library of Congress, Manuscript Division)

Morris, to whom he is much attached." The Marquis went on to declare Morris, fittingly, "an Epicurean philosopher." He concluded that Morris "has always played a distinguished part at table and in business," linking the two realms. In 1783, Harrison Gray Otis, then a wide-eyed Massachusetts law student, attended "a dinner of thirty persons," hosted by Robert Morris, "in a style of sumptuous magnificence which I have never seen equalled." Tax records from that year show the Morrises owned nine hundred ounces of silver plate (about five times that of the state's governor), surely adding to the glitter. Here was the Morrises' attempt to balance the distance between courtly French expectations and republican manners.[21]

After they vacated this house in November 1790 for the Washingtons, the Morrises continued their customs next door at the Stedman-Galloway House (fig. 2.3). This corner house had served as the residence of the president of the state's Supreme Executive Council, thereby becoming something like a governor's mansion until Morris bought it in 1786. Though the house was valued at less than one-third the cost of the Masters-Penn House, guests at the Morrises' new residence during the early 1790s gushed with hyperbole. Samuel Breck, who worked as a young merchant in the city at the time, recalled that Morris "did the honors of the city by a profuse, incessant and elegant hospitality. . . . There was a luxury in the kitchen, table, parlor and street equipage of Mr. and Mrs. Morris that was to be found nowhere else in America." Like so many others, Breck also compared the Morrises with the younger Binghams. "Bingham's was more gaudy, but less comfortable," Breck found. "It was the pure and unalloyed which the Morrises sought to place before their friends, without the abatements that so frequently accompany the displays of fashionable life. No badly-cooked or cold dinners at their table; no pinched fires upon their hearths; no paucity of waiters; no awkward loons in their drawing-rooms." They had made an ally in Breck.[22]

Breck's reference to "no paucity of waiters" underscored the dependence of such a household on the heavy efforts of nearly a dozen live-in servants. The 1790 census listed eighteen people in the Morris household; beyond the family, this included three white men, two white women, and four free black servants. City tax records also show the Morrises owned one female slave from the early 1780s until 1792, but it is not clear whether she resided in the household during this time. (Morris was largely silent on the issue of slavery in his letters. In some, he conveyed mild sympathy

Figure 2.3. The Stedman-Galloway House at the corner of Sixth and Market Streets, in which the Morrises lived in 1792. The Masters-Penn House, which the Washingtons were renting, was just past the lot on the left of this house. (Painted from memory by Charles A. Poulson, 1860. Courtesy of the Library Company of Philadelphia)

for abolitionist causes, but his previous experience in the slave trade and his ownership of slaves personally and through his industrial works into the 1790s suggest that those sympathies did not run deep.) Breck further mentioned his approval of the Morrises' staff as being "uniformly dressed," wearing livery, illustrating that these servants were not only the labor, they were also part of the display itself. This extended out into the streets, as Morris's coachmen assisted in keeping his five horses and two carriages suitably impressive and ready for the family's many travels.[23]

Both Robert and Mary took an active role in managing their servants. A revealing glimpse of their authority appeared during preparations for George Washington's move into the Masters-Penn House. The president's secretary, Tobias Lear, advised Washington that the room over the coach house could not be used to accommodate his stable workers, as the Morrises had done. "The whole is used as a Hay loft," Lear found, "and Mr. Morris' Coach-man has a bed in one corner where he sleeps; but neither a candle or fire could be carried there with any safety," given the risk of conflagration. "The Coach-man," continued Lear, "tells me that he is never suffered to carry a light into the loft[.] But," Lear suggested, "I beleive it would not be safe to trust your people under those circumstances, as they would be more apt to study their own convenience than the safety of the buildings." Lear thus concluded that Washington could not command the same kind of discipline from his slaves that the Morrises could command from their servants, since they had apparently been successful in keeping the coachman from the warmth or light of a fire in his unique quarters. Yet Morris's authority was not absolute. In late 1792, he advertised in the newspaper a $4 reward for the return or imprisonment of "an Irish servant lad, named George Reiley," who "Ran away," presumably from one of his industrial enterprises nearby. Morris could also demonstrate concern for the well-being of his servants, as when he once wrote to authorities on behalf of a jailed ex-employee whom Morris believed was innocent.[24]

In 1792, Robert and Mary enjoyed the services of Peter Bellizan (known as Constant) as their steward; Poirez as hairdresser; Acksia Guerin and Rosella as maids; Mrs. Christopher as washerwoman; and Robert Harris, Jacob Schwine, and James Dorsey as coachmen, among others. Most particularly, they enjoyed the work of Chaumette, a live-in cook direct from Paris who joined the Morrises in early 1792. Chaumette made use of what the family raised or bought locally, but Morris's account books also give some insight into

further delicacies. In the autumn, orders for the family's table included venison, raisins, apples, and "sweetmeats imported from Barbados." In the winter,
they purchased salmon, English cheese, and "Spanish segars." In the spring, it
was oysters and olive oil. In the summer, they enjoyed codfish, strawberries,
coffee, and beer. And always, it was wine, including Madeira, claret, and champagne. "I want these wines for my own use," Morris explained in one order to
his agent in Bordeaux, "and therefore send the best or none." As 1792 turned to
1793, the names of the coachmen and other support staff gradually changed,
but Constant, Chaumette, and Acksia remained fixtures.[25]

Morris's neighbor Washington had his own servant concerns, which
for him included runaway slaves. But the president acknowledged the Morrises' success in the realm of hospitality and fashion. He paid close attention
to the Morrises' decor and furnishings before he moved into their main
house, instructing Lear to heed the advice of Mrs. Morris in this regard, as
she was "a notable lady in family arrangements." When Washington placed
a complicated order for French tableware through then-diplomat Gouverneur Morris in Europe, he added these instructions: "If I am defective recur
to what you have seen on Mr. Robert Morris's table for my ideas *generally*."[26]

Morris also made the rounds at clubs outside his home, beyond the
Dancing Assembly. His favorite was perhaps the "Sons of St. George, established at Philadelphia, for the advice and assistance of Englishmen in distress," which he had helped establish before the war. Morris could relate
to the club's mission to help orphaned English emigrants, but what he most
enjoyed were its revelries. At the city's tavern rooms, members pooled resources and drank to their cause. Their highlight each year was St. George's
Day, April 23. In a letter to Mary from New York after this holiday in 1790,
Morris hinted at the usual celebrations: "Tell Doctor Jones that, remember-
ing his admonitions, I did not kill the Dragon on St. George's night altho I
sat from dinner untill Ten o'clock at night as merry as near anybody and as
much entertained with songs of Glee." Though not in his usual form, he still
needed an extra long walk the next day to work off that night's effects. Neither distance from home nor a spell of weak health kept him from the full-
throated party. Naturally, Morris often served as president of the Philadelphia
group, a position he held in 1792.[27]

A final, essential element for the Morrises' pleasure and hospitality in
the early 1790s was their beloved country retreat, known as "The Hills" (fig.
2.4). Reflecting a practice common among the city's elite, the Morrises had

Figure 2.4. A contemporary view of "the Hills," showing its stone house flanked by greenhouses, with a fenced garden in the foreground. ("Robert Morris' Seat on Schuylkill," watercolor by Jerry Paul, from *Original Drawings of Early Philadelphia* [1794–95]. Courtesy of the Historical Society of Pennsylvania)

purchased this estate just outside the city in 1770 to use as a breezier, shaded home during the summer months and also on special occasions. The Hills was located on the eastern bluffs of the Schuylkill River, about three miles from the city's center, with scenic vistas across the water. Beyond the two-story stone house, partially encircled by outlying work buildings, lay farm-land the Morrises had transformed into an abundant garden. Their fields provided vegetables, grains, and orchard fruit, as well as pasture for cattle, sheep, and assorted exotics. The family built extensive greenhouses, where they cultivated tropical fruits such as pineapples, oranges, and lemons. They installed ice houses, from which to freshen glasses of lemonade and punch in the summertime. They dug a decorative fish pond and stocked it with gold-fish. Mary Morris once wrote during wartime in 1777 that the family was soon "to inhabit the Hills, where we shall remain, if possible, in the enjoy-ment of all that's beautiful to the eye and grateful to the taste."[28]

As the family was reaching the height of their opulence in the 1780s and '90s, their joy in the villa had not dulled. Manasseh Cutler, a Congregational minister visiting the area from Connecticut, chronicled ongoing improvements at the Hills in 1787. His party rode a carriage westward out of Philadelphia "up the river several miles, and took a view of a number of Country-seats, one belonging to Mr. R. Morris, the American financier, and who is said to be possessed of the greatest fortune in America." The estate "is planned on a large scale, the gardens and walks are extensive, and the villa, situated on an eminence, has a commanding prospect down the Schuylkill to the Delaware." Later that same year, while Robert was in Virginia on business, he wrote Mary while homesick for the property. "I congratulate you on your frequent walks to the Hills[,] they will be usefull & I dare say are pleasant. I wish I could be with you in those excursions."[29]

An example of the couple's more strategic use of the Hills arose when Robert was in New York City. There, Robert had made friends with several wealthy New Yorkers who would soon set off for Philadelphia, and he made arrangements with Mary to return the hospitality they had shown him. ("These People are very Rich," he wrote to her, "but what is of much more consequence they are Worthy Good People, Hospitable, kind & Generous.") He asked Mary to "entertain them and shew them all those Civilities which you know so well how to bestow." He added, "I wish the Gentlm. to see the *Hills* & the Ladies too if they are so inclined." Robert recommended that the guests should taste a particular vintage of their wine, and instructed that "you must give them some of the best Fish & excellent Butter &c." Tellingly, he added, "I sometimes speake of these things." Later that summer, Mary shipped a gift box to Robert in New York, containing the first pineapple of the season from the greenhouses at the Hills, along with other fruits. He delighted over them, and treated those around him to a sample. "The raising of this very fine fruit makes me feel not a little proud," he admitted. And after the Dancing Assembly's presidential birthday ball a few years later, he used the house in spring 1792 to host a party of treaty-making Seneca Indians from upstate New York.[30]

As spring turned to summer that year, Morris was still facing criticism for his lifestyle and his politics. He may have justified his table, his homes, and the like in reference to his family's happiness, but, as with the Dancing Assembly's ball, other Americans saw more dangerous implications there. On the Fourth of July, a Vermont militia company issued a rousing toast, seemingly targeting Morris specifically: "May the American states be long defended from the inundation which is threatened by the increase of aristocrats," they said, "who wish for a rich metropolis and a poor peasantry; want a great personage's head on the current coin; and are advocates for keeping shut the doors of the Senate," the latter two points being recognizable positions held by Senator Morris. Within this atmosphere, Morris would turn his hand to the creation of a showy new mansion, and his choice of its designs could not be neutral.[31]

3. His Plans

Morris's lavish hospitality, his many servants, his houses, his fine things—all were built on something of a lie. True, many saw in Morris the personification of wealth, "the American financier . . . who is said to be possessed of the greatest fortune in America." Morris himself had done all he could to foster this image. Yet the reality was that Morris had labored under crushing debts since the mid-1780s, debts that threatened to strip his family of everything.

He had poignantly expressed his dilemma in 1788, upon his sons' return from their education in Europe. At the time, Morris was in Virginia on an errand to try to avert lawsuits and uphold his sinking credit. When he wrote home to congratulate Mary on the boys' return, he instructed her to immediately impress upon them the need now "to make their own way through the world." He continued by acknowledging that it would be difficult to convince them of the family's financial peril, "after what they have been told in Europe of my Fortune, what they see around them, and what will be told them by other People daily in contradiction of what we shall say, but they must still be convinced of the Truth, and we cannot begin too soon." These were the thoughts of a parent under duress; and Morris felt the weight of this tension between public façade and private "Truth." As he well knew, there were no private banks that might rescue him, and if Morris could not find enough money or time for his personal debts, he would be humiliated and sent to prison, and his family's property would be auctioned away. That he was not alone among his class in such straits was little comfort.[1]

His troubles had started almost as soon as he had resigned his position as superintendent of finance. During his years at the helm of the government, Morris had little time to organize his private affairs. He retained his hand as a senior investment partner in his merchant firms, which grew to include at least five major partnerships along the East Coast, from New York to Charleston, but his role had shifted from manager and trader to promoter and backer. When he returned to private life in 1784, he brought a renewed confidence to his entrepreneurial activities, along with an expanded worldview. Something about the superintendent position, or his wartime experiences, had stirred in him an appetite for action that would make his prewar mercantile risk-taking seem tame. A symbolic first step came in January 1784, when he helped launch the *Empress of China,* the first American ship to trade directly with China. Morris's share of the cost was nearly $60,000, and after the ship's successful return later that year, Morris orchestrated other voyages to China and India, with ships sailing eastward and westward around the globe.[2]

With this new boldness, he also demonstrated a lack of focus and, for the first time, a lack of acumen. While the *Empress of China* was sailing toward the Cape of Good Hope, Morris operated on a different hunch and struck an agreement with the Farmers General of France to monopolize the sale of *all* American tobacco to France for three years. This would have brought another fortune in itself. But it pitted his interests against those of southern planters, and the plan soon sparked a storm of difficulties: diplomatic, financial, logistical, and personal. Morris found himself overwhelmed, committed to supplying huge amounts of tobacco at unforeseen prices, in the midst of a rocky postwar economy with unstable currency. His letters from the period reflect his mounting strains. In November 1784, he confessed to his Baltimore partner, "I am in advance for so many People & so many objects that I begin to fear a want of money, to fullfill (with the punctuality I like) my engagements." By the following spring, he was making excuses why his advances "have been drawn to an extent that I never intended & ought not to have suffered." The drumbeat continued in 1786: "I feel most sensibly in the course of my business the general scarcity of money which deranges my operations a good deal." His affairs were also complicated by a lingering dispute with John Holker, French consul and a former business associate, over the value of old Continental money in their previous dealings together.[3]

This was not mere rhetoric. As Morris scrambled to right his vast tobacco contracts and settle his dispute with Holker, the worst happened in 1787.

In the late spring that year, a key partner in England, John Rucker, panicked and sailed home to America, leaving huge amounts of Morris's bills on him protested (unpaid). "In effect, his checks bounced," in the words of historian Elizabeth M. Nuxoll, thereby wrecking his credit, and quite publicly, in a world in which credit, the lifeblood of commerce, involved the ability to inspire confidence. Even worse, his failed bills were tied to the U.S. Board of Treasury, thereby hindering the Confederation government's relationship to foreign debtors. All of this transpired in Europe while Morris sat, solemn and perspiring, in the closed rooms of the Constitutional convention then taking place that summer in Philadelphia. When Morris heard in November the definitive news of the fate of his bills, he told Mary that "I am exceedingly hurt in my feelings, notwithstanding that my mind was previously prepared for this event." He was embarrassed and now would have to pay hefty damages and find a new way to fund his bills. He then spoke of "Fortitude" and "Fate" and "Grace," resolving that "I shall use every exertion to clear myself of this situation the soonest that circumstances can possibly admit." His brood was foremost in his mind; he hoped to have "sufficient left for My Family" and "to make you as happy as you can wish." The 75,000 florins' worth (approximately £80,000 sterling) of protested bills did not bankrupt Morris, but they did introduce a sense of personal crisis which would define the rest of his life.[4]

Into the 1790s, he remained haunted by his predicament. At various times, he inwardly felt "my disapointments and losses," "the recollection of difficulties and embarassments," "Reproaches and Complaints," and "my cares & anxieties." His scrape troubled his colleagues as well; one held that "Morris I think can't fail—if he does[,] ruin on Thousands will [result]," indicating how deeply embedded he was in the era's trade. Somehow, Morris's personality remained expansive, though, reinforcing his ability to abide public scrutiny and ridicule. "My successes and my misfortunes, which ever befall me, are equally the themes for abuse," he once mused to a friend. "However let them indulge their Spleen, if I had nothing else to disturb my repose, I should sleep much at ease." The setback did not dampen his tastes, as, for example, when he sat up laughing with club friends into the early morning hours or when he and Mary played host. What did disturb his sleep was his shaken financial expectation. As a consequence, Morris's entrepreneurial schemes grew more and more radical, confounding even his friends. By the early 1790s, Morris had involved himself in nearly every major arena of the young nation's economy, in a quest for supreme wealth.[5]

His prime enterprise, of course, became land speculation. Land fever—buying or claiming "unused" or "unsettled" lands to the west and then selling them to settlers or other investors for higher prices—had become something of an American obsession. Land was America's chief resource. Almost every notable figure of the era, including Benjamin Franklin, George Washington, James Madison, Henry Knox, Patrick Henry, Gouverneur Morris, Aaron Burr, William Bingham, and James Monroe, among hundreds of others, engaged in the hopeful practice. Indeed, private interests in land may have been one of the precipitating causes of the Seven Years' War and then the American Revolution, as European empires and then the British crown and its colonists butted heads over the issue. After the war, many army veterans received their back pay in the form of land grants from embattled state governments. A speculative boom followed in the late 1780s and into the 1790s, when Congress opened new lands it had acquired stretching to the Great Lakes and the Mississippi River. Land speculation had many critics, who charged that it concentrated vast amounts of property in the hands of a few. It seemed to enrich the speculator afar at the expense of the families actually carting their belongings into the forests and doing the work of settling and "improving" the land. It kept many settlers dependent on the credit, stores, and whims of their larger surrounding landholders. And it caused tensions among surveyors and state governments, to say nothing of Indian tribes, the primary (now displeased) inhabitants of the lands. Still, Morris and others saw the wave of speculation and settlement as a unique, certain opportunity, with the potential for huge returns.[6]

Surely Europe could be counted on for investments and loans. Yet the response from the Dutch, British, and French had been lukewarm. Morris redoubled his efforts in this area after his failed bills. "Flour & Tobacco still keep up at such high prices as render it impracticable for me to meddle with them," he wrote. "I must therefore turn the more eagerly towards that object which now seems the most likely to administer to my relief. I mean the sale of Lands." Gouverneur Morris, his old friend and business partner from the Office of Finance, was dispatched to Europe to serve as Morris's sales agent and to negotiate his bills directly, among other United States diplomatic duties. Gouverneur landed in France in January 1789 and immediately set to work selling what cargoes of flour and tobacco Robert could command, reloading his ships, soothing Parisian bankers, and laying groundwork while prospective maps were being prepared. Gouverneur came from a well-placed New York family and would bring a keen eye to Morris's tangled affairs. Concerned for his friend, he wrote warmly in April of his hopes that "the storms will at length ease their fury and we shall enjoy together the serenity of the evening."[7]

Perhaps salvation lay along the Genesee River in upstate New York. In August 1790, Morris, while bobbing in and out of the Senate's chambers, agreed to purchase one million acres of land in the western part of the state, just south of Lake Ontario. He was excited by reports of the quality of the land, and he believed the lands were more convenient and hosted more amenable Indian tribes than those in the Ohio country and beyond. He acquired the Genesee land for £30,000 Massachusetts currency (worth about $113,872), from Oliver Phelps and Nathaniel Gorham, two previous speculators who could not meet their installments. Morris intended to make payments on the transaction by quickly selling parcels to a European investment company in France or the Netherlands, as he said, "for the settlement of Foreigners who wish to live contiguous to each other." This would mirror the colonial pattern which had so defined Pennsylvania decades earlier, and there were good reports regarding the fertility of the lands. That winter, Morris purchased/mortgaged an additional four million acres, adjoining his original tract, from the Massachusetts state government for only $366,333 more, with the same goals in mind (fig. 3.1). Gouverneur Morris would take care of the sales, but to help, Morris also enlisted Benjamin Franklin's grandson, William Temple Franklin, as well as his own eldest son, Robert, Jr., to represent the land abroad. And his son Thomas, by now a lawyer, would serve as resident agent in the region.[8]

Beyond these enormous single tracts, Morris also accumulated an assortment of purchases throughout the country. These included hundreds of thousands of uncultivated acres in the late 1780s and early 1790s, mostly across Pennsylvania and southward, in Delaware, Maryland, Virginia, and beyond. Some lands he held, some he sold to American settlers or investors, and some he advertised in Europe with his New York property. Most land laws of the time—as in Pennsylvania's law of 1792—attempted to favor settlers over large speculators, and to prevent sales of lands to non-Americans, but these legalities were easily circumvented. To better reap this harvest, Morris began forming a number of new partnerships and real estate companies. Thus by 1792, Morris had transformed himself into real estate baron, attempting to rebuild his paper fortune with borrowed payments on the solid earth of his country. For him, this was not mere rapaciousness. In his view,

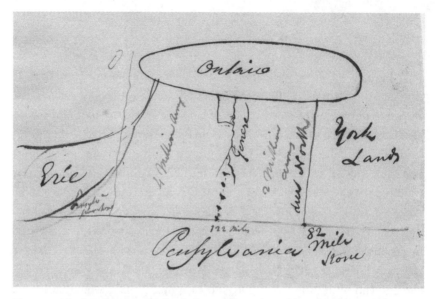

Figure 3.1. Map in Robert Morris's hand, showing the outline of the six million acres of Genesee land he purchased in western New York in 1790. The property was bounded by Lake Ontario on the north, Lake Erie and other lands on the west, and the Pennsylvania state line on the south. (Robert Morris to Gouverneur Morris, August 8, 1790, Gouverneur Morris Papers, Rare Book and Manuscript Library, Columbia University)

such activity was "calculated to promote public Good as well as private benefit." Through the promotional activities of investors and land companies, "uncultivated Lands will soon become settled & improved, and thereby the natural strength and wealth of the Country is increased." As always, he believed he was doing good.[9]

Morris's holdings also included a significant amount of "improved" property. Some, like "the Hills" and his Sixth Street residence in Philadelphia, were for personal use. Others around the city, such as the president's house, houses in Ton Alley, Minor Street, and Front Street, and a Springetsbury Manor estate adjoining the Hills, were leased to tenants. Further afield, his rural estates—like those near Trenton, New Jersey; Wilmington, Delaware; Hartford County, Maryland; and Goochland, Virginia—were leased to planters' families.[10]

Gouverneur Morris in France had misgivings about these sprawling designs, however. "I do not approve much of running in *Debt for Lands*," Gouverneur stated plainly at the outset in the summer of 1790. "You speak of my selling Land as if it were the easiest thing on Earth to perswade men to

give their money for they know not what," he chided Morris. Robert had not
sent him complete maps or titles, or even formal descriptions of the lands as
they piled up. American land schemes were becoming something of a farce
in Europe, where agents for a group called the Scioto Company, hawking
five million acres of newly opened land along the Ohio, came in for particular
abuse. Privately, Gouverneur worried to William Temple Franklin in 1791
that Robert was in a "dangerous situation." The following year, Gouverneur
told Robert that one of his potential backers in London "cried out that you
must finish by being ruind," upon being presented with "the glowing picture"
drawn by the exuberant financier. Indeed, Gouverneur found it necessary to
insist to such potential investors that "when once you are fairly out of Debt
you will abandon forever all new Projects and Pursuits," as he told Robert.[11]

But Morris put more wheels in motion. This merchant, banker, and
land speculator also became an industrialist. Morris's main manufacturing
operations were located at the falls of the Delaware River in Bucks County,
Pennsylvania, opposite Trenton. At this property, known as Morrisville, or
the Delaware Works, he drew power from the racing water nearby to oper-
ate various grist, saw, and rolling mills; a forge and iron works; a hat manufactory; a candle manufactory; a stone quarry; and a brewery. Further, he
leased several farms on the estate to tenants, and he established a fishery
there. In 1791 and 1792, he planted thousands of mulberry trees—dozens of
acres—which would provide food for a colony of silkworms, marking Morris's early attempts to begin producing commercial silk. Though the busy
works were valued at over £20,000 Pennsylvania currency in 1792, they
struggled to return the investment. A French aristocrat visited three years
later and observed of the manufactures that if Morris "was not so absorbed in
speculation, and if his affairs were not so embarrassed, he could give more
attention to these things and make them pay." Morris, frustrated with the
works' returns, hired and dismissed a succession of managers until late 1794,
when he finally appointed his eldest son, Robert, Jr., superintendent in an
effort to bring about profitability. Wage laborers, indentured servants, and
as many as six slaves owned by Morris also staffed the site. He, Mary, and
their other children visited the property often, staying in a comfortable house
kept for their use on the grounds. Elsewhere, beyond the Delaware Works,
when opportunities arose, Morris invested in steam engines and the development of new machine technologies. And he sponsored mining activities,
such as the Lehigh Coal Mine Company in Pennsylvania, the French Broad
lead mine in the Ohio valley, and copper mines in Maryland.[12]

In related moves, Morris also invested in bridge, canal, navigation, and turnpike companies. These would make his land and materials more accessible and perhaps turn a profit themselves. From 1788 into the early 1790s, he acquired shares in the Potomac Navigation Company, the James River canal project, the Dismal Swamp canal project, and canal projects between both the Susquehanna and Schuylkill Rivers, and the Schuylkill and Delaware Rivers. Indeed, Morris was more than an investor in these matters; he was among the founders of the Pennsylvania Society for Promoting the Improvement of Roads and Inland Navigation during his first years as senator, and in 1792 he served as president of the board of the Schuylkill and Susquehanna Navigation Company. A Philadelphia man recorded in a diary entry for 1791 that he went to a tavern one evening "and met the following gentlemen who are interested in making a turnpike road from the city to Vanderen's Mill: Robert Morris, Samuel Powell, [etc.]," with the result that "Mr. Morris was chosen chairman." We can imagine Morris sitting there among them, raising his glass and making big plans.[13]

Finally, Morris kept his hand in the realm of finance, actively purchasing and trading bills of exchange and public securities. His account books were littered with these transactions, as in January 1792, when his clerk recorded one purchase of $10,000 in government debts. The values of such IOU notes issued by the federal government or by the states rose and fell according to the times. The nation's money supply in the early 1790s was complex and controversial, and there were many opportunities for investors to profit from these shifting piles of paper. Congress authorized the nation's first mint in 1792, and it began sputtering forth silver half-dimes in October, but almost all economic transactions still took place in the form of individual credits and exchanges. Additionally, Morris invested heavily in bank shares, from the earlier Bank of North America to the Bank of Pennsylvania to Alexander Hamilton's newly established Bank of the United States, which provided him with sizable returns. He also bought at least one thousand shares in the new Insurance Company of North America.[14]

Such opaque transactions were viewed with suspicion by many Americans. They seemed manipulative, enriching a select few, and did not produce anything apparently constructive. Indeed, Morris hosted Hamilton, sitting secretary of the treasury, for private dinners, while Morris's votes as U.S. senator directly benefited his personal portfolio, much to the horror of political opponents. He defended these financial developments, as he had in the early 1780s, even when they seemed to swindle widows, veterans, and the public trust out of due compensation. Instead, he saw the Federalist structure of fully funded government debts and a national bank as setting the necessary conditions for a stable economy, and he saw it as just in regards to the government's outstanding obligations. "America has paid, and . . . the contest now is only, whether the whole shall reimburse the few, who sustain the advance," he explained. Funding the nation's debt would also reduce the profits foreign creditors reaped on it, Morris argued. Public securities afterward would then enter the free market. The opposition to this plain logic he attributed to the public not apprehending its "real interest" and to pandering politicians. He disarmingly phrased his view of his operations in a private letter to another American in 1789, by proposing that they join "friends in London" to "speculate in the American Funds . . . on such terms as will be usefull to them, beneficial to us, and consistent with principles of the strictest Integrity, Honor and the Public Good."[15]

Still, the practice of financial speculation, of making money with money, grew more suspect after the notorious William Duer failure in 1792. An arch manipulator, the New Yorker had helped initiate a bubble of inflating paper prices and a frenzy of credit-fueled buying in mid-1791, on the occasion of the first sales of stock in the new Bank of the United States. Crowds jostled in Boston, New York, and Philadelphia to attend the sales, while Duer and his associates worked to corner the market. After one month, the bank stock's initial buy-in price of $25 per share had risen to $325. Philadelphia became "a great gaming house," according to Benjamin Rush. Morris continued buying as more securities were drawn into the swirl, and by the year's end Morris was making payments of more than $7,000 every week on his shares in the Bank of the United States alone. The market crash came the following March, after prices had finally reversed, leading Duer to default on his $3 million in speculation-driven debts. The resulting panic and failures unsettled the coffeehouses, the economy, and the wary Jeffersonians. Duer went to debtors' prison, but Morris survived. If there were lessons there, Morris did not heed them. On April 28, 1792, Morris ordered $250,000 more in the government's "three percents" from John Nicholson, auditor and comptroller for the state of Pennsylvania and his future land partner.[16]

So by the end of 1792, Morris stood at the helm of a vast enterprise. He was at some level a silkworm cultivator, a miller, a quarry operator, a mining investor, a banker and financier, an agriculturalist, a canal backer and

Figure 3.2. Silhouette of Robert Morris, circa 1792. (Joseph Sansom, *An Occasional Collection of Physiognomical Sketches, chiefly North American, and drawn from the life; designed to preserve the characteristic features of personally, mentally, or officially Remarkable Persons, and the endeared Memory of Private Friends or Public Benefactors; with professional Notices &c.* [Philadelphia, 1790–92]. Courtesy of The Winterthur Library, Joseph Downs Collection of Manuscripts and Printed Ephemera)

company board president, a landlord, and a land salesman, in addition to being a U.S. senator (fig. 3.2). He also nominally remained a merchant, importing luxuries like wine, brandy, tea, molasses, and sugar, while exporting lumber, wheat, and flour. After his tobacco contract losses, he did not have the ability to put serious resources into the costly China trade. Instead, his ships sailed the Atlantic. Of his five major partnerships along the East Coast formed a decade earlier, four remained more or less intact, though Morris was starting to withdraw his stakes in them as he needed the funds. For all of these many details, Morris relied on the particular assistance of his main clerk, Garrett Cottringer, a Catholic and minor merchant in his own right who had worked under Morris since the 1780s.[17]

The glow of the new year of 1793 brought a rare, fleeting moment, when all this scratching seemed to bring real relief. And it came from the sale of lands. At the close of December 1792, Morris negotiated a confusing but hefty sale with a group of Amsterdam bankers, later organized as the Holland Land Company. The result put £75,000 sterling into his hands in exchange for two of his immense Genesee tracts, with the promise of more payments to follow. That same month, in Europe, Robert, Jr., secured his own, though less advantageous, sale to the same bankers of two more Genesee tracts for 1,250,000 florins, or $500,000. When informed, Gouverneur nicely summed up the effects of this sudden windfall: "Thus you are now completely clear of all troubles and incumbrances whatever on which I most heartily congratulate you." The two had been working toward this moment for years, with Gouverneur watching his friend squirm under the pressure of old debts and uneven returns, climaxing with impending payments that he knew he could not meet. So he renewed his call for Morris to "wind up your affairs and embark no more in any undertaking which can employ time or involve Hazard." "You are rich enough," he pleaded. "You have a fine family round you. You have an excellent woman for a wife who has gone chearfully along with you thro the fair and thro the stormy Days. For the sake of her of you and of them, may I add also for the sake of your friend enjoy now the calm." The French Revolution was then taking terrifying turns outside Gouverneur's windows and unsettling both sides of the Atlantic, making this advice particularly timely. In Philadelphia, Morris did relax some when he told his son Thomas that he would "now hold up & sell only to settlers, having sold already as much as will put me perfectly at ease in money matters." As for winding up his affairs, for abandoning forever all new projects, those proposals now seemed unnecessarily fearful.[18]

On the morning of January 9, perhaps in a mood of celebration, Morris stepped out with the rest of the city to see a highly advertised spectacle. For the past several days, Frenchman Jean Pierre Blanchard, fresh from European triumphs, had been in town stirring up excitement for his "Aerial Exhibition"—his planned launch of the first manned flight on the continent. Blanchard himself would be inside the basket of his experimental hydrogen balloon. At ten o'clock that morning, Morris and his family, along with the Washingtons and other notables in their specially priced front-row seats, arranged by Blanchard for this occasion, watched the yellow silk bag rise from inside the courtyard of the Walnut Street Jail.[19]

Into this picture stepped Peter Charles L'Enfant. And L'Enfant was not happy. The past fifteen years of the architect's life had led to this singular, explosive moment. It began when he first felt the pull of the American Revolution from across the ocean. Then, after arriving in America, he had risked his life on the battlefield. In victory, he had worked to persuade American leaders that the scale of the destiny that lay before them would be much more expansive than they had originally conceived, and he had finally received a glorious commission for his talents. But now, he had walked off, or had been pushed off, the Potomac project after a long-simmering confrontation with the new federal city's commissioners.

Like Morris, L'Enfant possessed an optimism that was difficult to keep down. Up until this point, it had served him well.

Born in 1754, L'Enfant was the son of a painter associated with the re-nowned Gobelins Tapestry Works. He grew up around the courts of Louis XV and XVI and received training, partially under his father, at the Royal Academy of Painting and Sculpture. When an American agent in Paris offered him the chance to join the Continental Army in 1777, L'Enfant took it, like other well-placed young men around him. He entered at the rank of lieutenant and soon joined the corps of engineers as captain. By the end of the war, he had anglicized his name from Pierre to Peter (and curiously added an apostrophe to his surname Lenfant). Six feet tall, he carried himself with what one observer called "military bearing, courtly air and polite manners." He had received a serious, lasting leg wound. And he had come to see tremendous prospects for the new nation.[20]

L'Enfant initially crossed paths with Robert Morris during the Revolutionary War. One day in April 1782, Captain L'Enfant called on Morris in the Office of Finance and, in Morris's words, "tryed hard to perswade me out of some Money." L'Enfant's request was not out of the ordinary, but Morris followed the necessary custom that served him on most such occasions, and he "refused peremtorily."[21]

At the time, L'Enfant was on the cusp of a major commission which would soon provide the two men with a more pleasant encounter. France's minister to America, the chevalier de La Luzerne, announced that same month the birth of the dauphin, the prince and heir to the royal throne. L'Enfant received the chevalier's commission to supervise and construct the setting for what would be the greatest party Philadelphia had yet seen. Any tension that may have underlain the new republic's salute to French royalty and aristocracy did not show in L'Enfant's hand. Working at the minister's rented Philadelphia residence on Chestnut Street, L'Enfant constructed a large colonnaded pavilion outside the main house, set within a lamp-lit garden. He added rich illustrations and tableaus with weighty national symbols, including a rising sun, thirteen stars, and noble Indians. On the evening of the fete, July 15, perhaps ten thousand people descended on the site, either as groomed, invited guests or as part of the celebrity-struck crowd. An orchestra played waltzes, thirty French chefs served delicacies, French and American officers toasted their alliance, fireworks were launched into the air from an outdoor stage, and spectators outside pressed against a special fence built to offer views of the scene. Morris attended, likely with Mary, and enjoyed himself. The party gave L'Enfant valuable exposure for his talents, and the French War Ministry covered the $5,000 total bill. It was the first hint of L'Enfant's ease with excess.[22]

L'Enfant and Morris developed a rough working relationship a year later, as fellow members of the Society of the Cincinnati. L'Enfant, promoted to the rank of major, was a founding member of the Society, formed by a core of Continental officers from the army and navy. In October 1783, Robert Morris was elected an honorary member of the Society. One of his first duties as such was finding funds for L'Enfant to go to France, to procure medals for the members. L'Enfant again showed up in Morris's well-worn office, and the two argued over money for the trip and pay. By November 8, the two had finally come to terms, and Morris saw L'Enfant off at the docks in Chester, where he was boarding the *General Washington* for Le Havre, France. Morris took satisfaction in these efforts on behalf of L'Enfant, being able, as he told the president of the Society's New York chapter, "to devise the Means of removing Difficulties which otherwise would have been insuperable and put it out of [L'Enfant's] Power to prosecute his Voyage to Europe." It may not have been the smoothest beginning, but each man could claim a benefit.[23]

L'Enfant returned to the United States in April 1784, having fulfilled his mission but leaving a trail of unpaid debts. He thereupon began sketching out a vision of his adopted country's future that meshed well with Morris's own. L'Enfant took the long view, promoting a blend of European traditions of power with New World opportunities, as in his statement to Congress in 1784, wherein he suggested that given financial constraints, it would take decades to build a new capital for the nation "in such a manner as to give an idea of the greatness of the empire as well as to engrave in every mind that sense of respect that is due to a place which is the seat of a supreme sovereignty." The following year, his hand came under Morris's direct supervision, as Congress appointed L'Enfant to do an initial survey of the lands along the Delaware River for a projected federal seat. Although the plan was halted shortly afterward, it gave the two an opportunity to share their visions. Small-scale farmers and agrarian idealists might be horrified at their visions of an American "empire," but the new Constitution in 1787 laid the groundwork for just such a structure. L'Enfant lived in New York City as an artist during that time, remaining close with Washington and Hamilton, and his renovation of New York's Federal Hall in 1788, with its grandeur, prominence, and symbolism, brought these political ideals into focus. The French ambassador at the time called the building "an allegory to the new constitution," in that "both have been entirely changed by their framers, who brought their interested clients a great deal further than they had thought to go." Naturally, Morris had admired the "Fine Federal Edifice" upon seeing it in 1789. Meanwhile, the Constitution's provision for establishing a federal district prompted L'Enfant to write pages more of proposals, mostly sent directly to Washington himself.[24]

In 1791, L'Enfant's impressive friendships, arguments, and experience paid off. He received the enviable commission to plan the federal city on the Potomac, and he quickly produced a correspondingly ambitious capital layout, carefully aligned with the district's topography for the most pleasing effects. In contrast with Jefferson's simple grid proposal, L'Enfant's city plan featured radial vistas, grand avenues, various parks, and a National Mall, with cascading fountains, monuments, a public church, and a "presidential palace." Here was a work suited to impress "the eyes of every other nation envying the opportunity deny'd them & will stand juge." Yet if his work on the Potomac confirmed his design genius, his nationalism, and his flair for what he called "sumptuousness," it also confirmed his testy temperament. Over several months, L'Enfant chafed under the directions of the city's three commissioners, who were responsible to the local landowners and city investors as well as to the miserly federal government. L'Enfant had taken his charge to build a city quite seriously; he had little tolerance for the foolishness of superiors who wished to build his plan around the whims of local proprietors with funds raised at auctions. Wooden stakes still marked the ground for the blocks and avenues when the city commissioners decided in February 1792 that they could no longer tolerate L'Enfant's insubordination—his hiring and dismissal of teams of project workers in defiance of orders, his refusal to allow a plan of the city to be printed and distributed when he felt the thing was not yet ready.[25]

By that time, L'Enfant had sadly reached the same conclusion. He had traveled to Philadelphia, arranging for his own engraving of the city plan, when he sent a report directly to President Washington that put the matter baldly. Washington, once one of L'Enfant's most enthusiastic supporters, then made a few attempts in the midst of his sixtieth birthday celebrations to persuade the engineer to remain on the job. But he concluded L'Enfant would continue in his ways to "be under the controul of no one." Engineering responsibility for the city was officially transferred from L'Enfant to the project's surveyor, Andrew Ellicott, on February 27, 1792. Ellicott and the commissioners would make a few alterations to L'Enfant's original plan, but his core ideas would remain. L'Enfant cut the project out of his life and passed through the district only once more during the 1790s.[26]

What does a man of L'Enfant's talents do when he loses the commission of his life? His companion Isaac Roberdeau, who had served L'Enfant loyally for the past year as secretary, assistant surveyor, and housemate, told a Potomac acquaintance that the pair "would go to Pennsylvania that they had offers from thence and could be employed when they pleased." After recouping over the summer, the two turned to a new and different project at the falls of the Passaic River in northern New Jersey, at the behest of Alexander Hamilton.[27]

Robert Morris was not involved, but he had his eye on the enterprise. Hamilton, as figurehead of the recently created corporation known as the Society for Establishing Useful Manufactures, had projected a complete industrial community along the river. Morris may have shared with Hamilton ideas from his own manufacturing experience. He did share staff, including an early partner and manager.[28]

Hamilton assured his Society's directors that L'Enfant was the ideal engineer for their job. He explained, "From much experience and observation of him, I have a high opinion of the solidity of his talents" and training. On August 1, 1792, while Morris was busily putting all his own speculative plans in motion, the Society's directors resolved to offer L'Enfant a one-year contract to engineer the waterworks, superintend construction of the buildings, and design the city plan at Paterson. L'Enfant was on the grounds by the middle of the month. And he soon brought up Isaac Roberdeau, having secured him a job on the project. The men's fortunes in Paterson would prove eerily similar to their fortunes on the Potomac. L'Enfant promised his patron Hamilton to remain mindful of the Society's finances, but he quickly became ensnared in the differences among the Society's directors, and he feuded with rival managers.[29]

By February 1793, the Society's staff had seen enough. Peter Colt, a factory overseer, complained to Hamilton that "several Buildings which have been ordered for manufactures, are extremely wanted." But "Majr. L'Enfant, to whom this part of the Business has been confided," was no longer present. Factory production slowed to a near standstill, and in March a director exclaimed to Hamilton, "What can be the Cause of Maj. L Enfants extraordinary long Absence? Will you speak to him and advise him to come forward immediately"? L'Enfant returned to Paterson at the end of the month, justifying his progress to Hamilton and bristling at the directors' decision to consult another regarding the waterworks. Still resolute in his own abilities, he fretted about the scenario unfolding yet again around him and despaired in his chopped English "that my whole labour is likely once more to be made a mean to gratify the petit Interest of some men to the Expulsion of me and the Subversion of all my views." He dismissed his assigned laborers and pushed toward a confrontation at the April meeting of the directors, wherein they became "seriously alarmed" at his "extensive plans & views." Colt then conveyed to Hamilton his opinion that L'Enfant would not adjust his plans "to square with the present Situation of the Funds of the Society." The directors reached the same conclusion. Hamilton would remain a friend to L'Enfant, but in June 1793 the engineer left his newest antagonists at Paterson, whom he saw shackling his artistic vision and interfering with impertinent questions. His one-year contract would lapse, and he would soon vow never to meet with the directors again.[30]

By that time, L'Enfant had found a new patron. He had been in and out of Philadelphia since the waning days of his federal city commission in late 1791. Most likely, he and Morris met and began plotting their magnificent new house for the family in late 1792 or early 1793, during L'Enfant's long absence from Paterson. L'Enfant occasionally took on additional commissions while engaged, and he had already begun to feel uneasy about his relations with the Society. He was seen that season in Philadelphia, chatting with disgruntled proprietors from the federal city. For his part, Morris wanted his family out of the Stedman-Galloway House, previously a rental property—a "sacrifice," despite their pleasant neighbors—and into something more suitable. Surely his family deserved better than the Binghams. It would have been easy for L'Enfant, seeking a new patron, to match Morris's vision, both for the nation and for Morris's place within it. And Morris could relate to L'Enfant's tales of unwarranted persecution. Presumably, over oysters, venison, and claret, the two put aside any lingering disagreements, and they began to plan. L'Enfant, though never one to be bound by budgets, quoted Morris an estimate for the whole project—perhaps $60,000—and Morris, flush with his recent sales, accepted.[31]

He had certainly engaged the major by May 9, 1793, when he sent a gently sarcastic letter to L'Enfant expressing his eagerness to move forward: "Dear Sir, I had like to have stopped my House for fear of wanting money, that difficulty being removed, it will now be stopped for want of Major L'Enfant." The next month L'Enfant walked away from the Paterson project, and the thing was begun.[32]

4. His House

In 1798, a small army of federal tax surveyors combed across the country to make inspections for a unique "direct tax" on citizens' private property. As they peered into doorway after doorway, the surveyors found that nearly three out of every four houses were so poorly built or so run down—valued at less than one hundred dollars each—that they did not even qualify to be taxed. Usually built of wood, these dwellings rarely had any window glass. Many had dirt floors, with holes in the roof in place of chimneys. Consisting of only a few rooms for even the largest families, the houses had cramped spaces, and the wind and cold blew through them.[1]

Cities boasted higher-quality houses on average, but the urban poor still lived in desperate, unhealthy conditions. In the 1790s, on Philadelphia's Third Street, just one block north of William and Anne Bingham's elegant mansion in the fashionable Society Hill neighborhood, a middle-aged widow/washerwoman named Susannah Cook ran a boardinghouse out of her wooden home. The entire two-story structure was only twelve feet wide and twenty-seven feet long. She and her two surviving children lived on one floor, while three boarders occupied the other. There, she cooked everyone's meals over an indoor hearth. Plenty of her neighbors did likewise, such as the family of tailor William Smith and his boarders, who made their home in an eighteen-foot-square, two-story frame house. On the northern fringe of town, mariner Richard Crips and his family huddled in an eleven-by-fourteen-foot single-story house. On the south, waterman Robert Moffatt made do with his single-room house at 33½ Catharine Street, set in the inte-

Figure 4.1. An example of Philadelphia's simplest housing stock, showing rear of Robert
Moffatt's house at 33½ Catharine Street, Philadelphia, a single-room frame house built circa
1790. (Historic American Buildings Survey PA.51-PHILA.359. Courtesy of the Library of
Congress, Prints and Photographs Division)

rior of its block, behind the street front (figs. 4.1 and 4.2). Near the city's
docks, the neighborhood of "Helltown" offered vagrants, prostitutes, the
insane, and escaped slaves and indentured servants even less comfort and
shelter. In the eyes of these residents, window glass and a spare room marked
the beginnings of a palace.[2]

Nor were size, finish, or neighborhood the only housing concerns.
There was also the problem of upkeep. In the mid-1790s, while living in
Philadelphia, the Frenchman Moreau de St. Méry complained that the homes
he had seen "always have broken windowpanes, doors without locks; and
leaks are common to every attic. These, the owners coldly insist, are impossible to prevent." Even worse was the problem of sanitation. In 1798, longtime

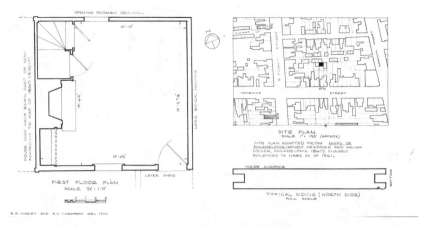

Figure 4.2. The one-room plan of 33½ Catharine Street, Philadelphia, with site plan showing position of the building on the interior of its city block. (Historic American Buildings Survey PA.51-PHILA.359. Courtesy of the Library of Congress, Prints and Photographs Division)

city resident Thomas Condie observed that though "there are few cities that can vie with Philadelphia in point of elegance or even cleanliness" overall, "there are several alleys in the city, which are also narrow, confined and filthy." In some areas, open sewers "exhale the most noxious effluvia; for, dead animals and every kind of nausea, are thrown into them, and there remain till they become putrified." At times in the crowded alleys, such as those near Walnut Street where Bishop William White's mansion stood, piles of filth stood so high that carts could not pass. Interior house furnishings, too, could be sparse. Doctor Benjamin Rush noted that in many of the "huts" of the poor he visited on his rounds, he had to "rest my weary limbs upon the bedside of the sick (from the want of chairs)." One-third of the city's residents owned no taxable property. Even something as simple as the use of spoons rather than forks at meals separated the lives of the poor from those of the refined. It was upon this broader foundation of common simplicity, as much as against the few aspiring town houses of the Binghams and others, that Robert Morris and Peter L'Enfant undertook their house project.[3]

The waterman Robert Moffatt's more prosperous neighbors, whose houses surrounded him on each side of his block, occupied an instantly recognizable style which formed the typical streetscape of the city. And this could be summed up by one descriptive term: "row house." From the early eighteenth century, Philadelphia's residents had carved the large city blocks into narrow lots on which London-inspired town houses of two to four stories stood shoulder to shoulder fronting the streets. Built individually, such houses featured symmetrical façades above the ground floor, gable roofs, double-hung windows, and, often, brick construction. Upon entering, one would step directly into the main room, as at Susannah Cook's, warmed by a fireplace and lit by a front window, with a winding staircase in a rear corner. Or, in more substantial row houses, like that of Bishop White's, one would step into a narrow side hall with a straight stair, which ran alongside the main room as well as a rear room, all connected by doorways offering greater privacy. The houses oriented their service spaces, including laundries and kitchens, to the rear yards, often connecting them to the main building by a slender "piazza." As most wealthy residents such as White conformed to the general house type, they distinguished their homes through elegance and detail, not bold dimensions or unusual forms (fig. 4.3). Indeed, the row house style grew so common as to draw complaints of monotony from visitors, an effect heightened by the city's gridded streets. "The regularity of Philadelphia is so great," observed one British traveler, "the streets are so much like each other & the houses so nearly the same size (being built of one coloured brick) that I do not think there is any thing else worthy of remark about it."[4]

But Morris would not be building a row house. Instead, he would seek to make a landmark, a residential equivalent to the State House, the library, the jail, the hospital, or one of the city's monumental churches, as the Binghams' mansion had done. For this, Morris had a special site in mind. His involvement with the property extended back to 1790, when John Dickinson approached Morris with a proposition. Dickinson owned essentially an entire city block between Chestnut and Walnut and Seventh and Eighth Streets, which he had acquired through his wife's Quaker family, the Norrises. Although only two blocks west of the State House and Congress Hall, the undeveloped block sat at the western edge of the built city (fig. 4.4). Beyond Ninth Street, the houses fell away to pasture, farmland, and trees. Indeed, Dickinson's block was known as the Norrises' pasture ground. Back toward the southeast, just across Walnut Street, was one of the four corner park squares on the city plan, which served as a potter's field—a burial ground for the indigent.[5]

Still, Dickinson's property was the closest undeveloped lot to the heart of the city's population core, which was radiating north, south, and west from the Delaware River and forming something of a triangle-shaped density. This block sat at the western tip of the expanding triangle. And the block offered an enviable proximity to the government's halls and offices

Figure 4.3. The Bishop William White House, built in 1787, located on Walnut Street near Third Street, Philadelphia. (Author photo)

clustering just east on Chestnut Street. In the first week of October 1790, Dickinson or his agent met with Morris, who was busy moving his family out of the Masters-Penn House on Market Street to make way for the Washingtons. "Would it not be more advantageous," asked Dickinson, to "take my Ground . . . for this purpose"? That is, "Buildings for the President's use" could "be erected in such a manner" on the latter ground "that in case of Congress's removal from Philadelphia, they could be conveniently divided into several Dwelling Houses for private Families, as the Savoy and Essex Houses were in London." In other words, Morris and the city's rental arrangement with the president seemed provisional. Washington's initial

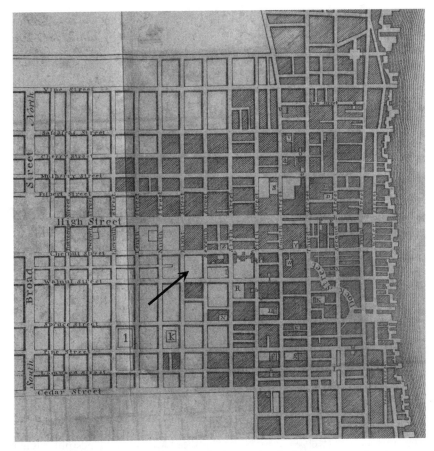

Figure 4.4. Plan of the city of Philadelphia. Shading on the plan indicates areas of settlement. The arrow added here indicates Morris's block, bounded by Chestnut and Walnut Streets, and Seventh and Eighth Streets (James Hardie, *The Philadelphia Directory and Register,* 2d ed. [Philadelphia: Jacob Johnson and Co., 1794]. Courtesy of the Library Company of Philadelphia)

lease ran only for two years, and the city council was already scouting locations where it could build a new house for the president. A presidential residence sited on Dickinson's block could be "magnificent, as the Front [on Chestnut Street] would be extensive," and "all the Back Rooms would front the South and the Gardens that might be laid out." This block rose higher than the surrounding lands, adding to the prospect.[6]

Morris, in full speculation mode, could indeed envision it. The land might serve for the presidential residence, or for his own use, or as a general investment property. "The Lot is very conveniently situated for me," he found, adding that he could make his money back "by means of dividing & cutting it up," like every other block in the populated part of town. So he agreed to Dickinson's proposal, which involved swapping one of Morris's rural estates worth £3,000 Pennsylvania currency, plus an additional £7,000 from Morris in the form of a seven-year mortgage. In exchange, Morris received the whole city block—396 feet wide by 510 feet deep—minus a tiny corner strip at Chestnut and Seventh, owned by the stubborn heirs of a local merchant who had died decades earlier. Morris's talk of subdivided lots and Dickinson's mention of the Savoy and Essex Houses indicated that neither initially saw the block as hosting a single private residence alone. Morris guarded himself against hopes of quick success, doubting that lots on the block could be sold for good prices soon, "for in this as in almost every other instance, there is too much of the commodity at market, and every owner of Lotts is striving to get the President[']s intended place of Residence on or near to his own property."[7]

The authorities indeed chose a different spot for their President's House construction. The city council had focused its search on the western portion of the city, and Morris's block made the short list of contenders. In the committee's words, his "Square adjoins the already paved Part of Chesnut Street," and "the Distance from the Public Buildings & built Parts of the City is not so great as to render it inconvenient." But in the end, after the state of Pennsylvania took over the project from the city and appropriated funds for the new building, Governor Thomas Mifflin looked one block farther northwest, perhaps for reasons of economy. The governor purchased and consolidated twelve lots on Ninth, between Market and Chestnut, giving his project commissioners a property 202 feet wide by 151 feet deep with which to work, significantly smaller than Morris's new block. Then, in October 1791, Mifflin invited Major L'Enfant, at work on the Potomac, to prepare a plan for the mansion—an ironic choice given that the Pennsylvanians were hoping their project might help "trap" the capital permanently there. L'Enfant may have submitted some ideas, having arrived in Philadelphia shortly after this invitation was issued. But when the builders broke ground in April 1792, employing a large, boxy, somewhat clumsy neoclassical plan, it seemed clear that any hand L'Enfant may have had in its design was slight. Still, as the three-and-a-half-story, five-bay structure took shape, it presented a unique appearance, built to stand alone, detached, unlike the city's typical, narrow row houses (fig. 4.5).[8]

The Morrises enjoyed living next to the Washingtons on Market Street. As workers pushed forward on the new Ninth Street residence into the sum-

Figure 4.5. "The House Intended for the President of the United States, in Ninth Street, Philadelphia," which was completed in 1797. (W[illiam]. Birch & Son, *The City of Philadelphia, in the State of Pennsylvania North America; As it Appeared in the Year 1800* [Philadelphia: W. Birch, 1800], plate 13. Courtesy of the Library Company of Philadelphia)

mer of 1792, even purchasing stone for the project from Morris's quarry on the Schuylkill, Robert likely began to think about moving along with the Virginians. He was not thinking of politics. In the thick of the past year, Morris had considered abandoning the Senate with two years left on his term. Rather, he was focusing on comfort and status—even monumental permanence. Meanwhile, masons, carpenters, plasterers, and painters shuffled in and out of his corner house on Sixth and Market, making substantial alterations in an indication that his family was still struggling to settle into their sacrifice. But Morris could not do anything bigger in 1792 while still so pressed for payments, before his balloon finally rose late that year with land sales.[9]

For the time being, Morris secured his new, empty block with a fence. He allowed it to lie idle into June 1792, when he paid workmen for making and hauling hay for his horses from its overgrown grass. Children could peer through the fence slats at their onetime trails.[10]

In the brightening of the new year of 1793, Morris returned his attention to what he called his "Lot on Chesnut Street." Writing in general terms, he told Thomas on January 2 that "I can now do those things which may be necessary to improve my Estate." More activity had begun to pick up along its streets; just east of Morris's block, on Chestnut Street, Oeller's Hotel had opened its doors in 1791. On the same block, the ambitious New Theatre was under construction. And George Clymer, a local gentleman and city official, made his home on this block, though none of the buildings west of the State House had numbers yet. Across the streets directly north, west, and south of Morris's block, residents had begun moving into modest homes, many of them built of wood. To the north lived a tax collector as well as a clerk of the House of Representatives; to the south, a carter, a hides worker, a painter, and a grocer. Immediately to the west, across Eighth Street, the widow Hannah Penington had opened a boardinghouse, in which many tradespeople lived, including house carpenters, a bricklayer, a tailor, and a dressmaker. It was a mixed neighborhood but clearly up and coming, "an improving part of the city," in the words of a local lot-seller. Around this time, L'Enfant drifted away from the Paterson enterprise and probably shared his fateful meal with Morris, with Morris's prime, empty lot enticing them as a fine canvas on which to paint.[11]

News of their grandiose plans spread quickly. Indeed, stories of the house would soon grow fantastic and take on a life of their own. But a seemingly accurate report circulated as early as mid-March 1793, when a relative of Dickinson's, Deborah Logan, was visiting with a neighbor near Germantown. There, Logan saw Henry Hill, a prominent city merchant, who "told us Robert Morris is going to build a superb house on the lot he purchased of cousin Dickinson[.] it is designed to be 140 feet front." Logan would have found much to talk about in this bit of news, beyond her family interest in the site. Hill himself owned one of the finest freestanding mansions in the city, located on Fourth Street in Society Hill, and it measured forty-eight feet wide by forty-eight feet deep, with 6,900 feet of living space in its three stories. The Masters-Penn house, in which President Washington lived, had even more space, though it measured only forty-five feet wide. Morris's new 140-foot-front would overshadow even the Pennsylvania State House, at 107 feet, to say nothing of the Bingham mansion, at 100 feet, or the President's House under construction on Ninth Street, also at 100 feet.[12]

Clues from L'Enfant's past hinted at their intentions. Earlier on the Potomac, L'Enfant had staked out a more ambitious foundation for his ill-fated "Presidential palace," as he referred to it in letters (though he named it the "President's House" on formal plans). L'Enfant had envisioned a seven-hundred-foot-wide structure with surrounding park, as "adding to the sumptuousness of a palace the convenience of a house and the agreeableness of a country seat." It was to be situated on a specific ridge, where it "will see 10 or 12 miles down the potowmack[,] front the town and harbor of alexandria[,] and stand to the view of the whole city." Every bit of this description would have appealed to the gregarious Morris, in thinking of his own residence. Further, L'Enfant had directed the President's House to be built entirely of stone, and it was to be integrally woven into the plan of the city by means of direct, radial avenues. Regarding its appearance, L'Enfant intended the presidential palace to feature a wide structure, with two curving, unattached wings (fig. 4.6). Isaac Roberdeau had begun digging out its cellars in mid-December 1791, but after L'Enfant's explosive resignation two months later, the house's design fell to another.[13]

L'Enfant's intentions for the presidential residence had aroused plenty of ire. As the engineer departed, David Stuart, a commissioner for that city, had voiced his and others' republican disgust with the proposed situation of the house. Targeting its extensive grounds, Stuart wrote that it "may suit the genius of a Despotic government to cultivate an immense and gloomy wilderness in the midst of a thriving city," but it would not do for the United States. Presumably, American landholders might build huge plantation

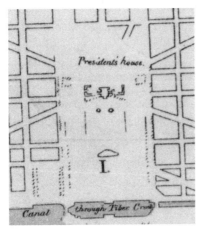

Figure 4.6. The intended "President's House" at the federal city. "I" is the "President's park." (Detail of image from Peter Charles L'Enfant, "Plan of the City intended for the Permanent Seat of the Government of t[he] United States," on the Potomac River [1791]. Facsimile produced by the United States Coast and Geodetic Survey [1887]. Courtesy of the Library of Congress, Geography and Map Division)

houses and dependencies, surrounded by miles of open property, but it was quite another thing to strike such a pose in the midst of a teeming city. Nevertheless, this was the prospect that L'Enfant and Morris were beginning to etch onto the city's grid at their block on Chestnut Street, as the redesigned President's House in Washington proceeded in parallel fashion.[14]

At the time Logan heard the news, L'Enfant had returned to Paterson, New Jersey, for his final season there. Still, Morris was able to move the work forward in his architect's absence. In March and April 1793, Morris directed more fencing to be put up on his lot and had the grounds surveyed and marked out. The momentum was also reflected in Morris's account books, where he retitled notations regarding the project from "Lot on Chesnut Street" to "House on Chesnut Street Lot." By May, when Morris sent his letter regarding the "want of Major L'Enfant," thousands of bricks and hundreds of bushels of lime had arrived at the site. Several blocks away, Pennsylvania's President's House project suddenly stalled for lack of funds, with construction up to the top floor and rafters. This sent men looking for work elsewhere, perhaps to Morris's site, where bricklayers and laborers were soon deep into the expansive foundations and cellars.[15]

Morris appointed his longtime contractor Burton Wallace to supervise the daily activity. Wallace was a master bricklayer. An active Methodist, he had worked on Morris's other properties, including both the Masters-Penn and the Stedman-Galloway houses on Market Street in 1790, and he regularly made improvements at the Hills. Morris trusted him. By June, Wallace had recruited teams of bricklayers and laborers and was directing their efforts as loads of earth were being moved around the site. By July, lumber had arrived, as had L'Enfant himself, after his final, dramatic departure from Paterson. Around the pair, workers dug wells and sinks, ran water pumps, and pushed wheelbarrows; deliverymen brought additional lumber, lime for mortar, tens of thousands more bricks, as well as the first blocks of stone. In August, stonecutters and carpenters descended on the site, squaring stones and setting up framing and scaffolding alongside the busy bricklayers. In all, Morris was paying the workers around £800 Pennsylvania currency a month ($2,144), with masons and bricklayers likely earning twelve shillings per day (nearly $2), and common laborers seven to eight shillings a day.[16]

A disquieting rumor followed L'Enfant's arrival. Though Morris had shown no signs of concern with his architect's earlier rocky relations with his clients, one visitor to Philadelphia that summer proclaimed the financier was now having second thoughts about his choice. The rumor spread from a biased source, the superintendent of operations in the federal city who had recently supplanted L'Enfant, Samuel Blodget, Jr. Blodget, then in Philadelphia on a financial errand, gloated in a letter back to his colleagues on the Potomac when he learned of L'Enfant's travails in New Jersey. The engineer had recently been dismissed from the Paterson manufactory, Blodget jeered, "for mistakes & a *Quixotic* Invention." He claimed this "has confirmd the Public in your opinion of this eccentric gentleman but Robt Morris did not know this when he contracted with him for his new house[.] he now begins to [become] alarmd & wishes he had never seen him." Was it true that Morris could be having second thoughts so soon? After all, the unflappable Morris had known the man for a decade, and only two months earlier, in May, he had called for L'Enfant's presence via letter. But perhaps it would be difficult even for Morris to project a palace without expressing a few reservations. No stranger to the charge of being quixotic, Morris settled into his choice of architects and flattered himself on his good fortune to land the man, despite what others might say.[17]

As L'Enfant adjusted to life alongside Burton Wallace and the rest of Morris's crew, the thirty-nine-year-old engineer was without his friend and former assistant Isaac Roberdeau. Roberdeau had struck up a romance with Susan Shippen Blair of Philadelphia the previous year, in the midst of the collapse of the federal city commission. The two married in November 1792, and they had likewise drifted back to town after the Paterson debacle. Soon, Roberdeau found a job with the state of Pennsylvania in the department of canals and turnpikes, probably with the aid of Morris.[18]

L'Enfant brooded over his finances. Surely Morris's commission would pay well, but for the moment the engineer was occupied with what he would call "the distress of my affairs." In 1790, he had balked at the ten acres of city land New York officials had offered him as his compensation for his work on Federal Hall. He had deemed it insufficient. Two years later, also on principle, he had refused the final compensation offered to him by the federal city commissioners: $1,150 plus a lot in the city. And he had left Paterson on equally bad terms, without receiving his full salary. Still, L'Enfant had managed to make a few investments along the way. He had purchased a prime lot near the President's House in the city of Washington, and he had recently converted his credit at the new Bank of the United States into a number of prized shares. L'Enfant began joining Morris for breakfast every other morning, at the latter's request, to discuss work on the house. He sometimes brought design drawings, which Mary reviewed with them. Looking forward, the trio flattered themselves on their prospects.[19]

With a one-time Frenchman at their breakfast table, a French cook in their kitchen, a French maid in their chambers, French tutors giving their daughters language lessons, Morris's best friend in Paris, and most of their accounts tied up in French banking houses, the Morrises were particularly attuned to the shifting destinies of France that year. But given recent events, the rest of Philadelphia, too, was alive to that country's fortunes. Diplomatic relations with this ally had taken a darker, divisive turn since the celebrations of peace in the 1780s. Louis XVI grumbled about the Americans' quick return to trade with the British, while his own subjects simmered with revolution. In 1789, with the storming of the Bastille in Paris, the prospects looked bright for republicans on both sides of the Atlantic, if not for the king. But leadership in France changed in spasms; the king was thrown in jail, its colonies around the globe opened their own violent rebellions, and thousands fled in the chaos.

Soon, Philadelphians found themselves awash in French speakers. The refugees joined a city already home to large numbers of non-English residents, particularly Germans and Africans. Still, the presence of the French was considerable, for by the end of the century they made up one in every ten people on the streets. The Comte de Moré famously dubbed the city "Noah's Ark" for his countrymen. And the French tended to cluster in certain neighborhoods, mostly near the waterfront, making their presence felt that much more strongly. Politics interested the émigrés, and their views were diverse, ranging from liberal aristocrats to radicals. Most would not settle permanently, though Robert Morris did what he could to interest them in his large hinterland tracts. Within the city, those without their own means worked as shopkeepers, artists, hairdressers, instructors, cooks, and servants.[20]

Their presence highlighted what was at stake, for France and for America. Secretary of State Thomas Jefferson and Congressman James Madison, among others, prominently celebrated the revolution, viewing the increasing violence in France as a temporary necessity or as the work of outsiders. Democratic-Republican clubs, including one founded in Philadelphia in April 1793, sprang up and agitated this perspective. On the other hand, Secretary of the Treasury Alexander Hamilton, Vice President John

Adams, and other Federalists recoiled from the revolution's anarchy and its proclaimed atheism. Such passions entered the streets, where hats and coats were decorated with different colors of cockades, paraders sang the "Marseillaise" and other republican songs, and, as at the Dancing Assemblies, toasts were made—or not—to the "Rights of Man." News of the king's beheading reached Philadelphia in the spring of 1793, and by April residents had learned that France, already battling Austria, Spain, and Portugal, had also declared war on Great Britain. President Washington, intending to keep the United States out of the conflict, promptly issued a Neutrality Proclamation. Its reception was mixed, as some critics charged him with turning his back on a sister republic. Meanwhile, the French warship *L'Embuscade* entered Philadelphia's port with two British prizes seized in American waters at the mouth of the Delaware Bay.[21]

On May 16, the colorful new French ambassador, Edmond Genet, arrived in the city after a successful tour up the coast from Charleston. For many, he seemed to embody the optimism of the revolutionary moment. One thousand Philadelphians crowded the streets to welcome him at his lodgings, and the young man returned their addresses with gusto. "Citizen" Genet would soon be enveloped in a season of what he called "perpetual fetes," stuffing himself and singing his cause from Oeller's Hotel to tables across the city. Two days after his arrival, he made his way to the Masters-Penn house to greet Washington. The president was not amused by the minister's increasing bravura. Genet, accompanied by Thomas Jefferson, entered Washington's drawing room and found the man with Mrs. Washington and Senator Morris, where they all shared an awkward moment in front of medallion portraits of the late king and imprisoned queen. In the stiff reception, Genet made bland political promises, and then returned to his own plans, one of which included outfitting an American expeditionary force to seize New Orleans and the Mississippi from the Spanish. A crisis loomed.[22]

Crowd activity brought these issues home to the Morrises. "An Old Soldier" writing to the *National Gazette* chastised the merchants' ostentatious support of Washington's Neutrality Proclamation as a type of "royal folly" and contrasted it with the "noble simplicity" of true republicanism stirred by Genet's arrival. "May the dignity of an American consist in virtue," he proclaimed, "and not in the externals of folly!" On the Fourth of July, while the fourth regiment of Philadelphia's militia sang the "Marseillaise" and processed to Genet's house, the Morrises spent the holiday upriver at the Delaware

Works. There, they treated workers, residents, and the local militia to a feast on the lawn, where the toasts celebrated the usual subjects, such as the day, liberty, the president, Congress, the state and governor of Pennsylvania, and the memory of fallen veterans. But the throng also toasted the "sister Republics of America and France," the National Convention of France, "the Fair daughters of the republics of America and France," and even Citizen Genet himself: "May he continue to be a worthy representative of the French republic." A newspaper reported that after the feast and songs, "the company unanimously agreed to wait upon Mrs. Morris"—wife of "that respectable patriot, Robert Morris," partisan to the president's neutrality policies—to give her the respects of the day. Ever the hostess and politician, she received the group "with her usual politeness and attention."[23]

By the time the Morrises returned to Philadelphia just a week or so later, Genet's momentum and mission had begun to disintegrate around him. Genet could not reconcile the public's enthusiasm alongside the Washington administration's failure to oblige his several demands for aid. He grew increasingly reckless, and by late July even Jefferson agreed that Genet must be removed, as his actions were threatening the sovereignty of the United States. Washington wanted to make public the full story of Genet's aggression; his cabinet divided on the issue, but Senator Morris promised Washington at dinner that he would "engage for all his connections" to support the move if taken. That fall, the question became moot as a new administration in Paris dismissed Genet. In the end, the affair served mostly as fodder for American intrigue; Hamilton used the controversy to attack the "faction" he accused of seeking to "overthrow" the standing U.S. government. In turn, Madison, prompted by Jefferson, wrote that Hamilton found support from "the foreigners and degenerate citizens among us, who hate our republican government and the French Revolution." Further, Madison argued that the president's Neutrality Proclamation, issued without a congressional vote, reflected "*royal prerogatives* in the *British government*" and therefore the monarchical views of its proponents.[24]

Late that summer, something else added to Philadelphia's poisonous air. At the end of July, while wharves were filling with the refugees from the West Indies, residents around Water Street began contracting a fever. Its effects were gruesome—spiking temperature, weak pulse, bloody vomit, stinking bile, headache, bloodshot eyes, delirium, and yellowing skin. Victims often died within days of their sudden symptoms. Philadelphia had seen fevers in previous decades, but not recently. The city's proud doctors debated the fever's cause and treatment, all to no avail as the disease began moving through other neighborhoods and sweeping off hundreds and then thousands. In the accompanying panic that peaked in September, the city came apart. In the words of one merchant, "the parents, the children, the domestics lingered and died, frequently without assistance. The wealthy soon fled; the fearless or indifferent remained from choice, the poor from necessity." And the disease was capricious; "those who were in health one day were buried the next." The federal government left the city in September, as did the Pennsylvania governor and the state assembly. Mayor Matthew Clarkson stayed on and helped organize a committee of residents charged with essential functions: burying the dead, removing the sick to makeshift hospitals, and supplying surviving residents with bread. Amid the "great human slaughterhouse," French volunteers and black members of the Free African Society distinguished themselves by carting and caring for the sick.[25]

The Morrises abandoned the city in September for their retreat at the Delaware Works. They took some servants with them, including their doorkeeper and their steward Constant. For good measure, they also brought medicinal bark said to ease the fever. Their son Thomas journeyed down from New York to meet them there, making for something of a frightened reunion. Mary Morris's brother, Bishop White, remained in Philadelphia to minister to the sick and dying, but he sent his own family away to a farm outside the city. L'Enfant left his duties at the house construction site and made for New York City. Morris, shaken by the horrors of the pestilence, wrote his absent architect in early October to rest "perfectly easy on the score of my building. I had rather it should stop than you or any other person should be exposed to the Contagious Fever which has proved so fatal to many worthy Citizens." Morris concluded that he thought it best "to close it as soon as we can for the season, taking care to secure it against damage by the winter."[26]

Yet construction on Morris's block did not entirely stop. Burton Wallace stubbornly kept a small crew going, even as other workers were taking ill, including John Sproul, head carpenter. In late October, after the weather had cooled and the sickness finally began to abate, Morris ventured back to the city, where he met with Wallace, inspected the beginnings of a front chimney, and instructed him to halt work on the building. The same day of his visit, Philadelphia's *Independent Gazetteer* reported yet another ill omen. Three workers at Morris's stone quarries on the Schuylkill River were killed in an explosion of rock. Two other men were severely wounded in the blast. The accident demonstrated that the building trades could be dangerous even outside an epidemic.[27]

With the November frosts, the sickness disappeared and the city began to reassemble itself. Morris returned home on the eighteenth, sending for Mary and their younger children after a few days. On November 24, he could write to assure their older son Thomas, back in New York, that they felt safe and that the fever had gone. Things had changed, however. Close friends had perished. Widows, widowers, and orphans remained. The city counted over four thousand dead, or one-tenth of its residents. Burial grounds, especially the potter's field southeast of Morris's Chesnut Street lot, filled to capacity with the awful corpses. Commercial houses had dissolved in an instant with their proprietors' deaths, leaving a tangle of unpaid accounts in their wake. Those that did not dissolve still ground to a halt, and the inability of survivors to exchange notes threatened the economy to such an extent that the Bank of the United States was forced to act for relief. The city's capital ambitions had taken a severe blow. And the gaiety which had characterized the previous seasons had gone. Preachers and journalists took the opportunity to lament the city's recent extravagance. In November, the printer Mathew Carey recalled that immediately prior to the epidemic, "Luxury . . . was gaining ground in a manner very alarming to those who considered how far the virtue, the liberty, and the happiness of a nation depended on its temperance and sober manners." The result was that "something was wanting to humble the pride of a city, which was running on in full career, to the goal of prodigality and dissipation."[28]

In all, it had not been a propitious year to break ground on a daring new mansion. Like Carey, the city's Lutheran minister was castigating "the luxury and dissipation among all classes of people," the theatergoing, and the "people who made their belly their God" for bringing on the yellow fever. "I look upon the whole," the minister exclaimed, "as a deserved punishment of a just, as well as merciful God." Meanwhile, with the ongoing French Revolution, the Democratic Society of Pennsylvania was insisting that its members were "no longer dazzled with adventitious splendor" and would "erect the temple of LIBERTY on the ruins of palaces and thrones." Nor were Morris's long-standing creditors impressed; late in the year, one wrote to the printer Thomas Bradford, asking him to "please inform me whether R. Morris's large House is still going on, for if so I propose to tell him of it & to insist that as an Honest Man he ought to pay his Debts instead of laying out his Creditors' Money in extravagance." All the while, widowed boardinghouse keepers like Susannah Cook and Hannah Penington were struggling to keep their walls sealed and fires lit.[29]

Across from the now-closed potter's field, Wallace's crew cleaned up Morris's site for the winter. They sorted the bricks and stone, and piled straw along the carefully set cellar walls to protect them from ice and snow. Toward the front of the plan, now dug into the ground, lay two huge, unusual projections, marking the building's wings. They puzzled the eyes of on-lookers and suggested a mystery of things to come.[30]

5. His Architect

Upon L'Enfant's return to the city in early 1794, he moved in with a curious friend. It would prove a mistake.

His housemate, Richard Soderstrom, was from Sweden. He had landed in Boston as a merchant fourteen years earlier and was appointed the Swedish consul in that city. In the process, he made very different impressions on those around him. One Bostonian described him as "a remarkably modest, unassuming man" who was "very honest and well disposed." Two other Swedes passing through the states sent back favorable reports of his activities. His Boston lawyer declared him "universally considered here as a character of the most honorable, amiable, and manly cast." But Secretary of State John Jay took issue with Soderstrom's initial protocol, calling it "disrespectful" to the United States government and recommending that the king of Sweden dismiss him. Soderstrom also became embroiled in a private lawsuit five years after his arrival, accused of improperly seeking diplomatic immunity. Further, Soderstrom's brother fled his home country in 1786 under suspicion of dishonest business transactions. These charges may have resulted from, as represented by one of his supporters, "a concurrence of ill-starred circumstances." In hindsight, they would appear as warning signs. Soderstrom's personality shimmered and flickered under different lights.[1]

It was clear to everyone, though, that Soderstrom was ambitious. And in this regard, the superintendent of finance proved a helpful contact. Robert Morris found the Swede agreeable and useful, and, after the war, he made sizable advances to Soderstrom in trading ventures. At one point, Morris would even acquire a ship named *Soderstrom*, while the consul occasionally acted as Morris's business agent. Into the 1790s, Morris made regular payments to Soderstrom, in the form of cash and by paying his orders on other individuals. Sometimes the amounts were rather small, while at other times they involved hundreds of dollars, eventually totaling over $14,000 by the end of 1793. The two shared a love of the table, and they also joined in land and bank speculations together. "Mr. Soderstrom is a very worthy honest man," Morris once told a business contact. "I have known him intimately for many years and have a great regard for him."[2]

L'Enfant entered Soderstrom's circle in 1786 or 1787, when the two crossed paths in New York. The two immigrants connected easily, as L'Enfant lent the Swede money the very next day. In 1790, L'Enfant and Soderstrom repeated the exchange, after the erstwhile consul had managed to land himself in New York's debtors' jail. Upon his release, Soderstrom continued in L'Enfant's confidences, with loaned money serving as the thread tying the men together.[3]

In the early 1790s, Soderstrom moved to Philadelphia. L'Enfant lodged at the same boardinghouse for a short while in 1793, until the yellow fever chased L'Enfant out. Morris, in his October letter to the major urging him to rest "perfectly easy on the score of my building," added the good news "that Mr. Soderstrom & his Son are recovered," apparently from the fever.[4]

So when in early 1794 Soderstrom rented a house on Filbert Street between Eighth and Ninth Streets, only three blocks from Morris's construction site, it was no surprise that L'Enfant decided to settle with him and his family there. But problems arose almost immediately. Though L'Enfant paid half the house rent, he maintained a sparse existence. He occupied only two rooms, one containing a pine bedstead and small table, the other with two old chairs and a broken table. L'Enfant tended to his own few clothes and his own rare fire, while he would later charge Soderstrom with "luxurious habits" in the remainder of the house—having multiple servants, multiple fires, horses and stables, a fine parlor room, free flowing liquors, and wild entertainments, which included paying for a "number of Harlots of his Friends." Even more, L'Enfant would accuse his companion of bullying, obliquely claiming that "when I wanted either to go to New York or elsewhere, he rather in anticipation of the time when I intended contrived to keep me distressed for money & prevented the Journey, then officiously proposed to me to give him power to recover for me." Soderstrom also began embarrassing

L'Enfant by telling friends that he had taken in L'Enfant charitably and was aiding him at great expense. Still, for the time being, the two managed to balance their lives in the house, loaning each other money and entering into their own speculations together and with their mutual friend Morris.[5]

Through it all, L'Enfant attended to Morris's project, three blocks away. His professional reputation indeed had suffered after Paterson; Samuel Blodget, Jr., had laughed at L'Enfant's dismissal and saw him now confirmed as an "eccentric gentleman." So the proud L'Enfant threw himself into his work (fig. 5.1). During the winter, the major had set up a contract with a local stonecutter, John Miller & Co., whose yard was near Tenth Street, in what would amount to a prize commission. Miller's hands were among the best in town; they had earlier worked stone for the city's still-unfinished President's House. By March 1794, carters around Chestnut Street were bringing in load after load of stone and other new materials in preparation for the year's work: lime, bricks, pine boards, and large wooden spars, plus new wheelbarrows and more fencing. Burton Wallace was back on site as superintendent for the bricklayers and day laborers, as was John Sproul, who had recovered from his illness the previous season and had achieved election to the city Carpenters' Company. The lot soon rang again with the banging, hammering, scraping, and shouts of gangs in a large work crew.[6]

Figure 5.1. The only known image from life of Peter Charles L'Enfant. Silhouette by Sarah DeHart, circa 1785. (Courtesy of the Diplomatic Reception Rooms, U.S. Department of State, Washington, D.C.)

Wallace worked well under L'Enfant. At one point during the project, while L'Enfant was away visiting New York, Wallace took up his pen and addressed the engineer, for "I presume nothing can be more pleasing to you at present than to hear how your building is going." The letter revealed no sense of rivalry or confusion—to Wallace, it was "your building." Proudly, he detailed how L'Enfant's specific orders regarding construction, outbuildings, and landscaping were being carried forward. And he made sure to reassure the major that there had been no damage done in a recent incident involving a minor fire atop an unfinished chimney. The fire was quickly extinguished and presented no trouble, but Wallace was concerned that if the news of it spread, L'Enfant might "on hearing it be uneasy not knowing the [full] truth of it." In closing, Wallace wished him "perfect health" and the long continuance of "every other happiness." The builder's obvious admiration for L'Enfant grew from his own close experience with the house's design, his knowledge that L'Enfant was capable of bringing a superlative building to Philadelphia, and the latter's devotion. Even Sproul, a product of the city's distinctly conservative carpentry tradition, dedicated himself to this unusual project for years.[7]

At the same time, L'Enfant took on side projects around the city. Some said he had assisted at the fashionable New Theatre on the next block down Chestnut Street, which had recently opened after a year's construction costing $135,000. If his hand showed anywhere on that building, it was in its fashionable elliptical interior, with three tiers of box seats, gilt railings, and an eagle hung above the stage.[8]

This was only the second theater in Philadelphia. Robert Morris had certainly applied his own hand there, as an early donor and proponent of the project. On February 17, 1794, after months of delay due to the previous year's yellow fever, the theater company had opened its doors to a packed opening night audience, featuring a comic opera titled "Castle of Andalusia." With Robert and Mary presumably looking on from a prime box, actors in Spanish banditti dress had stepped onto the stage and delivered the initial lines:

Here we sons of freedom dwell,
In our friendly, rock-hewn cell;
Pleasure's dictates we obey,
Nature points us out the way,
Ever social, great, and free,
Valour guards our liberty.

Perhaps more apropos for Morris and L'Enfant on that night would be the comedy which followed the opera, titled "Who's the Dupe?" But for now, the financier sat in luxury, and the architect's skills were in demand. Two months after opening night, in April, the theater's proprietors called on L'Enfant when a bench broke during a performance, creating an alarm regarding the building's safety. L'Enfant and two other men were called to survey the structure, with their findings published in the newspaper to reassure the wary public. After "a strict examination," the named committeemen could confidently pronounce the structure secure. L'Enfant's opinion still commanded a share of respect; the plays went on.[9]

In this light, L'Enfant was drawn into yet another local commission in April. Congress had finally appropriated funds to stiffen the nation's coastal defenses, a clear necessity after the Genet debacle, and a fort on Mud Island in the Delaware River guarding the capital city became a primary concern. Secretary of War Henry Knox named his comrade and fellow Cincinnatus, L'Enfant, to the position of temporary engineer for the defenses of Philadelphia and Wilmington on April 3, which mostly involved upgrading the makeshift Mud Island battery known as Fort Mifflin. Though immersed in the Morris project, L'Enfant took this new commission to heart, as it brought him back into military affairs. It also more closely matched his own description of himself in the Philadelphia city directory as "engineer of the United States." He set to it immediately, surveying the existing fort and then deeming its defensive angles useless. In its place, he insisted, an entirely new fortification must rise on the swampy land. So, over the summer months, he directed a campaign of demolition, retrenching, and infill. The island soon became so cut up "that a cart could scarcely be driven in any part of it," one resident recalled.[10]

Visitors, including Governor Thomas Mifflin and the new French minister, Jean Antoine Joseph Fauchet—Genet's replacement—ventured to the site to see the progress. And just as quickly, other state and federal officials voiced growing unease over the doings of the quixotic L'Enfant. In late June, Tench Coxe, a U.S. revenue commissioner, worried that "material injury to the Piers" and Philadelphia's harbor "will be produced by the new Works constructing by Major L'Enfant," due to the latter's dramatic leveling and dumping. Beyond concerns over potential harbor damage, some critics were even faulting the military effectiveness of the new design itself. "Some of our state officers," Coxe prodded Knox in July, think "that Mr. L,Enfant's plan is injudicious," given the works' reduced height. Further, the major used up all his allocated $12,000 by the end of the summer and was requesting more funds from the state and from the federal treasury.[11]

With a crisis approaching, the Pennsylvania legislature appointed a committee to investigate the project. By this point in his life, L'Enfant must have become accustomed to critics and the politics involved in government contracts. But, as always, he stood his ground and appealed to the highest authorities. In mid-September he put the matter directly to Secretary of the Treasury Alexander Hamilton: "After all possible exertions on my part, to progress the fortification at and near Mud Island," constrained by the "limited" means assigned, "it is with the greatest concern I am to inform you that those means, by proving too small, have long since forced me to relent of the progress." So, without further funds, "the whole must stop before any part is brought to that state of perfection necessary to be guarded against winter, and answer to some object of defence." It was an ultimatum. The complaints regarding the quality of his work, he felt, were not worth addressing. Would Hamilton again come to his aid?[12]

Still another project was giving L'Enfant and his clients fits that summer. This one involved the city's Dancing Assembly, which had been seeking to build a dedicated hall for its functions since the early 1790s. Naturally, Robert Morris, Henry Hill, Thomas Willing, and others opened their pockets to the project, and by 1794 the group was ready to make an attempt at construction. Deborah Logan, who had heard the first rumors of Morris's house, would later recall that "a number of Gentlemen" engaged Major L'Enfant in 1794 "to build for them a dancing hall. They bought a Lott and raised by subscription the money deemed requisite for its erection, which he entirely spent before he got the building raised." In turn, the gentlemen "were angry and disappointed and would not raise any more funds but sold the lott and building." Morris was silent on the effort, and the Assembly remained stationed at Oeller's Hotel, though the group was able to salvage something out of the attempt. It seems that L'Enfant's talents may have been turned to the interior of the Dancing Assembly's customary room in the hotel, where he refurbished it with elegant decorations, including wallpaper "after the French taste," pillars, and "groups of antique drawings."[13]

A final blow was in store for L'Enfant that summer. Stephen Girard, the French-born merchant and philanthropist who stood so tall in Philadelphia, had purchased a Water Street lot in the spring for the construction of a new town house. He thought of L'Enfant for the commission and wrote a mutual friend in Baltimore for a formal letter of introduction to the architect. A few months later his friend finally responded, with a decided lack of enthusiasm. "Enclosed you will find four lines to L'Enfant which you may use if you see fit to do so. You do not need to be warned by me not to allow yourself to be drawn into too great expenditure," he cautioned. The warning made an impression. Girard's resulting row house, finished the following year, was a plain, three-bay, four-story brick structure. It fit squarely within the traditional Philadelphia mold, suggesting that Girard had taken his friend's advice and avoided L'Enfant's creative but extravagant hand. At least the major may have been spared the knowledge of this loss. Surely, L'Enfant's recent frustrations—with the Dancing Hall and the Mud Island fort projects shut down, and the Paterson and the Federal City debacles still fresh—were enough. The progress being made on Morris's house buoyed L'Enfant's spirits during these seemingly inescapable conflicts. Even including his home at Filbert Street, it may have been the only place of solace for him that year.[14]

For his part, Morris seems not to have doubted the powers of his architect. Though by no means an artist, Morris had much experience in the role of patron. He had helped design the iconography for national coins while superintendent of finance. There were rumors that earlier Morris had even had a small hand in the design of the national flag created by Betsy Ross. More substantively, Morris sustained long relationships with notable painters, beyond that with Charles Willson Peale in the early 1780s. In 1784, Morris took an active role in the life of artist Robert Edge Pine, who had arrived in Philadelphia from England. Morris lent Pine money to build a house, which would feature a room for painting and, beneath a skylight, a gallery for exhibiting his works, whereupon Morris became a subject for Pine as well as landlord (fig. 5.2). After Pine died suddenly in 1788, heavily in debt, Morris even served as his dealer, selling off some of the remaining paintings while also assisting his widow. Dealing with Pine had probably prepared Morris to work with L'Enfant in another way as well; the European painter was described by contemporaries as of a "sensitive temperament" and having a "restless and litigious turn of mind."[15]

Morris had also displayed an interest in architecture, as illustrated in his many years upgrading the Hills and his Market Street houses. His detailed knowledge in this area was demonstrated in his instructions to George

Figure 5.2. Portrait of Robert Morris by Robert Edge Pine, circa 1785. (Courtesy of the National Portrait Gallery, Smithsonian Institution, Washington, D.C.)

Washington in June 1784 for the construction of an ice house at Mount Vernon. Washington's desire for an ice house, a partially subterranean out-building from which to serve ice year-round, was stimulated by his pleasure in the rare feature at Morris's Masters-Penn House in Philadelphia. Washington had failed in his first attempt, so he asked his friend for advice. Morris responded with detailed construction specifics, from walls "built of Stone without Mortar (which is called a Dry Wall)" to its floor of "Coarse Gravell," which "prevents the necessity of a Drain." "P.S.," he added below his signature, "Thatch is the best covering for an Ice House." Other in-novative features in Morris's buildings—such as indoor baths and boilers or greenhouse/hothouse combinations—also show his aptitude along these lines. He appreciated the solidity and security of his homes; once while on business in Virginia, he had despaired of the frame firetraps in which he boarded, writing, "I wish to God I was back at my Brick Mansion." Later, to his son Thomas, relocating to upstate New York in 1793, he promised to send "the plan of a good Pensylvania [*sic*] Barn."[16]

So when Morris selected L'Enfant for his house project, he could stand alongside his architect as a real partner. In their working relationship Morris was guided, as he once told L'Enfant, by "an inclination to indulge your genius," meaning that he would largely defer to the latter's judgment in design particulars. Like others in his circle, Morris remained convinced of L'Enfant's unparalleled skills. It was a conviction that had matured over time. Federal Hall in New York City had drawn Morris's wonder and his envy. The plan of the city of Washington had struck him as a singular achievement. Though Morris had not yet seen it in person, he had seen it published in March 1792. His high opinion of that plan would remain unshaken by L'Enfant's subsequent dramas. After all, Morris himself had dealt with all sorts of men and accusations. Whatever L'Enfant's difficulties, they were not enough to deter the financier; the engineer could deliver splendor. The bills stacked up, L'Enfant's troubled summer continued, but the two still joined for breakfasts together when they could.[17]

Those who knew L'Enfant only by reputation might have been tempted to imagine the French court inspiring his every design. Here was an enthusiast for the American Revolution, with a permanent leg wound to show for it, who created some of the nation's most vivid patriotic symbols. But it was true that he had been reared in the royal studios of Paris. L'Enfant's plan for Washington, D.C., had drawn inspiration from the baroque, ceremonial-oriented city layouts of Europe, including refashioned Rome and the spectacle of Versailles. In his design for Morris's house on Chestnut Street, L'Enfant turned explicitly to a Parisian theme, creating the most direct example of French art in his career.[18]

The specific model for Morris's house was the Parisian hotel. *Hôtel* is an elastic word in French, used to designate several types of major structures, from *hôtel de ville* as town hall, to *hôtel des ventes* as auction mart, to *hôtel-Dieu* as hospital, as well as simply an inn. But *hôtel particulier* stood for that class of urban mansions that had so defined city living for the French elite since the seventeenth century. These mansions brought something of the rural *château* into the city, with high walls, courtyards, dependencies, gardens, and formal stone façades. In dense areas, walls surrounding their property's exterior adjoined the walls of neighboring buildings, enclosing the main structure in a balance *entre cour et jardin*, between an inner court in the front and gardens in the rear. The buildings were monumental, but they were not wild; they created hierarchical spaces following the lead of Jules Hardouin-Mansart, Louis XIV's primary architect. Mansart's landmarks from the late seventeenth century featured regular rhythms, sculpted decorations, and distinctive, steep (mansard) rooflines enclosing their upper story. Their plans were usually wide, two rooms deep, showcasing an inner hall and stairwell, with grand salons facing the rear gardens. Owners traditionally allowed their architects much leeway in design, from buying the site to arranging the furniture. Into the eighteenth century, *hôtels particuliers*, once the exclusive province of the aristocracy, were increasingly adopted by the aspiring merchants and manufacturers of L'Enfant's homeland.[19]

Thus the footprint of Morris's house, so peculiar to Philadelphia residents as it took shape, made sense in a Parisian context. By midsummer 1794, visitors to the Chestnut Street site could see that the rising structure was massive and that it showcased an extraordinary amount of stone. It featured a central entrance facing Chestnut Street, set back from the street front, flanked by two curvilinear wings on each end, making its width much greater than its depth (fig. 5.3). To its rear, the stretch of the block swept back in what surely would become formal gardens. There was no other building plan like it in America's cities.

Perhaps the building most like it in Paris was the Hôtel Biron. Its original owner was Abraham Peyrenc de Moras, a wig maker and newly wealthy speculator who in 1727 commissioned noted architects Jacques Gabriel and Jean Aubert to build his family an impressive residence. This they delivered. The resulting Hôtel Peyrenc de Moras, its initial title, was a freestanding structure situated in an emerging neighborhood on the edge of the city, on the rue Varenne in the Faubourg Saint-Germain. Two stories tall, it featured twin projecting pavilions plus a central salon facing rear gardens, with tall, rounded windows offering plenty of light (figs. 5.4, 5.5, and 5.6). Sculpted reliefs overhung the window exteriors, below a pediment and customary steep roof. The structure was nearly 130 feet wide and two full rooms deep. A broad courtyard marked the entrance, flanked by support structures and additional gardens.

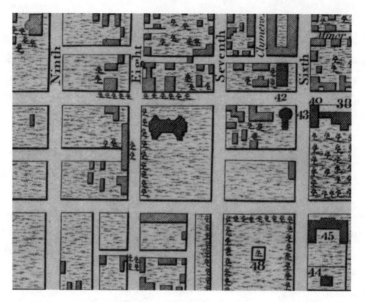

Figure 5.3. The footprint of the Folly (center), on Morris's block between Chestnut and Walnut Streets, during its construction. The block to the southeast was the old potter's field. (Detail of image from John Hills and John Cooke, *This Plan of the City of Philadelphia and it's* [sic] *Environs . . .* [Philadelphia: John Hills, 1797; London: John and Josiah Boydell, 1798]. Courtesy of the Library of Congress, Geography and Map Division)

Inside, the interior surfaces abounded in ornament, with arches and reliefs, paneling and plasterwork. In the second half of the century, the Duc de Biron bought the property and lavished the already-admired residence with care and visitors, thereby giving the hotel its permanent name. Its twin pavilions, tall windows, general plan, overall proportions, prominent roofline, rococo sculpture, and lush siting relate to that which would be seen in Morris's house, though the latter would show some important differences as well, marking it as a unique creation in its own right rather than a copy. L'Enfant's papers are silent regarding his design intentions for Morris's house, and he customarily insisted on his own inspiration for his works. Nevertheless, the Hôtel Biron appears as a rough model, a close representative of the genre.[20]

French art always had cachet among American audiences. Advertisements in nearly every Philadelphia paper at the time testified to this ongoing interest. In January 1794, the local firm Odier & Bousquet proclaimed that it was selling imports shipped on "the last vessels from Europe," including "House furniture, as Tables, beaureau chifonieres, dressing tables, &c. &c.

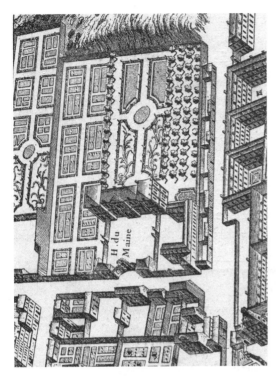

Figure 5.4. Hôtel du Maine (Paris, France), constructed in 1731 and later known as the Hôtel Biron. The hôtel's main building is situated between a front *cour d'honneur* and rear gardens. (Detail from "Plan de Paris," by Louis Bretez, under the direction of Michel-Étienne Turgot, 1739, reprinted in J. Vacquier, *Ancien Hôtel du Maine et de Biron en dernier lieu établissement des Dames du Sacré-Cœur* [Paris: Contet, 1909])

Figure 5.5. Garden front of the Hôtel Biron in Paris, now the Musée Rodin. (Photo by Adam Parrott-Sheffer and Chelsey Parrott-Sheffer, 2007)

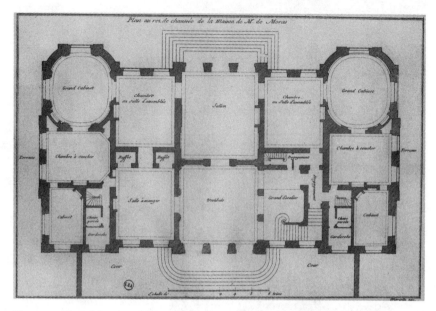

Figure 5.6. Plan of the ground floor of the "Maison de Mr. de Moras," later known as the Hôtel de Biron. (Jean Mariette, *L'Architecture français, reimpression de l'édition originale de 1727* [Paris: G. Van Oest, 1928], plate 214. Courtesy of James Branch Cabell Library Special Collections, Virginia Commonwealth University)

all in mahogany, covered with marble, of the last taste, A large quantity of super-fine looking glasses from Paris, with gilt frames," as well as silk umbrellas, fans, wines, clocks, glassware, "all sorts of French linen," in addition to "books French and English," among other goods. Despite republican anxieties and recent political tensions, Americans of all stripes understood that the civilization that had blossomed under the patronage of the Bourbon kings had distinguished itself as among the most cultured in the Western world. An appetite for its fruits hardly needed the stimulation provided locally in Philadelphia by merchants like Odier & Bousquet, officials like Fauchet, political refugees like St. Méry, showmen like Blanchard, and servants like the Morrises' cook, hairdresser, and tutors. In turn, American statesmen who voyaged to Paris, such as Benjamin Franklin, John and Abigail Adams, and Thomas Jefferson, returned full of talk about French culture and accomplishments, which persisted through the upheavals of revolution.[21]

Indeed, Jefferson returned with more than talk. When he finally departed Paris in September 1789, he brought with him over three dozen trunks full of goods: furnishings, sculptures, musical instruments, books, foods, clothing, and more. After another interlude of public service in Washington's cabinet, Jefferson returned to his home on the Albemarle County mountaintop in 1794 to rebuild Monticello along the lines of recent Parisian neoclassical masterpieces like the Hôtel de Salm, with its central dome and spreading wings. Morris's ambitious house project, undertaken while Jefferson served in Philadelphia, surely spurred his thinking. By the time Jefferson had come close to finishing his vision for Monticello in 1809, visitors could enter its foyer and discover an "interior arrangement . . . of the French character," in the words of American architect Robert Mills, to say nothing of eighty-six additional crates of fineries sent there from Paris. But few Americans would go the lengths of Jefferson or L'Enfant and Morris, especially on the tame external street fronts of Philadelphia. By the time that Jefferson's idiosyncratic vision fell into decay over his final years, and his survivors struggled to find a purchaser for the mansion, its immediate lesson would come too late. Trailing visitors to the empty house would soon declare Monticello "a curiosity—a monument of ingenious extravagance." L'Enfant's own radical designs proceeded unhindered, for now.[22]

In February 1794, shortly after receiving his college diploma, William Morris stepped off the ship *George Barclay* and made his way through the crowded London streets. It was his first visit to Europe, and political events there continued to disturb American waters. The impulsive William was twenty-one and already stout like his father. His speech reflected his youth: "I would advise all young Americans," he wrote his mother a few days after his arrival, "the least tinctured with aristocracy to pay a visit to Great Britain and I'll answer for it they will (like myself) undergo a complete [conversion]." Without a hint of irony, he praised instead revolutionary France, adding easily that "I hope and Believe that [in] America we shall not (at least in my time) need another Revolution. I go to Bath in a day or two Being already tired with London." The young Morris, with seven months' worth of allowance money from his father in his pockets, sampled the country's theaters, praising Drury Lane as "the only theatre in England superior to the one Philadelphia boasts [of]." He promised his mother that he would soon ship her desired purchases, and he wrote to her of England's ongoing war with France—"politics will not be considered by you as uninteresting," he knew. After Genet's machinations the previous year, subsequent British acts of war upon Yankee shipping had added a new sense of injury. William presumed the British cabinet would bow to American demands to stop harassing its neutral ships and preserve peace with the United States.[23]

His father, still a senator, agreed with his son's prediction. In March 1794, Robert decried "the British rapine & Insolence" but believed that nothing could justify American entry into the war. "When one considers the cost of war," he observed with some experience, "which is always a loosing [sic] Game to all concerned, it seems better to exercise Christian Patience and trust to time for gaining that reparation which is due for the injuries & insults received." He shared his countrymen's sense of outrage, but he reminded himself and his sons that "it is the interests of our country & not our Feelings that should influence our conduct." It was one arena of his life where he had consistently pursued moderation.[24]

Congress, however, was not so sanguine. Hundreds of American ships had been seized in the West Indies, and British forces edged into fortifications in the American northwest, where Indians found them a better ally. That spring, Congress approved the construction of new frigates, set L'Enfant and others to work stiffening coastal fortifications, and experimented with a brief embargo on all foreign trade. President Washington, whose views corresponded with those of Morris, sought to deal with the grievances before things came to blows. So he set about appointing a special envoy to Great Britain to plead the American case. The move, and the individual to be selected for the mission, quickly became controversial. On April 8, Washington consulted with Morris on the issue, and Morris, not shying from controversy, expressed a preference for Alexander Hamilton. A week later, Washington announced his more moderate choice of their friend John Jay, an experienced diplomat and the sitting Chief Justice of the Supreme Court. Jay knew the stakes were high for his young country: "I am rather inclined to think that peace will continue but should not be surprised if war should take place," he stated, ambiguously, before his departure.[25]

Jay settled in at London that summer. He was received by the court and the ministers, and he spent time visiting with fellow Americans when he could. Angelica Church, a charismatic New Yorker married to a wealthy member of Parliament, hosted Jay for dinner one evening in July. She reported to her sister Elizabeth, then in Philadelphia, that Jay had shared an interesting piece of news from home. It involved an update on the house project then under construction by their mutual friends the Morrises. Church wrote her sister: "Mr. Morris is building a palace, do you think Monsieur l'Enfant would send me a drawing of it? Merely from curiosity, for one wishes to see the plan of a house which it is said, will cost, when furnished £40,000 Sterling." This figure translated to nearly $200,000, at a time when Philadelphia laborers earned perhaps $300 yearly and could rent a small brick dwelling for under $80 a year. Even Church, who had lived so lavishly in London and Paris, expressed "curiosity" at the proposed scale of the house. Its scope had grown; the estimate was $140,000 more than the original said to have been proposed by L'Enfant, a fact only partially explained by the inclusion of planned furnishings in the new figure. Church also used a freighted word—"palace"—to describe the project. A "palace" denoted the official residence of a king or other ruler, but the word was also used at times for a splendid residence with palatial ambitions. The term fell out of use in the United States after the Revolution, when the imposing governor's palaces at Williamsburg, Virginia, and New Bern, North Carolina, faded into memory and ruins. Architect Charles Bulfinch had used the term pejoratively when applying it to the Binghams' London-inspired Mansion House in 1789. L'Enfant had tested the waters with the term at the President's House in the District of Columbia and then eschewed it. It would continue as a troublesome descriptor. In 1797, an American traveler in Salem, Massachusetts, would use the term uneasily to describe the lavish new town house of merchant Elias Derby, calling it "a most superb house, more like a palace than the dwelling of an American merchant." Angelica Church seemed mildly entertained by the idea, but what of, say, members of the Philadelphia militia companies? At a minimum, Church's exchange with Jay shows that the story was circulating and that L'Enfant's name was prominently attached to it.[26]

Jay seems not to have crossed paths with William Morris in London that summer. Jay knew the Morris children well, but William was suddenly in no mood for pleasantries. Rather, he was trying to save his eldest brother.

Around July, William heard that his father had just severed all connections with Robert, Jr. Shortly thereafter, the son in question arrived in England from Switzerland in a senseless fog.

The trouble involved a woman. The previous year, Robert, Jr., had stopped in Switzerland en route to Paris for a critical meeting with Gouverneur Morris to consummate a land deal. There, the young man fell for the daughter of his hosts in Geneva. "From that moment," his father stated angrily, Robert, Jr., "abandoned all attention to the Trust which had been committed to him and left me and my affairs to fate." His incredulous father recalled that until that moment, "he had ever been a dutiful Son, an affectionate Brother, and was a beloved member of a happy Family." The Morrises heard gossip that their eldest had become engaged, and then they heard wild reports of his flight alone, from Switzerland, to London, to Ireland, then back to London, "and then into the Country parts of England." In May 1794, the story was confirmed when Laurent Concler, the patriarch of the jilted family, wrote Morris a belligerent letter of outrage over the son's injury to his daughter and invited reparation. By the time William finally cornered his troubled brother in London, their father had felt forced to abandon "him who had so ungratefully abandoned me." William, in a flash of responsibility, persuaded his brother to go home immediately, as the only chance to reconcile with their father. So with a heavy heart, Robert, Jr., boarded a ship for Philadelphia in September.[27]

He arrived home in mid-November, just after the dust of the Whiskey Rebellion to the west had settled, in which George Washington and thirteen thousand troops had forced several hundred defiant farmers back in line. Faced with his own rebellion, Morris quickly forgave his son. The big-hearted financier "soon found myself inclined to make allowance for the conduct and consequences which arose from that passion which of all others has the strongest hold of young persons." He knew this himself. Probably speaking for Mary as well, despite their earlier "mortification" at their son's behavior, Morris once "having determined to forgive, I chose to do it completely without reproach or complaint." His son's conduct "displeased me," but "I did not suffer it to make a breach between us." Robert, Jr., would be taken out of the family land business and placed nearby, in a comfortable position at the Delaware Works, where he could do little harm. Likewise, the Whiskey rebels received their own pardons.[28]

Meanwhile, work on the Chestnut Street mansion led to its first achievement. Around the middle of 1794, the hands celebrated the completion of the site's substantial cellars. These would be recalled as marvels a generation later. Informed by hearsay, local antiquarian John Fanning Watson would write: "Immense funds were expended ere [the building] reached the surface of the ground, it being generally two and sometimes three stories under ground, and the arches, vaults and labyrinths were numerous." Three stories of intricate, brick-lined underground vaults indeed would have presented a sight. Their extent astonished one onlooker during their construction. In December 1793, James Kent, a visiting lawyer from New York, peered into their depths and recorded in his journal that "I viewed the *cellars* of Robert Morris['s] House which are just chalked out by Walls." He found that "the House is to be 160 feet long, & will be the most expensive & grandest private Building in the U. States. The Walls are 5 feet thick of Brick & Lime." His language was unequivocal. For two summers, Morris's workers had moved a great deal of dirt and poured a tremendous amount of bricks and mortar into the site— many houses' worth already—before the walls reached any height above the surface. As late as May 1794, a few of the hands were still digging and hauling dirt; from June through August, carters brought over 2,850 bushels of lime to the site to supply the busy bricklayers. Clearly Morris was making provisions for an extensive wine and food supply as well as servant spaces, probably including kitchens, below ground.[29]

As workers began raising the walls aboveground, L'Enfant placed more and more frequent orders for stone and stonecutting through John Miller. Morris paid for five of these large orders throughout that year into October. But beginning in November 1794, L'Enfant suddenly made two, three, and sometimes four orders for stone a month, with costs averaging around $400 per order. Brick foundation walls five feet thick were designed to support just such weights. Carters also brought lumber to the site, including five hundred feet of pine boards which arrived in February, plus "6 large spars" in April. Over 1,100 feet of poplar plank arrived in two shipments from Norfolk, in June and October. Burton Wallace and his crews toasted their progress on the Fourth of July with barrels of spirits supplied by Morris. Wallace was distributing about $500 per week to his laborers as wages during the busy summer, though work slowed for a short spell in August due to bad weather. John Sproul made enough headway on some interior walls to call for plaster of paris in September and November. Through it all, Morris was spending roughly $2,000 per month on the project's expenses.[30]

He must have felt satisfied about the progress, for he and Mary began discussing appropriate furnishings. Gouverneur Morris helped them with this from his position in Europe, where he was now free from official responsibilities, as James Monroe replaced him as the United States' minister to France in August 1794. Gouverneur had been overseas for five years, and his stay in Paris had not been calm. For example, that August, he dryly informed Robert that a client unfortunately "was guillontin'd before your bills on him reach'd me." But in October, before Gouverneur left France for a spell in London, he rounded up a huge shipment of goods for what he called the

Morrises' "new House." In some ways, the shipment exceeded that of Jefferson's. It included carpeting and tapestries from Beauvais and Aubusson, and a host of other furnishings, including "choice" looking glasses, six folding tables for card games, a marble commode, gilded andirons, and matching sets of sofas and chairs. Among it all, Gouverneur was particularly proud of two finds; first, there was a little China table "for Mrs. Morris to put her work on in the mornings." "She will find it handsome," Gouverneur reported with relish, "it served in that capacity to the Queen." Also, he sent a clock "which is single in the world and worth . . . at least a thousand Guineas." He added that "it cost originally much more to the King and the maker ruin'd himself by it." Gouverneur concluded with a message for Mary, offering that if not so busy he might have found things that would please her even more, "and if I had been possessed six weeks ago of the Plan of your House I would have sent out furniture for it compleat." Complete! There was no disguising the joy the otherwise pragmatic Gouverneur found in these relics of royalty. Writing from a city where regular executions of the aristocracy had taken place, Gouverneur could still envision a home for the world's most luxurious items in the Morrises' private town house. "I hope these articles will not be deem'd too rich," he stated facetiously. His calculations of their worth ran over £50,000 sterling, an unimaginable sum. Royal relics aside, they would be the envy of an entire shipment for a firm like Odier & Bousquet.[31]

There was a delay in their arrival; the cargo did not leave France for America until the winter. That season, the rest of the Morris brood continued well enough. The Morrises' eldest daughter, Hetty, had reached maturity and was receiving an allowance plus clothing and more art lessons. William had continued in his grand tour, traveling from London to Paris. Charles and Henry were at Philadelphia's university and receiving tutoring in French and arithmetic. Maria took art and riding lessons. Mary held things together: enjoying her children, orchestrating the servants, and paying the shopping bills. She even offered to take in Alexander Hamilton's children for a time while their mother was away in New York. All continued to enjoy the new theater and the old Dancing Assembly. They savored a newly commissioned landscape painting of their beloved greenhouses at the Hills.[32]

From afar, Gouverneur pondered all this. On the one hand, he indulged his friends' grandiose domestic fantasies. But on the other, he feared for their future. Robert's letters were still filled with hasty, ever-expanding land schemes and trading ventures. Gouverneur foresaw the risks associated with these in a way that his former partner could not. Why did Morris continue to subject himself and his family to these risks? Why would he not settle down and retire into the comfortable living that his family, his friends, his possessions, and his soon-to-be finished mansion offered? As the royal furnishings were en route, Gouverneur urged Robert to reflect. He put the matter as bluntly as he could in a letter that December: "In the name of friendship and of common sense let me ask you to what Purpose all this accumulation of Property with so much trouble and Labor and Anxiety? Why not pay off every thing & every Body and enjoy quietly?" For effect, Gouverneur nostalgically recalled their earlier exertions against the tobacco crisis of the 1780s:

> When I call to mind the many dreary Hours we past [*sic*] together in Virginia, when I consider how easy it is for you to liquidate all your affairs and preserve an immense Property[,] more than a wise man would wish to be plagued with the care of, much more, I own to you that I stand in admiration of that Inconsistency in human nature from which the best of its members are so far from being exempted.

He presented the problem to Robert in human rather than political terms, as more property than a wise man could wish. Gouverneur still thought the Morrises could maintain a respectable position, even at these heights, despite the populist undercurrents. But Robert needed to quit now. For those beyond Robert's table, the course seemed simple. Gouverneur concluded his letter with a wish—"May you see many and happy years and if possible some calm ones"—but it was an open question.[33]

Likewise, L'Enfant's activities by the end of the year were no less puzzling. His housemate Richard Soderstrom remained in Morris's pay, receiving thousands of dollars that winter in notes and loans, while L'Enfant himself loaned the financier twelve bank shares. More to the point, L'Enfant's efforts at Fort Mifflin collapsed. Pennsylvania's committee to investigate the controversial project met with L'Enfant in September and questioned his plans, which he naturally found insulting. L'Enfant saw his efforts as being thwarted by the maliciousness and disobedience of those around him. Hamilton directed another $1,000 toward the project, but it was not enough. Sometime that winter, L'Enfant quit the project in frustration, to be replaced by another engineer. Work on the fort continued in fits and starts, with the secretary of war reporting in 1796, echoing L'Enfant's previous clients, that the plan was now "much more circumscribed than was at first projected."[34]

6. His Folly

On March 21, 1795, a short article titled "The Folly of Pride" appeared in a Philadelphia weekly magazine, the *Minerva*. "Of all the passions that pervade the human heart," the article began, "there is none so certainly disgusting to the eye of sensibility as that of Pride." The author, signed only as "M.," then introduced imagery apparent to any resident of federal Philadelphia: "To see a well dressed gentleman or lady enter an Assembly, the attention of the whole audience is immediately fixed on them; they conceive their fine clothes have rendered them superior to the rest of the company." And, contrary to the American spirit, "if a stranger or a plain dressed person appears, they shun them with contempt, however great their talents or abilities may be." Here was an assault on the Dancing Assembly, the drawing rooms of the "Republican Court," the exclusive aspirations represented by the likes of Robert and Mary Morris. The assault was inspired and sharpened by luxurious exteriors; "M." saw something rotten behind such fronts. Perhaps with the Chestnut Street construction in mind, "M." concluded that "their outside is rich and fine, like the walls of their apartments; within there is often naught but meanness, baseness and poverty, and a frightful vacancy of all merit; and sometimes even this fine outward shew conceals the most enormous crimes, and shameful irregularities."[1]

Enormous crimes? Shameful irregularities? Robert and Mary certainly knew what made a fine outward show. Yet they would not recognize themselves in the eyes of "M." Robert was long accustomed to attacks, but this line of critique, framed much more pointedly than Gouverneur's gentle urges for him to wrap up his affairs, struck a different nerve. It added a defensive urgency to his exertions then taking shape on Chestnut Street.

The following month, Morris faced a related newspaper attack. This one threatened to reveal specific crimes and irregularities. It originated when two letters from America were published in Paris in late 1794. Both accused Robert Morris of attempting to swindle French émigrés by selling them false land titles. One letter was written by Jonas Fauche, an immigrant living in western Georgia who, in Morris's words, was the keeper of "a tippling house" there, where Morris had invested in land. The second letter was written by no less a personage than Jean Joseph Fauchet, the French minister to America, then in Philadelphia and an acquaintance of Morris. In April 1795, Morris received copies of these printed letters at the same time American newspapers began publishing them. Their language was bracing. The minister's letter warned of "intrigues practised by the great American Proprietors, to seduce French Adventurers to this country," in "a spirit of plunder" to sell them outrageously priced "territories to which they cannot prove their right." The minister then introduced Fauche's letter, effectively vouching for it, which named Morris directly. Fauche stated that, in his part of the country, "there are crowds of vile speculators" who survey the lands, whatever their condition or title, then collude with "the temporary Governors or Officers of State" for grants, to "sell their pretended property to the merchants, who dispose of them to Mr. Robert Morris, and he again to those French families who have already arrived, or who intend to emigrate into this country." The process, Fauche made plain, led to the settlers' "ruin." Such explicit charges, seconded by a high-ranking official, could wreck a speculator, to say nothing of the threat to one's public honor.[2]

Morris instantly struck back. He wrote to Minister Fauchet, to whom he "had not the most distant idea of any thing but friendly intercourse," denying the charges and demanding explanation and exoneration. And as to the tavern keeper Fauche, Morris threatened a libel suit. Minister Fauchet responded quickly, on April 20, pleading "an inexactness in the copy of my letter . . . which changes much the meaning of it." Still, Fauchet gave Morris something to think about, alluding to the earlier "victims" of William Duer's ill-fated "Scioto affair" and maintaining that he "trembles lest his fellow citizens should again be exposed to a like calamity." Then, Morris launched a public campaign. He collected testimonies from his clients, sellers, agents, and surveyors, and sent them on to the newspapers for a rebuttal regarding his Georgia transactions. And he circulated his own broadside, printed with all of the related letters and testimonials, which prominently featured his own offer to repurchase his land from any unsatisfied buyer at the original price, with 6 percent interest paid thereon.[3]

Morris, never one for duels, felt some satisfaction for the moment. But the whole flap pointed to an inescapable truth: his land affairs, as well as his public persona, were spiraling out of his control.[4]

Indeed, after Morris's windfall of relief in early 1793, he did not "wind up" his affairs and "enjoy now the calm," as Gouverneur had been insisting. Rather, he embarked on a pursuit of *more*. Perhaps emboldened by the initial money made from the Genesee land, Morris threw himself into the sparsely settled backcountry. On his own table, there was venison, ham, beef, oysters, salmon, olive oil, English cheeses, strawberries, cakes, sugar confections, and ice creams, along with coffee, tea, and bottles of champagne, Madeira, porter, and stout. On his account books there were lands in Georgia, Virginia, Maryland, Kentucky, Ohio, Pennsylvania, New Jersey, New York, Canada, and beyond, all being mortgaged and leveraged one unto another in the face of mounting odds.[5]

In April 1793, Morris had received urgent letters from Gouverneur Morris telling of the sudden bankruptcy of two major trading houses in London—first, Donald and Burton, and then John Warder & Co. Each held a significant amount of Morris's speculative bank stocks that he was attempting to resell, and the houses' failures amounted to an instant loss for Morris of over £20,000 sterling, or around $100,000. This was a blow his surprisingly thin pockets could hardly afford. That same month, he learned of the expansion of the European wars, while later in the summer Philadelphia's yellow fever epidemic ravaged the financial sinews of the city. Just as the markets regrouped in 1794, attacks on American shipping and the ensuing trade embargo produced further plagues. For Morris and many others, there was much at stake in Jay's ongoing treaty negotiations with Britain.[6]

Still, Morris plowed ahead. His confidence was bolstered by the likes of lawyer James Kent, who in late 1793 still counted Morris as one of "the richest Individuals in America," with "all the enterprising speculation of youth." So Morris kept a hand in the financial markets, even when the news was not good. In mid-1793, for example, Gouverneur found that his companion's

bank shares in Europe had fallen from an expected $800 apiece to less than $500, "so that if this has cost you $500 [each] you will not see your money again in a long time." The Delaware Works remained in full operation and provided a pleasant retreat for the family, where they repaired every other month, but it offered no profits. The mining, quarry, and canal projects were ongoing, as Morris continued to serve as president of two canal companies. But his merchant activity was now sputtering, as he had sold most of his ships, and he remained only a nominal partner in one major firm. In 1794, he had even sold his share in the old Willing, Morris, and (since renamed) Swanwick firm.[7]

Morris focused most of his energies on his new land partnerships, in which John Nicholson played an increasingly central role. The two were an odd match. Nicholson, born in Wales, was thirty-eight years old to Morris's sixty-one, and he belonged to the new, upstart Dancing Assembly rather than the old. During the Revolutionary War, the men had parallel experiences with the Continental Treasury—Morris at the national level and Nicholson at the state—as they were forced to deal with the discontent of unpaid soldiers and officers. But after the war, the two split over the Pennsylvania constitution and its party politics, with Nicholson receiving promotions and patronage under Morris's enemies. In 1782, Nicholson was appointed Pennsylvania's comptroller-general, through which position he supervised the disbursal of $27 million and millions of acres of state lands throughout the rest of the decade. The slender, blue-eyed man made good use of his inside information, ultimately leading to his impeachment trial the following decade. In the 1780s, Nicholson sparred on and off with the financier, working with friends in state government to defeat Morris's calls for more centralization under the Confederation Congress. Nicholson even attacked Morris personally in 1785 by filing suit against him on behalf of the state, renewing accusations that Morris mishandled state and federal funds, this time targeting the superintendent's pricing policies for wartime requisitions. The suit reached a happy resolution for both parties a year later, but these were not solid grounds for an alliance.[8]

By the 1790s, under the new state and national constitutions, Nicholson and Morris had found common ground in their ability to see fields of opportunity. Nicholson was never particularly dogmatic or troubled with party loyalty. Where he had originally opposed Morris's Bank of North America, he soon borrowed from it to fuel his speculations. Still, Nicholson could speak with high purpose; in one dispute with a colleague he expressed his hope that they could remain friends, but "I wish much more to preserve a conscience that will not reproach me thro life and torment me at death." For his part, Morris fed off Nicholson's exuberance. Here was a man who could keep pace. Some of their earliest deals together involved financial securities, such as the $250,000 in funded stock of the United States they exchanged in April 1792 or the $125,000 they signed for that June. With Gouverneur away in Paris and Morris's own affairs in disorder, Nicholson filled a surprising need for the aging yet still hungry financier.[9]

From 1792 to 1794, comptroller Nicholson and Morris together bought nearly two million acres of Pennsylvania land for just under $500,000. They attempted to fund much of this activity by forming a series of land companies. By pooling their holdings under the umbrellas of land companies, they envisioned a system that would help generate immediate profits to encourage sales and raise capital through stock shares. In May 1792, they incorporated their first outing along these lines, the Pennsylvania Population Company, finding investors that ranged from the Dutch banking houses and various state officials all the way up to the governor. The company secured its stock sales with 500,000 acres in northwest Pennsylvania, along the Ohio and Allegheny rivers, which Nicholson had helpfully preempted for himself when Pennsylvania first offered them for sale. Other artful techniques, such as the use of fictitious names on land warrants and bribes to surveyors and other officials, also smoothed the way. Nicholson, with 535 of the company's 2,500 shares, was the driving force behind the venture and served as its president. Morris, with only 100 shares, took a seat on its board in early 1793. The company's proposal spoke of establishing "a barrier to the frontiers" which would "enable the settlement of the other lands to be made in safety," with "great public utility," along with the promise of a "reward" for its undertakers.[10]

The prospect of foreign investors also called for land companies dedicated to such clients. In 1793, two years before Morris's 1795 newspaper embarrassments, French émigrés prompted Nicholson and Morris to put a new company in train, using lands along the upper Susquehanna River. Here, the two set aside tracts, in coordination with two prominent French aristocrats in Philadelphia who were seeking to resettle their royalist comrades, for what would be called the Asylum Company. The backers laid out a central village on the Susquehanna and even built a multistory *Grande Maison* made of hewn logs, with tall French windows and eight fireplaces, said to be intended to receive Marie Antoinette, as a lure. Settlement went slowly, though, boasting only forty residents in 1794. When the purchasers had trouble making payments, the company was reorganized in April 1794 on the basis of one million acres, with Morris as president of the board and Nicholson as one of the managers. The queen, of course, never arrived, but the managers kept working to sell its shares and lands.[11]

Most important, Nicholson and Morris partnered with James Greenleaf, a New England businessman, diplomat, and impresario who believed he had his hand on sizable initial loans from Amsterdam banking houses. In Holland, Greenleaf had already wooed the Baroness Antonia Cornelia Elbertine Scholten van Aschat et Oud-Haarlem, making himself something of a baron at twenty-three years old at their 1788 wedding, though he left his bride when he decided to return to the United States in 1793. Once returned, Greenleaf became fixated on the opportunities at the new city of Washington, and he directed the gaze of Morris and Nicholson there as well. The fledging city's problems had not abated with the departure of L'Enfant, as the district's commissioners were forced to rely on land sales, laughably lackluster since the first auction in 1791, to finance its development. Although the Capitol and the President's House were just under way, Isaac Roberdeau's wooden stakes still marked off key blocks, and lonely huts stood on vacant lanes intended as avenues. President Washington watched this comedy of city-building with unease. Into this vacuum Greenleaf and his newfound partners stepped as saviors. Despite Morris's boosterism for Philadelphia, he embraced the idea of investing in the future capital, perhaps thinking of the boom he had observed with its initial relocation to his own community, in addition to his faith in L'Enfant's city plan. The three men reached an agreement sometime before October 1793. By December, they had entered a contract with the commissioners of the district to buy six thousand lots (40 percent of the city's total) for $480,000 total, to be paid in annual installments, with the requirement that the three begin building brick or stone houses on a number of their lots. The first installment of $68,000 would be due in May 1794, when Greenleaf's Dutch funds were expected. From Paris, Gouverneur naturally disapproved, not only in the scope of all these land schemes but in Morris's choice of partners. They were a far cry from Thomas Willing; Old Square Toes was then sitting as president of the Bank of the United States.[12]

Nicholson's unpleasant impeachment trial for financial irregularities in the spring of 1794 hardly slowed the three down. One historian fairly judged Nicholson's final years in the comptroller's office as a "crime spree," which was abetted by Pennsylvania's unstable governor, Thomas Mifflin. Nicholson's defense team included William Bradford, then attorney general of the United States, and Philadelphia lawyer Edward Tilghman, both of whom held speculative lands themselves. Secretary of the Treasury Alexander Hamilton appeared as a witness for Nicholson during the trial. On April 5, 1794, the Pennsylvania Senate voted to acquit Nicholson on all seven charges, though this hardly proved his innocence. Indeed, at least one of the "not guilty" votes came from a fellow stockholder in the Pennsylvania Population Company, in which Nicholson sat as the company president. Nicholson's network of support helps explain the involvement of Morris—heretofore rigidly sensitive to questions of character—with such a man. Gouverneur saw through the mist, which was making a mockery of their supposedly virtuous republic. Nicholson resigned his office the week following the verdict and, with Morris, turned his full attention to lands.[13]

These speculative plans, convoluted as they were, could be made easily enough on paper. But with the new year of 1795, it became clear that the trio had overextended themselves and that returns would not be on the order of Morris's earlier Genesee sales, for which he still was under obligation to remove Indian claims. As expressed in the letter of Jonas Fauche, there were complications involved in selling and settling millions of acres of unseen land. The French Revolution did not spur a new wave of settlement in the American backcountry, whatever the Asylum Company's plans. True, the American population itself was growing and spreading west, but American squatters preferred to take matters into their own hands and leverage their own claims under state improvement laws, or to simply keep moving. The Iroquois and other Indian nations still controlled key areas. Titles were unclear. Taxes continually came due on the vast tracts of unsold lands. Surveyors and land agents required ongoing payments. The British seized or blocked American shipping, thereby preventing streams of income from reinforcing the land speculators. And Morris had still not recovered from the British banking failures of April 1793. Nicholson's cash flow fared no better.

Their Washington city enterprise would bring unique distresses. Like unsettled backlands, investments there required surveys, taxes, administration, and improvements. A great deal hinged, personally and politically, on the thousands of lots for which the partners had signed. Within a year of their initial 6,000-lot purchase, the partners had added to their burden 1,234 lots bought from private landholders in the federal city. From this pool, the partners made an encouraging early, profitable sale to Thomas Law, a British mogul who had recently arrived from the East India Company and, with his associate William Duncanson, took about one thousand city lots off their hands. But the rest of the news from the Potomac, as L'Enfant could have predicted, was bad. In a twist, James Greenleaf turned out to be the villain Morris could blame for an increasingly tense predicament. First, Greenleaf's promised Amsterdam loans—the main prompt upon which Morris had entered the deal—evaporated. Even worse, Greenleaf himself drew largely upon Morris's remaining credit without the latter's knowledge. He misappropriated the trio's money for his own use. And he defaulted on their notes, leaving Morris and Nicholson hanging on a number of hooks. By early 1795, his actions made Nicholson look something like a saint in comparison.[14]

Just as this scenario was becoming clear to the other two partners, the three men cast their respective lots into their penultimate venture, the North American Land Company. This company was founded in February 1795 in near desperation to make their mounting payments and to organize their efforts. Into this entity they rolled most of the millions of acres they had signed for from Pennsylvania to Kentucky to Georgia, with a total cost of $1,233,867. With lands not selling quickly or easily enough, perhaps shares would go better. Shares could also be dangled as security for potential loans. The trio pitched it as a populist approach, so "all persons who had money might, if they pleased, participate in the advantages resulting from the purchase, sale and improvement of valuable estates." It was structured as a formal corporation, with trustees, a secretary, and a board of managers. Further, its board of managers would improve the properties for sale, establishing roads, towns, farms, mills, and other enticements amid its acreage. They planned for $3 million in capital stock and guaranteed 6 percent in annual dividends.[15]

The shifting continued into the year. In the spring, Nicholson bought out Morris's shares in the Pennsylvania Population Company for $20,000 and in the Asylum Company for $487,375, all on credit. In July, Nicholson and Morris finally made arrangements to buy out Greenleaf's position in the Washington properties, though the lots themselves were used as collateral for their promissory notes. And so it continued—buying out and expanding ever outward with notes swapped among the partners and mortgages made on other mortgages, pledged to other creditors (fig. 6.1).[16]

The sums made no sense. The trio's treatment of creditors, large and small, who were willing to put money into their hands made no sense. Morris's letters revealed little psychological insight into his decisions. They floated

Figure 6.1. Promissory note from Robert Morris to John Nicholson, June 2, 1795, for $4,000, payable in three years—one of many such notes generated between Morris and Nicholson during this period. (Society Small Collection, Robert Morris section, Historical Society of Pennsylvania)

along on bravura salesmanship. "I am on the point of bringing into operation one of the best plans that ever was formed," he wrote a longtime colleague, unsmilingly, announcing the North American Land Company in February 1795. "As soon as it is printed I will send you a Copy, and . . . I pledge my Reputation that those who engage will receive beside the annual Interest of Six pCent a return of at least four times & more probably ten times the Capital they invest." He added, "I expect that you will wish a pretty handsome Concern in it." Such confidence would echo in his angry rebuttal to Fauchet and Fauche that April. Yet Morris also could no longer ignore a familiar, creeping distress. He began January 1795 with an apology to a middling creditor for not attending to the latter's demands; "Heavy disappointments repeated one after another has brought me behind my Engagements and I am day by day labouring for the means of facing them." He did not intend to deceive; he somehow remained deluded as to the real value of his scattered investments. "With ample wealth," he insisted, "I find it next to impossible to get the possession of Ready money at this season." Into March, he sang the same tune to another creditor, writing, "I have not any money, but if I can get any you shall have part. Who in Gods name has all the money," he wondered. "Every body seems to Want." That month a draft of $10,600 fell due to a Boston creditor whom he could pay only with an apology and a land company prospectus. In April, he described himself to a friend as "in a constant state of Exertion." Into this morass, his own accounting tactics did him no favors.

He expected, *needed,* peace in Europe so that the flow of capital and shipping would resume.[17]

The visages of Robert and Mary were captured at this time in a pair of portraits. Morris commissioned them from noted artist Gilbert Stuart. Stuart's shop sat one block down from Congress Hall on Chestnut Street, where Morris and his wife must have sat for the painter in early 1795. The resulting, somber paintings illustrate the intervening years that had passed since their more exuberant precursors in the Peale portraits of the 1780s (figs. 6.2 and 6.3). Robert's gaze is still steady, but more guarded. His hair, snowy white, falls loose to his shoulders, while his jowls sink into his shirt collar. Mary's expression presents a greater contrast. No longer the decorated dancing companion, she now seems almost modest, even plain. Her portrait was never completed; Stuart worked in her eyes, nose, white hair, and trim mouth, but left her surrounding frame in an unfinished cloud. Looking into her eyes, one would find it difficult to tell how much she contributed to Morris's growing folly. In February, the visiting Duc de la Rochefoucauld-Liancourt did not find her plain. He wrote privately upon meeting her that she "imagines herself queen of America because she is in a beautiful salon, she has a beautiful dress and her husband . . . is building her a beautiful house." This was a description to which the couple could hardly object. In March, Mary placed an order for nearly $300 worth of new porcelain from Canton and then ordered additional porcelain from Paris, indicating she was as reluctant as her husband to acknowledge any real difficulties.[18]

Robert did make one major accommodation to his circumstances that season. In January 1795, he informed his state legislature and the public that he would not stand for the U.S. Senate again. His six-year term was expiring in March, and he reasoned that "having devoted a large portion of my time to public service for twenty years past, and being now arrived at that period of life, when it becomes essential to my own peace of mind, and to the interest of my family, that I should wind up very extensive private concerns, I think it my duty to retire into a private station." The move was not sudden. The federal government had come a long way since Morris's initial bumpy carriage ride to New York City, and Morris acknowledged, in the wake of his retirement, that "my time has latterly been so much engaged that I found it impossible to pay that attention to Public Business which it had been my Custom to do." One of his final priorities in office had been to promote the U. S. Navy, which had always been pitifully small. Secretary of Treasury

Figures 6.2 and 6.3. Portraits of Mary Morris and Robert Morris
by Gilbert Stuart, circa 1795. (Courtesy of the Historical Society
of Pennsylvania)

Alexander Hamilton resigned in January also, for different reasons, but Morris toasted their moment together in a celebration the following month at the City Tavern. Before Hamilton left town shortly thereafter for New York City, he stopped at the Morris house for final good-byes, to thank the family for their kindness and support, and to see about collecting a $10,000 personal loan from the prior year. Robert was not home. The debt went unpaid.[19]

Amid this storm, Morris hoped his Chestnut Street project would soon offer refuge. Sensing momentum toward its completion, Morris in late 1794 began searching for purchasers interested in buying his current homes. The search was not difficult. As early as December 1794, at least two potential purchasers appeared for the Stedman-Galloway House on the corner of Sixth and Market Streets, in which his family then resided. Two days after Christmas, Morris concluded a deal with William Bell, a merchant and neighbor on Market Street, who agreed to buy the house and most of its lot for $17,000. Bell intended to rent out the home, next door to the Washingtons, and he quickly found an eager tenant in George Hammond, the British minister to America. After the sale was finalized in February, Hammond asked about moving in, so Morris consulted with his wife and his architect to decide when the family could vacate the house for Chestnut Street. Although construction there had been ongoing for two full years, the three could only tentatively determine that they would be ready to move out by December, with the Morrises paying Bell a stiff rent in the meantime. Even the December date would involve "some risque of Inconvenience," Morris believed.[20]

In March, Morris sold the Masters-Penn House next door to Andrew Kennedy, also a Philadelphia merchant, for $37,000. The "President's House" construction project on Ninth Street had resumed, but it was clear the Washingtons would remain in the Masters-Penn House until retirement, so Kennedy would be a landlord as well. Thus Morris, the largest landholder in America, had become a tenant in his own city, eager to project the confidence he could still summon in a monumental new mansion.[21]

Indeed, the Chestnut Street mansion was beginning to present its impressive façade, as brick walls interlaced with stone now stood aboveground. The thick walls curved in the outline of two massive wings, dubbed the east and the west wings, connected by a central hall. Construction in the 1795 season resumed early. Loads of lumber, sand, bricks, and stone arrived over the winter, while L'Enfant added new stonecutters, including the firm of

James Thornbier, to join alongside John Miller & Co. In March, stoneworker Joseph Musse delivered 14,992 marble slabs, worth $2,998.40, with visitors comparing the stone favorably to that found in Italy. At the federal city, L'Enfant had made clear his preference for stone over bricks. The bricks in Morris's foundation and those framing the stone in the walls were begrudging, rare gestures toward practicality. Until the roof was put on, L'Enfant surmised, there was always the possibility of adding more stone.[22]

The laborers showed up in March as well, with Burton Wallace's crew wielding shovels, spades, trowels, wheelbarrows, and tubs alongside the hammers and saws of John Sproul's crew. Their numbers soon swelled to one hundred, with hands teeming around the rising walls. At the helm, L'Enfant observed the shape of the new walls and began thinking about window settings. Workers carefully unloaded six chests of prized window glass from Europe. Each chest held fifty-five large squares of "fine Crown Glass 24 by 18 inches," the size and quality of which indicated they would not be set in Philadelphia's typical double-hung frames.[23]

Another sign of distinctive details appeared when an unusual craftsman showed up on the site in January, an Italian stucco worker named Giusepe Proviny (or Provigny). Philadelphia artisans had a tradition of working in plaster to create mantle surrounds, ceiling medallions, and other interior decorations, but their most celebrated creations were still seen as lesser substitutes to the models produced in France, Italy, and Britain. L'Enfant relished the opportunity to employ expert European craftsmen, and Morris needed little persuading on this point. Proviny had done some work earlier on the public buildings of the federal city of Washington, preparing his molds and forms inside a small outbuilding there. But within a few months, either the pull of L'Enfant or the push of the chaos surrounding the federal city brought the Italian north to Chestnut Street. L'Enfant provided Proviny a place for him to set to work prepping models. As some of the house's first-floor rooms neared completion, Proviny would begin installing his decorative handiwork. He earned about $100 each month that year for his skills.[24]

Proviny's equivalent in stonework was a pair of Italians, presumably brothers, listed in Morris's accounts as "J. & A. Jardella," who arrived on-site in late spring. "Joseph" (Giuseppe) and "Andrew" Jardella (or Iardella) were true sculptors when American sculpture was in its infancy. Most figurative works at the time, excluding gravestones, were being done in wood and painted white or gray to imitate stone. And though Pennsylvania was blessed with an abundance of local stone, buildings of hewn stone in Philadelphia were rare. Almost all were wood or brick, though the best featured undecorated stones in key places such as steps and lintels. Stoneworkers at Morris's house were cutting and setting marble in more than these usual places: in the foundation, up huge portions of the exterior walls, around each window opening, and presumably throughout the interior. William Bingham had earlier gotten around the obstacles of expense and skill when building his Mansion House in 1787 by importing bits of "Coade stone" from England, a fabricated composite material intended to look like true stone. Some of these he placed on exterior walls. Now Morris would show him the use of the real thing. The Jardellas were tasked with creating ornamental reliefs in stone to adorn the exterior, to be fixed over windows and doors in the Renaissance or Parisian manner. Such detailed surface decoration also fit within the orbit of London's neoclassical style, such as that of Robert Adam during the previous decade. For themes, the Jardellas would turn to classical portrayals of the arts: "Music," for example, and "Drama" and "Painting." There was no Philadelphia equivalent.[25]

Meanwhile, into the summer, development around the Chestnut Street property brought more foot traffic. Rickett's Pantheon Circus and Amphitheater opened one block east on Chestnut Street, next to Oeller's Hotel, creating a popular counterpoint to the latter's refined assembly rooms. In the newspapers, developers advertised residential lots facing the south side of Morris's block, across Walnut Street, as "very advantageously situated for building" and "facing the valuable improvements" of Robert Morris. Having closed the potter's field for interments, city leaders were transforming it into the public square it was originally meant to be and began a fresh planting of rows of trees. The public gardens behind the State House at Sixth and Chestnut streets drew increasing crowds of pleasure seekers. In the midst of this, by July Morris's own site could boast the beginnings of its own recognizable garden, in place of earlier construction debris.[26]

Naturally, the site drew visitors. All saw it for the spectacle it was, even if they were unsympathetic, as in the *Minerva*. Jacob Hiltzheimer, a longtime resident and state assemblyman who was familiar with Morris's project, brought his daughters and guests from out of town to visit the site one day in May 1795. In his diary, Hiltzheimer recorded simply that they "visited the house being built for the President [on Ninth Street], and also Robert Morris's great house." Isaac Weld, a Dubliner visiting America that summer, recorded a stronger reaction. Weld ranked Morris's project among the only three Philadelphia houses "that particularly attract the attention," but "little beauty is observable in the designs of any of these. The most spacious and the most remarkable one amongst them," he discovered, "stands in Chesnut-street, but it is not yet quite finished. At present it appears a huge mass of red brick and pale blue marble, which bids defiance to simplicity and elegance." So much for L'Enfant's purported genius. Weld also demonstrated that tales involving its cost, and therefore too its meaning, continued to circulate. "This superb mansion," Weld added, "according to report, has already cost upwards of fifty thousand guineas," or $252,000, "and stands as a monument of the increasing luxury of the city of Philadelphia." Moreau de St. Méry concurred that pride was at work in the construction. That year, he informed his countrymen, "Only a few houses in Philadelphia deviate from the regulation shape and size that characterize all of them, but some are much larger; and some, even, are decorated with marble." He named Robert Morris's house as one such building, but concluded that it and others "which Americans build for ostentatious display are not sufficiently beautiful to merit the name of mansions. Never can marble columns . . . beautify the gloom of a brick structure. Pride can make an effort in this respect, but good taste will always nullify it." One might have expected St. Méry to have a more sympathetic view of the gesture, but it seems that L'Enfant's translation—especially his rare accommodation by using some brick—struck him as awkward. For all these observers, the financier's perceived pride and attempts at luxury overrode all other considerations.[27]

Such visits further spurred the stories circulating around the house. "Young Americans are for the most part, excessively silly company," observed Dietrich von Bülow, in his wanderings later that year. "Of Germany in particular they have the absurdest ideas. They enquire, for instance, whether there are stone houses in Germany, and whether a house as big as that of Robert Morris, is to be met with there?" In this instance, Morris's unfinished mansion stood in for the largest conception of a house provincial Americans could imagine. Their question to von Bülow betrays awe as well as a degree of national pride. But the most extraordinary report came from Edinburgh, Scotland, where an American medical student commented on a letter he had just seen from Philadelphia. The letter "surprised me a good deal. It was this[,] that the large house building at present by Robt. Morris was desired for the reception of George 3rd in case the French should drive him from Great Britain."[28]

A retreat for King George. The "palace" label earlier applied to Morris's construction by Angelica Church and others had thus given way to a full-fledged royal fantasy. The exiled heirs to France's throne already dined at the Morrises' board; Marie Antoinette's sewing table and other furnishings graced their chambers. One like item attracting particular interest in Philadelphia was the royal couple's gold clock, having finally arrived from Gouverneur Morris. In June 1795, the clock sat in the shop of an immigrant clock maker for repair. There, it played twenty different tunes for curious passersby, who well knew its owner and the item's enormous cost. Surely the Morrises did not start the King George rumor, but they do seem to have been encouraging such untimely associations. This Edinburgh rumor was especially odd, given Morris's well-known heroics during the War for Independence. Could the recent royal scourge of the colonists find a comfortable home in L'Enfant's vision on Chestnut Street? Would this recommend it to city residents?[29]

At the end of the summer, Morris showed the first hint of modesty regarding the house. And it brought about his first serious strain with L'Enfant. That such a strain should develop was hardly surprising, especially given the financial duress under which Morris was laboring, all the while writing notes every week for the project's tremendous expenses. On July 21, for example, Morris gave Burton Wallace $1,000 for two weeks' worth of laborer's wages alone. That week, Morris also addressed carpenter Sproul's huge order for lumber scantling to the Norfolk dealers. He was paying high rent for the Stedman-Galloway house and faced the prospect that its new owner might want it "before I have a place to go into." L'Enfant's living situation on Filbert Street was no better, as his relationship with Morris's colleague Richard Soderstrom was steadily deteriorating. Finally, it did not help that Morris was attempting to foist North American Land Company shares onto L'Enfant, in place of cash. There were no more friendly breakfasts.[30]

In September, the situation exploded in a fight. The summer had seen good progress on the house, with Wallace, Miller, Sproul, the Jardellas, and the rest working hard to finish the exterior walls, and Morris taking the opportunity to make more furniture purchases. But the progress had not gone far enough, and worse, L'Enfant's decisions confounded Morris. Morris confronted his architect to demand that a roof be placed over the structure that fall, which was essential for the interior work to be finished the following year (the December deadline for moving into the house was now impossible to meet). When Morris returned to the site shortly thereafter, on September

23, he saw that the walls were not going to be ready, and the duo exchanged words. The following day Morris sat down to write, still in a temper. "Sir," he wrote, picking up the thread of their recent exchange, "my sole motive for being urgent proceeds from an anxiety to get a roof over the west wing of the House." He reminded L'Enfant of his "assurance six weeks ago that the House should be covered this Fall," and explained that he did not have the leisure then to keep monitoring L'Enfant's progress. "Consequently," Morris continued, "when I came yesterday and found both by my own observation & by the answers obtained to questions which I put to Mr. Wallace that there was no chance of getting the whole building covered," the financier was outraged. Morris then seized upon his architect: could the west wing, at least, be covered soon or not? "To this question you very abruptly told me to ask Miller if he could do his work in time and that a roof could not be put on without the outside wall. This answer," a sarcastic one, Morris fumed, "I think was extremely improper from you to me. I certainly have a right to enquire, to examine and to be satisfied and if you do not think I am entitled to receive satisfaction from you, it is high time to part." Here, finally was the threat, which L'Enfant was always ready to see. Morris reviewed his summer instructions again, making his preference now for expediency plain. He would have the walls "run up with Brick should delay in waiting for marble be likely to prevent the covering of it."[31]

This issue pointed to the larger fault line developing between them. Morris stated it here: "Although it was not my intention or desire to have the marble you have introduced into this building, yet an inclination to indulge your genius induced me to permit so much of it (before I knew the extent to which you meant to carry it) as seemed to call for the remainder." Thus the troublesome, extensive stonework had been L'Enfant's design. Morris, somehow unaware of its extent, went along with the plans due to his confidence in his architect, but he could no longer afford the time or funds to "indulge" L'Enfant's genius. Increasingly harried, he now drew a distinction between what he called "my intentions instead of your own." L'Enfant responded in kind, revealing again his delicate sense of honor, and accused Morris of wishing to sacrifice the architect's fame and fortunes. But Morris, the patron extraordinaire, would have none of it. "I do not wish you to sacrifice any thing to or for me," Morris retorted, "but if I am to pay, I am entitled to every information I may think proper to ask, and I have an unquestionable right to expedite my building & lessen my expense if I choose so to do."

Morris had the patience to explain this basic point to L'Enfant, who, in turn, envisioned himself guiding the equivalent of a Parisian nouveau riche. For Morris, there was one way forward. "I prefer that the west wing & of course the whole building should go on under your directions, but with this proviso, that you will positively have it covered this Fall. If not I would rather abandon all the marble & finish with Brick, therefore if you agree, follow it up & get the thing done, if you do not agree my orders to the builders must be obeyed."[32]

L'Enfant valued Morris's patronage, and he believed in this creation. He did not want to lose either one. But he shot one more arrow the next day in a response to Morris's tirade, offering the suggestion that the delay had had to do with Morris's inability to pay the workers. Morris retorted that the accusation was more "ingenious than just—Mr. Miller alone has received from me a sum equal to what you told me in the outset the whole Building would cost." Morris did acknowledge that "Mr. Wallace has sometimes been a little neglected, but I believe he always had as many men at work as you or he thought necessary." The financier waived further observations in light of L'Enfant's fresh assurances. So the project continued with this uneasy understanding, and Morris promised his family "a House to live in the next spring."[33]

When John Jay's treaty with Great Britain finally arrived in Philadelphia on March 7, 1795, it, too, contributed to the farce of Morris's expectations. "We are daily expecting some good Tidings of Mr. Jays mission," he had told an associate a few months earlier, "having been led to believe that all points will be adjusted to mutual satisfaction and Benefit." Rather, the treaty upended the city.[34]

It was not necessarily the details of the treaty that wreaked such havoc. Jay had kept quiet over the substance of his negotiations in London during the summer and fall of 1794, sending back only vague statements of optimism. He had faced an imposing task, to persuade the British that the outrage of their former colonies was a force on the same magnitude as their current preoccupations with wars across Europe or the collapse of the French monarchy. American grievances had not been dealt with for years, and though they were daily increasing there was little leverage Jay had at his disposal. His task was made even more difficult when the British read reports of James Monroe, the new American minister to France, embracing the president of the National Assembly in Paris and publicly celebrating the successes of French troops. Jay's deliberations continued until he finally signed a treaty on November 19, 1794, which required Britain to abandon its posts on American land, compensate traders for earlier seizures, and offer limited access to the West and East Indies. In return, America would grant the British most-favored-nation trading status and arrange for repayment of prewar debts. The French would see it as an ally's abandonment. When President Washington finally got his hands on the treaty, he chose not to release its contents publicly until the Senate had considered it for ratification in a special session scheduled for June 1795. For Washington and his Federalist allies, there were serious sticking points, but it was perhaps the best that could be hoped for now. At a minimum, it was better than war, and it offered a program on which to build in the future. Morris and other leading merchants closed ranks behind the president.[35]

Republicans stepped into this breach, assailing the secrecy with which Washington shielded the treaty and making good use of details as they leaked out. Their jabs found an audience, as some newspapers began attacking the treaty on principle. Even as such attacks increased, however, some Republican politicians still wondered whether they could defeat the treaty against the "President, twenty Senators, funded gentry . . . and a gregarious tribe of sycophants and rum-mad speculators."[36]

One rum-mad speculator, William Bingham, had taken Morris's seat in the Senate, and his was one of the votes needed for the Senate's two-thirds majority to accept the treaty. When the Senate emerged from its closed deliberations on June 26, it had indeed ratified the treaty along strict party lines, though with the proviso of a formal objection to one of the articles restricting the American export trade. The treaty then went to the president's desk for his action on the matter.

The timing was terrible for Washington; it was only a week before the Fourth of July. Philadelphia's Republicans held mass meetings leading up to the holiday, and their newspapers scooped the administration by publishing the treaty, with damning commentary, before authorized copies reached the streets. On the fourth, across the country rioters marched in protest, from Boston to Charleston, with effigies, fires, and mock executions, stirring Federalist fears of a Jacobin uprising. In Philadelphia, five hundred shipbuilders and other artisans marched from Kensington, on the city's northern outskirts, into downtown, carrying aloft an image of John Jay and fawning senators shown selling American liberty for British gold. On Market Street, surrounded by a crowd, this group was blocked by city cavalry before it could reach Washington's house. It then returned to Kensington, where it burned the image and repelled the cavalry attempting to disperse its proceedings.[37]

Unrest culminated in an organized protest in the State House yard on July 23. There, prominent Republican leaders, including Morris's one-time partner John Swanwick, rallied thousands to vote for a memorial to President Washington urging him to block the treaty. Afterward, in the words of eyewitness Oliver Wolcott, Jr., the treaty itself "was thrown to the populace, who placed it upon a pole; a company of about three hundred then proceeded to the French Minister's house, before which some ceremony was performed." Fauchet had since sailed back to France, replaced by Pierre Adet, who kept a reserved silence that day indoors. Nevertheless, the crowd continued on to the house of the British minister, George Hammond, "and burnt the treaty with huzzas and acclamations; the same was done before Mr. Bond's and Mr. Bingham's houses," the former being the British consul in the city. The Binghams' Mansion House, here, became a political target, where "some glass was broken by the mob" and its inhabitants physically intimidated.[38]

The action against the Mansion House was not lost on the Morrises, but they rode out the trouble on an enjoyable retreat up the Schuylkill. Indeed, Robert was so broad-minded a Federalist that he could write a cheery, complimentary letter that June to the Republican figurehead, Thomas Jefferson. As it happened, the Morrises were not staying at the Hills. The Delaware Works, now being called Morrisville, had become a new favorite, so earlier in the year Morris took an opportunity to lease the Hills to its long-time caretaker. Instead, the Morrises gathered the entire family, except for William, who was in Paris, at a neighboring Schuylkill villa, owned by James Greenleaf, called Lansdowne. There, they all celebrated Hetty's recent marriage to James Marshall, brother of prominent Richmond lawyer and future Supreme Court justice John Marshall. Morris mused to the absent William that it would not be long before the group "shall separate and disperse again." Robert, Jr., would return to Morrisville, Thomas to Canandaigua in New York, and Hetty would perhaps go to London with her husband. At home, "Charles is preparing to take his degree at the University & then for the study of the Law, Maria & Henry of course remain with us." Morris wanted William to soon "set down in the Federal City of Washington which promises to be a fine and flourishing Place," as the family's agent there. In the meantime, "I will pay your Bills" in Europe, he intoned, "upon your assurance that you are not extravagant." At the same time, Morris sorted through yet another lawsuit brought on by his attempts to help son-in-law Charles Croxall, living with Polly and the couple's children in New Jersey.[39]

Amid these diversions, Morris developed his views on the treaty. He agreed with the Senate's decision to ratify all but the export trade article, the assent to which by Jay surprised him. Morris also understood that when the Senate voted to suspend this offending article, it "of course suspends the execution of all the rest, and opens a door to renew negotiations." But he hoped the path of neutrality would continue, and he insisted that "a general Peace must take place in Europe the ensuing winter," with the "combined Powers" recognizing France's right to "form such a Government as they please." As to the city's demonstrations, he already had enough private trouble on his own plate to concern him, and he directed those who asked "to the news Papers for Politics, news Treaties Riots &c &c."[40]

It fell to President Washington, whose desk had been flooded with antitreaty petitions, to make the final decision. The Senate's ratification with an objection made the task no easier, nor did the sudden news that Great Britain had resumed predations on American shipping in direct conflict with the terms of the treaty. By late summer, Washington chose to ship the full treaty out with his signature. War in Europe, and the grievances which were its byproduct, would continue, but with cooler weather into the fall, tensions in America over the treaty would finally ease. The following spring, the House of Representatives would narrowly vote to make appropriations for the treaty, while members of both parties geared up for the nation's first true presidential campaign.[41]

By the end of 1795, it was clear that Morris's projects—his fortune, his mansion, his party's politics—had begun to take on the appearance of folly. It was the word and concept that would come to define his legacy. In the eighteenth century, "folly" was a delightfully versatile term, one related to "fool." As a noun, "folly" denoted a foolish act, or ridiculous conduct. It could also stand for foolishness personified, the opposite of Wisdom. Less frequently, the term indicated lewdness, wickedness, or madness. The Morrises themselves used the term in its more typical formulation throughout their lives. For example, in 1785 Robert stated, "It is a Folly to repine of past events," while reflecting upon his indulgence of his errant son-in-law Charles

Croxall's schemes. Likewise, in 1790, Robert warned Gouverneur Morris against taking any action in the then-depressed tobacco market, because "upon these terms you will see it would be Folly in the extreme to execute any thing." That was also the year he consoled his once disappointed daughter on "the vanity, folly & uncertainty of Human affections & pursuits." And in June 1795, while the family enjoyed Lansdowne, Morris used the term in a letter to the family his son jilted in Switzerland: Robert, Jr., "acknowledged his Folly and misconduct, regretted it exceedingly, but his mind was made up" against a marriage with the girl. That summer, Morris also claimed "Mr. Fauchet repents of his Folly" in the latter's newspaper accusations. In such a way, a London author could publish a broadly satiric poem titled "The Age of Folly" in 1797, a theater company in Baltimore could perform the play *Folly as It Flies* the following decade, and the *Philadelphia Minerva* could treat "The Folly of Pride" in 1795.[42]

But "folly" had other, more specific connotations, especially relating to architecture. Since at least the early eighteenth century, members of the English gentry had erected little ornamental buildings on their estates, nestled amid grottoes and ponds and garden lanes, in search of the picturesque. Some of these "follies" featured a medieval theme, some classical, some Turkish, some Egyptian, some Chinese, others eclectic, but all proudly showcased the eccentricities of their owners. These small shelters or towers grew so common as to command the attention of pattern-book authors, and the various examples tended to arouse sentimentality in their owners and observers.[43]

Such a term easily slid into an additional meaning—a monumental structure of any sort demonstrating the foolishness of the builder. This is the origin of the term by which "Morris's Folly" would come to be known. A prominent early example arose in Annapolis, Maryland. In 1744, Governor Thomas Bladen planned the construction of a new mansion, for which the legislature awarded £4,000. Bladen brought in a Scottish architect for the job, and construction was well under way when Bladen went back to the legislature for an additional £2,000 to finish the enormous, three-story brick structure. The legislature declined, and Bladen returned to England in 1747, leaving the structure's shell behind, which quickly became known as "Bladen's Folly." In 1762, a visitor from Philadelphia wrote that he "Viewd Bladens Folly as the Inhabitants Call it, the ruins of a Spacious Building began by Govr Bladen but carried on no further than the Brick Work & Joists 2 stories

High but if Finished would have been a Beautifull Edifice." The building remained unfinished and abandoned for forty years, until it was turned into a school. Bladen's Folly was the result of the governor's grandiose scale and expenses, as well as his inability to finish his project.[44]

Other follies earned their title by the curiosity of their construction or their location. One example was built overlooking the Schuylkill River outside Philadelphia in the mid-eighteenth century by William Smith, provost of the city's college. Smith was able to complete his vision and reside in it, but his residence was built so far into the woods, and its semioctagonal shape (with matching outbuildings) was so unusual, that residents referred to it as "Smith's Folly." Most such examples were houses, though the type was not restricted to residential constructions. A commercial example appeared in Philadelphia around 1793, when Jacob Cooke, an English-born goldsmith, built a four-story building at the corner of Third and Market Streets that he hoped to sublet to a number of shopkeepers. It was a forward-looking retail hub, with nine front bays, its ground floor open with tall display windows, and its several upper and lower floors housing apartments and offices. But residents thought it odd, few shopkeepers took up his call, and Cooke lost his investment in spectacular fashion, so it assumed the mantle of "Cooke's Folly" until its demolition in the early nineteenth century. Elsewhere in the late eighteenth century, Manhattan had its own Smith's Folly, Boston had Harris's Folly, and Danvers, Massachusetts, had Browne's Folly, all of which saw the ruin of their creators.[45]

This newer architectural use of the term "folly" retained the old associations with wealth, individual personality, and emotion, but it lost its innocence. These follies were troublesome constructions—associated with extravagance and out of step with their neighbors, in form or in fortune, or both. Often, these buildings went unfinished due to underestimated costs or overconfident financial planning at the outset. Notably, one could not set out to build a folly of this type. Rather, the categorization arose in the eyes of beholders. Even so, the constructions became closely associated with a patron's identity, as in Bladen's Folly, Smith's Folly, or Cooke's Folly. One historian has found that within this rather loose architectural category, the "thing that characterizes all these works . . . is the seriousness and intensity by which the builders tackled their tasks." All tell a story of misguided ambition.[46]

Robert Morris was increasingly haunted by such a vision of his future. He could see that his story had the makings for a folly, despite L'Enfant's protestations that the work was in hand, and despite his own sunny assurances to his investors. He had to acknowledge plainly in late summer that "it is not in my power to meet my engagements." With his architect, he had projected a one-of-a-kind house on an entire city block, with an irregular plan, elaborate sculptured marble, a mansard roof, and detailed plastering, to be stocked with the curios of royalty. Such a gesture in the midst of financial failure would make him a laughingstock or worse, especially if left unfinished. For the next two years, Morris set about trying to save it and his family from such a fate.[47]

7. His Entreaties

Thomas Morris faced a dilemma. Somehow he had to bring the Seneca Indians to the council fire; his father's earlier Genesee land sales to the Dutch stood in the balance. By the terms of those sales, involving millions of acres and over a million dollars, Morris had agreed to extinguish Indian claims on the land. In effect, this meant purchasing the land from the resident Senecas. "I must depend on you," Morris instructed Thomas in early 1796, "to think well on the subject & put every thing in the best possible train with the Indians."[1]

The Senecas had already made significant concessions to Americans, and they had little motivation to sell more land. Thomas Morris, whom they had named *Otessiawne*—"always ready"—during a moonlit ceremony a few years earlier, was well aware of their reluctance. At twenty-five years old in 1796, he was his father's primary agent in northwestern New York, which the older man still had not seen with his own eyes. Thomas had settled in the small frontier village of Canandaigua, a depopulated Seneca site, in 1792. There, he built himself one of the only frame and brick houses among the region's log huts and quickly became a leading citizen. He cultivated friendships with Red Jacket, Farmer's Brother, Little Billy, Cornplanter, and other area leaders, and he helped the U.S. government host occasional, anxious treaties of friendship with the Six Nations of Iroquois, which included the Senecas. Although a growing number of settlers like him had succeeded in edging into the Iroquois' western territory, the Senecas kept the Americans off balance by playing them off the British. They also maintained relations with tribes to the west that the whites called hostile, such as the Miami and the Shawnee, then in outright war against the United States.[2]

The Senecas' position began to soften in late 1794 when U.S. forces under General Anthony Wayne dealt the Miami, Shawnee, and Delaware tribes a disastrous defeat at the Battle of Fallen Timbers in the Ohio country. After that defeat, Thomas observed, members of the Iroquois "became completely cowed and, from that time, all apprehensions of a war with them vanished." New motivation also arrived with the conclusion of the Jay Treaty between the United States and Great Britain in 1795, which promised the removal of friendly British forces from nearby Fort Niagara as well as from other forts to the north and west in 1796. These setbacks magnified internal disagreements among the scattered Iroquois, pitting stalwart chiefs against the more pliable Cornplanter and Little Billy. Robert Morris crowed privately to General Wayne that "the Check which you have given to the Savages and the Treaty which Mr. Jay has negotiated with the Court of Great Britain" would end their troubles in that quarter.[3]

Yet the matter was not so simple. The Senecas remained resilient, the last of its once-proud league still in possession of a thickly forested homeland of rolling hills, rivers, and lakes. President Washington and Congress, with so much already on their plates, did not wish to provoke them for the mere sake of Robert Morris's ledgers. This was especially true after stories filtered in from the Senecas that they did not wish to treat with the financier. "We are much disturbed in our dreams about *the great Eater with a big Belly* endeavoring to devour our lands," Red Jacket told the new American commander at Fort Niagara later in 1796. "We are afraid of him, believe him to be a conjurer, and that he will be too cunning and hard for us, therefore request Congress will not license nor suffer him to purchase our lands." These were direct words, and the famed orator spoke from experience, having dined at the Hills in Philadelphia four years earlier, hearing Morris's hearty laugh for himself (fig. 7.1). Morris pressed on, however, intending to use all his powers to entice the negotiations forward. By U.S. law, any Indian treaty required the presence of a commissioner nominated by the president and confirmed by the Senate. And Washington refused to appoint a commissioner until the Seneca themselves made the request. "*The task of procuring from them, this request,*" Thomas noted with trepidation, "*devolved on me.*" So Thomas found himself setting out by foot to greet the Senecas in their villages and to ask them to ask

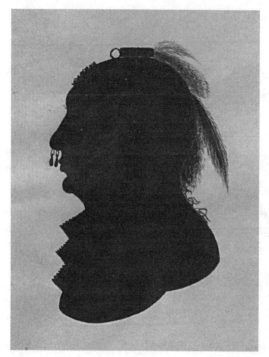

Figure 7.1. Silhouette of "Tseku-yeaathaw, Or the Man that keeps you awake, Chief Speaker of the Five Nations" [Red Jacket], circa 1792. (Joseph Sansom, *An Occasional Collection of Physiognomical Sketches, chiefly North American, and drawn from the life; designed to preserve the characteristic features of personally, mentally, or officially Remarkable Persons, and the endeared Memory of Private Friends or Public Benefactors; with professional Notices &c.* [Philadelphia, 1790–92]. Courtesy of The Winterthur Library, Joseph Downs Collection of Manuscripts and Printed Ephemera)

him for a treaty. There was no other option. Meanwhile, his father was busy treating with an incoming rush of parties closer to home.[4]

It was a long line. John Nicholson had asked him the previous summer, "Does this rainy weather keep off your duns? Mine come thro the *water* & would I suppose the fire if it lay between." The intervening year had only increased the duns' resolve. First in line were the foreign creditors on whom Morris had depended all these years. He owed British capitalist John B. Church nearly $100,000 from a 1793 loan and for which Church's brother-in-law Alexander Hamilton acted as intermediary. To London banking firm Bourdieu Chollet & Bourdieu, Morris had accumulated debts of nearly $400,000. He owed a total of hundreds of thousands more to London firms J. Henry Cazenove Nephew & Co., Bird Savage & Bird, and the Pulteney Associates, as well as to Paris's Le Couteulx and Amsterdam's Willink brothers, in addition to outstanding title obligations to the Holland Land Company and smaller land purchasers. The interest payments alone on these debts threatened to sink him in 1796. Lands were not selling, so to meet these payments, he offered handfuls of shares in the North American Land Company, which no one wanted, and he tried to buy more time by securing the debts with mortgages on his lands, as he did for various creditors with a multiply-burdened reserve in the Genesee territory. Morris also scrambled to recover his tens of thousands of pounds sterling in lost bank shares from the ongoing bankruptcy proceedings of John Warder & Co. from 1793.[5]

In turn, Morris sought domestic lenders to help him meet these interest payments. This move had the unfortunate effect of essentially compounding his debts. To the Bank of Pennsylvania, Morris owed over $100,000; to the Bank of North America, his own bold creation over a decade earlier, he owed nearly half a million dollars; to the Bank of the United States and the new Bank of Columbia, thousands more. There was also the Insurance Company of North America, whose agents sought the return of $100,000 advanced to Morris. He also owed significant sums to private citizens. Local Philadelphians such as William Hamilton, Thomas Fitzsimons, Isaac Hazlehurst, Joseph Ball, Standish Forde, and James Yard had advanced more than $200,000 among them. Smaller sums, but more poignant, had been drawn on Morris's brother-in-law William White, exposing the bishop to embarrassment, and even on his own daughter Hetty Marshall, as he borrowed her inheritance from her maternal grandmother. In addition, Morris, with his partner Nicholson, still owed payment on the notes they had endorsed for their toxic partner James Greenleaf. One Philadelphia broker alone held over $194,000 of Greenleaf's defaulted notes for which Morris remained liable. Eventually, eighty-six individuals out of a much larger crowd would come forward to prove claims totaling $2,948,711.11 against him from this time.[6]

Lastly, Morris's line of impatient creditors included government agencies seeking payment for the ongoing taxes on his millions of acres of land. And those same government agencies clamored for the original payments Morris had promised in his purchase contracts. The most insistent of these were the commissioners of the District of Columbia, themselves desperate to keep their city-building project afloat. In May 1796, Morris and Nicholson finally excised Greenleaf by giving him their signatures for nearly $600,000 of empty credit, such as he had given them. "Mr. Greenleaf led Mr. Nicholson & myself into this last scrape," Morris grumbled. "He was under contract to supply us with money equal to all the objects when we first undertook the purchases." Yet the financier spent little time on recriminations. With Greenleaf out, the remaining partners still owed the strapped city commissioners $40,000 on past due installments, with another install-ment—$62,214—due in May 1796, all of which was needed in order to keep laborers, artisans, and city surveyors from walking off. Further, the original contract's stipulation that the partners build 370 brick houses across their six thousand lots within four years still held, requiring hefty, separate outlays to meet the deadline. Morris, Nicholson, and Greenleaf had hired architects and builders to construct these houses, but when pay fell behind, their labor-ers gathered for mass meetings of protest and then petitioned the Maryland legislature to force their employers to pay overdue wages.[7]

Inevitably, this whole spectrum of creditors began to turn to the courts to force payment out of Morris's assets. So Morris and Nicholson added law-yers' fees and settlement costs to their burdens, as they moved to pacify their once sanguine investors. Morris settled a case with Alexander Lymondton in March and with stone cutter John Gullen in April 1796. The Bank of Penn-sylvania won a judgment against him in March for nearly $21,000. In May, he attempted to put off James Smith's threatened suit by explaining, "I pay as fast as I can and am always willing to pay when I can, therefore he that insti-tutes a Suit against me throws the money he would otherwise receive into other hands." The District of Columbia's commissioners repeatedly threat-ened to seize Morris and Nicholson's lots and resell them at auction, while individual proprietors in the district proceeded with their own actions. Doz-ens of other cases followed into the autumn. "There is not stopping of the Torrent," Morris lamented to Nicholson.[8]

The tremors of this situation shook the nation's economy. The entire structure involved one creditor leaning upon others, and the pillars soon be-gan to fall. Although Morris and Nicholson's situation was extreme, theirs was not a solitary pursuit. In Philadelphia alone, examples of other signifi-cant speculators included William Bingham, now a U.S. senator; James Wil-son, Supreme Court justice; Tench Coxe, U.S. commissioner of the revenue; John Hoge, member of the Pennsylvania Senate; Walter Stewart, merchant and former army general; George Meade, merchant; Thomas Ruston, physi-cian; William Irvine, former army general and member of the House of Rep-resentatives; Blair McClenachan, member of the House of Representatives; Albert Gallatin, merchant and eventual U.S. secretary of the treasury; Andrew Ellicott, surveyor; Phineas Bond, the British consul; Théophile Cazenove, Dutch investor; Thomas Mifflin, governor; and even, to an extent, George Washington, president. The list went on. Scandals involving the president of the Bank of Pennsylvania further stirred financial worries. Benjamin Rush would observe that in one six-week period, 150 failures had occurred in the city toward the end of 1796. Sixty-seven debtors went to prison within two weeks. The debts of "Morris and Nicholson," Rush exclaimed, "said to amount to 10 millions of dollars, were currently sold for 2/6 in the pound," as holders of their notes hurried to exchange them with others who remained optimistic.[9]

In these depths, Morris still had allies to rally, beyond Thomas in the Genesee. One of his most long-standing, Gouverneur Morris, was in London preparing to return home. Gouverneur described what he had heard of Morris's situation as "painful in the Extreme," but he believed the financier's affairs could yet be salvaged, perhaps with the help of outside trustees. Gouverneur overlooked the debts between himself and Robert and promised to help effect a settlement of the latter's accounts upon landing, retaining a belief in "the integrity of his Heart in which my Confidence remains unimpaired." Morris's new son-in-law, James Marshall, secretary of the North American Land Company, also put his shoulder to the cause, having been dispatched to London on a sales mission, accompanied by his now pregnant wife. A number of other commissioned salesmen, including William Temple Franklin, joined the effort on behalf of Morris and Nicholson to filter across war-torn Europe touting the pair's lands and inquiring about further loans. Morris drew upon Marshall and Franklin for large sums in anticipation of their success. Also in Europe, Morris's third son, William, extended his stay while attempting to sell whatever he could of his father's properties.[10]

At home, Morris worked to retain the strongest ally he could—the president—whose patience with him now strained to its limit. The fate of Washington's beloved federal city had become deeply enmeshed with the fate of the troubled financier. President Washington first channeled his temper over the affair in 1795 through the intermediary of Edmund Randolph, then secretary of state. Without receiving a satisfactory response, Washington took up his pen that September to put his complaints directly to Morris, with a letter that cited "private friendship" as well as "ruinous consequences" and a "hurtful situation" regarding the federal city. Washington characterized the results of the initial sale to Greenleaf and then "the subsequent one in which you are concerned" as having produced a "disagreeable spectacle" and indirectly chastised Morris for irresponsible speculation.[11]

Morris addressed the charge instantly. To Washington he acknowledged "severe mortification" at owing the commissioners arrears and offered as his excuse his inability to obtain ready money. "I have long & unceasingly endeavored to procure it and have offered to make sacrifices that sufficiently prove my anxiety," he insisted, but he also had "immagined that a little delay was not of any *real* importance," an impression that was now corrected. He also blamed the malfeasance of James Greenleaf and the interruptions occasioned by the French invasion of Holland. As to the charge of speculation, Morris gave the president a dose of plain talk: "No body can suppose that Mr. Nicholson or myself entered into these engagements with an expectation of holding the property." Rather, "It was from the beginning & is now our intention to resell when it can be done to our satisfaction & I believe the interest of the city will be more certainly promoted by interesting a number of Individuals, than by any one or two men, continuing to hold a large number of Lotts." As in his western speculations, Morris continued to emphasize the good that would come with such backing and publicity. As for future payments due, "in those we do not expect ever to be delinquent." More promises. By summer 1796, Washington commiserated with his commissioners that "the continual disappointments of Messrs. Morris & Nicholson are really painful. One would hope that their assurances were not calculated for delay," he fumed, "yet they seem to admit of hardly any other interpretation." Still living next door to the financier, Washington could see the man was harried, but his table gave little evidence of such extreme want. The president turned the city commissioners toward a search for foreign loans as a solution, and he swallowed his suspicions about Morris.[12]

Nearby, Morris's primary staff remained on board. He had a couple of lawyers working for him, Edward Tilghman and James Gibson, though he found them useless. More valuable was Garrett Cottringer, who worked long hours to handle office correspondence and accounting, while the clerk's own finances became entangled with those of Morris. In the Morris household on Sixth Street some old faces remained, including the maid Acksia and a few coachmen, but there were new faces, too. The family's longtime chef, Chaumette, retired from employ and was replaced by another Frenchman, named Louis. Mr. Secard was still dancing master, while Poirez remained hairdresser. The Morrises' steward, Constant, had dropped out in favor of a new one, James Tate, who had a fearsome temper toward underlings which, in Morris's words, "saved me the trouble with subordinate Servants." Morris's eldest son, Robert, Jr., had married "a charming, amiable young woman." Mary visited the couple at Morrisville occasionally, while Robert continued to draw from his wife's support. "I am never so happy as when you are with me," he told her.[13]

Finally, a few key colleagues remained. Morris's former partner Thomas Willing, head of the Bank of the United States, advanced Morris a few personal loans while maintaining his professional distance. From New York City, Morris's old colleague William Constable lent the financier his ear, advice, and, at times, money. Richard Soderstrom continued exchanging sporadic notes, though the Swede was still more debtor than creditor. Other foreign investors who had relocated to Philadelphia, such as Théophile Cazenove and Charles Maurice Talleyrand de Périgord, offered some hope for future land sales. And though tension remained in Morris's relationship to L'Enfant, the major remained on the Chestnut Street job site. In December 1795, Morris responded politely to a request from L'Enfant for pay. With some resourcefulness, given the gravity of the financier's situation, he sent $600, adding, "I am sorry you did not mention your wants to me, as I am disposed to accommodate you whenever I can, therefore in future tell me when you want money & I will with pleasure do what may be in my Power for your accommodation." The major could best help by finishing the house, thereby staunching that flow of funds.[14]

But of course Morris's closest business ally remained John Nicholson. And Nicholson, though a fount of financial creativity, did far more harm than good. That Morris was not in good hands was evident in his partner's recent brush with the Widows Fund Corporation of Nicholson's own Presbyterian church. The fund had placed its accumulated donations—intended for the widows of veteran soldiers, no less—under the comptroller's supervision a few years earlier. By late 1795, Nicholson had "borrowed" $37,166 from the fund for his own speculations, and when the congregation discovered the fact, it brought a formal suit. Nicholson registered astonishment, insisting that the funds were secured with generous mortgages on lands whose titles seemed good, with promising returns. In the end, Nicholson could not meet these promises, and another category of unhappy creditor—veterans' widows—joined the line. Morris knew about his partner's dealings with the likes of the widow's fund, but, unlike the Presbyterians, Morris tended to believe the comptroller's promises of ultimate redemption. So the two locked arms and assumed the same pose against the onslaught of creditors. Four years later, in hindsight, Morris would blame his friend for their troubles, though without malice. "With the purest Intentions, [Nicholson] unfortunately laid a train that ended as it hath done. I here say that he laid the train, because there are living Witnesses that I opposed as soon as I knew it; altho' from Infatuation, Madness, or Weakness, I gave way afterwards." Surely for the affable Morris, it was all three.[15]

Somehow the pair continued to venture other schemes for moneymaking beyond land sales. Nicholson owned an industrial complex at the falls of the Schuylkill River, a complement to Morris's manufacturing works at Morrisville, both of which brought in some income but also continually required capital. Their mining, canal, and bridge investments held some promise but served primarily to spur development rather than to raise the needful. The pair shipped out occasional loads of flour to international markets, even as war and ship seizures made such attempts unreliable, and Morris ordered a few shipments of dry goods from England for Philadelphia merchants. None of this bustle gave them any traction.[16]

In these troubles, the two allies hit upon the only way to keep themselves going, beyond kiting payments on their salesmen in London. They began exchanging their own notes—countersigning promises to give the appearance of security—and then sending those notes out to creditors at sixty days or longer. When those became due, the process repeated itself. The pair's correspondence from the time suggests the operations of a printing press. In 1795: Nicholson to Cottringer, "I request the 4,000 Dollar notes if Mr. M. has signed them." Morris to Nicholson, "I ask your name as endorser to the note herewith of this date signed by me in your favr for $2500." Nicholson to Morris, "This is to take up my note of 8080 Dolls & [interest] with your indorsement in Norton Pryors' hands—I request your indorsement hereon." Nicholson to Morris, "Inclosed are the notes 20,000 Dollars for which I charge you." And in 1796: Nicholson to Morris, "Inclosed are my 113000 Doll which you were kind enough to agree to indorse for me." Morris to Nicholson, "I have made a purchase in consequence of which I want $500,000 in your notes of this date in my favor payable in two years."[17]

In 1796, these countersigned notes became known as "M & N's," after their signatories (see fig. 6.1). They circulated as a type of depreciating money. Joseph Cooke, Philadelphia's enterprising goldsmith, advertised in April 1796 that the M & N notes would be "received in payment at their current value" for his goods. Like the old Continentals with which both men had been so plagued during the Revolution, the glut of the notes on the brokers' markets led to their almost total loss of real value. "I . . . think that

Machine will not work much longer," Morris acknowledged to Nicholson in November. As early as February 1797, the notes traded for ten cents on the dollar, though their signatories remained indebted for their full value. Later that year, Nicholson's note for $8,000 would command only $135.[18]

Under these strains, Nicholson took to a habit of "drinking Porter & Water & Sugar at night—it has a pleasing effect," which helped him sleep. Morris began dipping into several volumes of Shakespeare, perhaps skipping the tragedy of King Lear, while continuing to console himself at the St. George Society. M & N rarely bickered; rather, they attempted to humor themselves and vented their frustrations outward. They exchanged bawdy jokes—"you shall no more lay your profane hands on Tristram's *knocker*," Morris said to Nicholson of one of their bankers, "but leave it to a softer hand for *chaster* purposes." And they made detached witticisms regarding their situation; "I find a number of your notes are coming in for Payment, and of course go to the Fraternity of 'Notarius Publicus,'" Morris teased in late 1796, "and as the Supreme Court is now sitting, honorable mention will be made of our names." Behind it all, they remained philosophical, or delusional, living out Morris's advice to his son-in-law, who was soon frustrated by a lack of European sales: "I think I can perceive a little symptom of despondency in your letters," Morris instructed in July 1796, "but I beg you not to give way to it, keep your Expectations alive, and never suffer disappointments to make the Impression on your mind." On the contrary, "cherish with confidence the Expectation that you are to succeed, make every attempt you can think of, and one day or other, perhaps when expectation is at the lowest Ebb, you will succeed." The approach worked for Morris and Nicholson for a time, but it did not work for their duns.[19]

Awaiting a commissioner for Morris's treaty with the Senecas, and with the North American Land Company dead in the water, the pair put their remaining energies into their Washington, D.C., lots. Nicholson took command of their operations and moved there for an extended stay in August 1796. Morris traveled down for his first visit in early September. He wrote to Mary that the city exceeded all of his expectations. "The City is so far fixed that it must go on & the property we now hold will hereafter be up a value beyond calculation," he believed. His view of the city contrasted sharply with those of European travelers that year, who saw nothing but thick woods, rough roads, and the occasional construction site. But Robert found that "the property here is of immense value and my confidence in it is perfect." Morris did his best to pacify the commissioners and proprietors, make new sales, and coordinate his house-building activities, which an agent told them that the "people here laugh at." He and Nicholson did manage to see the completion of twenty of their brick houses, thereby finishing the only complete street front on any of the city's squares. They celebrated by treating their architects and two hundred workmen to a gleeful on-site barbecue.[20]

After two months away, Morris at last set out for home, hurrying to beat back "the infamous lies" circulating there about Nicholson and himself. It had been his first protracted spell away from the Philadelphia region since his time in New York City with the first federal Congress. And the trip itself was no kinder; he swung west to avoid suits against him in Baltimore. Setting out north from Frederick, Maryland, one morning in the rain, he was thrown over his horse when it stumbled, sending him sprawling and injured on the ground. The following morning, at the river near York, Pennsylvania, the local ferrymen refused to risk the high gale and waves until Morris persuaded them with "a good Breakfast, a good Drink and a hard Dollar." Tired and homesick, he soon made his "triumphal Entry" into Philadelphia "to the great Joy of some and vexation of others, for I really came in the nick of time to defeat the malevolent designs" that had been formed against him. It hardly matched his memories from his return to the city with the capital six years earlier.[21]

By mid-1796, it had become commonplace for observers to make connections between Morris's distressed circumstances and the edifice on Chestnut Street. Political pamphleteer James T. Callender delighted in them. Callender wrote in 1796 that "a person is just now building, at an enormous expense, a palace in Philadelphia. His bills have long been in the market at eighteen pence or a shilling per pound." Callender used the scenario to lambast the favorable treatment of elite debtors compared with those in Philadelphia's jail, "many of whom are indebted only in petty sums." The charged term "palace" also appeared in the diary of Thomas Lee Shippen, who knew of what he spoke, having seen Versailles several years earlier. Shippen's observation was occasioned when he rode by "Mr. Morris's palace" on Chestnut Street during a January pleasure outing. An English visitor used the term while admiring Philadelphia's brick houses with their marble window and door surrounds. He distinguished Morris's construction apart from these, noting that "Morris is building a house that appears like a Palace." The visitor followed this with the observation that "Ranks in Society are strongly marked" and "preserved with proud jealousy." That same year, Irish traveler Harman Blennerhassett marveled at the Americans' eagerness for speculation, "on principles no better than horse-jockeying." His prime example was "Mr. Morris, of Philadelphia, who, in the last war, had more credit than the Union altogether," and whose paper was then "selling at 4s 6d. in the pound, though he still continues proceeding with a house that can not cost less than £200,000," the equivalent of roughly $1 million. None of these observers registered the architectural effect intended by L'Enfant and Morris. The comments of Shippen and the Englishman were neutral yet telling. Callender and Blennerhassett went more to the point, with farce. This American "palace," set within the context of Morris's distressing accounts, invited mockery, both republican and aristocratic. The idea that the house caused Morris's ruin was only a short step from there.[22]

Representatives in Congress, still meeting in Philadelphia, pitched parallel criticisms of the grandiose public buildings then under construction in the federal city. Protesting a loan to bail out the strapped commissioners, John Williams of New York complained that the district's public buildings "had been begun upon a wrong principle—upon a plan much too magnificent; they were more so than any palace in Europe: they would cost a million of dollars more than calculated." Williams then worried that "the officers who go into those palaces must have their salaries proportioned to the grandeur of their habitations." Such complaints echoed those raised by David Stuart in the federal city four years earlier. Continuing the charge, William Branch Giles of Virginia, who had recently seen the 170-foot-long President's House then under construction, asserted that it "was much too magnificent, much more so than was intended. Every one thought so who saw it." Indeed, Isaac Weld affirmed "many persons find fault with it, as being too large and too splendid for the residence of any one person in a republican country." One new resident of the federal city mused that the President's House teetered close to folly. A North Carolina congressman vowed he would "vote any sum that was necessary to pull down the President's house and to build one on a proper scale." The House even voted to inquire into the possibility of doing so. Though no action was ultimately taken, these sentiments demonstrated that pretentious houses mattered as much to the public as to their owners. The buildings inflamed the anxieties of the age.[23]

Morris felt the sting of these stories. He went to view his construction site when he could, sometimes standing to discuss the spectacle with friends.

Later writers would recall that "Mr. Morris, as he became more and more sensible of his ruin in the above building, was often seen contemplating it, and has been heard to vent imprecations on himself and his lavish architect." Not all the publicity was bad; the city directory for 1796 celebrated the boom in new constructions, "of which the principal are, ROBERT MORRIS's Esq. by Major L'ENFANT," touted alongside the first Presbyterian Church and the new Bank of the United States. But the answer to the increasingly negative attacks was to finish the house and move in gracefully, just as the answer to those impatient creditors with "malevolent designs" was to triumph in repayment.[24]

This would prove a difficult strategy. In the summer of 1796, the diarist Jacob Hiltzheimer walked with a friend "to Robert Morris's house, which attracts the attention of every one who sees it. One of the workmen told me that it could not be finished under five summers." Despite the tens of thousands of dollars then being expended on it, progress was maddeningly slow. Getting a roof over it still presented a problem. Part of the difficulty lay in the design of the roof itself. L'Enfant had chosen a mansard-style roof for the construction, featuring steeply sloping sides. The style would eventually become widespread in America by the late nineteenth century, but in 1796 it was unheard of. Certainly these Philadelphia builders had never completed one. In May, the hands began erecting the roof's frame, which Morris intended to cover with slate, another Philadelphia anomaly. Morris soon changed course and decided to go the quickest route and use local shingles. Then, after more delay, he reconsidered again in August and placed a large order for New York slate, which finally arrived in the fall. For the uppermost, horizontal rooftop, workers rolled, hammered, and cut sheets of copper to try and cover the massive edifice as the north, west, and east walls became ready, while leaving openings for several artfully placed iron-framed skylight lanterns.[25]

Below, the ground had changed. Morris's team was making greater use of the block's stretches of open field, with laborers developing the gardens to the south and setting paving bricks, while carpenters erected outbuildings. Morris also directed masons to build a brick wall around the exterior of the block, but their work was delayed by city regulators who deliberated over an authorized height. The city tax books registered the improvements. In 1796, the property was listed for the first time in public records as a having a "house" rather than a just a "lott," all valued at $15,000. That valuation was a fraction of visitors' estimates and the actual cost. But when compared to valuations of more common properties, even decent ones such as foreman

Burton Wallace's nearby three-story brick house valued at $400, the figure made more sense.[26]

Wallace himself was no longer on the job in 1796. His absence explained another aspect of the house's uneven progress: Morris's inability to pay his workers. Until then, Morris had made regular payments for the Chestnut Street site's labor and materials, week by week, in good times and bad. For example, he had signed over $5,000 in wages alone for his biweekly payment on October 5, 1795. But he increasingly fell behind, and the pay he did offer by early 1796 was worth less and less. He was forced to make smaller payments "on account," as contractors absorbed more of the costs of the construction while they waited for the balance. Many, including Burton Wallace, would never receive their payment in full, and their names appeared among lists of other unsatisfied creditors. The master bricklayer and supervisor grew tired or sick or pessimistic, so he walked off the commission in April 1796, somehow even leaving his tools behind. Morris tried to assure him a few months afterward: "I intend to relieve your wants as speedily as possible." Morris could sound easy, but the loss of Wallace's leadership was significant. Master carpenter John Sproul did not even last that long, having been replaced by Matthew Crozier in November 1795. Stoneworkers also began suffering. By October 1796, Morris was likewise apologizing to his longtime stone dealer John Miller, stating that he was "sorry that Mr. Cottringer has not been able to supply money as fast as you want it." After more promises, Morris told Miller, "Go on therefore my Friend with vigor & dispatch and I will soon come to your relief."[27]

Miller and others, including the Jardella brothers and the plasterer Proviny, did continue. Cart after cart brought massive quantities of materials: hundreds of bushels of lime, tens of thousands of bricks, tens of thousands of feet of lumber, and so much stone that Morris paid for overflow storage offsite, surely more for security or the stoneworkers' convenience than for any true lack of space on his block. L'Enfant managed to add noted Philadelphia mason James Traquair's skills to the project, fresh from his commission on the city's President's House. Glaziers began hanging the windowpanes in the spring of 1796, while carpenters got up to the structure's cornices. Even a few steps were taken inside, as carpenters began making mahogany installations and preparing lath and plaster walls, while painters, including the Frenchman Peter Beauvais, plied their brushes in adding color and decoration. In the midst of it all, one worker—William Callegan—was shockingly maimed in the course of the work, after which Morris paid him a $30 "donation." But Crozier kept the rest of the men at it, and Morris helped motivate the hands with occasional barrels of rum and gin.[28]

The biggest challenge to the house's completion involved Morris's relationship with Major L'Enfant. An earlier associate working with L'Enfant at Paterson, New Jersey, had complained that the engineer could not confine "his views to those things which are essential instead of what is ornamental." As in that episode, L'Enfant, confident in his training, driven in his goals, restless in his private life, and uncompromising in his executions, could not adjust his visions to Morris's reverses. A monumental achievement must have felt tantalizingly within his reach. Although Morris could not even properly pay L'Enfant's own fee, the engineer proceeded to build and shape so long as there were men and materials to command. And Morris, himself still convinced of ultimate success, had a hard time persuading his engineer of his poverty. But in August 1796, Morris flew into a rage when he saw the latest work on his building. "It is with astonishment," he exclaimed to L'Enfant, "I see the work of last fall now pulling down in order to put up more marble on my House, on which there is already vastly too much." Morris had reached a point on the project that he called "intolerable" and accused L'Enfant of being naïve in regard to the availability of money. "If you persist in exposing yourself to censure & me to ridicule by alterations and additions," he prophetically warned, "you will force me to abandon all Expectations of getting into the House and to stop the work." He still clung to expectations. In response, L'Enfant wondered that his patron had suddenly urged economy and dispatch. It struck him as a new note. L'Enfant reminded Morris of earlier conversations regarding the marble in question, prompting Morris to acknowledge that "your Explanation in the letter of yesterday is satisfactory, except that you seem to tax my memory with serving badly." Thus the cycle of the pair's relationship continued, mutually enabling one another's flights, even to the onrushing end of construction.[29]

That end came only one season later.

"You can form no idea of what I daily suffer," Morris fumed to Nicholson in December 1796, in the chill of the winter frosts. The building was still not secure, despite all the attention to the roof and the vast quantities of slate and copper purchased. The family could not move in. Without funds, all the laborers were dismissed except for a few carpenters. The hands had known this day was coming. Morris then dejectedly signed over the house as it stood to his creditors the Willinks in Amsterdam, on a mortgage to prolong their patience. Into the new year, Morris, along with other visitors, continued to stroll by and stare at the dark edifice, at what would have been "the most expensive & grandest private Building in the U. States," for which the financier was still paying back accounts to laborers and suppliers. Crozier drifted away. Proviny set up shop on Second Street, to exhibit wax figures and to advertise for his composition work. One of the Jardellas ventured south to the city of Washington.[30]

After a few months of ruminating, in May 1797 Morris bitterly summed up the situation for a colleague. "You touch me to the quick in regard to the Building Subject—I have expended ten times the sum I was told my House was to cost & the Roof is not compleat, the south Front not carried up nor a single floor laid or wall plaistered and now I am out of money and Credit, so that all stands still, and unless Times change the work cannot be resumed by me." Ten times the sum of $60,000, if that indeed was what L'Enfant had first suggested, equaled $600,000, a fair estimate of most of the expenditures on the unfinished house's construction. Nearby, the state's President's House project, which itself had cost a staggering $110,000, had been completed in March, adding to Morris's sense of frustration. And so the Chestnut Street mansion's career as a public morality lesson began. "Thus you may judge how sufficiently I am Chastized for my folly," Morris added. Morris's Folly was born.[31]

The remaining contact between L'Enfant and Morris dealt with money, not art. In May, they acknowledged to each other that "that unfortunate building in Chesnut Street" would not continue. Morris had borrowed thirteen shares of valuable bank stock from L'Enfant, and he also owed him for his services. L'Enfant never delivered Morris a formal account, but he did seek some payment and the return of his bank shares, to which Morris could only reply, "Sorry I am that it is not in my power to comply instantly with your Wishes," while deflecting some blame back on the "extravagant expenditures" of the construction. Morris's attitude toward L'Enfant's services would increasingly harden, and by 1801 he would describe his Chestnut Street site as one "upon which Major L'Enfant was erecting for me a much more magnificent house than I ever intended to have built." Still, Morris acknowledged his debts to the major and felt them, especially as he saw that L'Enfant was also in financial distress. Richard Soderstrom took up the role of intermediary, while L'Enfant lapsed into depression. He would receive only one more architectural commission afterward.[32]

This did not mean that the pair had accomplished nothing. The house stirred unease and drew ridicule, but it also inspired awe, and it hinted at greater possibilities for the city. This combination of feelings colored the only surviving image made of its façade.

The man responsible for this lasting image was William Birch, a forty-three-year-old enamel painter who had arrived in Philadelphia from England in 1794. Birch had immediately looked to the city's elite for their patronage. William and Anne Bingham took up that role, giving Birch his first commissions in the Mansion House. After three years of growing success, Birch moved his family back out of the city to a series of outlying villages to hatch something even bigger.[33]

It was in one of these rentals that he outlined an ambitious work to be titled *The City of Philadelphia, in the State of Pennsylvania North America; As it Appeared in the Year 1800.* Created with Birch's grown son Thomas, the twenty-eight engraved plates therein would celebrate the flourishing city. The sweep of the collection ensured its fame for the next two hundred years; Birch later bragged that during the whole of Jefferson's presidency the book laid on the sofa of the White House parlor "till it became ragged and dirty, but was not suffered to be taken away." Published as a complete volume in 1800, Birch's engraved views illustrated the elegance, order, and prosperity of the city. The views included scenes of the streets (wide and lined with substantial buildings), the docks (full of laden ships), the State House (with pleasure gardens in the rear), and the market (spacious and organized), as well as other public buildings and a few notable houses.[34]

One of those houses was Morris's empty mansion. The only other house featured individually in the entire series was the monumental "House intended for the President of the U.S. in Ninth-Street," then being taken up by the University of Pennsylvania for its use (see figure 4.5). As such, the Ninth Street house was more public work than private residence. Another plate, titled "View in Third-street from Spruce Street," featured the Binghams' Mansion House prominently on the left side, behind a long wall, though the frame centered on the street with its fashionable pedestrians. Thus the solitary image completed in 1800 of Morris's house, after the building's final sale, titled innocently "An Unfinished House, in Chesnut-street," was a curious choice of subject for the volume's otherwise polished city attractions.

With pen, ink, and watercolor, the young Thomas Birch sketched a preliminary view of the mansion from a vantage near Eighth Street, setting it in the middle ground of his picture (fig. 7.2). He framed his image on the left with a night-watch box, a common city feature, where a lamplighter with a ladder and oilcan walks into the frame accompanied by a dog. Two slender trees split the scene in the foreground, echoed by two trees in the background of the otherwise barren work yard. To the right, the peculiar mansion is surrounded by a number of visitors: a gentleman flanked by two ladies (one with a parasol, one veiled) and a child; also two men conversing, one standing with a cane while staring toward the building. Another man follows a woman holding a child off to the right. Three slabs of stone lean against a lamppost at the corner of an unfinished courtyard. Other city buildings fill the distant background of the picture, with a number of structures to the left of the house and a traditional row house just visible on the right frame of the image.[35]

A closer look at the house itself reveals several unique details captured by Birch's hand. Its mansard roof, two main stories, extensive marble ornament, and red brick walls are immediately apparent. On top of the roof, two iron skylight frames stand empty of their glass. Likewise, two incomplete brick chimneys peek above the right wing of the building, presumably echoed on the opposite wing. The brickwork on some sections of the walls remains unfinished or scarred, especially in the front-center section, above wooden planks marking what would have been a portico entrance. Small porticos and columns mark several corners of the wings as the wall planes undulate in geometric sections around the house. The many tall windows showcase the imported glass and suggest the luxury of light inside. Sculpture adorns the window openings, and stone makes up nearly the whole face of the end wall. The building's basement rises just above the grade of the rough ground, hinting at the vaults there. Viewed from this perspective, the double-winged house was in almost every way a contrast to Philadelphia housing traditions. Even as curvilinear lines and tall windows were then becoming fashionable on high-style American houses, those features were carried to such extremes on Morris's house as to sever all connections with the more static attempts nearby.[36]

All of these details made it into the final copper engraving of the image in 1800, which is nearly identical in composition to Thomas's initial study

Figure 7.2. Artist's study [by Thomas Birch?] for "an unfinished house in Chesnut Street, Philadelphia," circa 1798–1800. (Courtesy of the Library Company of Philadelphia)

(fig. 7.3). The Birches were fascinated by the building, both as an architectural construction and as a public spectacle. The public, too, was fascinated; beyond those observers personified in the image itself, there were those who paid $1.50 for a single, colored print of the "unfinished house" and those who lingered over it in Birch's completed volume. Birch knew when he published his volume that the house would never be completed. His affinity for the city's leading gentry led him to celebrate Morris's vision, even as he carefully removed any direct associations with its once-mighty patron in the print's studiously bland title and in the absence of the rotund Morris from the scene. In doing so, he attempted to walk an apolitical line through party rancor, economic ruin, and republican concerns. With his eye for art, Birch even purchased at auction two of the Jardellas' decorative bas-reliefs, which Birch described as "beautiful." One figuratively represented painting, and the other represented sculpture. Birch adorned the front of his own house with them. Even more, when he issued a subsequent, revised edition of the views in 1804, he included the "Unfinished House" plate while dropping the plate depicting Bingham's house on Third Street. All of this demonstrated that while Morris's house was not destined to last on the Philadelphia landscape, it would last in the imaginations of its observers—as a monster, or perhaps a promise, but always hovering near destruction.[37]

With the abandonment of this construction, Morris had to decide what to do with all its intended furnishings. Where to put the queen's clock and sewing table? Where to store the Gobelin tapestries? In the spring of 1797, the Morrises learned they would have to return their current Sixth Street residence, the Stedman-Galloway House, to landlord William Bell. Further, they also knew that their personal assets were likely to be seized anytime by the sheriff to satisfy unpaid debts. So they signed over nearly the entire inventory of their household to longtime friend and creditor Thomas Fitzsimons. Doing so was a legal fiction; Fitzsimons would allow them to continue the enjoyment of the same, wherever the family ended up, and he would sign the goods back to the family when the storm cleared. Or, should the worst happen, he would have some security for his many outlays on their behalf.[38]

The eight legal sheets itemizing the inventory, totaling $20,211.81, represented a lifetime of memories and hospitality. These goods had enabled the Morrises to maintain their social station. Mary Morris played a large role in the assemblage, as Robert deferred to his wife in this regard. The inventory

Figure 7.3. "An Unfinished House, in Chesnut Street Philadelphia." (W[illiam]. Birch & Son, *The City of Philadelphia, in the State of Pennsylvania North America, As it Appeared in the Year 1800* [Philadelphia: W. Birch, 1800], plate 14. Courtesy of the Library Company of Philadelphia)

also suggested in broad strokes how the couple had intended to begin furnishing the now-doomed mansion.[39]

Like all elite households of the time, the Morrises arranged their furnishings in a hierarchy of spaces, from public parlors to private servant rooms. In
the Stedman-Galloway House, their most expensive items—beyond the 2,240
ounces of silver plate—were located in the two ground floor parlors and the
second story front room (though their dining room, laden with costly pieces,
was not represented on the inventory). In these comfortable settings, visitors
and the family relished European, Asian, and local furnishings that featured
high-quality materials and craftsmanship. The royal clock stood in the front
parlor, as did mahogany card tables, chairs, sideboards, and knife cases, as
well as bamboo stools. A harpsichord offered additional entertainment below
gilt sconces, framed paintings, and large mirrors. In the back parlor, more
card tables were arranged around the walls, creating space for movement
around silk-lined sofas and armchairs, an inlaid writing desk, two chande-
liers, another clock, two urns, and two gilded girandoles, all watched over by
"a likeness of Genl. Washington in wax." The girandoles in particular illustrated the family's engagement with cosmopolitan art; these wall hangings
were made in England or America of carved wood and plaster, with dinner-
plate-sized mirrors in the center to reflect their candlelight into the communal
spaces of the room. Their craftsmen had celebrated the tastes of American
consumers by carving an eagle with spreading wings on top, flanked by eagle
masks on each piece's sides. At the same time, the pieces' delicate lines suggested the latest international trends toward classical design, while the ebony
rings encircling the mirrors signaled an exoticism not available to all.[40]

This pull between the exotic and the familiar continued throughout the
rest of the house. In the back bedchamber on the second floor sat two China
"mandarines," a "set of China ornaments," and a Japanned box and mirror.
A Turkish carpet was intended for the second floor, the Gobelins tapestries
(worth $1,600) were stored for the time in the garret, and the family could
choose to eat off any number of sets of Chinese or French porcelain. The
family also owned two globes of the world. Yet they also sat on common
Windsor chairs, slept on Philadelphia bedsteads, stored clothes in Philadelphia chests, and gazed upon a plaster sculpture of John Paul Jones, paintings
of their two eldest sons, and paintings of Gouverneur Morris and John Jay,
in addition to another formidable wax visage of Washington.[41]

Such ensembles would have required careful positioning to blend with the aggressive structural details of the Chestnut Street house. The painter Beauvais, the plasterer Proviny, and the sculptors Jardella worked to create vigorous finishes that would have been softened only slightly by the Morrises' nods to domestic references. Two chimneypieces later attributed to the Chestnut Street construction suggest the house's approach. The first chimneypiece, of white marble, shows a nearly square fireplace opening, with rich rococo motifs (fig. 7.4). Between carved horizontal cornices, swirls of leaves and buds encircle bowls of fruit. The chimneypiece presents a showcase for the female form, with a stark face in each of the upper corner blocks and squatting nudes in high relief at the bottom of each column. The central figure at the top is the erotic "Leda and the Swan," in which the seated woman of Greek myth receives a kiss from Zeus in the form of a swan (fig. 7.5). It would provoke conversation. As in other houses of Philadelphia's so-called Republican Court, additional wall and ceiling decorations would have tied its form together with the rest of its room in a harmonious whole. Appropriately, the other surviving marble chimneypiece from the Folly showcases Apollo and the nine muses (fig. 7.6). This piece is larger and more substantial, in line with the dimensions of the house.[42]

Figure 7.4. "Leda and the Swan" marble chimneypiece, attributed to Robert Morris's mansion. Currently installed at Lemon Hill mansion, Philadelphia. (Photo by Jordan Fugeman)

Figure 7.5. "Leda and the Swan" chimneypiece (detail), Lemon Hill mansion, Philadelphia. (Author photo)

A large focus of the Morrises' furnishings involved food and entertaining. In their rear kitchen, their French cook Louis could draw upon over a dozen copper or brass stew pans, an assortment of frying pans and pots, fish kettles, a copper coffeepot, a sugar boiler, waffle irons, roasting irons, and Dutch ovens, all for two different stoves. There were also pots for making ice cream. The family enjoyed tea, and so had several tea trays and tables. Beyond sets of China, they owned a Wedgewood dinner service, fruit baskets, salad dishes, punch bowls, and an astonishing 122 wine glasses plus twenty-one champagne glasses. These were complemented by damask napkins worth $126 and dozens of ornamental table cloths. The focus on dining in the Chestnut Street house would have been even greater.

Much of the remainder of the Stedman-Galloway House—the fourth floor garrets, the pantries, the back buildings—was given over to their large staff of servants. Here were old chairs, easy chairs, multiple bedsteads, fire buckets, clothes irons and presses, and other tools. These would have been relocated to the vast cellars in the house on Chestnut Street, alongside the wine and food to be stored there. In the rear of the family's Sixth Street yard, a stable held a coach, a chariot, and a coachee, as well as harnesses and saddles for the family's five horses. The house steward, the intimidating James Tate, lived in a room in a back building, furnished with a silk sofa, two

Figure 7.6. "Apollo and the Muses" marble chimneypiece, attributed to Robert Morris's mansion. (In the collection of the Philadelphia History Museum at the Atwater Kent, installed in the Historical Society of Pennsylvania. Photo by Jordan Fugeman)

mahogany chairs, a bed, and six pictures on his walls. He had a fireplace for warmth in the adjoining hall. Would Tate have moved inside the main mansion on Chestnut Street, or would he again settle in an outbuilding?

Unlike the Chestnut Street mansion's unusual massing and external details, this interior ensemble related to the contours of the existing Republican Court. The Morrises lived like elite Philadelphians, after all. The Binghams, for example, adorned their Mansion House with French girandoles, a harpsichord, satin window curtains, sets of French and Chinese porcelain, mahogany knife cases, "Mandarin Figures," Japanned furnishings, an "Elegant clock," busts of Revolutionary heroes such as Benjamin Franklin, local mahogany bureaus, desks, and card tables, the expected tools and servant goods, and nearly two thousand ounces of silver plate. The Morrises counted 122 wine glasses; the Binghams counted 133. The main differences between the two households' goods were the Morrises' emphasis on recently available royal relics, the quality of some of their built-in features (the Mansion House's composition Coade Stone for entablatures, mouldings, and sculptures lost some of its luster), and the sheer bulk of goods that would be needed to fill the Chestnut Street mansion's larger spaces.[43]

William Bell and Thomas Fitzsimons took down this inventory, and they would see nothing surprising in the dazzling roomfuls of furnishings. But the effect of the rooms on the uninitiated was different. One young woman in Henry Hill's Philadelphia house, for example, admired the beauty of a carved chimneypiece there but concluded that "it was quite too nice, ever to be used." Julian Niemcewicz, a more seasoned tourist from Europe, visited the Binghams in 1797 and testified that the "pompous appearance" of the Mansion House "wounds a little the spirit of equality and excites envy." Following this understatement, he narrated his impressions of its grand interior and reiterated that the "opulent" house "attracts attention, criticism and envy." He concluded darkly, "Woe for the country if it ceases to astonish, if it ceases to be pointed out."[44]

As it happened, Robert Morris, a prime victim of that envy himself, never got to hold on to his beloved furnishings. In early June the Morrises moved out of Sixth Street with all their belongings to a large rental house on Chestnut Street near Eighth, across the street from their abandoned mansion. There, as they and their servants unpacked their crates of furnishings, the temporary arrangement with Fitzsimons—now their next-door neighbor—began to dissolve under legal scrutiny. Creditors were rightly skeptical that Morris had actually conveyed the goods. So in August, Morris responded by sending over to Fitzsimons the family's silver plate and "such other valuable things as Mrs. Morris & you may fix on." Robert also proposed to deliver to Fitzsimons the key to their current rental house, which might satisfy the lingering concerns about legal possession of the remainder of the inventory. Morris's lawyers were looking into the matter. In the meantime, they, like the rest of the public, could peer into the Folly's empty rooms. The following year, visitors would get inside and see its layout. But for now the mansion stood as the forbidding shell in Birch's drawing.[45]

Even more than trying to save his Chestnut Street mansion and its intended furnishings that summer, Morris was focused on trying to save himself and Nicholson from debtors' prison. In 1797, there was no general bankruptcy law in Pennsylvania. Debtors were considered to be morally as well as financially responsible for repaying their debts. Thus, following English common law, if a creditor brought a due claim before the sheriff, the debtor in question who could not answer that claim faced punishment. And punishment in Phila-delphia meant incarceration in the Prune Street debtors' apartment, a stone house separated from the main Walnut Street prison by an inner wall between their respective yards. There, now-criminal debtors languished, whether they owed fifty dollars or thousands, until their proved debts were repaid or the creditor was satisfied with other securities. The dread of Prune Street was not just its shame and relative discomfort but the pall it cast over one's affairs and the ironic limitation it placed on the ability to rectify the debt. As William Duer had learned, it was difficult to make money from inside a prison.[46]

Only the forbearance of Morris's current legions of creditors and his own weighty reputation had kept him out of Prune Street so far. "Domestic attachment is still a little talked of against you," Morris had warned Nicholson in November 1796, "but he must be a hardy Fellow that will take the oath in my presence." Morris's creditors, themselves squeezed by others, grew more and more hardy. Only a month later, Morris equivocated; "I think my Per-son safe," he told Nicholson, while instructing his partner to sneak into the city upon his return from the federal city. Creditors in Philadelphia and else-where had assumed Nicholson had fled the country for England or Germany. Rumors that Morris himself was in prison circulated in Boston and New York in December 1796. Several creditors obtained judgments against Mor-ris at the March 1797 court term which authorized seizure of his person, in the hopes of scaring him into payment or at least, in Morris's words, "that the first that laid hold of me would be the first paid." Morris indignantly reiter-ated his willingness to pay as soon as he had the means, and asked his law-yers to treat with his enemies in order to persuade them to hold their writs of seizure until August. "Should any of them refuse," he instructed, "hand me a List of their names that I may make personal Application." In the meantime, he turned over all his remaining local property, now itself at risk of seizure any day, into his newest ruse, the "Pennsylvania Property Company," from which he attempted to placate his creditors with shares. In March this com-pany listed $1 million in holdings on its books, which included the Hills and Morrisville. Some creditors played the game, including James Biddle, a state court justice, and William Bell, both of whom served as the company's two trustees, but the company would soon experience the same fate as the North American Land Company and those before it. Across the ocean, the Bank of England shrank the credit markets even further by halting specie payments in response to a run on its own holdings. So the Morrises hardly felt secure in their new rental house. Their landlord, fellow speculator David Allison, was sent to Prune Street in July, another victim of the financial bust.[47]

Under these conditions, the Morrises at last halted their social rounds. Parading their freedom at the Dancing Assembly, even if they felt like dancing, would only stoke the anger of their creditors. Morris acknowledged in early 1797 that he "cannot go to Public places or amusements," and he did not wish "to mix much in society whilst harassed." Observers took note of their absence. In February 1797, the Morrises were absent from the city's "Birth night ball" for President Washington. Mary must have been particularly chastened not to join Martha at the annual event. However, the family did continue to entertain guests at private dinners. Robert still desired "to see my friends at my own house," where they could somehow meet "a chearfull welcome." Indeed, John Marshall came to Philadelphia that summer and enjoyed dining with the family. "That family receives me with precisely the same friendship & affection as formerly & seems to preserve in a great degree its vivacity," Marshall told his wife. "A heavy gloom hangs around them which only their good sense restrains them from showing." Remarkably, the family still lived "most elegantly," the main change being "the cro[w]d of company which formerly frequented it." Marshall also spent some time with the fashionable Binghams. Remarkably, for a man himself so overextended in lands, Bingham voiced his pleasure that the panic had "put an end to the various extravagant speculations, which disgraced the country; many of those who engaged deeply are ruined and involved great numbers in their misfortunes." His latter phrase may have tipped his real concern. Marshall found Anne Bingham elegant, yet disapproved of the way her "sleeve [does] not reach the elbow or the glove come quite to it. There is a vacancy of three or four inches & just [above] the naked elbow is a gold clasp." Marshall wrote his wife that he much preferred the genuine "warmth & cordiality" which he found among the secluded Morrises.[48]

For George Washington's final dinner hosted as president, however, the Morrises made an exception. Party spirit had run high the previous fall, as Adams and Jefferson vied for the position, despite Washington's attempt to soothe such divisions in his famed Farewell Address. A choice barb appeared in Philadelphia's *Aurora General Advertiser* during the election when it sounded an "Alarm," stating, "John Adams, the advocate of a kingly government, and of a titled nobility to form an upper house, and to keep down the swinish multitude . . . would deprive you of a voice in cho[o]sing your president and senate, and make both hereditary." Washington's retirement meant more than just the nostalgic exit of the Revolution's greatest figure; it also suggested the partisan rancor to come. On March 3, 1797, the afternoon before Adams's inauguration, the Morrises joined the Washingtons and other esteemed guests in the dining room of their old house. Morris said his toasts, and Washington reciprocated his devotion, with recent difficulties put aside. After the inauguration, when the family cleared out for Mount Vernon, Washington offered Mary the parting gift of a "lustre"—a tabletop piece that had sat in the main drawing room of the Masters-Penn house—"as a small testimony of our Affectionate regard for you, Mr. Morris and family." Mary received it gratefully, and the sparkling treasure struck an emotional chord. In May, she expanded on her thanks for the gift, writing that "you have not, neither has Mrs. Washington an Idea how much I miss your removeall from hence." Their removal deprived her of two "most valued friends" and neighbors at an unfortunate time, "when I have less inclination than ever to go further from home." She packed the lustre off with the family's other treasures to Fitzsimons's house.[49]

Her husband's activities descended into chaos. Suits came in, forcing Morris constantly to arrange and rearrange creditors according to the most demanding. Meanwhile, James Greenleaf and John Nicholson tore at each other in the newspapers, publishing column after column of accusations and bile. Morris was disgusted by the newspaper war, which he thought only damaged their common schemes still barely afloat. This attitude gave way when Morris finally set his own pen to work in April 1797. Writing to James Greenleaf on the pages of *Porcupine's Gazette,* he jeered that "it is my duty to refute the charges of having made an improper sale of some of *your land*" and "a misappropriation of the money." Morris ended his column-length recitation of transactions dating to 1793 with an offer to submit their differences to arbitrators. It hardly settled the matter. Greenleaf, nearing debtors' prison himself, launched suits against his former partners. In June 1797, the mess of the trio's federal city lots was placed in the hands of a group of interested trustees called the Aggregate Fund. These creditors, largely composed of fellow Philadelphia merchants, attempted to provide for the whole by forestalling foreclosure. Morris and Nicholson, now without the power to make their own lot sales, fed the trustees land company shares and Kentucky lands while the Fund took up the negotiations for time and loans. The long-suffering federal city commissioners were unimpressed.[50]

Through it all, Morris managed to keep his eye on the proposed treaty with the Seneca. After all, the Genesee lands had saved him once before. Concluding the purchase would bring the final £37,500 due from the Holland Land Company, and it coincided with his wish for fairness for his faithful Dutch creditors. Maybe they could be persuaded to do still more. Morris also retained a few remaining parcels in the area he hoped to sell.[51]

Over the past year, his son had made good progress on his errand. Thomas had given speeches to the Indians; he had scouted the best location to hold a treaty; and he had soothed British traders in the area who might otherwise make trouble. In February 1797, Thomas had even convinced the Seneca leader Cornplanter to trek to Philadelphia for some softening with the great Eater, though he could not convince Red Jacket nor Farmer's Brother to go. His father paid Cornplanter's traveling expenses, and he found the Indian upon arrival receptive to the idea of exchanging some land for annuities. Cornplanter's arrival finally prompted President Washington to authorize a treaty commissioner, and he submitted a name to the Senate two days before Adams's inauguration. Cornplanter left town "well satisfied as I believe with me," Morris announced, and he vowed "the promises I have made to them I shall sacredly perform." Yet they all still had to get the whole of his people "in the Humour to sell."[52]

This Thomas accomplished in May. From his home in Canandaigua, he set out on a 270-mile trek by foot to Buffalo Creek and then Niagara and back, during which he visited the Seneca chiefs and appealed to their sense of trust and "friendship" with Morris over the years. While there, Thomas even confronted Red Jacket about his earlier jab at the devouring financier, whereupon the Indian orator retracted the big belly statement as one made in jest. Thomas then suggested to the group a formal "Interview" with Morris at which the Seneca could hear "proposals" regarding their lands, without necessarily committing to a sale. His appeal worked, as the Seneca, prodded by the likes of Cornplanter and other sweetened leaders, notified the authorities a month later of their willingness to meet, and the place was set for Big Tree, a village later known as Geneseo, in August.[53]

Robert Morris instantly began scratching up the funds to provide the enormous quantities of whiskey, tobacco, food, and gifts customary for such treaties. The whiskey itself would run to twenty-five gallons, or 1,500 rations. Attending personally along with the goods would be tricky. Thomas thought his father's presence would help but agreed he could handle the negotiations in his stead. In the end, Morris was simply too harried to leave Philadelphia. So he shipped out two wagons' worth of delicacies in July to supplement his son's purchases at Albany. "Brothers of the Seneca Nation," Morris stated in an opening speech to be delivered on his behalf, "It was my wish and my intention to have come into your country and to have met you at this Treaty but the Great Spirit has ordained otherwise and I cannot go." He continued with frankness: "I grow old[,] am corpulent and not very well and am fearfull of travelling so far during the hot weather in the month of August. I am also obliged to attend to much business here otherwise my affairs would suffer greatly during my absence. I hope therefore that you will excuse me for not coming as I intended and as I formerly told some of you I would do." With the draft of this speech, which went on to outline his intentions and arguments for the sale, Morris also sent Thomas his powers of attorney. Additionally, he appointed Charles Williamson, a trusted Genesee resident, to serve as co-negotiator with Thomas. Morris authorized them to offer as much as $75,000 for the land, plus individual payments to key chiefs. "I shall intrust the business to you & him," he wrote Thomas, "in full confidence that your Prudence & good sense will produce as good consequences as if I were present."[54]

When Morris wrote these instructions and explanations in mid-July, he was a prisoner in his own house. He had negotiated for a stay of execution until August, but now that month was upon him, with fresh writs joining the queue. Morris chose neither to flee the region nor to surrender himself to the authorities; rather, he avoided service of these writs by "keeping close," the practice of barricading oneself inside one's home, thereby preventing the sheriff from serving them. Writs were required to be served in person, and authorities could not legally break and enter for such a purpose. For Morris, this meant retreat to the Hills estate outside the city on the Schuylkill, where the broad grounds would expose any stray visitors long before they could arrive at the locked door. He moved there in July, in the midst of his final preparations for the treaty and only days after James Greenleaf was seized and thrown into the Prune Street debtors' prison, casting the options in stark relief. A few weeks later, Morris was already suffering the absence of his family, whom he had left behind in the rental house on Chestnut Street. "I want sadly to do away that distance and to go boldly home again," he repined, while remaining confident that "time which brings about all things will effect this also." Mary, Maria, young Henry, and his grown sons visited with him occasionally, mostly on Sundays, when no writs could be served, and at times he risked the streets himself. Charles had incurred his father's displeasure earlier that year for wastrel habits and then lit out "to the westward," returning just as suddenly to rally to the family's cause. William, too, had returned home to Philadelphia and his father's affairs. John Nicholson kept close with Morris inside the Hills for a few weeks to conduct their business together until he retreated to his own estate on the Delaware River at the end of August. The two initiated a frenetic correspondence, sending letters and instructions between the Hills—which they dubbed "Castle Defiance"—and Nicholson's house—which became "Castle Defense"—as fast as William, Charles, and the other couriers could carry them.[55]

Despite its relative loneliness, Castle Defiance was not a bad place to be (fig. 7.7). It had been in the hands of a tenant until earlier that year, and a new canal now cut through its three hundred acres, but its longtime gardener, David Landreth, kept it in bloom. Recent visitors still raved about the orange, lemon, and coffee trees and the pineapples growing in the greenhouse and hothouses there. Beyond the surrounding orchards, the land rolled, with sheep and cattle grazing in fenced pastures. The main house, a "large and elegant Stone Building," as Morris termed it, adjoined the greenhouse. This nine-room complex retained its grandeur, offering several beds, dressing tables, and four different dining tables with seats and place settings for eighteen. Its windows opened out to a view of the river below. The Hills was also well stocked with supplies necessary for Morris's stand: bottles of liquor and casks of Madeira, as well as writing paper, two spyglasses, and guns. A servant named Jenny and "a black cook" stood on hand to provide victuals. However, it was dispiriting when a sheriff auctioned lots in mid-August from Morris's adjoining estate of Springetsbury. Morris wrote that "the Sale was thinly attended and as I am told not well conducted." Just downriver, officials were organizing tent cities to remove the poor from the city's crowded alleys, as another yellow fever epidemic threatened in the August heat, recalling the terrible memories of 1793. Morris thought the danger of the fever overblown, venturing into Chestnut Street on August 20 before a near capture sent him hurrying back to the Hills. Whether his family remained on Chestnut Street or retreated from the fever in the other direction, up the Delaware to Morrisville, the financier believed they would be in a safer position than behind the doors of his airy castle.[56]

Three hundred miles away, over the mountains, Thomas was at Big Tree surrounded by 1,200 camping Senecas and other Iroquois plus an assortment

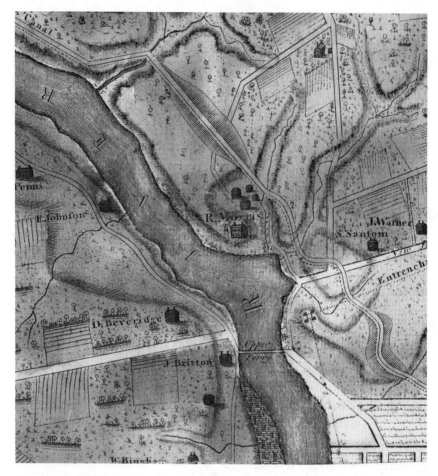

Figure 7.7. "The Hills," renamed "Castle Defiance" by Morris, on the Schuylkill River just outside Philadelphia, seen here as "R. Morris" in the center of the image. (Detail of image from P. C. Varlé, *To The Citizens of Philadelphia This Plan of The City and its Environs is respectfully dedicated By the Editor* . . . [Philadelphia, (1794)]. Courtesy of the Library Company of Philadelphia)

of government officials, land surveyors, translators, secretaries, and bankers, as well as spectators and hawkers selling goods. On August 28, Thomas lit the council fire and initiated the customary Condolence Ritual to start proceedings. Cornplanter stood to give a speech, then American officials gave their speeches, then Thomas delivered his father's speech plus some words of his own, to all of which Red Jacket responded darkly with words discouraging a sale. Proceedings continued fitfully over the next several days with heavy drinking, private conferences, and more speeches until matters completely stalled on September 6. Thomas had upped his father's proposal to $100,000 for the whole, or three cents an acre, but Red Jacket, speaking for the chiefs, countered with a final offer to sell only a tiny fraction of the lands, which Thomas rejected as unacceptable. Red Jacket then seized the moment, standing up and roaring that the council fire should be covered and the parties depart without a deal. In the ensuing confusion and apparent end of the gathering, Thomas, in a last-ditch effort, sidestepped Red Jacket and appealed to the chief women. Privately, he emphasized the benefits of the sale to them, promising them a life of ease and comfort on the annuities. Cornplanter and the warriors, too, came to Thomas's aid, with the result, to the great surprise and relief of Thomas and his delegation, that an agreement was reached just a few days later. In sum, the Seneca would retain certain reservations of a few hundred square miles total while transferring the rest of the state in exchange for $100,000 worth of stock in the Bank of the United States. The bank's much-vaunted interest rates would generate $4 per Seneca per year.[57]

Morris, named at the treaty "Big Bear," was elated at the news of the Treaty of Big Tree, which was signed September 15, 1797. Although the cost was higher than he had hoped, indeed higher than almost any Indian purchase to date, he told his son, "I am much rejoiced and am perfectly satisfied that *you have managed this business as well as it was possible & perhaps better than if I had been there.*" Morris believed it to be in the interest of the two nations, and he had made sure with the Hollanders' cash advances that it was in the interest of Cornplanter, Farmer's Brother, and other leaders. Even the outspoken Red Jacket received $600 in hand plus $100 annually for his signature, given at Big Tree on the sly, thereby accepting push for the lands before more white settlers came to shove. A sorry life on reservations awaited them all. Morris, in his own straitened position, hoped that his Philadelphia creditors could likewise be made to bend.[58]

But the news of the treaty could not beat back the storm besetting him at the Hills. A week before the treaty was signed, Morris saw his Chestnut Street mansion as well as the Hills advertised for sale by the sheriff. Morris managed to prolong their auction with advances from the Treaty dealings, even while wondering aloud, "How are all these things to end?"[59] Thus began a plaintive soliloquy. That fall, in a stream of letters to whomever would listen, the one-time superintendent of finance exclaimed at his writing desk:

> I am in great distress, without as yet seeing relief at hand.
> Altho I am here secluded from personal intercourse with the world,
>   I am not allowed one moment of uninterrupted leisure.

> By Heaven there is no bearing with these things, I believe I shall
>   go mad, every day brings forward scenes & troubles almost
>   insupportable and they seem to be accumulating so that at
>   last they will like a torrent carry every thing before them.
> God help us, for men will not, we are abandoned by all but those
>   who want to get from us all we yet hold.
> Ours is a hard fate. I fear my Chesnut Street house and lot will fall
>   a sacrifice and if so, the rest will follow.
> There can be no better security in America than that which is
>   bound for these debts.
> Good heavens what vultures men are in regard to each other.
> I never in the days of prosperity took advantage of any mans
>   distresses and I suppose what I now experience is to serve as
>   a lesson whereby to see the folly of Humane & Generous
>   conduct.[60]

His words revealed a soul still convinced it was right—even humane and generous. He acknowledged trustworthy individuals, though they were set against a cruel new landscape. Things soon turned violent. In November, while the Philadelphia sheriff auctioned off the remainder of his other local properties, creditors and their hired hands prowled the grounds, hoping to catch the financier out of doors or even at a window. They lit fires for warmth while staking him out. Just after Christmas, six men with sledgehammers and pickaxes rushed the Castle, to be repelled by a show of nearly "every Pistol & Gun in the house" as much as by the timely interceding of a friend. Two days after the new year, Morris learned that an undersheriff "is to attack me to day" and took precautions to have him interrupted before the man could rage up the Schuylkill. Later that month, aided by his spyglass, Morris observed that "a French man" hoped to shoot him through a window.[61]

He identified as among his most relentless foes the Bank of North America and George Eddy, a minor Philadelphia creditor. To the Bank of North America, Morris offered its now-estranged directors a shuffling and reshuffling of his deck of local properties. To Eddy, he issued a rare, sullen threat. Morris told Eddy that he was aware of the latter's attempts to imprison him, and if successful, "you will in doing so prove yourself the greatest enemy I have in the world and you will neither benefit yourself nor any one else by it." Morris promised Eddy he would regret this course, for if Morris were imprisoned, "you may rest assured that I shall never come out alive." Rather, Morris suggested that Eddy visit his grounds for a talk from the upstairs window, promising his tormentor ultimate repayment and indemnification from his own debts.[62]

But Eddy, figurehead for a hundred distressed colleagues, achieved his triumph shortly thereafter. By that point, Morris was worn down. "I shall now prepare for Prune Street," he acknowledged to Nicholson on February 5, 1798, in response to Eddy's latest summons. Neither Garret Cottringer, his son William, nor his lawyers could prolong the attachments or find anyone else willing to stand bail. And sheriffs near and far were sweeping all his remaining property away. "My money is gone my furniture is to be sold I am to go to prison & my family to starve—good night," he spat. In that moment, the reality of it all finally hit home. He could acknowledge this "hard & cruel Fate" was deserved punishment for "my imprudence in the use of my name & loss of credit." He even contemplated suicide, but held his hand in consideration for his family. "On *their* account I would do any thing to avert" prison, "except an act that would still affect them more deeply," he concluded darkly.[63]

So on the evening of February 14, 1798, five years after he had toasted Blanchard's balloon launch, Morris unlatched and opened his door to the sheriff, as well as to George Eddy and Eddy's brother Charles, "the most hardened villain God ever made." The following day, the sixty-four-year-old financier walked in custody from the Hills to his family's city rental in Chestnut Street, where the formal arrest would take place. Mary had had a long time to prepare for this moment, and she had received a calm note from her husband the previous day informing her of the process. He was resolved to be stoic, but his appearance there broke Mary's genteel composure after the strain of it all. One resident described their arrival as causing the family to exhibit "a dreadful scene of distress." Mary was practically "frantic": she lost control and "flew upon the Person who was his bail and who bro't him to town and would have committed violence but was prevented." On February 16, with her sobs still in his ear, Robert was led down Sixth Street to Prune Street, where he entered like so many other lesser debtors whose plans for prosperity in the new republic had gone foul.[64]

"Brothers," he had told the Seneca in his written speech that August, as he may have reminded those crowding about him now, so many imprisoned because of his failures, he wished only "that mutual fair dealings and Justice shall take place. . . . I desire nothing but fair open and honest transactions." It must have been cold comfort for them all.

8. His Ruins

At a crowded city coffeehouse on Saturday evening, December 9, 1797, the sheriff's gavel fell on the Chestnut Street property. It was the beginning of the house's strange demise.[1]

A friend, fellow Philadelphia merchant William Sansom, brought some hope just before the sale. Thirty-four years old, Sansom came from a long-standing Quaker family in the area and traveled in many of the same circles as Morris. He was even something of a neighbor, as his Schuylkill estate stood near the Hills. Beyond their ordinary acquaintance, Sansom had particular insight into Morris's distress, for he also served as a member of the board at the Insurance Company of Pennsylvania and at the Insurance Company of North America, two major creditors of the failing financier. Sansom shared Morris's enthusiasm for their city's prospects, but he was a more prudent investor. His trade was profitable and his securities were sound. At the time, he could tell fellow Quaker John Dickinson, to whom Morris still owed £7,000 Pennsylvania currency for his original Chestnut Street purchase, that "I have come forward in the theatre of Life in some measure," and that "Providence hath indulged me with an ample fortune." In this position, Sansom took pity on Morris. He felt "compassion for the Family of an unfortunate and imprudent man; who have seen days of great splendor and apparent happiness & wealth." Sansom could express such sentiments even as Morris owed him a personal debt of $16,000. So in response to Morris's pleas, Sansom promised to try to help save the financier's homes, provided it did not entail undue risk. He was able to interest two more of Morris's creditors:

Joseph Ball, president of the Insurance Company of North America and member of the board of managers of Morris's Pennsylvania Property Company, plus a local merchant firm, John Reed & Standish Forde, who combined stood to collect $44,000 and rising. At the sheriff's sale, with potential purchasers skittish about the title and the nature of the properties, Sansom's group planned to buy and hold the Chestnut Street property as collateral while Morris continued scrambling.[2]

On the night of the auction, Sansom "managed the thing to a charm," in Morris's estimation. A hostile creditor turned up late to the coffeehouse, intending to bid and take the property, only to go away disappointed and angry, despite Sansom's attempts to soften him on his way out. The mansion and lot, subject to a mortgage held by the Willinks in Amsterdam in addition to Dickinson's principal, sold for only $25,600, just slightly more than Morris's original purchase price of the block alone in 1790. This fact was not lost on William Bingham, who believed the lot itself was worth nearly $90,000 a year earlier. Morris had never been able to purchase the sliver of property at the northeast corner of the lot, then owned by Peter Rick, so that was not included in the sale. The Hills, under a mortgage to the Insurance Company of Pennsylvania, was also sold that night to Joseph Ball and Standish Forde, who immediately leased it back to Morris, thereby enabling his continued stand inside Castle Defiance for a few more months.[3]

Morris's reprieve was temporary and conditional. For any hope of retaining control of the properties, he needed to replace Sansom, Forde, and the others with long-term creditors. For that he turned abroad, pitching new schemes based on the two properties to the representatives of his Amsterdam bankers in Philadelphia and New York. He also tried the Bank of North America again, an unlikely source, as he stood so much in their debt already.[4]

Morris, barricaded inside near a smoky chimney in the winter cold, soon saw subdivision of these massive estates as the only possible solution. It was a rejection of his earlier vision. "I believe the [Chestnut Street] House and lot if properly divided may sell so as to produce $250,000 or more," he told one representative. The Hills "may also be divided into lots so as to produce 150,000 or more," with sales beginning as early as the spring. But his colleagues were spooked, and no one took him up on his propositions. Within weeks, Morris understood the properties would be lost.[5]

By the end of January 1798, lesser creditors ("vultures," in Morris's words) had moved in on the movable property on both estates. On January

25, the financier observed that not only were all the tools and building supplies on the Chestnut Street lot threatened, but "tomorrow they are to break open the doors" of the mansion "and levy on every thing within not fixed to the building." Further, "tomorrow the Sherriff is to come out here," to the Hills, "and levie upon the furniture (miserable as it is) in this House and upon the Green House Trees, Shrubs, Plants &c." In an attempt to defeat this plan, Morris signed over all the Chestnut Street house's movables to William Sansom for $3,000, and he signed over movables at the Hills to Standish Forde for $2,000. Forde now owned the wines, cups and dishes, furniture, and spyglasses in his hands, as Fitzsimons owned those of Morris's family in town.[6]

A few weeks later, just before going to Prune Street, Morris received an ultimatum from Sansom, Ball, and Reed & Forde. Until the last hour, the financier kept casting about for a solution to "rescue" his estates from their "dreadfull sacrifice," needing $65,000 in hand for the immediate purpose, with his son Charles hand-delivering his pleas. But he failed, and he entered Prune Street with the tepid promises of Sansom and the others to return any surplus from the resale of these estates. His costly architectural vision and his pleasure grounds were now reduced to someone else's ledger entries.[7]

In March, Standish Forde explained his group's plans for the Chestnut Street property to Morris. Naturally, this would involve cutting up the city block, to maximize the available lots for sale and to integrate them into the surrounding neighborhood. Despite four years of L'Enfant's lavish hand, no purchaser could be found to move into the estate as it stood. The same could be said of the state's erstwhile "President's House" erected for George Washington on Ninth Street, the bulky frame of which would stand empty for years after John Adams declined its use. On either side of Morris's Folly, a street ran parallel between Chestnut and Walnut Streets westward from the State House at Sixth Street to the edge of the city. Now William Sansom intended to cut this street, named George Street (or "St. George's Street" or "Little George Street"), through the middle of Morris's block, although he planned to shift its position slightly. Morris took notice, and his wounded pride felt the slight: "George Street is to be continued through the Chestnut Street Lot," Morris informed John Nicholson, "but Mr. Sansom's ambition has led him to change the name & position." Specifically, "it will be nearer to Walnut Street so as to shorten the Depth of his Lots," and "the name in the future 'Sansom Street.'" In doing so, Sansom would imprint his name onto the city's grid more permanently than Morris could (fig. 8.1). George Street

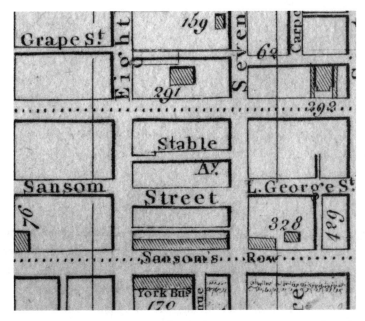

Figure 8.1. Philadelphia street plan in 1810 showing Sansom Street cut through
Morris's old block, with Sansom's Row fronting south to Walnut Street. (Detail
of image from John Adems Paxton, [The stranger's guide]: an alphabetical list
of all the wards, streets, roads . . . wharves, ship yards, public buildings, &c. in the
city and suburbs of Philadelphia, with references for finding their situations on an
alphabetical plan [(Philadelphia): Edward Parker, (c1810)], opening insert.
Courtesy of the Library Company of Philadelphia)

as a whole would come to be called Sansom Street into the twenty-first century, becoming a residential and commercial landmark. Sansom's imprint
there erased many of the public associations of Morris with the site. He
achieved this geographical reorientation surprisingly quickly.[8]

Four months after the sheriff's sale, on a stormy day in March 1798, a tall,
bespectacled European wandered onto the abandoned construction site.
Benjamin Henry Latrobe had been in America for two years. Born in England, he had traveled in Germany, Italy, and France as a young man, receiving a formal architectural education in the process, making him the most
sophisticated architect on American soil when he landed. Here was a true
peer of L'Enfant, in terms of international exposure and training. Latrobe
had recently come north from his new Virginia home for a trip to Philadelphia to learn more about the Walnut Street Jail, after receiving a commission

to build a penitentiary in Richmond. He also wanted to see the other sights of the metropolis, including the Chestnut Street mansion about which he had heard so much already. His conclusion after seeing the Folly: "It is impossible to decide which of the two is the maddest, the architect, or his employer. Both of them have been ruined by it." Latrobe returned to the site wide-eyed several times during his Philadelphia stay.[9]

The traveler recently had a brush with architectural infamy himself. Upon his landing in Norfolk in 1796, Latrobe had made a friendly wager with the local merchant William Pennock, who challenged the newcomer to design a symmetrical house for his family on an awkwardly shaped Main Street lot. Latrobe made some ambitious designs and drawings in response, showing the requisite arrangement, and then left for Richmond. There, in a tavern, he was stopped short by a dining companion's tale: "A Frenchman was at Norfolk, who had given Captn. Pennock the most preposterous design, which he had ever seen; that Captn. Pennock had been mad enough to attempt to execute it, and that having carried up part of the Walls he was now perfectly at a stand, as none of the Workmen knew how to proceed." To his shock, Latrobe suddenly realized that he was the "Frenchman" under discussion; Pennock had tried to build the design in his absence with local craftsmen. Latrobe returned to Norfolk to wrestle the house to completion, though its refined brickwork, spiraling entrance stair, garden-front bow projection, and siting toward the rear of its lot made it a poor fit for Norfolk's timber-frame houses and shops. Latrobe blamed the provincial workmen for its unhappy execution and destiny. Pennock moved out of the house five or six years later to a different Main Street address. His "preposterous" house, valued at $12,000 plus an accompanying kitchen building, was destroyed sometime in the nineteenth century, possibly at the time of Pennock's move. It had narrowly missed receiving the appellation of "folly." Meanwhile, Latrobe was able to renew his reputation with a series of high-profile, successful commissions, beginning with the state penitentiary.[10]

Perhaps this initial experience alerted Latrobe to the stakes involved in designing houses for the young nation's ambitious merchants. It certainly did not predispose Latrobe—who saw architecture through the lens of a restrained, proportioned neoclassicism—to enjoy L'Enfant's work for Morris. Amid the rain, he wandered around the structure and "gazed upon it with astonishment," trying to make sense of what he was seeing. He also ventured inside. The house would make as deep an impression on him as on anyone.[11]

When he finally returned to Richmond a month later, he confided to his journal why he waited until then to jot down his observations on the house and its "violently ugly" features. "I knew not what to say about it in order to record the appearance of the monster in a few words. Indeed I can scarcely at this moment believe in the existence of what I have seen many times, of its complicated, unintelligible, mass." He made a rough sketch of the floor plan alongside his notes, but he protested that he could not identify the parts of the building intended in the plan, even after querying friends acquainted with Morris and L'Enfant (fig. 8.2).[12]

Latrobe's sketch indeed highlighted the Folly's complicated layout. Latrobe acknowledged that his drawing shortened the building's extensive breadth, "but I believe its outline is otherwise correct as to its *ins* and *outs*." It shows the building's two main wings, with projecting bows at all four corners. He offered a lettered key to explain certain features. "At *A*," the north front of the building facing Chestnut Street where the main entrance would have been, "is a recess, across which a Colonnade of One story columns was

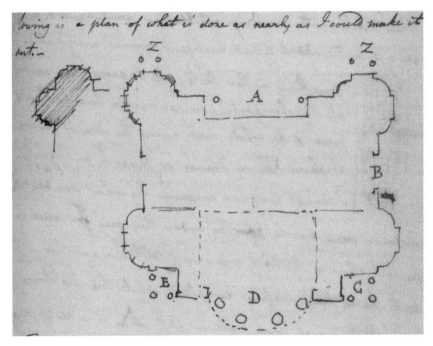

Figure 8.2. Benjamin Henry Latrobe's sketch of the Folly's plan. (Detail of image from Benjamin Henry Latrobe, Virginia Journals, entry for April 26, 1798. Courtesy of the Maryland Historical Society)

intended, the two lateral ones being put up, with a piece of their Architrave reaching to the Wall; I cannot guess what was intended above them." Flanking *A* were two bows at *Z*, formed by alternating curvilinear and flat lines, with tall windows in each of the latter. Latrobe's attempts to sketch and re-sketch their lines in the upper corner of the drawing reveal their peculiarity. On the south, garden entrance of the house, "*The bow* at *D* is open to the roof, the bases only of 4 Columns being laid in niches, as in the front of St. Peters at Rome, from which I hope [L'Enfant] copied them, as such a madness in modern architecture stands in great need of a powerful apology" (fig. 8.3). There was no way to view this building dispassionately. Inside the bows flanking the unusual portico at *D* were two "angle porches" at *E* and *C*, "irresistibly laughable things." Finally, on the east side, "At *B* is a wide opening with an *Eliptical* rough arch in the brick wall. Conjecture is entirely baffled here, nor could I obtain the smallest information what could be intended." Latrobe was not acquainted with the Morrises; otherwise he might have guessed that the opening was intended to connect with a hothouse or some outbuilding, as at the Hills. The interior of the drawing's plan is a blank—Latrobe did not even try to delineate room divisions or stairwells he might have seen. Nor did he venture down into the dark cellars. He estimated the whole structure as "very large"—at least 120 feet long by at least 60 feet deep. Unbeknownst to Latrobe, its plan's outline presented an uncanny resemblance to the emerging plan of Monticello, which Thomas Jefferson, so familiar with Philadelphia's buildings, had just undertaken to

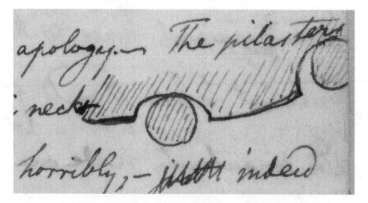

Figure 8.3. Latrobe's sketch of the Folly's columns-in-niches, placed around the rear bow. (Detail of image from Benjamin Henry Latrobe, Virginia Journals, entry for April 26, 1798. Courtesy of the Maryland Historical Society)

renovate. In 2002, architectural historian James D. Kornwolf would identify Morris's Folly as an elaborate "H" plan, popular in France for two hundred years. Kornwolf conceived eleven major rooms on each floor, with double stairwells on either side of a central salon. Surely L'Enfant had planned something interesting below each of the "3 or 4" skylights Latrobe observed.[13]

The building's exterior struck Latrobe as haphazardly unfinished, "although," he acknowledged, "much of the marble dressing is entirely complete in patches." Miller and the Jardellas' work did not inspire. The windows were "cased in White Marble with mouldings, entablatures, architraves and sculpture mixed up in the oddest and most inelegant manner imaginable: something in this taste," he wrote alongside his sketches (fig. 8.4). Latrobe believed that "all the proportions are bad" and that "the whole mass" brought to mind the reigns of Louis XIII in France and James I in England. Again, the royal references hung around the building like a vapor. Moving from the

Figure 8.4. Latrobe's sketch of the Folly's windows and window casings. (Detail of image from Benjamin Henry Latrobe, Virginia Journals, entry for April 26, 1798. Courtesy of the Maryland Historical Society)

exterior window treatments, Latrobe proceeded to describe the columns, porticoes, and pilasters, surrounded by "a profusion of wretched sculpture" in marble. Soffits were "inriched with pannels and foliage," while the "Capitals of the Columns are of the worst taste." He called the Ionic-inspired capitals' design, featuring scrolls and swags, "a sort of composite" and compared them with extravagant Roman examples (figs. 8.5 and 8.6). Lastly he took note of the roof, "an immense *Mansard*," though by this time he had little spleen left to vent and he did not opine on the choice. In sum, there was nothing about the building he liked. He could acknowledge that some people admired it or at least boasted of it; he sneered that he was told "in Virginia, that it was the *hand*somest thing in America." And he himself was drawn to spend plenty of time ruminating over its form and meaning. In the end, he could satisfy himself that beyond the ruin of the structure's mad patrons, "It is now sold to Mr. Sansom of the Pensylvania [*sic*] bank, who means to convert it, as I was told into five houses." The monster would not stand.[14]

What was the root of Latrobe's outrage over the house's aesthetics? It may have signaled a whiff of jealousy from the ambitious newcomer, who would soon purchase loads of its "wretched sculpture" and stone to decorate his own commissions. It may have indirectly involved politics; while in

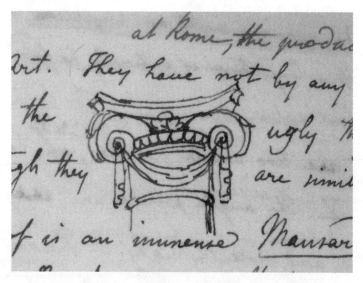

Figure 8.5. Latrobe's sketch of the Folly's capitals. (Detail of image from Benjamin Henry Latrobe, Virginia Journals, entry for April 26, 1798. Courtesy of the Maryland Historical Society)

Figure 8.6. Salvaged capitals from Morris's Folly, in a stone yard outside Philadelphia. (*"The Georgian Period": Being Measured Drawings of Colonial Work* [Boston: American Architect & Building News Co., 1902], part 9, p. 23. Courtesy of James Branch Cabell Library, Virginia Commonwealth University)

Philadelphia, Latrobe observed that political "fanaticism" was at its peak. Upon arrival, this newly minted Virginia democrat suffered the scorn of the Philadelphia Federalist establishment, so recently stirred by developments following John Adams's 1796 election. Relations with France had again charged the air; in the wake of Jay's Treaty and the election of the Federalist candidate Adams, the French envoy had been withdrawn from Philadelphia, the American minister in Paris was expelled, and French ships preyed on those of America on the seas. Most ominously, a peace mission Adams had dispatched to France had recently been humiliated, and this news was released just as the architect with the French surname stood on Morris's lot. On April 3, the Federalist *Porcupine's Gazette* jeered at the activities of Latrobe ("son of an old seditious dissenter") and suggested "he is very likely to be the *first tenant*" of his new Richmond penitentiary when complete. Latrobe complained that one must cow to the British ambassador in the city, or risk being marked a democrat and an outcast. On the defensive, he may have been lashing out at Morris as Federalist pillar. But most likely Latrobe's vitriol really did come down to a question of taste. There was nothing of the baroque in Latrobe. L'Enfant's vision was entirely out of step with the clear volumes and lines Latrobe showcased in his own work. And the Greek temple forms beginning to pop up in towns across the nation testified that Latrobe was not alone.[15]

Nor were the moral aspects of his critique unique. The recoil from the house's extravagance was already commonplace. Around the same time, Polish traveler Julian Niemcewicz echoed these points by stating plainly that "the house of Robert Morris, recently sold, is a monument to the folly of this man who, in spite of all his genius for commerce, has finished by becoming bankrupt. He undertook it in a spirit of rivalry with Bingham. He took as his architect another fool, Major Enfant. He built for him a real confection which was to be covered with white marble. The undertaking was abandoned in that state most suitable to show all its extravagances." Here, like Latrobe, Niemcewicz distilled the key elements: folly, bankrupt, abandoned, extravagances. The only element Niemcewicz had missed was "palace," captured by Latrobe in the latter's references to Louis XIII, James I, and St. Peter's. So Latrobe's reaction resonated with the cumulative judgments, from Deborah Logan in 1793 to Isaac Weld in 1795 to James Callender in 1796 to Niemcewicz in 1798, notwithstanding the more ambivalent treatment that William Birch would soon release. Latrobe's statement that the house "ruined" its authors and his general condemnation of the structure became primary slants for the house's long shadow.[16]

These judgments did not stop residents at the time from picking prizes out of the abandoned site. Morris had been selling materials off the lot since October 1797, after his work crews had dispersed. The sheriff seized unused building materials lying on the lot into 1798. Despite this, and despite Sansom's move to cut his street through the block, the house stood relatively intact through 1798 and even into 1799, while Birch was preparing his engraved views of the city. In the words of one observer following Latrobe's visit, it "remained for some time uninhabited, a dreary, lonely, and forlorn monument of absurd taste and capricious prodigality." The house had received a stay of execution because the multiple new owners could not agree on its division.[17]

In late 1799, Joseph Ball, Reed & Forde, and William Sansom finally moved to divide the property and dismantle the Folly. Morris remained bitter about their plans. "It seems to be in the way of bidding me adieu," he complained of its dissolution, "without leaving a vestige for me to remember it unless by the account of cost in my books." The owners hired laborers to begin taking down the building's walls and to prepare the materials for resale. The Chestnut Street lot then became a brickyard and a stone-yard, offering

easy prices intended to repay its new owners. The buyers who showed up
were familiar faces, among them: James Traquair, the stone dealer who had
worked with the Jardellas for Morris; John Miller, Morris's primary supplier
who still held his outstanding bills; Sansom himself, taking 45,000 bricks for
the row houses he was having built nearby; and Benjamin Henry Latrobe,
who had returned to reside in Philadelphia. Latrobe surely thought he could
put the cubes, lumps, and carved stone to better use than had L'Enfant, and
his purchase alone totaled $5,322. From January to June 1800, Reed & Forde
and the others sold over 800,000 bricks and thousands of feet of stone (483
perches plus those taken by Latrobe). It was a mountain of materials. The
owners sold other scraps, too—copper, boards, iron skylights. All of these
would be absorbed into new constructions, such as Latrobe's Bank of Pennsylvania, begun that year and built in marble in the form of a Greek temple, or
the rows of houses Sansom would erect. One Philadelphian, Joshua Francis
Fisher, recalled a sense of justice in this dispersal. He held that Morris's "mechanics, who were not paid for their work, divided the materials for their par-
tial indemnity, and the blocks of houses on Chestnut, Walnut, Sansom and
Locust Streets, erected on speculation by the associated mechanics, aided by
funds from Wm Sansom, and others, in the end exhausted all the stone, bricks
& timber that could be used." Fisher's memory held a grain of truth. Associations with the site began to fade, as builders turned the occasional bit of sculpture remaining on blocks inward. The only things the lot's owners could not
sell were the yawning basements, which Sansom and the others attempted to
cover with fill, leaving of the Folly nothing but a hole in the ground.[18]

Yet not all material relics of the Folly were snuffed out. Indeed, sometimes these associations were celebrated, as ordinary citizens toyed with bits
of the financier's onetime vision. The most recognizable remnants were survivors from the Jardellas' series of bas-reliefs in marble, for which they completed at least six works, likely intended for exterior decoration of the house,
or for interior overdoors. The reliefs were six feet wide by three and a half
feet tall. They depicted pairs of putti, or childlike spirits from classical imagery, on clouds adorned with laurels, celebrating the various arts. During the
early Renaissance, Florentine sculptor Donatello had revived these *spiritel-
los*, imagined to animate life and the body with sudden joys, passions, panics, and other sensuous swoons. Their innocent yet mischievous antics
typically offered relief from the seriousness of religious and political themes.

In other words, in these playful sprites the Jardellas offered an ideal figure-head for the gregarious, dancing Morrises and their mansion.[19]

Even Latrobe enjoyed them, in his own way. Among the finished pieces he purchased from the site, he selected two of the Jardellas' rectangular reliefs in marble, presumably titled "Drama" and "Music" (fig. 8.7). The first featured winged putti handling the masks of comedy and tragedy, adrift on clouds while also tugging on swags of leaves. Their plump bodies roll. Likewise, in the second relief, one childish sprite plucks a harp's strings while another holds aloft an open book of music. Appropriately, in the early 1800s, Latrobe installed the two panels on the front of his refurbished New Theatre on Chestnut Street. There, they overlooked the street directly above the doors on the building's flanking wings (fig. 8.8). Figural sculpture of any kind was still rare in America, as demonstrated by the theater's companion pieces of two full-sized female sculptures done in wood. Latrobe did not seek to hide the origins of "Drama" and "Music," which had been hauled from Morris's block just down the street. Their themes fit the spirit of the theater, as did the local stories which followed the pieces. Latrobe confidently dem-onstrated that his eye for proportion led him to treat such adornments much differently than had Morris and L'Enfant. Nor did the lives of "Music" and "Drama" end there. After the destruction of the theater in the 1850s, the two reliefs ended up in private hands, by this time cut into lunette semicircles. The reliefs were installed inside a row house on Philadelphia's Delancey Place, as choice artwork with ties to the city's history.[20]

William Birch likewise purchased two Jardella reliefs, presumably titled "Sculpture" and "Painting," "from the ruins of the Building," as he stated. He used them to decorate the front of his rural cottage, Green Lodge. "Sculpture" then became lost, but "Painting" survived when it was moved sometime later to the home of a quarry owner just outside Philadelphia. By the early twentieth century, the relief was built into the exterior wall of a Butler Pike stone house, between the second story windows. As a result, the structure became known to locals as "Angel House," with its painting putti catching the eyes of pass-ersby. In this relief, a third angelic head emerges between the two central fig-ures. Above it, the painter's oval shield features the faintest outline of a woman, who gently embraces a winged putto at her feet (fig. 8.9). In the 1920s, when the Philadelphia Electric Company demolished this house to make way for an electricity line, utility company executive J. Alexis Shriver took the relief for his private home in Joppa, Maryland, known as Olney. He proudly installed it

Figure 8.7. "Drama" (top) and "Music" stone reliefs, attributed to Giuseppe Jardella, circa 1795. Each measures thirty-six by seventy-two inches. (Author photo)

Figure 8.8. The "Drama" and "Music" reliefs, seen on each of the New (Chestnut Street) Theatre's entrance wings, directly above the arched doorways. (William Strickland, "New Theatre, Chestnut Street," 1808. Courtesy of the Pennsylvania Academy of Fine Arts, Philadelphia. Gift of Mr. and Mrs. William Jeanes)

above the house's rear entrance. There, he reflected on the ability of Morris's doomed, so-called cupid doorhead to speak to philosophical themes.[21]

Two final reliefs in the series ended up in South Carolina sometime prior to the 1880s. The reliefs are nearly identical, each depicting two chubby, winged sprites showcasing a central medallion or shield intended for inscription. The story of their acquisition is not clear, but they may have arrived as early as 1800, when wealthy Charlestonian Peter Smith undertook extensive renovations to the William Gibbes House on South Bay (now Battery) Street. One of the reliefs was thereafter installed on a brick wall in the site's rear gardens. It is more likely that this installation occurred after 1834, when one of the Smith descendants, John Grimké Drayton, inherited the house. Drayton married Julia Ewing of Philadelphia and moved with her to Magnolia Plantation, the Drayton family's Ashley River estate just outside Charleston. When his wife became homesick, Drayton dedicated himself to beautifying the estate's gardens to help soothe her. A prime feature of these riverfront gardens was the Drayton family tomb, upon which stood a rectan-

Figure 8.9. "Painting," stone relief attributed to Giuseppe Jardella, circa 1795, mounted on the exterior of Olney House, Maryland. The relief measures forty-two by seventy-one inches. (Author photo)

gular monument. Here, the companion Jardella relief to that at the Gibbes house was mounted, with the Drayton family name now emblazoned on its central shield (fig. 8.10). Though the Drayton family had corresponded with Robert Morris on business as early as 1795 and had long-standing Philadelphia connections, John Grimké Drayton and his wife, Julia, probably acquired the two pieces together, in a nostalgic effort to surround themselves with bits of the city's lore as much as its craftsmanship.[22]

We can imagine all six of these sculptures, and perhaps more, intended to ring the walls of the Folly, following Parisian style and indeed the precedent of the Binghams' manufactured pieces. Perhaps the Jardellas even had time to install these pieces on the Folly, as seen in Birch's 1800 print of the "Unfinished House," in which the rectangular carvings above the house's ground-floor windows seem to match with the slight arch at the base of the surviving pieces (see fig. 7.3).

In addition, less singular sculptures from the Folly washed across the region. James Traquair, whose marble yard was located nearby on Tenth and

Figure 8.10. The Drayton family tomb at Magnolia Plantation, near Charleston, South Carolina, showing a stone relief attributed to Giuseppe Jardella. The relief measures forty-one by seventy-one inches. (Author photo)

Market Streets, decorated his establishment with other carved relics from the Folly. Joshua Francis Fisher confirmed in the 1860s that "fragments of [its] sculpture were in various stone-yards 'till within a few years." He believed the marble door frames and columns of a house at Market and Tenth Streets came from the Folly. He identified a set of its capitals placed on the entrance gate to a nearby cemetery. Another contemporary journalist pointed to a row of houses on Race Street near Eighth Street with exterior tablets featuring festoons of flowers as relics of the Folly. Sixty years after their disbursal, even mundane pieces still hinted at their origins.[23]

Aside from exterior sculptures, interior pieces surfaced as well. These included two marble chimneypieces. Henry Pratt, a member of Morris's long-suffering "Aggregate Fund," seems to have bought one—"Leda and the Swan"—around 1800. He soon installed it in his "Lemon Hill" mansion on the Schuylkill River, which took the place of the Hills, Morris's old hideout (see fig. 7.4). Meanwhile, Elias Boudinot, then director of the U.S. Mint and longtime Morris acquaintance, bought "Apollo and the Muses" for his home in Burlington, New Jersey, around 1808. In the late nineteenth century, the piece was donated to the Historical Society of Pennsylvania as a relic of the Folly (see fig. 7.6). A set of large paneled cherry doors featuring silver knobs said to have been part of Morris's Folly ended up at a country house built in Bucks County, Pennsylvania, in the first quarter of the nineteenth century. William Maris, the owner, had been a merchant in Philadelphia. He named his house Cintra, after a royal palace in Portugal. In a nod to the financier, locals renamed it Maris's Folly when Maris failed in 1834.[24]

Finally, the furniture intended for the Chestnut Street mansion circulated widely. Thomas Fitzsimons, himself in financial duress, began selling off the family's inventory in July 1798. From prison, Morris lamented that he could not save it from being sold piecemeal. Even worse, in May 1799, a formal auction of the estate goods was held from Mary's town house, surely not soothing her nerves. In January 1802, on behalf of Fitzsimons, Morris wrote to then-president Thomas Jefferson to offer him a dozen of the family's French chairs that Fitzsimons still held. Morris believed the chairs elegant and suited for the White House, and Fitzsimons tellingly added that they were "better adapted to the President[']s than to a Private House." Jefferson declined them, but furnishings boasting a provenance of Morris's Folly were trumpeted elsewhere into the 1870s, as when a Philadelphia newspaper described a state chair, covered with Gobelin tapestry, then on display in a Chestnut Street shop. The reporter claimed the tapestry was one which Gouverneur Morris had purchased in Paris during the French Revolution and shipped to Morris for use in the famed house. A cabinetmaker, Joseph Barry, had purchased several of the rare tapestries at the original auction and passed them down carefully through his descendants.[25]

Part of this impulse was natural enough—furniture was valuable, bricks and stone could be reused, while decorative sculptures executed by an experienced hand were rare enough to warrant interest. Further, some of the new owners had a right to Morris's property, and probably took their pieces as payment toward their debts. Yet there was something ironic about a populace so repulsed by the Folly, as exemplified in Latrobe, yet so willing to seize and mount bits of it here and there. The dismantling of Morris's house was not mob action. It was not the kind of smashing glass, splitting doors, emptying mattresses destruction unleashed during the tax protests of the 1760s and 1770s on the houses of Tory officials throughout the seaports. (And which had threatened to resurface in Philadelphia in the attack on the Binghams' house during the Jay Treaty protests.) The attack on Morris's Folly did blur personal identity with property as in those earlier house assaults; it involved public shaming; and it even related to the practice of plunder. But the sundering of the Folly took an entirely different approach, in that friends, merchant peers, political enemies, as well as common laborers took part in a more communal, consensual, legal approach. The dismantling of Morris's mansion within two years of its seizure resulted in a reintegration of the threatening monster into more comfortable domestic bounds, where the pieces became merely curiosities, and their removal reinforced the general boundaries of republican ideals shared by almost all parties. These pieces, along with Birch's print of the "Unfinished House," equated the palace with ruins, just as the very concept of ruins—whether classical or medieval—was becoming an increasingly important theme as a subject unto itself. The process did not heal existing divisions, but it did solve a particular problem. These lingering associations proved that bits of the Folly could survive as a solution; Sansom would finish the job on the Chestnut Street lot shortly.[26]

The Hills fared little better than the Chestnut Street palace. Its new owners, including Standish Forde, reckoned with a $30,000 mortgage owed to the Insurance Company of Pennsylvania, after the debts to Reed & Forde were cleared. In the summer of 1798, Joseph Ball and Forde asked the imprisoned Morris for final delivery, so Morris sent his son William to survey what effects remained on the estate. William found that the gardener had moved into one of the main house's empty bedrooms. There was little else beyond the plantings. A few items remained in the gardener's house, which Mary Morris asked to be returned to her directly. The bulk of the furnishings, in Forde's possession, were auctioned away in January 1799.[27]

Ball and Forde worked to divide the property and then sell parts off. In 1799, the sheriff made sale of the main estate to Henry Pratt of the Aggregate Fund. Pratt, a city merchant, reveled in the property. The following year, he oversaw construction of an elegant new mansion overlooking the Schuylkill, notable for its elliptical, projecting bay featuring oval interior rooms and fittings. This mansion sat within sight of Morris's older stone house. Pratt renamed the estate "Lemon Hill," thereby adjusting the name by which the property had been known (fig. 8.11). He expanded Morris's greenhouse/hothouse complex into an extraordinary botanical conservatory, cultivating plantings and fishponds around it. Pratt also opened his gardens to an eager public. One local publication in the 1850s touted that, as

Figure 8.11. A view of Henry Pratt's new mansion, Lemon Hill, on the left, and the remnants of Morris's "The Hills," with flanking greenhouses, on the right. ("Lemon Hill," by John Woodside, 1807. Courtesy of the Philadelphia History Museum at the Atwater Kent, the Historical Society of Pennsylvania Collection)

"Pratt's Garden," it was "the pride and pleasure of our citizens." Following decades of Pratt's ownership, the site fell into some disrepair, to be purchased by the city in 1844 in order to shield the nearby waterworks. The estate was then incorporated into the city's string of other nearby villas to create Fairmount Park in the 1850s. By then, residents could recall the property with some nostalgia, mistakenly describing Pratt's now-empty house as where "the great financier, whose guests were Washington and Franklin and Jefferson, held his Republican Court."[28]

In another auction, held June 1798, the sheriff sold the Delaware Works and the family's other holdings around Morrisville. The financier's 2,500-acre Bucks County estate, whose industries he had nurtured since the beginning of the decade, was subject to a mortgage of $73,000 and interest owed to the Insurance Company of North America, as well as a $25,000 mortgage to George Clymer, a fellow signer of the Declaration of Independence. As with all the auctions heretofore, Morris observed that the

purchasers agreed "to apply any surplus to the final discharge of the mortgages," with anything remaining to go to Morris's other creditors, but these
were mere wishes. The purchasers turned out to be Clymer and Fitzsimons,
who, prompted by Morris, paid $41,000 for the burdened factory town. In
turn, Robert Morris, Jr., packed his new family up from the "elegant frame
house" they presided over with its carriage houses and stables—"probably
the best . . . in America," his father had once boasted—and moved into a
Philadelphia town house on Market Street.[29]

Morrisville's new proprietors kept the works running. Oddly, the busy
estate soon attracted several well-to-do French immigrants. Louis Le Guen,
a French merchant operating in New York City, established a seat there in
1799, followed six years later by the French general Jean Victor Maria
Moreau, who moved his family into Morris's old grove-side house. In 1811,
that house burned down, thereby eliminating another relic of Morris's landscape, and Moreau returned to Europe. Still, Morrisville, incorporated as a
borough in 1804, continued as a manufactory center, and Morris's name lived
on there, in road signs, at least.[30]

The close associations with the family these properties carried did not
protect them and may have even sped their transformations. The Genesee
country and the City of Washington on the Potomac would eventually pros-
per, but even there Morris's property did not escape the ruin of his downfall.
In 1800, Morris observed from prison that on many of his lots in the federal
city, the dozens of brick houses he had struggled so mightily in 1796 to erect
had "suffered great damage by Neglect, Pillage &c. &c., so as to be now in a
most ruinous situation." Some of his houses there were "pulled to pieces &
plundered." Or, it felt like plunder to him. Any plunderers in the federal city
surely were not looking for souvenirs from the financier's projects per se. But
their actions did show that no one's property in the early republic—not even
that of a vaunted founder—was immune from retribution.[31]

In the depths of Morris's failure, it was difficult to mourn such destruction.
William Sansom certainly wasted no tears. By mid-1799, he was already finishing eleven three-story brick houses on the property, with two others just
begun on the south end of the block fronting Walnut Street. Sansom, a director of the Bank of Pennsylvania, commissioned Latrobe to design twenty
adjoining row houses across the length of Walnut Street between Seventh

and Eighth Streets. Though Latrobe downplayed their significance—
"These houses were built in the most economical manner for sale," he later
told prospective clients—the structures were part of a bold plan. Sansom
envisioned complete row house developments, built together as single units
of construction across the entire block's street fronts, rather than the piecemeal, staggered construction that had previously filled in so many of the
city's narrow lots. Latrobe employed time-tested traditions, with narrow,
side-hall plans and brick construction, but the overall effect created something elegantly new: "Sansom's Row."[32]

Sansom soon had twenty-two additional houses built on the row's
rear, across a small alley, facing north on the newly cut Sansom Street. For
this strip, he contracted with Thomas Carstairs, a local carpenter, who
drafted a rigid yet handsome plan and elevation for the unit (fig. 8.12). Its
row featured houses forty feet deep and no more than eighteen feet wide,
with hall entrances and two rooms, heated, on each main floor of the houses'
three stories with cellar. Each house shared party walls with its neighbor.
Exterior decoration consisted of red brick, stone entrance steps, doorways
flanked by simple columns, stone belt courses, and wood cornice. The roofs
were gable, not mansard. Using materials from the Folly, these were completed by 1801, to be let for $200 per year (fig. 8.13). Sansom also enticed
residents to this edge of the city by paving Sansom Street at his own expense. Many moved in soon after, including merchants James Barckley and
Alexander Miller, bricklayer Timothy Andrews, sea captain John Ashmead,
doctor Jonas Preston, widows Martha Caldwell and Rebecca Lawrence,
and "gentlewoman" Anna Moore. One new renter, the young merchant
Thomas Cope, enjoyed his move from Mulberry Street because he found
the air there "freer." His pleasure was not due to any of the site's associations with Morris; in his diary Cope noted that the "house stands on the
Square on which Robert Morris had erected his very uncouth & expensive
edifice, which is now erased."[33]

In May 1801, Sansom continued his development of the block with an
auction of lots in the northwest quarter, along Chestnut and Eighth Streets.
Here, eleven strips with the familiar narrow dimensions—some only seven-
teen feet wide—were bought and sold (fig. 8.14). Henry Pratt took two of the
lots as investments. House construction followed, though more slowly than
along the planned fronts of Walnut and Sansom Streets. By 1806, thirty-seven

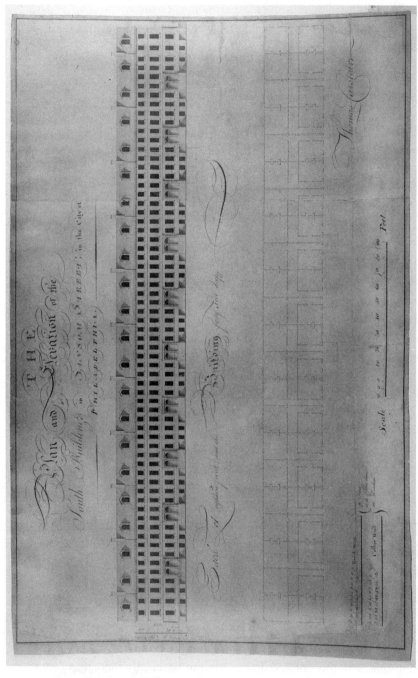

Figure 8.12. Front elevation and floor plan of William Sansom's row house project, which took the place of Morris's Folly. (Thomas Carstairs, "The Plan and Elevation of the South Buildings in Sansom Street, in the city of Philadelphia," circa 1800. Courtesy of the Library Company of Philadelphia)

Figure 8.13. Surviving houses from Sansom's Row, 730 and 732 Sansom Street, Philadelphia. (Photo by Jordan Fugeman)

buildings, mostly houses, fronted both sides of Sansom Street. Later in the nineteenth century, a diminutive alleyway in the middle of the northern section of the block was renamed: Morris Street.[34]

The city responded favorably to Sansom's projects. As renters and purchasers were moving into the site, longtime Philadelphia resident Stephen Moylan described Sansom's new houses as being "in the modern taste." And the city directories offered public praise. In 1804, the *Philadelphia Directory* commended the houses raised by Sansom, "whose well laid plans have greatly

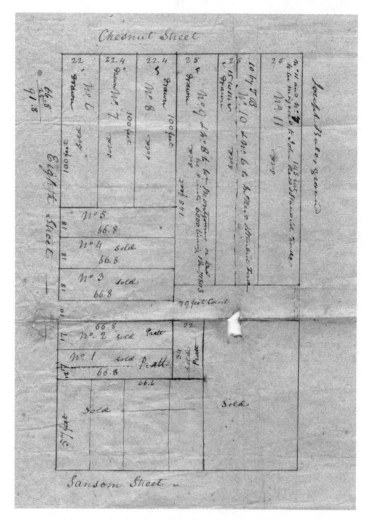

Figure 8.14. Plan of lots divided on Morris's Chestnut Street block, May 11, 1801. (Reed and Forde Papers, Robert Morris section, Historical Society of Pennsylvania)

improved the City, particularly in Walnut Street [and] in Sansom street, the first that has been built in America with a strict attention to uniformity." The directory linked these to the city's traditions, explaining generally that "the private buildings in Philadelphia are generally three stories high. They are built of a clear red brick, and generally ornamented . . . with facings, key stones and flights of steps, in white marble," thereby sketching the template followed by Sansom's rows. The directory reiterated this praise in the next several editions. It was echoed in *The Picture of Philadelphia* in 1811, when the author approvingly judged that the houses on Sansom Street were "built agreeably to [William Sansom's] plan, strictly uniform in height and external appearance." Along with Sansom's houses facing Walnut Street and another of his rows on Second Street, these "have greatly tended to ornament the city, and accommodate the inhabitants." Visitors, too, singled out Sansom's projects for praise, as one Englishman noted that "in some of the new streets uniformity is observed, particularly in Sansom-street, which may vie with those fashionable parts of London."[35]

Modern, uniform, and popular—Sansom's rows were in many ways the opposite of Morris's mansion. Where Morris's mansion claimed the whole block with the idiosyncratic façade of a single house, Sansom's narrow row houses were identical to each other. The survival of portions of these houses to the present testifies to the success of this speculator in gauging his city and its mood.

But the remains of the house would not rest easy. As the circulation of the Folly's materials attests, stories of the house survived and even flourished for a time. A generation after its fall, John F. Watson cast the story of "Robert Morris' Mansion" in his first edition of the *Annals of Philadelphia* in 1830. In doing so, Watson consolidated the tales circulating about the house since Latrobe. Watson, who worked at the Bank of Germantown, had been writing his broad tome for a decade. When released, the *Annals* defined its genre, proceeding into additional editions for nearly one hundred years. Its subtitle suggests its casual flavor: *Being a Collection of Memoirs, Anecdotes, & Incidents of the City and its Inhabitants from the Days of the Pilgrim Founders . . .* [36]

Watson's treatment of Morris's Folly ran only two pages, sandwiched between pieces on "Norris' House and Garden" and "Loxley's House." Still, it rang like a bell. In opening this section, thirty years after the house's demise, Watson wrote, "This great edifice, the grandest ever attempted in Philadelphia for the purposes of private life . . ." For Watson, the tale was amusing, but the lesson was still clear. Morris's ambitious house proved, in Watson's words, "a ruinous and abortive scheme," largely because of Morris's architect, according to the annalist. With "a palace in effect fronting upon Chesnut Street . . . it must have had a signal effect," Watson imagined. He told of its extensive grounds, its massive underground vaults, and its marble ornament. He did not mention Morris's vast speculations, pointing instead to Morris's "ruin in the above building." Unlike Niemcewicz, Watson made little attempt to relate Morris's strivings against the context of the 1790s, whether in terms of common housing, rivalry with the likes of the Binghams, or specific political ideals. In a later section of the book, returning briefly to Morris's block, Watson repeated his essential theme, that the block on Chestnut Street was "made into Morris' square, to ruin him in the erection of an intended palace."[37]

Watson's relatively brief account became the single most important source for the legend of Morris's Folly. Two years later, the Philadelphia magazine *Atkinson's Casket* ran the same story on "Morris' Folly," repeating Watson's version of the tale. The magazine accompanied the story with an image based on Birch's view. The story continued to circulate that decade in other publications and private letters. Meanwhile, Birch's original plate depicting the mansion found its way to a local bookseller, Robert Desilver, in the early 1840s. In 1841, Desilver issued a short biography of Robert Morris, "the Great Financier," with equal emphasis given to "the Celebrated House, Partly Erected in Chestnut Street." Desilver offered an agreeable portrayal of Morris, shadowed by the old story of the mansion told through Watson's lens. In this venture, Desilver sensed continuing curiosity regarding Morris's plan. He reprinted Birch's "Unfinished House" engraving, and sold it to a new generation, less overawed by its stature.[38]

After Watson, the second most important treatment of the legend came after the Civil War, in Thompson Westcott's 1877 book, *The Historic Mansions and Buildings of Philadelphia*. Here, the tale of "Morris's Folly" reached its summation in the stirrings of the nation's centennial. A Philadelphia lawyer and newspaperman, Westcott was well informed regarding his city's history; he would soon co-author an exhaustive history of its founding and development. For Westcott, Robert Morris merited two long chapters: one on the Folly, and the other on the Hills. In a sympathetic portrait emphasizing the financier's accomplishments and hospitality, Westcott nevertheless made clear the threat the Folly presented to the city. Borrowing some from Watson's *Annals*, Westcott asserted that Morris's "ambition to erect this splendid mansion, which far exceeded anything at that time to be seen in the city, attracted much attention, and was considered a scheme of extravagance." He followed this with his most biting observation, recalling that its palatial form "was looked upon as offensive to plain and simple people. Hence, as the building progressed it was the talk, the wonder, and on many tongues the censure, of the town." This language sounded something like a Greek chorus, as Westcott gave voice to the moral center. Westcott then explained the birth of the legend: "When it became evident that the house could not be finished, the appellation of 'Morris's Folly' was given to it, and the pride and vanity of the projector were a subject of frequent ridicule, heightened by improbable stories of the character and peculiarities of the building." At a time when the legacies of founding fathers were rarely called into question, Westcott could not avoid the "offensive" tone struck by the building. On the other hand, Westcott resurrected somewhat the reputation of L'Enfant, "who has been made the scapegoat for Mr. Morris's imprudences." Westcott portrayed the architect as a victim of the Folly in the damage Morris's failure did to his reputation. This distinguished Westcott's reporting from that of Watson and Latrobe. But all shared the belief that the Folly was an important outlier and a threat. Thirty years after Westcott, at the turn of the twentieth century, another local historian confirmed the lingering power of this tale when he found that all anyone could recall of the financier was the erroneous belief that he died in debtors' prison and that "he built a marble house in Chestnut Street which he could not complete." Morris's Folly had eclipsed all else in the patriot's life.[39]

In the end, the mansion found its primary use through its metaphor-laden destruction. And that destruction was necessarily incomplete. Even today, remains of the storied building lurk below the city's sidewalks. Near the basements of Jeweler's Row on Sansom Street, or beneath the office buildings just to their north, Burton Wallace's vast masonry vaults likely lie buried, disturbed only by the occasional utility line. Latrobe's legacy of clear, neoclassical refinement is celebrated in the city's architectural heritage, while the work of L'Enfant, Wallace, Sproul, Proviny, and Jardella hides belowground, inside a sunroom on Delancey Place, or on far-flung estates in Maryland and South Carolina. As the process of making these ruins began in 1798, the man behind them sat in his cell, awaiting release.[40]

9. His Release

Robert Morris—fatherless apprentice, merchant prodigy, affectionate husband, Revolutionary financier, government minister, Episcopal pew holder, unapologetic banker, merry clubman, art patron, capital mover, U.S. senator, manufactory proprietor, land baron, treaty maker, fool, and downcast defaulter—entered prison on February 16, 1798. He walked with the sheriff that winter day from his family's rental on Chestnut Street past the Folly and then two short blocks to the Prune Street debtors' apartment at the corner of Sixth Street.

"This gloomy mansion," as Morris would call the stone prison, had been filled to capacity ever since the previous year's financial panics laid low so many merchants and aspiring traders. It could be a rough place. Inmates sometimes bullied others out of clothes and belongings, while criminals exercised in the yard just across the wall to the apartment's rear. Its doors were open to prostitutes, who took turns through the house's rooms, and to those selling liquor, fueling gambling and the occasional suicide. None of these conditions prevented angry creditors from entering and confronting the inmates in their rooms, to continue threatening or cajoling to the best of their abilities. But friendly faces, and business associates, could visit as well. The whole noisy establishment was overseen by a keeper and a Board of Inspectors, supplemented by a Society for Alleviating the Miseries of Public Prisons, whose members included Benjamin Rush (Morris's doctor), William White (his brother-in-law and priest), and John Swanwick (his onetime mercantile partner). The Society generally focused on the criminals across the wall, and the keeper of the debtors' apartment, Jacob Hofner, had little incentive to clean up the crowded quarters.[1]

At first, Morris could find no space in which to settle. "I sleep in another person's bed, I occupy other people's rooms, and if I attempt to sit down to write it is at the interruption and inconvenience of some one who has acquired a prior right to the place," he explained to John Nicholson, who keenly followed his partner's progress. Prisoners themselves were responsible for paying their own board, rent, and fuel, and Morris immediately set to work on Hofner, trying to arrange a private room. In a few weeks, he found his way into a room he described as "the best in the house," for sixty precious dollars a month, and it took him several more weeks before he could get reliable furniture with his working papers at hand. Even then, he faced the "torture" of constant harassment from his duns and was forced to set a policy refusing to see any visitors until their names and business were announced at his door.[2]

Morris had friends there, such as his onetime landlord David Allison as well as Henry Banks, a fellow merchant. But there were enemies too, most notably the "scoundrel" James Greenleaf, whose room was across the hall and whose nearby pacing added to Morris's frustrations. William Bingham was prevented from joining them only by the heroic support of his London bankers. Garrett Cottringer continued in service, and Morris's sons William and Robert, Jr., and occasionally Charles, helped by bringing him needed papers and carrying his messages throughout the city, as he continued trying to raise his sunken ship.[3]

There was no more talk of suicide from Morris, though. He took stock of his remaining blessings in his family and resolved to accept his fate. Breaking the news of his imprisonment to his son Thomas, he promised "to meet the bad as well as the good with Fortitude, and to make the best of whatever happens. Thank God I can do all this," he exclaimed, "my Health is good, my spirits not broke, my mind sound & vigorous." So he pledged to do all he could "consistently with the principles of integrity to make the best of my affairs & extricate myself as well as I can." He held on to the hope that he could still salvage some wealth out of his tangled affairs.[4]

A regular morning's walk around the yard helped. By March, he had measured out a circular walk of three miles by lapping the prison's enclosed garden fifty times. Each day, he did the circuit, dropping a pebble every round to mark the distance. William Wood, a young actor also imprisoned for debt, observed the financier on his rounds one morning: "His person was neat, and his dress, although a little old-fashioned, adjusted with much care." Wood knew him as "the financier of the Revolution," and gave him deference; "Mr. Morris appeared cheerful, returned my salutation in the politest manner, but in silence, continuing his walk." One day, Morris "suddenly stopped, inquired whether I was ill, and added, with something like severity: 'Sir, this is but an ill place for one so sickly, and apparently so *young*.'" Wood offered him no explanation, but the two struck up a friendship. Wood later remembered Morris's kindnesses, demonstrating that the man could still make friends as easily as ever.[5]

Morris could manage inside. But as he well knew, his wife had a severe task outside. News of his failure had charged the city. Mary, shaken by the arrest, and stripped of her husband, dressmakers, chefs, and most servants, bore the brunt of the public's scrutiny. On February 19, wealthy Philadelphia Quaker Elizabeth Drinker gasped to her diary that Robert Morris "is actualy gone to Jail within this day or two." Congressman Harrison Gray Otis, who fifteen years earlier had met the Morrises at their dinner for thirty, took the moment to sermonize on the couple, as "an example of the folly and vanity of human grandeur." Where Mary had once "ruled the world of fashion with unrivalled sway," Otis projected that Robert "will now probably moulder away a few remaining wretched years in prison, and her joys & comforts have probably forever vanished."[6]

Others confirmed the gloomy outlook along with Mary's burdens. Abigail Adams, wife of the president, provided the most harrowing description of the family. Writing shortly after Morris was taken to prison, she agreed that if ever "I had felt a disposition to extravagance, I should have been cured by a visit to Mrs. Morris." Adams explained to her sister: "Two years ago, Mrs. Morris was a remarkable well looking woman, [daughter] Maria, my companion, gay and blith as a bird, blooming as a rose in June." But "I went to visit Mrs. Morris, & met her without knowing her, so alterd that I was shockd. Maria pale, wan, dejected & spiritless. Such is the change." Abigail's pity was instantly aroused. She concluded that "all speculative wealth has a shallow foundation, but that its foundation has always been shallow is no mitigation of disappointment, to him who had only viewed it in its superstructure, nor is its downfall less terrible to its visionary elevator because others had seen it from the beginning as a folly or Chimera." Mary partook of that folly with her husband, and Abigail understood her sense of loss. The prim first lady had never been particularly close with the family; the effect of Mary and Maria's visages on their better friends must have been greater.[7]

Still, Mary bore her burden uncomplainingly. She was used to running a household, and her husband managed to continue paying rent on their house while also somehow providing about $100 each month for her expenses. This was a sizable amount, certainly a ransom's worth in the eyes of the few servants she managed to keep on board, allowing her to maintain what appearances she could for visitors like the president's wife. Her intimacy with Robert held up under the strain, and Mary began visiting her husband regularly with Maria that summer at the jail when things settled down. The auction of her furniture and fineries from beneath her in July was a bitter pill, but by then the family had adjusted somewhat to their new routine.[8]

The city as a whole suffered a blow that July, when yellow fever again appeared along the docks of the Delaware River. This season's epidemic would rival that of 1793. It came on the heels of lingering fears from the fever the previous year, during which nearly two-thirds of the city's residents had fled, and it effectively ended the city's aspirations as national capital. During the first week of August 1798, fifty-three people died of the fever, with cases increasing every day. Men, women, and children packed what they could and headed out of town, at least as far as the tents arranged for the poor outside the city along the Schuylkill River, while the prisoners at the Walnut Street Jail watched helplessly from their windows. For a time, Morris could make light of the scare as "Doctors Fever."[9]

That levity soon vanished. George Washington, from Mount Vernon, sent his offer to host the Morris family on August 19, but of course Morris could not leave, nor would Mary and the children. Garrett Cottringer fled to Trenton, keeping in contact through the mails. James Greenleaf, still slippery, had effected his own liberation from Prune Street a few months earlier by a successful appeal to the state legislature under its insolvency law. As the fever spread into early September, Morris's son William began feeling ill, alarming the family on Chestnut Street. Around the fourteenth of that month, the pestilence struck Walnut Street Jail like a hammer. Inmates of the main jail began dying, leading to panic throughout the crowded complex, prompting the head jailor and staff to flee and the prisoners to riot. A city alderman took charge, and two prisoners were shot and another stabbed before a shaky order was restored. Aided by the remaining turnkeys, the alderman took precautions by moving lesser criminals—"the vagrants, and prisoners confined for petty offences," in the words of a journalist—"to Morris's Buildings," meaning the vacant, unfinished Folly and its outbuildings. In doing so, city leaders hoped to ease crowding in the jail and remove low-risk prisoners to this huge empty structure nearby. Morris himself would have joined them, marking a mean twist of fate, but neither he nor the other debtors were allowed to do so. So male and female "vagrants" took up enforced residence inside the Folly's walls, probably housed respectively in each of the building's two wings. It was a practical move, but the message it sent—the inversion of the structure as a palace—was long remembered.[10]

By September 25, the fever had entered the debtors' apartment. Several came down with the disease, including Morris's dining partner David Allison, whose "French Doctr." ordered him to be sweated and bathed rather than bled and purged as recommended by most of the city's physicians. Neither remedy worked, and more than eighty deaths occurred in the city each day. Morris, struggling himself with a different kind of ailment—scraping together dollars to forestall what he called "the Starvation Fever"—was confounded by the doctors' conflicting suggestions for his ill companions. He tried to keep his distance in the house from the sick, while reporting in daily letters to John Nicholson in town, whose family was likewise visited with sickness. Morris's son William was still at home, afflicted with an ill-defined sickness. Mary sent meals to Morris when a courier could be found. In early October, William rallied somewhat and rose to make an appeal for his father's temporary release. The sheriff held eight suits against Morris at the time and told William that he needed permission from all eight parties. Five agreed, but in the city's upheaval William could not locate the other three.[11]

The young man's energy did not last. As he faded, the physician Benjamin Rush and others came to blister and purge him in hopes of recovery. His mother was distraught, and Morris ached to be with them, frantically writing the chief justice and haranguing the sheriff. Their hopes were dashed on October 10 when Robert received word that William had died that day of what they called a "Billious remitting Fever," not the prevailing yellow fever. Morris cried to Nicholson, "Do not letter copy the Fate of my poor son of whom I can not help thinking constantly his image being ever present to my mind." He acknowledged that "Mrs. Morris & Maria are . . . dreadfully hurt." The boy's wayward delays in Paris were forgotten, and the father deemed the loss of this son and companion "irreparable." Friendly inmates tried to console Morris, offering him what brandy they could find. The greatest consolation arrived the following day, when Mary and Maria took the risk to come and embrace him in person.[12]

Meanwhile, yellow fever continued tearing through the debtors' apartments. Allison and others died in their own vomit and filth. The keeper, Hofner, caught the disease shortly after William's death, and on the afternoon of October 15 he stumbled into the room where Robert was sitting with Mary and Maria. They saw that "he was pale & ghastly, horror in his countenance, & I fear, terror in his mind." Hofner's ugly death just three days later, along with the sickness of the remainder of the staff, prompted Morris to prohibit his family from further visits to the jail. That night, seven prisoners in the main jail dug beneath the outer wall, and five successfully escaped. Morris himself scrambled to change rooms, as Hofner had lodged directly across from his own. Even so, he held fast to his earlier acceptance. "I hope my life will be spared for the sake of my Family untill I get my affairs settled," he wrote coolly. "I shall submit patiently to my Fate be it what it may." Mary could not be so stoic, while Maria offered to serve her father as runner around the city as she was able, which deepened her protective father's sense of shame. Charles had fled to join Thomas in New York, and Robert, Jr., and Henry were also gone away. A remaining servant in Mary's household took himself to the hospital and died.[13]

Finally, cooler weather in later October signaled the passing of the fever. The city's population slowly returned, as did the federal government's offices, which had relocated to Trenton in August. Then sermons, studies, and spin began again in the epidemic's aftermath as in 1793. Morris was probably spared reading one sermon circulating that season, Thaddeus Brown's *An Address in Christian Love, to the Inhabitants of Philadelphia; on the Awful Dispensation of the Yellow Fever, in 1798*. Reflecting on five years of decadence and disease, Brown viewed it all as a judgment from God for a variety of the citizens' sins. He tore first into the sin of Pride, notable among those "who would be thought rich." And then there was Covetousness and Injustice, exacerbated by the speculators. Brown worked over the latter, exclaiming against "Overgrown nominal estates—foundations for princely palaces—and a variety of vast speculative schemes and arrangements." At the same time that prisoners were being removed from temporary quarters in Morris's Folly, Brown warned that "Injustice, and speculation . . . has a direct tendency, by example and otherwise to infect a whole community." Morris himself needed no further shaming, though he did not blame God. He returned to quiet turns in the prison's garden. "Let us believe . . . that Providence has reserved us for the enjoyment of future Independancy and happiness," he consoled a fellow debtor who had likewise survived the storm.[14]

That November, a political show took the place of the fever. "The Great & Good man from Mount Vernon," as Morris observed, arrived in Philadelphia amid the preparations for war with France. Since the American humiliations in Paris that spring, Federalist leaders had moved the country closer to open confrontation with every additional affront on the seas. They had also pressed their momentary advantage in a bid to silence the Democratic-Republicans for good with the Alien and Sedition Acts, used to imprison or deport their opponents. That fall, the new army drilled nearby under the eyes of Washington and Alexander Hamilton, as the epidemic had done nothing to slow the train.[15]

But Morris had long lost all stomach for such jockeying, and Washington respected the family's recent losses. As soon as the general had arrived in the city, Morris heard he intended to pay a visit. But Washington was busy with official greetings and duties, or else dissuaded from venturing into the jail until absolutely safe, so it was not until the end of his stay, on November 27, when Washington strode the several blocks to Prune Street. He took his quiet meal there in Morris's room, in the familiar presence of Mary and Maria, all of them under the watchful eyes of a house full of prisoners and surrounded by stacks of Morris's letters and account books. As candles shone on the room's new whitewash, the two men made a playful pledge to each other not to die before the year 1800. Soon enough, they toasted their good-byes, which would prove to be their last.[16]

Nearly one year later, in September 1799, the Washingtons reiterated their offer to host Mary at Mount Vernon, reassuring her of "the most affectionate regard for you, Mr. Morris, and the family." But Mary and Maria's brief travels did not enable a stop, and the old general died at home in bed in December. Washington's death sent the nation into a frenzy of mourning, as processions, speeches, and commemorative souvenirs conveyed tributes for years after the event. Washington died a recognized hero, despite the tumult of his last years in the presidency. His rigid attention to character and the cautious ambition he displayed throughout his long life earned him the respect he wished. It cemented the model he hoped to project. Morris, toasting the general's passing from his cell, knew a different fate awaited him.[17]

At the time, Major P. Charles L'Enfant had yet to hit bottom. Since the dissolution of the Chestnut Street project, he had continued to rent his two meager rooms in Richard Soderstrom's apartments near Eighth Street in Philadelphia. Like everyone else, he needed money, and he did not have immediate prospects. The self-styled "engineer of the United States" would consider working for select patrons only. He had written a few more appeals to the financier during the latter's standoff at the Hills, making his necessities clear, but the bank stock he had loaned Morris was still maddeningly out of reach. Oddly, L'Enfant showed signs of land fever and made a few proposals along these lines to the failing Morris in late 1797. Morris arranged for a lien in L'Enfant's name on some Genesee investments, but this was the best he could do. A year later, with the nation's stirrings of war against the Directory-controlled France, L'Enfant felt the tug of patriotism and opportunity like so many others and applied unsuccessfully to George Washington for a commission in the newly mobilized army.[18]

In 1799, the passing of Washington, the central patron of L'Enfant's life, worked a strange effect on the loyal engineer. It seemed to free him to begin petitioning the federal government for what he believed proper compensation, mostly for services in the federal city. So after Washington's death, L'Enfant suddenly took up his pen to seek payment for what he called the "laborious pursuits of twenty two years services to the United States." His housemate, Soderstrom, sensing the possibility of new income, was eager to help. In September 1800, the pair set up for a season in a Washington tavern, and L'Enfant's first formal petition landed in the House of Representatives a few months later. He asked for nearly $100,000. The petition was denied, but L'Enfant remained at the Potomac to continue pleading his case to Congress for the next twenty-five years.[19]

The Morris family became involved with his petitioning in 1801. By that time, the financier's relationship with Soderstrom had foundered, with Morris observing that the consul owed him $18,000 for fraudulent sales and debts, including money he had advanced the Swede for several years' subsistence. In January 1801, Thomas Morris offered to intercede with Alexander Hamilton in "poor L'Enfant's business." Acting under power of attorney, Thomas would request funds for the Federal Hall project of twelve years ago. L'Enfant might have been richer by ten acres of Manhattan land had he accepted the city's original offer, but he had found his sense of honor more valuable. So Robert, working through his son, delighted in telling L'Enfant that authorization for a new payment from the city of up to £1,000 was "in good train." One week later, Morris heard that the council would offer L'Enfant only $750. The financier suggested the major leave Washington and go to New York in person to press for a higher amount. L'Enfant could not afford travel expenses, so the matter remained unresolved, and L'Enfant remained poor. Morris himself was still counting the surplus dollars he believed would be coming to him. Though their lives had been turned upside down, the pair may as well have been back at the dining table together in 1793. Their final exchange took place one year after L'Enfant's refusal of New York's $750 offer. In 1802, L'Enfant complained bitterly to Morris that, among other insults, his Genesee assignments had yielded nothing. This triggered the latter to protest that such reproaches could do little good. Morris concluded by assuring him, "If I had means I would relieve you [and] do at once what you propose." He could not, and the pair left it at that.[20]

L'Enfant's new surroundings in the federal city did not cheer his spirits, either. The Democratic-Republicans who had gained power differed entirely in their view of what the city should look like. So they let the struggling village lie as it was, leaving L'Enfant's extensive plans on paper. L'Enfant, tall and gaunt, shuffled around the region, dodging lawsuits and writing his petitions. The ugliest blow occurred in 1804, when the primary relationship in L'Enfant's life, that with Soderstrom, blew up. Soderstrom struck first by bringing suit in federal court against L'Enfant for over six years' worth of back rent and expenses amounting to $7,300. The infuriated major, still hampered by his weak language skills, scrambled to draft a statement in response. He sputtered out his disbelief at the audacity of his onetime spendthrift roommate to accuse him of financial irresponsibility. L'Enfant would ask the consul: had he not loaned him money regularly, even from the date of their first acquaintance? Had Soderstrom not used L'Enfant's name and assets to his own benefit? L'Enfant wondered, in his broken English, at "the impertinance of the tale which he affects to tell every one—that all he has done for me was not charity," and pointed to "real advances I made him for what I received from him." L'Enfant "expected a more Gentleman regard of circumstances than he has manifested." L'Enfant did acknowledge he had been negligent in his own record keeping, leaving himself open to the purportedly petty, opportunistic Soderstrom. The major had even offered to submit their dispute to gentlemen, including Robert Morris, for arbitration, but Soderstrom declined and pressed his case forward. So L'Enfant vented his passions over several pages, painting himself as a prisoner, largely helpless against Soderstrom's many manipulations "to render me dependent upon the assistance which he afterward afforded."[21]

Soderstrom prevailed. When Congress in 1808 finally authorized a settlement with L'Enfant for $4,600 plus a city lot, the Swedish consul took over $4,000 of that sum by lien. Most of the remainder went to L'Enfant's lawyer and creditors. So L'Enfant nursed yet another wound. By then, architect Benjamin Henry Latrobe had taken over many of the design responsibilities in the federal city. Latrobe described seeing the "miserably poor" L'Enfant wander the city daily as "the picture of famine." "He is too proud to receive any assistance, and it is very doubtful in what manner he subsists," he observed.[22]

Somehow, L'Enfant remained alive and free from debtors' prison into the presidency of James Madison, at which time a glimmer of hope appeared. In 1812, members of Madison's cabinet offered L'Enfant a post at West Point as a professor of engineering. L'Enfant was flattered but declined—he did not like young people or faculty blowhards. But Secretary of State James Monroe came through for L'Enfant again by offering a commission to rebuild fortifications on the Potomac River in 1814. To this, L'Enfant eagerly agreed. The radical report that resulted from his work on Fort Warburton, located on the north bank of the river across from Mount Vernon, plus L'Enfant's familiar litany of personal complaints, were tabled. Just as quickly, L'Enfant was mustered out of service from his final commission.[23]

But his work on the site proved fortuitous, for it enabled him to grow familiar with the proprietor of Warburton Manor, Thomas A. Digges. Digges took pity on the sixty-year-old veteran, whom he moved into his Maryland household with the latter's old trunk of papers. There the two lived together for several years after L'Enfant's ouster from Fort Warburton. Digges offered a description of L'Enfant, "quiet, harmless and unoffending as usual," in 1816, nine years before the major's death: "I fear from symptoms of broken shoes, rent pantaloons, out at the elbows, etc. etc. etc. etc. that he is not well off—manifestly disturbed at his getting the go by, never facing toward the Fort, tho' frequently dipping into the eastern ravines and hills of the plantation—picking up fossils & periwinkles. Early to bed & rising— working hard with his instruments on paper 8 or ten hours every day as if to give full & complete surveys of his works &ca." Digges's description revealed that the major still felt an intensely personal connection to his work, "never facing toward the Fort" nor any other of the numerous projects that had not achieved his intentions.[24]

After Digges's death a few years thereafter, L'Enfant received an invitation from another branch of the family, William Dudley Digges and his wife, Eleanor, to move to Green Hill, a Maryland estate adjoining the federal district. While there, L'Enfant offered some designs for the estate's gardens and again took to strolling the grounds, "smelling of the flowers and looking at the sky." With the flowers, the sky, and his rambles, he seems to have found some philosophy. L'Enfant died at Green Hill at seventy years old in June 1825, to be buried on the grounds alongside the Digges family servants and slaves in an unmarked grave. Few beyond the estate took notice.[25]

Likewise philosophical, Morris had applied himself to his tangled accounts and chased plans for his own release. He made little progress on either front, and by the spring of 1799, one season after George Washington's visit, Morris despaired all his property would be lost. He had heard that one of his estates, worth $100,000, sold at $800 for overdue taxes. "As to saving property from being sacrificed I see plainly that it is impossible," he observed; "one thing goes after another and so will continue untill the whole shall vanish and none know what is become of it." At the time, Morris faced bigger problems, such as finding "means to pay for bread to sustain" himself and his dependents. In want, he was surrounded by gloomy companions, including a "Capt. Bazing," who "paid his debts with a dose of laudanum" one day after the two men drank together. Morris also heard of the recent death of speculator William Duer in New York, and he observed "thereby another unfortunate is released." Still, Morris remained relatively free at heart. "I shall with resignation wait the call of him that sent me here," he wrote in April. Compared to the yellow fever scare and the loss of William, the rest seemed tame.[26]

In August 1799, Morris was joined in prison by his most frequent correspondent and occasional Sunday guest, John Nicholson. The pair's creditors had finally put hands on the evasive Nicholson, completing the besieged comptroller's inevitable arrest. He was over $4 million in the hole. Nicholson and Morris tried their best to make merry, and Nicholson even launched a short-lived news sheet from Prune Street, titled *The Supporter, or Daily Repast*. It did them no good to know their nemesis Greenleaf was then out in the federal city, boarding with his charitable brother-in-law while knocking into courts and creditors there. Greenleaf's outstanding debts of $9 million made the other two partners look nearly thrifty. Once Nicholson was inside, the spirits of the forty-three-year-old did not hold up. The mercurial young man died in prison on December 5, 1800, leaving a wife and eight children to contend with his debts. So Morris said good-bye to another friend and wrote his "fellow sufferer" a sympathetic obituary. "Without being stimulated by avarice or ambition," Morris intoned, "he became too ardent (from habit) in the pursuit of wealth" and "lost a fortune that ought to have contented him." Partly true, for the both of them.[27]

Nicholson's passing would leave Morris back in the hands of his old companion Gouverneur Morris, recently returned from Europe. Still a bachelor after ten years away, Gouverneur had made the most of his own homecoming and then traveled to Philadelphia earlier in April 1799, making good on his earlier promise to look after his friend. Gouverneur acknowledged the real damage Robert did to his creditors. He even shamed the financier directly for the blizzard of irresponsible M & N notes, observing that news of them had halted Gouverneur's initial attempt to raise rescue funds. But the jovial, caring New Yorker showed great kindness to the family when he met them in prison. He was anguished by their ordeals. Mary's state of mind worried him particularly, and he took pains to visit with her and the rest of the family at her home. He believed she "put on an air of firmness which she cannot support, and was wrong to assume." So Gouverneur offered the Morrises diversions, conversation, and hope. It helped Robert, at least. "His only business here is to see me," Morris boasted. "He will occupy a good deal of my time whilst he remains here." When Gouverneur took his leave after several days, he insisted on keeping the family stocked with spirits, and he shipped them a case of claret upon his return to New York. The following year, in 1800, Gouverneur entered the U.S. Senate for his home state, which would entail more trips through Philadelphia and perhaps a more material opportunity to aid his friend.[28]

Indeed, after much deliberation, Congress passed its first Bankruptcy Act in 1800. The states, including Pennsylvania, had been tinkering with bankruptcy and insolvency laws, but this was the first of its kind at the federal level, and still highly controversial. It was driven by the spectacle of Morris and other notable figures in prison, such as William Duer, Supreme Court justice James Wilson, Congressman Blair McClenachan, and New

York gentleman John Pintard. These were prominent, commercial debtors whose imprisonment cast the traditional associations between indebtedness and immorality in a new light. The act's proponents argued that it would discourage fraud and more effectively satisfy competing creditors. Its opponents saw it as another Federalist bow to monied interests. Either way, the Act proved the key to Morris's freedom.[29]

In contrast to James Greenleaf, Morris had resisted applying for release under the existing Pennsylvania state insolvency law. Although this might get him out of prison, it would require the forfeit of *all* his tangled assets as well as any claims on future property until all legal disputes were resolved. This arrangement would guarantee penury for his family. Further, Morris did not relish the idea of being hauled before the Court of Common Pleas and laid open before the bar.[30]

But the Bankruptcy Act offered a smoother, and sometimes involuntary, release. Some observers thought the Act was passed specifically with Morris in mind. It may as well have been, for it offered no relief for petty debtors owing less than $1,000, who were left to stew where they were. Morris did not appreciate the gesture. After the Act passed, he worried about "being made a Bankrupt" if any of his creditors "issue process against me." How, after three years in prison, did he find it hard to accept the title of "bankrupt"? Why did Morris not seek its relief immediately, since Mary's concerns for him weighed so heavily on his mind? A full year after the Act took effect, Philadelphia merchant John Huston, who held $283,790 in overdue M & N promissory notes, submitted his petition in July 1801 for Morris to enter bankruptcy proceedings. "Some of my creditors are trying to make a Bankrupt of me," Morris reiterated after he got this summons. He did not put up much of a fight, though. He braced against "some disagreeable scenes" he knew lay before him in the proceedings, but he quickly realized "after what I have sustained, what is to come seems as nothing." Success would mean the loss of his current property claims but a clean discharge. As the proceedings started, the judge ordered Morris's jailors to turn him out of prison. So on the fine summer evening of August 26, 1801, Morris had the "inexpressible satisfaction" of walking out of Prune Street and into the arms of his family.[31]

He stepped out into a changed world. Philadelphia was no longer a capital. The state government had relocated west to Lancaster. The federal seat was now in Washington, D.C. Napoleon ruled France, and President Adams had signed a peace treaty with its ministers, thereby removing that threat on the seas and fears of a land invasion. In early 1801, Thomas Jefferson had succeeded Adams as president, and his fellow Republicans promised a return to Revolutionary principles celebrating the common man. The nation's west now meant the Mississippi and beyond, even to the Pacific.

Morris's home had changed as well. Walking back from Prune Street, he joined Mary in her rental on Eighth and Chestnut. It faced across the street from the worksite now headed by William Sansom, where the Folly had recently been leveled. Though still eating and sleeping on borrowed furniture, Morris found his home richer, in one way. He was now a grandfather. Mary had relished her role as grandmother; she had spent time with Hetty Marshall's four children at their Virginia home and often hosted Thomas with his new wife and daughter in Philadelphia. Maria courted merchant Henry Nixon, whom she would marry the following year, to her parents' pleasure. Wandering Charles had taken to the sea; and the couple's youngest, Henry, had entered an apprenticeship with a local trading house. Morris looked forward to getting to know the new additions. Though "without one cent that I can call my own," he somehow found the resources to hire a cook.[32]

The fortunes of the Binghams, which had done so much to spur the Morrises and the rest of Philadelphia society, reflected a change as well. Earlier in the year, in February 1801, the lovely Anne Bingham had developed a dire cold. Senator Bingham rushed home from Washington to attend her. Her doctors recommended warmer climes, so her family prepared a ship for Madeira. On April 13, the thirty-seven-year-old Anne was carried onboard the *America* on a litter, swaddled in bedclothes, before somber crowds. Her condition worsened after they set off, so her distraught husband directed the ship to nearby Bermuda, where Anne died that May. In August, near the day Robert Morris walked out of prison, William Bingham and his unmarried daughter left Philadelphia to live in England. He would die there in 1804. Though Bingham was able to craft an impressive trust to convey his securities to his descendants, the famed Philadelphia Mansion House would find no more of a foothold in the city than Morris's Folly. In 1805, the mansion would become the scene of a noisy public auction, as all of its luxurious contents—its gilt china, its birdcages, its composition stone sculptures, its harpsichord, its settees, its satin curtains, its silver plate, Anne's canopy bed—were displayed before curious crowds. No individual buyer stepped forward for the house itself, and it was purchased by a group hoping to establish a coffeehouse there. Those plans fell through, so for the next forty years the building operated as a hotel—the "Mansion House Hotel." When a fire consumed it in 1847, a row of brownstones took its place.[33]

Morris, in his bankruptcy proceedings, drafted an account of his own property for the court. His resulting statement ran to seventy-four pages. "I shall begin," he stated in its opening lines, revealing a mind still ill-tuned to the public spectacle of his gluttony, "with the Lands purchased in the Genesee Country, acknowledging that if I had contented myself with those purchases, and employed my time and attention in disposing of the lands to the best advantage, I have every reason to believe, that at this day I should have been the wealthiest citizen of the United States." The bankruptcy commissioners received this report and heard eighty-six of Morris's creditors who took the time to step forward and make claims that totaled $2,948,711.11. Most involved the cursed M & N notes, dating as far back as December 1794. The claimants, some insolvent themselves, included many merchants, an innkeeper, tailors, brokers, a bookseller, an apothecary, and even Pierce Butler, recently senator from South Carolina. Two women recorded their claims, Mary Geery and Agnes Rutherford, who ran a boardinghouse on Walnut Street. In August, just before departing for England, William Bingham appeared before the commissioners to state that Morris owed him $40,500 by promissory notes. Old shadows from the Chestnut Street project also came forward. Peter Carron, blacksmith, employed on the site from 1795 to 1797, claimed $1,266 for work done there. Burton Wallace, foreman and bricklayer, claimed $2,492 outstanding, for work spanning more than three years. John Cromwell, who took Wallace's place, claimed $716, while the estate of Robert McGee, lumber dealer, claimed $872 outstanding. By December, the commissioners had heard enough. The judge discharged Morris on December 4, leaving his creditors to find a way to make any of the tangled old assets pay.[34]

Anger over his failure remained. President Jefferson's lament in 1801 that he could not appoint Morris to his cabinet acknowledged the plain truth that "R. Morris has fallen from his height of character" in the eyes of the public. Gouverneur Morris concurred. He noted "Mr. Ross speaks to me of Robert Morris's situation, and says he behaved very ill. Mr. Fitzsimmons tells me that he is completely ruined by advances to Robert Morris. Another man has sunk $80,000 in the vortex." One young city merchant described Morris as "loaded with the curses of thousands whom his overgrasping & inconsiderate speculations have reduced to poverty & wretchedness." Decades later, lawyer Joshua Francis Fisher recalled Morris unflinchingly: "Grasping round as all mighty speculators do, to save him-self, he involved all his friends, & almost all our business community, my Uncle among the number,—for who had not then confidence in the integrity and great resources of Robert Morris?" The results remained raw: "His bankruptcy was like a little earthquake, every body trembled and feared their roofs would fall about their heads." Among these, "My Uncle trusted everything of his own to his friend and patron, and lost all except the house which had been bought four years before in his wife's name." The voices were not unanimous; some residents could not cast stones at the patriotic clubman. In the depths of his 1798 troubles, Daniel Brodhead, the state's surveyor general, claimed Morris's "truly magnanimous conduct towards me formerly made impressions which no lapse of time can efface," and Brodhead longed for "the power to speak peace & comfort to his wounded mind." And from Scotland, a Philadelphia woman wrote her sister about Morris's imprisonment with concern, recalling his generosity and sincere friendships. But Robert and Mary would pay the costs of their follies for the remainder of their lives.[35]

The Morrises found a small stream of income from the Genesee transactions. Gouverneur negotiated on their behalf with the Dutch to secure Mary, who had also signed the documents, a lifetime pension of $1,500 a year. Soon after his release, Robert traveled to see Gouverneur in New York, who found him "lean, low-spirited, and as poor as a commission of bankruptcy can make a man," but sent him home "fat, sleek, in good spirits," and possessed of this pension. Morris continued his tour, venturing to the Potomac, to see friends, family, and colleagues there. He dined with President Jefferson and James Madison, who were "very Polite, very attentive, but that is all," and he stopped to pay his respects at Mount Vernon. Returning to Philadelphia, he tinkered with the markets but found the mercantile community closed to him. Soon he and Mary made their last move together, farther west to South Twelfth Street. There, on the edge of the city's settlements, they made their home in a rented, three-story brick row house, two bays wide (fig. 9.1). It sat next to that of Paul Busti, agent of the Holland Land Company. Morris took to walking with his grandchild Sally to nearby "Dunlap's corner," strolling past his neighbors—a midwife, a weaver, a painter, as well as his old gardener, David Landreth.[36]

For the remaining few years of his life, Morris continued to indulge in follies. He floated a new subscription scheme for the Washington lots. He

HOUSE WHERE ROBERT MORRIS LIVED AND DIED

Figure 9.1. "House Where Robert Morris Lived and Died." The Morrises' final house, on Twelfth Street in Philadelphia. (Undated newspaper clipping from Castner Scrapbooks, vol. 6, p. 69. Courtesy of the Free Library of Philadelphia)

met with proponents of a new commercial bank, intending to serve as its president, but it never got off the ground. He and Robert, Jr., went "*high go mad,*" in Morris's words, "for settling & making fortunes in East Florida" for a time and planned a reconnoitering trip there to consider planting cotton. And they also dabbled in the wine importing business, seeking out an elusive second taste of a delightful, drained cask.[37]

More pragmatically, in 1804, Morris made out his will. The small collection of items he was able to bequeath reflected his sentiments. To his eldest son, he gave his father's gold watch, "left to me at his death" and "carefully kept and valued by me ever since." To Thomas, he gave a gold-headed cane, the head of which was given to Morris by John Hancock when the latter was the president of Congress. Henry would get his copying press and writing paper that was a gift from a London colleague, while Hetty and Maria got pieces of family silver which Morris had been able to repurchase after bankruptcy. To Gouverneur Morris, Robert bestowed a French spyglass. Lastly, he gave "my dearly beloved wife Mary," whom he named as executrix of his estate, the remainder, trusting her to dispose of it all afterward as she saw best. He then took the opportunity to apologize. "Here I have to express my regret at having lost a very large fortune acquired by honest industry, which I had long hoped and expected to enjoy with my family during my own life and then to distribute it among those of them that should outlive me. Fate has determined otherwise, and we must submit to the decrees, which I have done with patience and fortitude." The public man's world had become quite private. In this apologetic gesture in his will, he also bequeathed his unparalleled personal *story*—the story of his follies—to posterity. He finalized all of these thoughts in his last surviving letter, to Thomas, in 1805. In it, he thanked God for his blessings, considered himself as happy as circumstances would permit, and recommended his children to keep their desires within their means. "As fortune slipped out of my hands I hope such of them"—his children—"as feel the want of it will be able to make it for themselves, or what is perhaps still more desirable that they will be able to restrain their desires or wants within such bounds as the means they do or may possess will be competent to gratify and then they also will be contented."[38]

In April 1806, the St. George Society of Philadelphia toasted Robert Morris at the group's annual revelry. The following month, at seventy-two years old, Morris lay on his sickbed. A "tedious and lingering illness" pestered him until the night of May 8, 1806, when he knew he would die. He looked up calmly at his huddled family. It was a life full of flights. A day later, his obituary—one short sentence in the local papers—mentioned his Revolutionary War contributions. In a quiet service, his body was interred alongside his son William in the family vault at Christ churchyard. The contrast with the passing of Washington, Franklin, Hamilton, and other lights was pronounced, but Morris's survivors were by then thankful for the obscurity. Robert, Jr., informed the Croxalls in New Jersey, while Mary retreated into mourning at her Twelfth Street home. She would survive her husband by two decades.[39]

Gouverneur Morris continued reaching out to Mary and the family. Appropriately enough, he had offered a better reflection on his friend's fate the previous year. Gouverneur served as a trustee at Columbia College, and in 1805 he was prompted to deliver a formal "Oration on the Love of Wealth" for the benefit of students there. As one of the architects of the U.S. Constitution, Gouverneur knew the subject's importance for these rising citizens.

At the same time, his oration must have also offered a moment to contemplate the financier's decline. Gouverneur was given to eulogies, having done the honors after Washington's death in 1799 and, most recently, Alexander Hamilton's in 1804. So in 1805, he stood at his podium, looking down at a roomful of young men's faces, and intoned out an indirect reflection on his friend Robert. His oration dealt with the condition of a man driven to purchase millions of acres of land, to carve out an entire city block for a private palace, to scratch toward phantom opportunities until the end, and therein Gouverneur found pity.[40]

The dilemma arose easily before the eyes of Columbia's finest. Was this passion for the love of wealth—which Gouverneur described as so universal in this "festive Land," in "every populous Town"—essentially vicious? What was the proper response to it? First, Gouverneur sorted out the love of wealth as expressed by members of different classes. Surely the poor could be forgiven cravings for necessities and comforts beyond their meager hearths. Moving up the social ladder, a love of wealth among the middling classes involved the search for independence and reputation. At the top of the order were those "who grasp at Gold as the Means of Power" and then those in self-enforced penury because they could only hoard, not spend. Oddly, neither of these latter ends—hunger for power or miserly hoarding— was a particular problem for the financier. Still, Gouverneur's friend could be recognized in the oration, as one of those entering the upper classes seeking "the Consideration and applause of his fellow-men." Surely, Robert Morris could be faulted for his extravagant plans, but, in Gouverneur's generalized query, "Shall we not rather pity than blame that Being who glows with a love of fame but is cramped and shackled by the social institutions of a Country which leaves no Road to Distinction except thro the Regions of Plutus," the Greek god of wealth? In other words, the American experiment, he suggested, offered few official means of recognizing and celebrating greatness; it had no titled aristocracy. Gouverneur's formulation overlooked other opportunities for distinction, such as military glories and public service. Instead, he rallied behind his friend by implying that Morris and others like him felt compelled to publicly establish their own esteemed position themselves, through their use of private wealth, which entailed certain risks. Hence an upstart palace. "Unhappy state!" Gouverneur exclaimed in observing the results, "where talents excite Envy instead of inspiring Respect, where Defamation is the Reward of Merit, where Virtue meets the need of Folly." The orator then rambled, discussing the fruits of ambition, until he reached his final climax, in which he refused to decry the love of wealth itself but rather the lack of other vibrant passions alongside it. So it came down to a sense of balance. "We must not then blame the Love of Wealth but pity the absence of every other Love," he claimed. No one could accuse Robert Morris of not having other loves: his wife and children, his food and drink, his country, city, and club. Somehow, Gouverneur had found that Robert was not truly the victim of a love of wealth. Rather, he had pursued industry, accomplishment, and then an old age "rewarded by opulent Ease," as was natural, only to run up against the boundaries of his nation's polity and the shoals of economic forces. Gouverneur's ringing conclusion would sound over the grave of his friend: "Let us not be ashamed to love Wealth as it ought to be loved and seek it as it ought to be sought, that we might possess the Comforts which become our Station in Life, the means of that Independence which is essential to Freedom and the Power of indulging a generous Mind in Acts of Benevolence."

Comforts, independence, benevolence—all noble and loyal sentiments, and true to the financier's concept of himself. Robert's children could find consolation in these words. But they were surprisingly evasive, coming from the worldly Gouverneur. In contrast, other Americans, such as William Sansom and the purchasers of his new homes on Sansom Row, saw the unmistakable folly of a man run mad through his own sense of conquest, through his appetites, who could not tailor his vision to his surroundings. Even esteemed Revolutionary leaders could prove fools; even men with worthy intentions could go very wrong. For common citizens, American liberty did not mean the freedom to cast off all limits, to supersede one's own society, to explode the free market. It also required ongoing responsibilities. Yet such critics could not extinguish Morris's appetites, or even truly their own (fig. 9.2). Morris's unique vision for wealth and art died with him, but the ambition he personified would live on, in a populace dedicated to better, faster, bigger. His house became a cautionary tale for a reason. Indeed, he had founded the nation, in more ways than one.

Figure 9.2. Tony's Paradise jewelry store, resting on top of Morris's Folly at Eighth and Chestnut Streets, Philadelphia. (Author photo)

Notes

Abbreviations Used in the Notes

COLU   Rare Book and Manuscript Library, Columbia
University, New York City, New York

HSP   Historical Society of Pennsylvania, Philadelphia,
Pennsylvania

HUNT   Huntington Library, San Marino, California

LOC   Manuscript Division, Library of Congress,
Washington, District of Columbia

MDHS   Maryland Historical Society, Baltimore, Maryland

NYHS   New-York Historical Society, New York City,
New York

NYPL   New York Public Library, New York City,
New York

OIEAHC   Omohundro Institute of Early American History
and Culture (previously Institute of Early American
History and Culture)

PROLOGUE

1. *Claypoole's American Daily Advertiser* (November 12, 1798) (quotation);
Donald Jackson and Dorothy Twohig, eds., *The Diaries of George Washington* (Charlottesville: University Press of Virginia, 1979), 6:322–26.
2. Detail based on descriptions in Charles Brockden Brown, *Arthur Mervyn;
Or, Memoirs of the Year 1793*, edited with an introduction and notes by

Philip Barnard and Stephen Shapiro (Indianapolis, Ind.: Hackett Publishing Company, 2008), 194.

3. "Inventory of Articles found in the Possession of Robert Morris in his Rooms, Debtors Apartment," [Robert Morris], *In the Account of Property* (Philadelphia [1801]), 25; John T. S. Sullivan, ed., *The Public Men of the Revolution, Including Events From the Peace of 1783 to the Peace of 1815. In a Series of Letters. By the Late Hon. Wm. Sullivan, LL.D.* (Philadelphia: Carey and Hart, 1847), 141; William B. Wood, *Personal Recollections of the Stage, Embracing Notices of Actors, Authors, and Auditors, During a Period of Forty Years* (Philadelphia: Henry Carey Baird, 1855), 37–39; Mrs. Armine Nixon Hart, "Robert Morris," *Pennsylvania Magazine of History and Biography* 1 (1877), 341–42; and Bruce H. Mann, *Republic of Debtors: Bankruptcy in the Age of American Independence* (Cambridge, Mass.: Harvard University Press, 2002), 99–101.

4. Robert Morris to John Nicholson, November 14, 1798, Dreer Collection, Robert Morris letters, HSP (quotation, emphasis in the original); "Serious Disturbance at the Gaol," *Gazette of the United States, and Philadelphia Daily Advertiser* (September 19, 1798); Thomas Condie and Richard Folwell, *History of the Pestilence Commonly Called Yellow Fever, Which Almost Desolated Philadelphia, in the Months of August, September & October, 1798* (Philadelphia: R. Folwell, 1799), 9, 52–95, 108.

5. George Washington Parke Custis, *Recollections and Private Memoirs of Washington, by His Adopted Son, George Washington Parke Custis, With a Memoir of the Author, by His Daughter* . . . (Philadelphia: William Flint, 1859), 436.

6. Jackson and Twohig, *The Diaries of George Washington*, 6:326.

7. Alexander Garden, *Anecdotes of the Revolutionary War in America: With Sketches of Character of Persons the Most Distinguished, in the Southern States, for Civil and Military Services* (Charleston, S.C.: A. E. Miller, 1822), 334–37; Redwood Fisher, "Revolutionary Reminiscences Connected with the Life of Robert Morris, Esq., the Financier," *The American Review: A Whig Journal of Politics, Literature, Art, and Science* 6 (July 1847): 68–81; Diary of Robert Morris, September 1–5, 1781, in E. James Ferguson, ed., *The Papers of Robert Morris, 1781–1784* (Pittsburgh: University of Pittsburgh Press, 1975), 2:172–75.

8. Robert Morris to John Nicholson, October 10, 1798, No. 2, Dreer Collection, Robert Morris letters, HSP (first quotation); George Washington to Robert Morris, August 19, 1798, in W. W. Abbot, ed., *The Papers of George Washington: Retirement Series* (Charlottesville: University Press of Virginia, 1998), 2:535 (last quotation).

9. Benjamin Henry Latrobe, Virginia Journals, entry for April 26, 1798, MDHS.

10. Condie and Folwell, *History of the Pestilence,* 75–76 (first quotation); Thompson Westcott, *The Historic Mansions and Buildings of Philadelphia With Some Notice of Their Owners and Occupants* (Philadelphia: Porter and Coates, 1877), 356 (last quotation).

11. Robert Morris to Thomas Morris, February 24, 1798, Collection of Papers of Robert Morris, HUNT (quotation). I follow Kenneth Bowling's observation that, once in America, the engineer rendered his own name as Peter, not Pierre, as he also added the apostrophe in L'Enfant. See Kenneth R. Bowling, *Peter Charles L'Enfant: Vision, Honor, and Male Friendship in the Early American Republic* (Washington, D.C.: Printed for the Friends of the George Washington University Libraries, 2002).

12. Jane Kamensky's *The Escape Artist: A Tale of High-Flying Speculation and America's First Banking Collapse* (New York: Penguin, 2008) provides one next step in this process, which stretches through Thorstein Veblen, *Citizen Kane,* and the 2008 financial crisis. See also Steve Fraser and Gary Gerstle, eds., *Ruling America: A History of Wealth and Power in a Democracy* (Cambridge, Mass.: Harvard University Press, 2005). An inversion of this issue is traced in Scott A. Sandage, *Born Losers: A History of Failure in America* (Cambridge, Mass.: Harvard University Press, 2005).

    My historiographic intentions in this work are threefold. First, no complete study of this architectural landmark has been attempted, nor a dedicated study of Morris's financial failure. The best studies of Morris's late career are Elizabeth M. Nuxoll, "The Financier as Senator: Robert Morris of Pennsylvania, 1789–1795," in Kenneth R. Bowling and Donald R. Kennon, eds., *Neither Separate nor Equal: Congress in the 1790s* (Athens, Oh.: Published for the United States Capitol Historical Society by Ohio University Press, 2000); Barbara Ann Chernow, "Robert Morris: Land Speculator, 1790–1801" (Ph.D. diss., Columbia University, 1974); and the last two chapters in Charles Rappleye, *Robert Morris: Financier of the American Revolution* (New York: Simon and Schuster, 2010), though none deals much with the Folly. The only extended study of the Folly is found in Westcott, *Historic Mansions and Buildings of Philadelphia,* first published in 1877.

    Second, I have consciously employed the narrative method here, in an attempt to highlight this underutilized tool's value for architectural history. For the method's rationale and context, see Ryan K. Smith, "Building Stories: Narrative Prospects for Vernacular Architecture Studies," *Buildings & Landscapes* 18:2 (Fall 2011): 1–14.

Last, I believe Morris's story contributes to recent attempts to present a more rounded view of American founders, and it further reveals the anxieties of the republican experiment, themes explored in works from Stanley Elkins and Eric McKitrick's *The Age of Federalism: The Early American Republic, 1788–1800* (New York: Oxford University Press, 1993) to Nancy Isenberg, *Fallen Founder: The Life of Aaron Burr* (New York: Viking, 2007), among many others, though these themes have yet to displace old assumptions in the public imagination.

CHAPTER 1. HIS CAPITAL

1. Robert Morris to Mary Morris, March 4, 1789, Collection of Papers of Robert Morris, HUNT.

2. For William Maclay's personality, background, and diary, see Kenneth R. Bowling and Helen E. Veit, eds., *Documentary History of the First Federal Congress of the United States of America*, vol. 9, *The Diary of William Maclay and Other Notes on Senate Debates* (Baltimore: Johns Hopkins University Press, 1988), xi–xviii, 431–41.

3. Robert Morris to Mary Morris, March 4, 1789, Collection of Papers of Robert Morris, HUNT.

4. Robert Morris to Gouverneur Morris, March 4, 1789, in Charlene Bangs Bickford et al., eds., *Documentary History of the First Federal Congress of the United States of America*, vol. 15, *Correspondence: First Session, March–May 1789* (Baltimore: Johns Hopkins University Press, 2004), 11–12; Kenneth R. Bowling, *The Creation of Washington, D.C.: The Idea and Location of the American Capital* (Fairfax, Va.: George Mason University Press, 1991), 32–68, 79–80, 127–38; Ron Chernow, *Alexander Hamilton* (New York: Penguin, 2004), 180–83, 324–27.

5. Gouverneur Morris to Robert Morris, May 8, 1789, Gouverneur Morris Papers, LOC; Robert Morris to Mary Morris, August 28, 1789, and September 6, 1789, Collection of Papers of Robert Morris, HUNT; Bowling and Veit, *The Diary of William Maclay*. See also Bowling, *The Creation of Washington, D.C.*, 127–60. Morris had served in 1785 as one of the three commissioners charged by the Confederation Congress with overseeing the creation of a federal residence at the falls of the Delaware River, near Trenton. The commission was short-lived, though, as the Congress failed to appropriate funds for the project and the issue was postponed.

6. Robert Morris to Mary Morris, March 4, 1789, Collection of Papers of Robert Morris, HUNT (first quotation); Robert Morris to Gouverneur Morris, March 4, 1789 (second quotations), and Frederick Muhlenberg to Benjamin Rush, March 5, 1789 (last quotation), in Bickford et al., *Correspondence: First Session, March–May 1789*, 11–12, 37; Linda Grant De Pauw et al., eds., *Documentary History of the First Federal Congress of the United States of America*, vol. 1, *Senate Legislative Journal* (Baltimore: Johns Hopkins University Press, 1972), 3.

   For Federal Hall, see Louis Torres, "Federal Hall Revisited," *Journal of the Society of Architectural Historians* 29 (December 1970): 327–38; James D. Kornwolf, *Architecture and Town Planning in Colonial North America* (Baltimore: Johns Hopkins University Press, 2002), 3:1413–15; Bickford et al., *Correspondence: First Session, March–May 1789*, 26–31; and Scott W. Berg, *Grand Avenues: The Story of the French Visionary Who Designed Washington, D.C.* (New York: Pantheon Books, 2007), 57–64.

7. Robert Morris to Gouverneur Morris, March 4, 1789, in Bickford et al., *Correspondence: First Session, March–May 1789*, 11–12 (first quotation); Robert Morris to Henry Drinker, March 23, 1789, Henry S. Drinker Papers, HSP; Robert Morris to Gouverneur Morris, March 30, 1789, in Bickford et al., *Correspondence: First Session, March–May 1789*, 160; De Pauw et al., *Senate Legislative Journal*, 3–11; John Page to St. George Tucker, April 5, 1789, in Bickford et al., *Correspondence: First Session, March–May 1789*, 201–2 (last quotation); William Constable to Gouverneur Morris, April 7, 1789, in ibid., 219–20; "Letter from New York," *Massachusetts Centinel*, April 11, 1789, in ibid., 211–12; William Maclay to Richard Peters, April 16, 1789, in ibid., 274–75.

8. De Pauw et al., *Senate Legislative Journal*, 7–11; Robert Morris to George Washington, April 6, 1789, in Bickford et al., *Correspondence: First Session, March–May 1789*, 209–10 (quotation).

9. George Washington to James Madison, March 30, 1789, in Bickford et al., *Correspondence: First Session, March–May 1789*, 163; Robert Morris to John Jay, April 20, 1789, John Jay Papers, COLU; *The Federal Gazette and Philadelphia Evening Post* (April 22, 1789); *The New York Daily Gazette* (April 25, 1789); Douglas Southall Freeman, *George Washington: A Biography* (New York: Charles Scribner's Sons, 1954), 6:169–74; David Waldstreicher, *In the Midst of Perpetual Fetes: The Making of American Nationalism, 1776–1820* (Chapel Hill: Published for OIEAHC by the University of North Carolina Press, 1997), 117–26.

10. Robert Morris to John Chaloner, May 2, 1789, Chaloner and White Papers, HSP; De Pauw et al., *Senate Legislative Journal,* 42–53; Robert Morris to Mary Morris, May 13, 1789, Collection of Papers of Robert Morris, HUNT; *The Pennsylvania Packet and General Advertiser* (May 25, 1789); Susan Dillwyn to [William Dillwyn?], May 2, 1789, Dillwyn Manuscripts, 1770–1793, HSP; *Gazette of the United States* (May 27–30, 1789).

11. Robert Morris to Francis Hopkinson, July 3, 1789, Hopkinson Family Papers, HSP. For the Morrises' and Washingtons' theater attendance in New York, see *Gazette of the United States* (June 3–6, 1789).

   For a sampling of Morris's positions on these political issues, see Robert Morris to Edward Tilghman, June 21, 1789, Tilghman Family Papers, MDHS; Robert Morris to Francis Hopkinson, July 3 and August 15, 1789, Francis Hopkinson Papers, HSP; Robert Morris to Richard Peters, August 24, 1789, Peters Papers, HSP; Robert Morris to Levi Hollingsworth, August 29, 1789, Hollingsworth Family Papers, HSP; Benjamin Goodhue to Samuel Phillips, Jr., September 13, 1789, in Charlene Bangs Bickford et al., eds., *Documentary History of the First Federal Congress of the United States of America,* vol. 17, *Correspondence: First Session, September–November 1789* (Baltimore: Johns Hopkins University Press, 2004), 1528–30; and, for Morris's general view of congressional debates and his role as a senator, Robert Morris to Anthony Wayne, July 9, 1789, in Charlene Bangs Bickford et al., eds., *Documentary History of the First Federal Congress of the United States of America,* vol. 16, *Correspondence: First Session, June–August 1789* (Baltimore: Johns Hopkins University Press, 2004), 988. See also De Pauw et al., *Senate Legislative Journal,* 62–145; Bowling and Veit, *The Diary of William Maclay;* "Robert Morris, Senator from Pennsylvania," in William Charles DiGiacomantonio et al., eds., *Documentary History of the First Federal Congress of the United States of America,* vol. 14, *Debates in the House of Representatives: Third Session: December 1790–March 1791: Biographies of Members* (Baltimore: Johns Hopkins University Press, 1995), 766–73; and Elizabeth M. Nuxoll, "The Financier as Senator: Robert Morris of Pennsylvania, 1789–1795," in Kenneth R. Bowling and Donald R. Kennon, eds., *Neither Separate nor Equal: Congress in the 1790s* (Athens, Oh.: Published for the United States Capitol Historical Society by Ohio University Press, 2000).

12. George Partridge to Samuel Holten, May 20, 1789, in Bickford et al., *Correspondence: First Session, March–May 1789,* 600 (first quotation); George Clymer to Benjamin Rush, June 18, 1789 (second quotation), Peter Muhlen-

berg to Benjamin Rush, August 10, 1789 (last quotation), in Bickford et al., *Correspondence: First Session, June–August 1789*, 804–5, 1279–80; Bowling, *The Creation of Washington, D.C.*, 127–36.

13. Robert Morris to Mary Morris, September 6 (first quotation) and September 9 (last quotations), 1789, Collection of Papers of Robert Morris, HUNT; Robert Morris to Richard Peters, August 9, 1789, Peters Papers, HSP; Bowling and Veit, *The Diary of William Maclay.*

14. Robert Morris to Gouverneur Morris, September 27, 1789, in Bickford et al., *Correspondence: First Session, September–November 1789*, 1626–28 (first quotation); De Pauw et al., *Senate Legislative Journal*, 181, 187–203 (second quotation); Bowling and Veit, *The Diary of William Maclay*, 155–70 (last quotation, p. 163). Maclay observed that Morris had spent that eventful day during deliberations "running backwards & forwards like a Boy, taking out one Senator after another" for bargaining.

15. On the eve of the bill's failure, Morris wrote to Gouverneur: "We have been playing hide and seek on the banks of the Potomac, Susquehannah, Conegocheague, &c &c. It has constantly been my view to bring the ramblers back to the banks of the Delaware, but the obstinacy of one or two, and the schemes of some others, prevented my getting them so high up as the Falls." Robert Morris to Gouverneur Morris, September 27, 1789, in Bickford et al., *Correspondence: First Session, September–November 1789*, 1626–28. For the critical response in Pennsylvania to Morris's moves, see *Independent Gazetteer* (October 2, 1789) and John Armstrong, Jr., to Frederick William Steuben, October 4, 1789, in Bickford et al., *Correspondence: First Session, September–November 1789*, 1669–70. Yet Morris was defended at the time by "Morrisites"; see *Independent Gazetteer* (October 3, 1789). See also Charles Rappleye, *Robert Morris: Financier of the American Revolution* (New York: Simon and Schuster, 2010), 462–67; "Robert Morris, Senator from Pennsylvania" in Di-Giacomantonio et al., *Debates in the House of Representatives . . . Biographies of Members*, 772; and Bowling, *The Creation of Washington, D.C.*

16. William Grayson to James Madison, October 7, 1789 (quotations), and James Madison to George Washington, November 20, 1789, in Bickford et al., *Correspondence: First Session, September–November 1789*, 1675–77, 1715–16.

17. Mary Morris to Robert Morris, December 12, 1787 (first quotation); Robert Morris to Mary Morris, May 22, 1790 (second quotation); Robert Morris to Mary Morris, July 2, 1790 (last quotation), Collection of Papers of Robert Morris, HUNT. See De Pauw et al., *Senate Legislative Journal*, 395–97; Bowling and Veit, *The Diary of William Maclay*, 309–21; Stanley Elkins

and Eric McKitrick, *The Age of Federalism: The Early American Republic, 1788–1800* (New York: Oxford University Press, 1993), 155–61; Joseph J. Ellis, *Founding Brothers: The Revolutionary Generation* (New York: Knopf, 2000), 48–80; Nuxoll, "The Financier as Senator," 105–7; Rappleye, *Robert Morris*, 476–80; and, more broadly, Bowling, *The Creation of Washington, D.C.*, and T. L. Loftin, *Contest for a Capital: George Washington, Robert Morris, and Congress, 1783–1791, Contenders: Dramatized Events of America's Founding Years* (Washington, D.C.: T. Loftin Publishers, 1989).

Rumors circulated that Washington had offered Morris the position of secretary of the treasury but that the latter deferred in favor of Hamilton. A newspaper article from June 1789 stated that the "eyes of many would be turned towards Mr. Morris" for the treasury position "if it was not thought incompatible with his Senatorship," a reference to a constitutional bar on congressmen holding executive office. The author added that even without this objection, "there would be others raised which would require attention from other circumstances if not from their merits. There are prejudices against as well as for him." See "Letter from New York," [Philadelphia] *Independent Gazetteer* (June 9, 1789) and widely reprinted elsewhere; Bickford et al., *Correspondence: First Session, June–August 1789*, 706–7; George Washington Parke Custis, *Recollections and Private Memoirs of Washington, by His Adopted Son, George Washington Parke Custis, With a Memoir of the Author, by His Daughter* . . . (Philadelphia: William Flint, 1859), 349–50; and Nuxoll, "The Financier as Senator," 91, 99. Morris reacted positively to Hamilton's appointment, sending the news to his wife before the official announcement. See Robert Morris to Mary Morris, September 6, 1789, Collection of Papers of Robert Morris, HUNT.

18. The 1790 print showing Morris with Federal Hall was probably engraved by Henry G. Jenks. See R. W. G. Vail, "Notes and Documents: A Rare Robert Morris Caricature," *Pennsylvania Magazine of History and Biography* 60 (April 1936): 184–86; Margaret C. S. Christman, *The First Federal Congress, 1789–1791* (Washington, D.C.: Published by the Smithsonian Institution Press for the National Portrait Gallery and the United States Congress, 1989), 189–95; Bowling, *The Creation of Washington, D.C.*, 200–202; and Nuxoll, "The Financier as Senator," 105–7.

Two more versions of this cartoon also appeared at the time but do not survive. In one, Morris was portrayed shouldering Federal Hall, crowded with small congressmen, to a wharf, as a devil standing atop the ferry house for New Jersey shouts, "This way, Bobby!" This print was described by

earlier historians such as Benson J. Lossing, *Mount Vernon and Its Associa-
tions, Historical, Biographical, and Pictorial* (New York: W. A. Townsend
and Company, 1859), 244; John S. C. Abbott, *Lives of the Presidents of the
United States of America From Washington to the Present Time* (Boston:
B. B. Russell and Co., 1867), 89; James Parton, "Caricature in the United
States," *Harper's New Monthly Magazine* 52 (December 1875): 32; Martha J.
Lamb, "The White House and Its Memories," *Magazine of American History* 17 (May 1887): 370; and Ellis Paxson Oberholtzer, *Robert Morris: Patriot and Financier* (New York: Macmillan Company, 1903), 258–59. The
other version pictured the heavy-laden Morris with small versions of Hamilton, John Jay, and Henry Knox in Morris's pockets, while Madison swings
from his watch chain and Jefferson serves as his walking staff. See Theodore Sedgwick to Pamela Sedgwick, July 4, 1790, Theodore Sedgwick Papers, Massachusetts Historical Society, Boston, Massachusetts, and William
A. Duer, *Reminiscences of an Old Yorker* (New York: 1867), 76–77.

19. Christman, *The First Federal Congress*, 189–95; Bowling, *The Creation of
Washington, D.C.*, 200–202; and Nuxoll, "The Financier as Senator," 105–7.
For contemporary comments on these cartoons, see *New York Morning Post*
(July 8, 1790), *Columbian Centinel* (July 14, 1790), and *New Hampshire Re-
corder* (August 26, 1790). Philip Freneau's "The Removal" appeared in the
New York Daily Gazette on August 10, 1790 (emphasis in the original). The
poem was reprinted in the *New-York Journal & Patriotic Register* (August 10,
1790) and in papers further abroad, as in Charleston's *The City Gazette, or
the Daily Advertiser* (September 11, 1790).

An exception to the primary focus on Morris was "The Valedictory,"
which though it lampooned "Bawdy *Bob*" for "fobbing the Pence," it singled out Pennsylvania Representative Thomas Fitzsimons, who "has more
influ'nce whenever he wills; Then staggering *Bob* with his *noted* long bills."
[New York] *Morning Post* (August 21, 1790). See Nuxoll, "The Financier as
Senator," 105–7, and Edward M. Riley, "Philadelphia, the Nation's Capital," *Pennsylvania History* 20 (October 1953): 360–62.

20. Robert Morris to Mary Morris, July 2, 1790, Collection of Papers of Robert
Morris, HUNT. William Maclay recorded his disapproval of Morris's
bawdy speech in a diary entry for May 17, 1790: after dining with the Pennsylvania representatives that afternoon, he recalled "I never heard such a
Scene of Beastial Ba[w]dry kept up in my life. Mr. Morris is certainly the
greatest Blackguard in that way ever I heard open a Mouth." Bowling and
Veit, *The Diary of William Maclay*, 270. In the 1860s, Joshua Francis

Fisher, whose elder family members had known Morris well, recalled that "Mr. Morris was a man of very loose morality," basing this judgment on Morris's own illegitimate birth, his fathering of an illegitimate daughter, his "Epicurean life," and his "coarse conversation." Joshua Francis Fisher, "A Section of the Memoirs of Joshua Francis Fisher, Philadelphia Social Scene from the Time of the Hamiltons to the Early Part of the Nineteenth Century," Cadwalader Collection, Series 9, Joshua Francis Fisher Papers, Box 10, HSP. For an example of this speech, see Rappleye, *Robert Morris*, 391.

21. Henry Wynkoop to Reading Beatty, July 2, 1790, quoted in Joseph M. Beatty, Jr., "The Letters of Judge Henry Wynkoop, Representative From Pennsylvania to the First Congress of the United States," *Pennsylvania Magazine of History and Biography* 38 (April 1914): 201 (first quotations); "We are informed," [Philadelphia] *General Advertiser and Political, Commercial, and Literary Journal* (April 27, 1791) (last quotations).

22. "Extract from the Mss. Narrative of the Principal incidents of Jeremiah Banning of Talbot County Maryland," 1793, HSP; "Robert Morris, of Oxford, Md.," *Boogher's Repository* 1 (March 1883): 45–50; Elizabeth M. Nuxoll, "Illegitimacy, Family Status, and Property in the Early Republic: The Morris-Croxall Family of New Jersey," *New Jersey History* 113 (Fall/Winter 1995): 3–4; Rappleye, *Robert Morris*, 7–11; Oberholtzer, *Robert Morris*, 1–8; and William Graham Sumner, *The Financier and the Finances of the American Revolution* (New York: Dodd, Mead, and Company, 1892), 1:1–4. Morris inherited £2,500 from his father. Rappleye offers a useful and entertaining overview of the historiography on Morris in the epilogue of *Robert Morris*.

23. Clarence L. Ver Steeg, *Robert Morris, Revolutionary Financier: With an Analysis of His Earlier Career* (Philadelphia: University of Pennsylvania Press, 1954), 2–4, and Rappleye, *Robert Morris*, 9–14. For Morris's early involvement in the slave trade, see *Pennsylvania Gazette* (October 9, 1755); John F. Watson, *Annals of Philadelphia, Being a Collection of Memoirs, Anecdotes, & Incidents of the City and Its Inhabitants From the Days of the Pilgrim Founders* . . . (Philadelphia: Carey and Hart, 1830), 482; James A. Rawley with Stephen D. Behrendt, *The Transatlantic Slave Trade: A History*, rev. ed. (Lincoln: University of Nebraska Press, 2005), 343; and Joe William Trotter, Jr., and Eric Ledell Smith, *African Americans in Pennsylvania* (Harrisburg: Pennsylvania State University Press, 1997), 70.

24. Mrs. Armine Nixon Hart, "Robert Morris," *Pennsylvania Magazine of History and Biography* 1 (1877): 333–34; Rappleye, *Robert Morris*, 17–21; Thomas M. Doerflinger, *A Vigorous Spirit of Enterprise: Merchants and Economic Develop-*

ment in Revolutionary Philadelphia (Chapel Hill: Published for the OIEAHC by the University of North Carolina Press, 1986), 26–27, 236–40; and Oberholtzer, *Robert Morris*, 9–13.

25. Charles Henry Hart, "Mary White—Mrs. Robert Morris," *Pennsylvania Magazine of History and Biography* 2 (1878): 157–84; William White Wiltbank, "Colonel Thomas White, of Maryland," *Pennsylvania Magazine of History and Biography* 1 (1877): 420–38; Thomas H. Montgomery, "Colonel Thomas White," *Boogher's Repository* 1 (April 1883): 72–75; and Oberholtzer, *Robert Morris*, 13–15 and 261–63. For examples of their pet names, see Robert Morris to Mary Morris, March 4, 1789, and Mary Morris to Robert Morris, February 28, 1777, Collection of Papers of Robert Morris, HUNT.

26. Rappleye, *Robert Morris*, 27–72; Hart, "Robert Morris," 334–35; Ver Steeg, *Robert Morris*, 6–7; Oberholtzer, *Robert Morris*, 9–13; Sumner, *The Financier and the Finances of the American Revolution*, 1:188–97.

27. Robert Morris to Benjamin Rush, February 15, 1777, Folder 1777–1786, Box 18, Robert Morris Papers, LOC (quotations). In late 1776, Morris served as Congress's prime representative and acting minister in Philadelphia after that body had flown from the advancing British military forces. He sent his family away for safety as well. They all returned the following year. Ver Steeg, *Robert Morris*, 7–36, and Rappleye, *Robert Morris*, 80–91.

28. Ver Steeg, *Robert Morris*, 7–36; Oberholtzer, *Robert Morris*, 17–59; Sumner, *The Financier and the Finances of the American Revolution*, 1:197–238; Rappleye, *Robert Morris*, 173–97. See also generally E. James Ferguson, *The Power of the Purse: A History of American Public Finance, 1776–1790* (Chapel Hill: Published for OIEAHC by the University of North Carolina Press, 1961).

29. Robert Morris diary entry for February 21, 1781 (first quotation), and Robert Morris to George Washington, May 29, 1781 (last quotations), in E. James Ferguson and John Catanzariti, eds., *The Papers of Robert Morris, 1781–1784* (Pittsburgh: University of Pittsburgh Press, 1973), 1:8–9, 96; Robert Morris to the President of Congress, January 24, 1783, in John Catanzariti, ed., *The Papers of Robert Morris, 1781–1784* (Pittsburgh: University of Pittsburgh Press, 1988), 7:368; Ver Steeg, *Robert Morris*, 58–63; Rappleye, *Robert Morris*, 229–39; and Sumner, *The Financier and the Finances of the American Revolution*, 1:262–69. Two years into the position, Morris maintained the same attitude toward public service, writing: "At present I fill the most important office in the American Government but am trying to get rid of it because I want ease and indulgence to Compensate for a life of Labor and Bustle." Robert Morris to Ralph Forster, August 8, 1783, in

Elizabeth M. Nuxoll and Mary A. Gallagher, eds., *The Papers of Robert Morris, 1781–1784* (Pittsburgh: University of Pittsburgh Press, 1995), 8:405–7.

30. For Morris's role as superintendent of finance, see "Introduction" in vols. 1 and 6–9 of *The Papers of Robert Morris, 1781–1784* (Pittsburgh: University of Pittsburgh Press) (vols. 1 [1973] and 6 [1984] edited by E. James Ferguson and John Catanzariti; vol. 7 [1988] edited by John Catanzariti; vols. 8 [1995] and 9 [1999] edited by Elizabeth Nuxoll and Mary Gallagher); Ver Steeg, *Robert Morris*, 62–186; Rappleye, *Robert Morris*, 307–57; Sumner, *The Financier and the Finances of the American Revolution*, 1:278–91, 2:1–63, 94–134; Oberholtzer, *Robert Morris*, 60–209; and John Dos Passos, "Robert Morris and the 'Art Magick,' " *American Heritage* 7 (October 1956): 86. A sense of Morris's experiences as superintendent comes through in his interaction with General Arthur St. Clair from Pennsylvania, who, among others in distress, showed up in Morris's office in September 1782 and walked away with Morris's personal notes worth $320 in his pocket. Diary entries for September 14 and 16, 1782, in John Catanzariti and E. James Ferguson, eds., *The Papers of Robert Morris 1781–1784* (Pittsburgh: University of Pittsburgh Press, 1984), 6:377, 379.

31. Charles Coleman Sellers, "Portraits and Miniatures by Charles Willson Peale," *Transactions of the American Philosophical Society* 42 (1952): 146–48; Charles Coleman Sellers, "Charles Willson Peale's Portrait of Robert and Gouverneur Morris: A Convergence of Politics and Art," *Antiques* 99 (March 1971): 404–6. Morris had apparently commissioned a miniature of himself from Peale earlier, in 1778.

32. Sellers, "Portraits and Miniatures by Charles Willson Peale"; Doris Devine Fanelli and Karie Diethorn, *History of the Portrait Collection: Independence National Historical Park* (Philadelphia: American Philosophical Society, 2001), 242; and Kenneth Hafertepe, "Banking Houses in the United States, the First Generation, 1781–1811," *Winterthur Portfolio* 35 (Spring 2000): 1–52. The building in the portrait may also suggest an upgraded design intended to replace his Bank of North America's storefront quarters on Philadelphia's Chestnut Street.

33. Nuxoll, "The Financier as Senator"; "Introduction," in Elizabeth M. Nuxoll and Mary A. Gallagher, eds., *The Papers of Robert Morris, 1781–1784* (Pittsburgh: University of Pittsburgh Press, 1999), vol. 9; Ver Steeg, *Robert Morris*, 193–99; Rappleye, *Robert Morris;* and Oberholtzer, *Robert Morris*, 214–25, 353. Jefferson's lament is found in Thomas Jefferson to James Madison, March 12, 1801, in Barbara B. Oberg, ed., *The Papers of Thomas Jefferson*

(Princeton, N.J.: Princeton University Press, 2006), 33:255–56. Morris had earlier done his part in this relationship, assuring Jefferson sincerely on March 2, 1801, that "my esteem & Respect for your personal Character has never abated from party considerations," in ibid., 121–22.

The controversy surrounding Morris's motives and his alleged profiteering has proved a staple issue for nearly all his observers and biographers. Among them, historian William Graham Sumner provided a useful estimation: "The public sought his services in the position of a statesman, not because he was a statesman, but because he was a merchant and banker, and they wanted the professional services of a merchant and banker. What his high-principled critics demanded was that in his public capacity he should be both public man and private man, but that in his private capacity he should abstain from any knowledge or opportunity of the public man" (*The Financier and the Finances of the American Revolution*, 1:205). For a different view, see Terry Bouton, *Taming Democracy: "The People," the Founders, and the Troubled Ending of the American Revolution* (New York: Oxford University Press, 2007), 70–75. For examples of the public controversies surrounding Morris's financial affairs into the late 1780s, see Nuxoll and Gallagher, *Papers of Robert Morris*, vol. 9, appendices, and Nuxoll, "The Financier as Senator."

34. Thomas Fitzsimons to [Miers Fisher?], July 15, 1790, and Thomas Fitzsimons to Miers Fisher, July 16, 1790, Miers Fisher Papers, HSP; Robert Morris to Walter Stewart, July 28, 1790, No. 59 in *G.51.7.4, Boston Public Library, Boston, Massachusetts; Robert Morris to Mary Morris, April 25, 1790, Collection of Papers of Robert Morris, HUNT.

35. Russell F. Weigley et al., eds., *Philadelphia: A 300-Year History* (New York: W. W. Norton and Company, 1982), 1–155; George B. Tatum, *Penn's Great Town; 250 Years of Philadelphia Architecture Illustrated in Prints and Drawings* (Philadelphia: University of Pennsylvania Press, 1961), 17–52; Kenneth R. Bowling, "The Federal Government and the Republican Court Move to Philadelphia, November 1790–March 1791," in Bowling and Kennon, *Neither Separate nor Equal*, 3–33; Doerflinger, *A Vigorous Spirit of Enterprise*; Billy G. Smith, *The "Lower Sort": Philadelphia's Laboring People, 1750–1800* (Ithaca, N.Y.: Cornell University Press, 1990), 150–75; and Emma Jones Lapsansky, *Neighborhoods in Transition: William Penn's Dream and Urban Reality* (New York: Garland Publishing, 1994).

36. Edward Lawler, Jr., "The President's House in Philadelphia: The Rediscovery of a Lost Landmark," *Pennsylvania Magazine of History and Biography* 126 (January 2002): 5–95.

37. Minutes of the Philadelphia Common Council, August 9 and 30, 1790, Philadelphia City Council Minute Book (1789–1793), Collection 1411, HSP; "Report of the Comm[itt]ee of Aug. 9th & 23 for the Accommodation of the President," November 22, 1790, Etting Collection, Independence Hall, Catalogued Items, HSP (quotations); George Washington to Tobias Lear, September 5, 1790, in Mark A. Mastromarino, ed., *The Papers of George Washington: Presidential Series* (Charlottesville: University Press of Virginia, 1996), 6:397–99; and Lawler, "The President's House in Philadelphia," 23.

38. "Report of the Comm[itt]ee . . . for the Accommodation of the President"; Robert Morris to Gouverneur Morris, October 31, 1790, in Jared Sparks, *The Life of Gouverneur Morris, With Selections From His Correspondence and Miscellaneous Papers* (Boston: Gray and Bowen, 1832), 3:17–19 (quotations). The city was allowed to deduct the cost of additions and repairs "permanently useful & ornamental to the Buildings" from the rent due Morris. For the Stedman-Galloway house, see Chapter 2 and Lawler, "The President's House in Philadelphia," and Weigley, *Philadelphia: A 300-Year History*, 109–55. The Stedman-Galloway house was valued at £1,835 in 1792, less than one-third the value of the Masters-Penn house. See Tax Assessor's Ledger, 1791, Middle Ward, City Archives, Philadelphia, Pennsylvania, and entry for June 4, 1792, in "Journal, 1791–1801," Robert Morris Business Papers, HSP.

39. George Washington to Tobias Lear, September 5, 1790 (first quotations, emphasis in the original), George Washington to Robert Morris, September 9, 1790, Tobias Lear to George Washington, September 12, 1790 (second quotation, emphasis in the original), Tobias Lear to George Washington, November 4, 1790, and Tobias Lear to George Washington, November 21, 1790, in Mastromarino, *Papers of George Washington: Presidential Series*, 6:397–99, 410–11, 419–23, 622–25, 678–82; Robert Morris to Gouverneur Morris, October 31, 1790, in Sparks, *The Life of Gouverneur Morris*, 3:17–19 (last quotation); and Tobias Lear to Miers Fisher, September 20, 1791, Miers Fisher Papers, HSP. See also Lawler, "The President's House in Philadelphia," 22–25.

40. Tobias Lear to George Washington, October 14, October 17, October 24, October 28, October 31, November 4, and November 14, 1790, in Mastromarino, *Papers of George Washington: Presidential Series*, 6:557–59, 569–70, 603–7, 622–25, 655–58; Lawler, "The President's House in Philadelphia," 22–48.

41. Bowling, "The Federal Government and the Republican Court Move to Philadelphia"; Anna Coxe Toogood, "Philadelphia as the Nation's Capital,

1790–1800," in Bowling and Kennon, *Neither Separate nor Equal*, 34–60; Riley, "Philadelphia, the Nation's Capital"; DiGiacomantonio et al., *Debates in the House of Representatives . . . Biographies of Members*, xi–xiii; Rufus Wilmot Griswold, *The Republican Court, or American Society in the Days of Washington* (New York: D. Appleton and Co., 1854), 253–72.

42. Robert Morris to Gouverneur Morris, October 31, 1790, in Sparks, *The Life of Gouverneur Morris*, 3:17–19 (quotation); Nuxoll, "The Financier as Senator"; "Robert Morris, Senator from Pennsylvania," in DiGiacomantonio et al., *Debates in the House of Representatives . . . Biographies of Members*, 766–73.

CHAPTER 2. HIS FAMILY

1. Lynn Matluck Brooks, "The Philadelphia Dancing Assembly in the Eighteenth Century," *Dance Research Journal* 21 (Spring 1989): 1–6, and Charles Coleman Sellers, "Portraits and Miniatures of Charles Willson Peale," *Transactions of the American Philosophical Society* 42 (1952): 148–49. On Mary Morris's position during Washington's presidency, see William Maclay's diary entry for June 11, 1789, in Kenneth R. Bowling and Helen E. Veit, eds., *Documentary History of the First Federal Congress of the United States of America*, vol. 9, *The Diary of William Maclay and Other Notes on Senate Debates* (Baltimore: Johns Hopkins University Press, 1988), 73–75; Rufus Wilmot Griswold, *The Republican Court, or American Society in the Days of Washington*, rev. ed. (New York: D. Appleton and Company, 1856), 162–63; and Charles Henry Hart, "Mary White—Mrs. Robert Morris," *Pennsylvania Magazine of History and Biography* 2 (1878): 172. For an example of Mary Morris's thoughts concerning formal balls in Philadelphia, see Mary Morris to Robert Morris, January 13, 1788, Collection of Papers of Robert Morris, HUNT.

One of Mary's dresses apparently survives in the collection of the Philadelphia Museum of Art. It is a bluish-green silk satin, short-sleeved, trimmed with satin and embroidered, with V-neckline, court train, and a floral theme, of French origin. See accession number 1890-25. See also accession numbers 1897-666 (for a fragment of a silk dress imported for her from China) and 1929-175-3 (for a goat fleece shawl imported for her from India).

2. Robert Morris to Mary Morris, August 1, 1790, Collection of Papers of Robert Morris, HUNT (quotation). For Washington's birthday, see Simon P. Newman, *Parades and Politics of the Street: Festive Culture in the Early American Republic* (Philadelphia: University of Pennsylvania Press, 2000),

44–82; David Waldstreicher, *In the Midst of Perpetual Fetes: The Making of American Nationalism, 1776–1820* (Chapel Hill: Published for OIEAHC by the University of North Carolina Press, 1997), 109–76; Scott W. Berg, *Grand Avenues: The Story of the French Visionary Who Designed Washington, D.C.* (New York: Pantheon Books, 2007), 188–90; and Richard Norton Smith, *Patriarch: George Washington and the New American Nation* (Boston and New York: Houghton Mifflin Company, 1993), 128–29.

3. Abigail Adams to Abigail Adams Smith, December 26, 1790, in *Letters of Mrs. Adams, the Wife of John Adams*, 4th ed. (Boston: Wilkins, Carter, and Co., 1848), 350–51 (first quotations); Molly Tilghman to Polly Pearce, February 18, 1787, reprinted in J. Hall Pleasants, ed., "Letters of Molly and Hetty Tilghman," *Maryland Historical Magazine* 21 (1926): 146 (last quotation). See also Griswold, *The Republican Court*, 253–63; Russell F. Weigley et al., eds., *Philadelphia: A 300-Year History* (New York: W. W. Norton and Company, 1982), 168–80; Kenneth R. Bowling, "The Federal Government and the Republican Court Move to Philadelphia, November 1790–March 1791," in Kenneth R. Bowling and Donald R. Kennon, eds., *Neither Separate nor Equal: Congress in the 1790s* (Athens, Oh.: Published for the United States Capitol Historical Society by Ohio University Press, 2000), 3–33; Susan Branson, *These Fiery Frenchified Dames: Women and Political Culture in Early National Philadelphia* (Philadelphia: University of Pennsylvania Press, 2001); and Amy Hudson Henderson, "Furnishing the Republican Court: Building and Decorating Philadelphia Homes, 1790–1800" (Ph.D. diss., University of Delaware, 2008).

4. Julian Ursyn Niemcewicz, *Under Their Vine and Fig Tree: Travels Through America in 1797–1799, 1805 with Some Further Account of Life in New Jersey*, trans., ed., and with an introduction and notes by Metchie J. E. Budka (Elizabeth, N.J.: Grassmann Publishing, 1965), 36–37 (first quotations); George Washington, diary entry for May 21, 1787, in Donald Jackson and Dorothy Twohig, eds., *The Diaries of George Washington* (Charlottesville: University Press of Virginia, 1979), 5:159 (last quotation). The grounds occupied nearly three acres. See Robert C. Alberts, *The Golden Voyage: The Life and Times of William Bingham, 1752–1804* (Boston: Houghton-Mifflin, 1969), 157–64; Henry A. Boorse, "The Third Street House in Philadelphia by William Birch: The Inside Story," *Imprint* 14 (1989): 11–17; Henderson, "Furnishing the Republican Court," 92–101.

5. [Benjamin Franklin], *The Way to Wealth*, 1757, in Kenneth Silverman, ed., *Benjamin Franklin: The Autobiography and Other Writings* (New York: Pen-

guin Books, 1986), 215–25 (quotation, emphasis in the original). See Laurel Thatcher Ulrich, *The Age of Homespun: Objects and Stories in the Creation of an American Myth* (New York: Knopf, 2001); Richard L. Bushman, *The Refinement of America: Persons, Houses, Cities* (New York: Knopf, 1992), particularly 181–203; and David S. Shields, *Civil Tongues and Polite Letters in British America* (Chapel Hill: University of North Carolina Press, 1997). William Penn himself had warned against "inexcusable" superfluities of construction and furnishing in his city. See Wayne Andrews, *Architecture, Ambition, and Americans: A Social History of American Architecture*, rev. ed. (New York: Free Press, 1978), 48.

6. Charles Lee to Robert Morris, August 15, 1782, in E. James Ferguson and John Catanzariti, eds., *The Papers of Robert Morris, 1781–1784* (Pittsburgh: University of Pittsburgh Press, 1980), 5:212 (quotation). Philadelphia's *Columbian Magazine* presented this view clearly in November 1787, in a piece stating that "luxury . . . may be permitted in an absolute monarchy, without injury, whilst the introduction of it into a commonwealth will terminate in its destruction." Quoted in David L. Barquist, "'The Honours of a Court' or 'the Severity of Virtue': Household Furnishings and Cultural Aspirations in Philadelphia," in Catherine E. Hutchins, ed., *Shaping a National Culture: The Philadelphia Experience, 1750–1800* (Winterthur, Del.: Henry Francis du Pont Winterthur Museum, 1994), 327. See also *Aurora* (February 15, 1796), cited in Stuart M. Blumin, *The Emergence of the Middle Class: Social Experience in the American City, 1760–1900* (New York: Cambridge University Press, 1989), 18; Gordon S. Wood, *The Creation of the American Republic, 1776–1787* (Chapel Hill: Published for OIEAHC by the University of North Carolina Press, 1969), 65–70, 413–25; and Cathy Matson and Peter Onuf, "Toward a Republican Empire: Interest and Ideology in Revolutionary America," *American Quarterly* 37 (Autumn 1985): 496–531.

7. James Warren to Elbridge Gerry, April 19, 1789, in Charlene Bangs Bickford et al., eds., *Documentary History of the First Federal Congress of the United States of America*, vol. 15, *Correspondence: First Session, March–May 1789* (Baltimore: Johns Hopkins University Press, 2004), 287–88 (first quotation); Robert Morris to Matthew Ridley, October 14, 1781, in E. James Ferguson and John Catanzariti, eds., *The Papers of Robert Morris, 1781–1784* (Pittsburgh: University of Pittsburgh Press, 1977), 3:57 (second quotation); William Bingham to Thomas Willing, quoted in Alberts, *The Golden Voyage*, 157 (third quotations); George Washington to Tobias Lear,

November 14, 1790 (fourth quotation, emphasis in the original), in Mark A. Mastromarino, ed., *The Papers of George Washington: Presidential Series* (Charlottesville: University Press of Virginia, 1996), 6:655–58; George Washington to Catherine Sawbridge Macaulay Graham, January 9, 1790, in Dorothy Twohig, ed., *The Papers of George Washington: Presidential Series* (Charlottesville: University Press of Virginia, 1993), 4:551–54 (last quotation). For a broader review of these concerns, see Stanley Elkins and Eric McKitrick, *The Age of Federalism: The Early American Republic, 1788–1800* (New York: Oxford University Press, 1993), particularly 46–50. Even such a connoisseur of fine dining, furnishing, and living as Thomas Jefferson could fret that at Washington's inaugural ball, the president's sofa became "wicked" in its inappropriate placement above others in the room, as it hinted at a throne. See Franklin B. Sawvel, ed., *The Complete ANAS of Thomas Jefferson* (New York: Round Table Press, 1903), 127–28, and Henderson, "Furnishing the Republican Court," 108.

8. François René Chateaubriand, *Memoirs of Chateaubriand* (London: Henry Colburn, 1848), 1:255 (first quotations); Charles Bulfinch quoted in Alberts, *The Golden Voyage,* 163 (last quotation); and Margaret C. S. Christman, *The First Federal Congress, 1789–1791* (Washington, D.C.: Published by the Smithsonian Institution Press for the National Portrait Gallery and the United States Congress, 1989), 200. Niemcewicz disagreed with Bulfinch's equation of the Bingham mansion to European structures, but he agreed that the house drew censure in America. Bingham's house, he stated, "as opulent as it is, would never be pointed out in the big cities in Europe, but here it attracts attention, criticism and envy." Niemcewicz, *Under Their Vine and Fig Tree,* 37. See also Ethel E. Rasmusson, "Democratic Environment— Aristocratic Aspiration," *Pennsylvania Magazine of History and Biography* 90 (April 1966): 155–82.

9. M. L. E. Moreau de St. Méry, in Kenneth Roberts and Anna M. Roberts, trans. and eds., *Moreau de St. Méry's American Journey, 1793–1798* (Garden City, N.Y.: Doubleday and Co., 1947), 333 (first quotation, emphasis in the original); a subscriber, "For the *General Advertiser,*" [Philadelphia] *General Advertiser* (February 16, 1793) (last quotations, emphasis in the original). A response countering this attack was published in the *General Advertiser* on February 21, 1793. See also Lynn Matluck Brooks, "Emblem of Gaiety, Love, and Legislation: Dance in Eighteenth-Century Philadelphia," *Pennsylvania Magazine of History and Biography* 115 (January 1991): 63–88. For an example of the longevity of these particular tensions, see "A Representa-

tive of Thousands," *A Few Reflections upon the Fancy Ball, Otherwise Known as The City Dancing Assembly* (Philadelphia: G. R. Lilibridge, 1828).

10. Stephen Kingston, [Fran] West, J. M. Nesbitt, Joseph Redman, and J. Swanwick, to the Managers of the New Dancing Assembly, February 13, 1792, "City Dancing Assembly of Philadelphia," oversize folio, AM.3075, HSP (quotations); "Philadelphia, Friday, 24th Feb.," *General Advertiser* (February 24, 1792); "On Wednesday the 22d Instant," *Federal Gazette and Philadelphia Daily Advertiser* (February 24, 1792). See also John F. Watson, *Annals of Philadelphia and Pennsylvania, in the Olden Time; Being a Collection of Memoirs, Anecdotes, and Incidents of the City and its Inhabitants, and of the Earliest Settlements of the Inland Part of Pennsylvania, From the Days of the Founders* (Philadelphia: Penington and Hunt, 1844), 1:285–86.

    The ball of the "New Dancing Assembly" took place in the "New Rooms in Chesnut Street," at Oeller's Hotel. See "The Gentleman who changed his hat" and "On Wednesday the 22d instant," *Federal Gazette and Philadelphia Daily Advertiser* (February 24, 1792), and "Philadelphia, Feb. 23," *The Mail; or, Claypoole's Daily Advertiser* (February 23, 1792). The sources do not state where the "old" Assembly's February 21 ball took place, although it was probably at its usual rooms in Oeller's. See "Philadelphia, 24 November," *Federal Gazette and Philadelphia Daily Advertiser* (November 24, 1790); "Philadelphia Dancing Assembly," *General Advertiser* (October 26, 1791); Thomas Willing Balch, *The Philadelphia Assemblies* (Philadelphia: Allen, Lane and Scott, 1916), 100; and Peter Thompson, *Rum Punch and Revolution: Taverngoing and Public Life in Eighteenth-Century Philadelphia* (Philadelphia: University of Pennsylvania Press, 1998), 190.

11. "Philadelphia, 23d February, 1792," *Federal Gazette and Philadelphia Daily Advertiser* (February 23, 1792); "Philadelphia, Feb. 25," *The Mail; or, Claypoole's Daily Advertiser* (February 25, 1792); "Yesterday was Celebrated," [Philadelphia] *National Gazette* (February 23, 1792); "On Wednesday the 22d instant," *Federal Gazette and Philadelphia Daily Advertiser* (February 24, 1792); and Brooks, "The Philadelphia Dancing Assembly."

12. "Philadelphia, Feb. 25," *The Mail; or, Claypoole's Daily Advertiser* (February 25, 1792).

13. Robert Morris to Robert Morris, Jr., December 19, 1792, Collection of Papers of Robert Morris, HUNT (quotation). For Thomas Morris, see Charles Rappleye, *Robert Morris: Financier of the American Revolution* (New York: Simon and Schuster, 2010), 97–137. For Polly Croxall, see Elizabeth M. Nuxoll, "Illegitimacy, Family Status, and Property in the Early Republic:

The Morris-Croxall Family of New Jersey," *New Jersey History* 113 (Fall/
Winter 1995): 3–21. For an example of Mary Morris's correspondence with
Polly, see Mary Morris to Robert Morris, December 12, 1787, Collection of
Papers of Robert Morris, HUNT.

14. Edward Lawler, Jr., "The President's House in Philadelphia: The Rediscovery of a Lost Landmark," *Pennsylvania History and Biography* 126 (January 2002): 16–19; Robert Morris Diary, June 11, 1782, in E. James Ferguson
and John Catanzariti, eds., *The Papers of Robert Morris, 1781–1784* (Pittsburgh: University of Pittsburgh Press, 1980), 5:376; Hart, "Mary White—
Mrs. Robert Morris," 173; Oberholtzer, *Robert Morris*, 76–77. Catherine
(Kitty) Livingston, sister of John Jay's wife, Sarah, and daughter of Governor William Livingston of New Jersey, also lived with the Morris family in
Philadelphia around this time.

15. Robert Morris to Hugou de Bassville, July 29, 1786, Collection of Papers of
Robert Morris, HUNT (quotation); Gouverneur Morris to Robert Morris,
December 30, 1791, Gouverneur Morris Papers, LOC. See also Hart, "Mary
White—Mrs. Robert Morris," 169–71, 184.

16. Robert Morris to Edward Tilghman, June 21, 1789, Tilghman Family Papers, MDHS (quotation); Robert Morris to Matthew Ridley, November 5,
1783, in Elizabeth M. Nuxoll and Mary A. Gallagher, eds., *The Papers of
Robert Morris, 1781–1784* (Pittsburgh: University of Pittsburgh Press,
1995), 8:729–34; Robert Morris to Mary Morris, December 12, 1787, Collection of Papers of Robert Morris, HUNT; entries for January 29, April
21, and May 12, 1792, in "Journal, 1791–1801," Robert Morris Business Papers, HSP; Oberholtzer, *Robert Morris*, 268–71.

17. Hetty Morris to Robert Morris, February 10, 1787, Box 18, Robert Morris
Papers, LOC; Robert Morris to Mary Morris, November 15, 1787, Mary
Morris to Robert Morris, December 12, 1787, Robert Morris to Mary Morris, July 12, 1789 (first quotation), and March 4, 1790 (last quotation), Collection of Papers of Robert Morris, HUNT; Mary Morris to Gouverneur
Morris, June 9, 1791, Gouverneur Morris Papers, COLU (second quotations); Robert Morris to Matthew Ridley, November 5, 1783, in Nuxoll and
Gallagher, *Papers of Robert Morris*, 8:729–34; entries for November 26,
1791, April 21, 1792, June 4, 1792, July 14, 1792, and March 19, 1793, in "Journal, 1791–1801," Robert Morris Business Papers, HSP.

18. Mary Morris to Robert Morris, January 13, 1788, Collection of Papers of
Robert Morris, HUNT (quotation). For Mary's illnesses and worries, see,
for example, Hetty Morris to Robert Morris, February 10, 1787, Box 18,

Robert Morris Papers, LOC; Mary Morris to Robert Morris, January 13, 1788, and Robert Morris to Thomas Morris, November 29, 1792, Collection of Papers of Robert Morris, HUNT; Tobias Lear to George Washington, October 14, 1790, in Mastromarino, *Papers of George Washington: Presidential Series*, 6:557–59. For an example of Mary's European shopping orders, see Mary Morris to Gouverneur Morris, June 9, 1791, Gouverneur Morris Papers, COLU. For her Philadelphia purchases and orders, see entries throughout 1792, for example, in "Journal, 1791–1801," Robert Morris Business Papers, HSP. For context regarding women as "silent partners" in their husbands' business pursuits, see Susan Branson, "Women and the Family Economy in the Early Republic: The Case of Elizabeth Meredith," *Journal of the Early Republic* 16 (Spring 1996): 47–71.

19. Robert Morris to Gouverneur Morris, January 2, 1791, quoted in Hart, "Mary White—Mrs. Robert Morris," 181 (first quotation); Robert Morris to Ralph Forster, August 7, 1783, in Nuxoll and Gallagher, *Papers of Robert Morris*, 8:406 (second quotation); Mary Morris to Gouverneur Morris, June 9, 1791, Gouverneur Morris Papers, COLU (last quotation). For Esther White's burial, see Edward L. Clark, *A Record of the Inscriptions on the Tablets and Grave-stones in the Burial Grounds of Christ Church, Philadelphia* (Philadelphia: Collins, 1864), 15. Robert and Mary also paid pew rent at times at St. Peter's Episcopal Church. See entry for April 17, 1792, in "Journal, 1791–1801," Robert Morris Business Papers, HSP.

   Morris's letters are filled throughout with loving sentiments toward his wife, and they indicate that the affection was returned. See, for example, Robert Morris to Mary Morris, March 4, 1789, and Robert Morris to Mary Morris, September 6, 1789, Collection of Papers of Robert Morris, HUNT.

20. For full explorations of these issues, see Bernard L. Herman, *Town House: Architecture and Material Life in the Early American City, 1780–1830* (Chapel Hill: Published for the OIEAHC by the University of North Carolina Press, 2005); Shields, *Civil Tongues and Polite Letters in British America;* Catherine Allgor, *Parlor Politics: In Which the Ladies of Washington Help Build a City and a Government* (Charlottesville: University of Virginia Press, 2000); Bushman, *The Refinement of America;* Barbara G. Carson and Kym S. Rice, *Ambitious Appetites: Dining, Behavior, and Patterns of Consumption in Federal Washington* (Washington, D.C.: American Institute of Architects Press, 1990); Rasmusson, "Democratic Environment—Aristocratic Aspiration," 155–82; and Henderson, "Furnishing the Republican Court." For

the Morrises' interest in card games, see J. M. Fenster, "Nation of Gamblers," *American Heritage* 45 (September 1994): 34–51.

21. Marquis de Chastellux, *Travels in North America, in the Years 1780–81–82* (New York: White, Gallaher, and White, 1827), 99–100 (first quotations). The original English translator added that Morris had made "great additions" to the Masters-Penn house on Market Street, suggesting that Morris "is the first who has introduced the luxury of hot-houses and ice-houses on the continent." The translator also believed that Morris's "luxury" was not "to be outdone by any commercial voluptuary of London" (99). Harrison Gray Otis to Rev. Dr. Lowell, November 10, 1846, reprinted in "Letters Relating to the Character and Services of the Hon. J. Lowell," *Historical Magazine* 1 (September 1857): 262 (last quotations); Tax Assessor's Ledger, 1783, Middle Ward, City Archives, Philadelphia, Pennsylvania; Sumner, *The Financier and the Finances of the American Revolution*, 2:222–25.

   See also Prince de Broglie, quoted in E. W. Balch, trans., "The Narrative of the Prince de Broglie," in "Notes and Queries," *Pennsylvania Magazine of History and Biography* 1 (1877): 224; Henderson, "Furnishing the Republican Court," 67; and also James Brown to William Magee, June 8, 1787: "We spent last evening with Mr. Robert Morris. . . . He is a large fat man, very sociable & easy in his manners. The party at his house consisted of about forty of both sexes; no language I am master of could convey an idea of the elegance of the entertainment. Mr. Morris' house is furnished in a stile superior to anything I have ever seen. The company being so numerous I had an opportunity of seeing all the apartments. The evening was spent at cards and the celebrated Mr. (Francis) Hopkinson (or more probably Joseph) gave us several pieces of music on a harpsichord of the newest invention. Some of the ladies also played and sung. Rich lemonade was brot round in silver urns, and a little before supper a profusion of iced creams was served to all the company, but when supper was announced we were introduced to a table, more resplendent than any I had ever beheld." Quoted in E. James Ferguson and John Catanzariti, eds., *The Papers of Robert Morris, 1781–1784* (Pittsburgh: University of Pittsburgh Press, 1973), 1:173–74.

22. H. E. Scudder, ed., *Recollections of Samuel Breck With Passages From His Note-Books (1771–1862)* (Philadelphia: Potter and Coates, 1877), 203 (quotations). Lawler, "The President's House in Philadelphia," 17–22; Griswold, *The Republican Court*, 271; Thompson Westcott, *The Historic Mansions and Buildings of Philadelphia With Some Notice of Their Owners and Occupants* (Philadelphia: Porter and Coates, 1877), 354–55; Oberholtzer, *Robert Morris*, 294–95.

As William Maclay's comments on Morris's bawdy talk (cited in the previous chapter) make clear, some observers associated an unpalatable edge with these entertainments. Historian Ethel E. Rasmusson found that "Mrs. Bingham punctuated her conversation with oaths and facetious anecdotes, and the after-dinner conversation at the Morrises was reputed to degenerate sometimes into vulgarity." See Rasmusson, "Democratic Environment—Aristocratic Aspiration," 167.

23. *First Census of the United States 1790: Pennsylvania* (Washington, D.C.: U.S. Government Printing Office, 1908), 227; Scudder, *Recollections of Samuel Breck*, 203 (quotation). See also Rufus W. Griswold, *The Republican Court, or, American Society in the Days of Washington* (New York: D. Appleton and Company, 1867), 311.

Robert Morris's fullest views on slavery are expressed in a 1786 letter to George Washington. In his letter, Morris recounted his support for the return of a friend's slave but noted that the Quaker "Society which attacked him tread on popular ground, and as their Views are disinterested as to themselves, and *sometimes* very laudable as to the objects of their Compassion, it is not a very pleasant thing to Attack them." Robert Morris to George Washington, April 26, 1786, in W. W. Abbot, ed., *The Papers of George Washington: Confederation Series* (Charlottesville: University Press of Virginia, 1995), 4:29–30. The federal census showed no slaves in the Morris household in 1790. Philadelphia city tax records showed that Morris owned one slave valued at £60 in the early 1780s. By 1785, this slave was listed as a "Negro woman," and the family was also taxed for one black indentured servant. The indentured servant does not appear after the 1786 assessment. Despite the enslaved woman's absence in the 1790 census record, the tax records show that Morris still owned her in 1791, but the family must have sold or freed her in 1792 (or she died), as neither she nor any other slaves would be listed in their tax assessments after that year. Tax Assessor's Ledgers, Middle Ward, 1783, 1785–1787, 1789, 1791–1793, Philadelphia City Archives. In 1793, Morris's accounts show that he paid "John Miller for a mulatto Boy named [Tonas?] who is to serve me eight years" and he paid Patrick Colvin "for negroes and other property bought of him." It is not clear where these slaves worked nor when this transaction originated. Entry for April 18, 1793, "Journal, 1791–1801," Robert Morris Business Papers, HSP. See Chapter 3 for Morris's use of slaves at his industrial works.

The same Philadelphia tax records above show that in 1789 the family owned one "coach," one "chariot," one "phaeton," and one "pleasure waggon," in addition to five horses. By 1791, the family had sold the phaeton, and by

1793, the family had sold one of the horses. In 1784, Morris thanked William Bingham, then in London, for "sending me the Crests for my Carriage," presumably heraldic. Robert Morris to William Bingham, January 19, 1784, in Elizabeth M. Nuxoll and Mary A. Gallagher, eds., *The Papers of Robert Morris, 1781–1784* (Pittsburgh: University of Pittsburgh Press, 1999), 9:39–40.

24. Tobias Lear to George Washington, October 17, 1790, in Mastromarino, *Papers of George Washington: Presidential Series*, 6:569 (first quotations); "Four Dollars Reward," *The Mail; or, Claypoole's Daily Advertiser* (November 30, 1792) (last quotations); Robert Morris to William Coates, November 30, 1796, Robert Morris Papers, LOC. In a related transaction on September 3, 1792, Morris noted in his records that he paid "L. Farmer for Indenting George Nicholas Surbahn who is to serve me 4 years" at his Delaware Works industrial site. Entry for September 3, 1792, in "Journal, 1791–1801," Robert Morris Business Papers, HSP.

Mary Morris's direct involvement with the servants is recorded in Robert Morris's account books, where he occasionally notes that he has "paid Mrs. Morris to pay" various household workers. For example, see entries for August 18, 1792, and April 26, 1794, "Journal, 1791–1801," Robert Morris Business Papers, HSP. In 1801, Robert noted that cleanliness was something his wife deemed "highly important," and the couple valued servants who could meet Mary's standards in this regard. He added more generally that "I attributed to Mrs. Morris the merit of an attentive superintendence which caused the performance of domestick duty" among their many servants. Robert Morris to Thomas Jefferson, March 2, 1801, in Barbara B. Oberg et al., eds., *The Papers of Thomas Jefferson* (Princeton, N.J.: Princeton University Press, 2006), 33:121–22.

25. Robert Morris to John Bondfield, April 20, 1795, Robert Morris Papers, LOC (quotation). All the rest of this information is from "Journal, 1791–1801," Robert Morris Business Papers, HSP. "Poirez" seems to have been spelled "Poives" by Morris in 1792.

26. George Washington to Tobias Lear, October 27, 1790, in Mastromarino, *Papers of George Washington: Presidential Series*, 6:589–91 (first quotation); George Washington to Gouverneur Morris, October 13, 1789, in Twohig, *Papers of George Washington: Presidential Series*, 4:176–79 (last quotation, emphasis in the original).

27. Robert Morris to Mary Morris, April 25, 1790, Collection of Papers of Robert Morris, HUNT (quotations); [Philadelphia] *Independent Gazetteer* (April 30, 1791); James Hardie, *The Philadelphia Directory and Register* (Philadel-

phia: Dobson, 1793), 205; and Deborah Mathias Gough, *Christ Church, Philadelphia: The Nation's Church in a Changing City* (Philadelphia: University of Pennsylvania Press, 1995), 92. See also entries for September 18, 1792; November 10, 1792; May 11, 1793; March 10, 1794; May 30, 1796; in "Journal, 1791–1801," Robert Morris Business Papers, HSP.

28. Mary Morris, quoted in Hart, "Mary White—Mrs. Robert Morris," 161 (quotation). Philadelphian Jacob Hiltzheimer reported buying "a little pig imported by Mr. Morris from the East Indies" at the Hills on June 15, 1789. See Jacob Cox Parsons, *Extracts from the Diary of Jacob Hiltzheimer, of Philadelphia, 1765–1798* (Philadelphia: William F. Fell and Co., 1883), 153. In 1794, Morris's groundskeeper at the Hills advertised his sale of "a fresh and general assortment, of garden and flower seeds, with a variety of ornamental and flowering shrubs and plants, and also early vegetables," *The Philadelphia Gazette and Universal Daily Advertiser* (March 6, 1794), 2. In 1795, Thomas Jefferson's interest was piqued by the imported Spanish sheep grazing on the property. See Robert Morris to Thomas Jefferson, June 1, 1795, Robert Morris Papers, LOC.

A detailed description of the Hills can be found in "Schedule of Property within the State of Pennsylvania conveyed by Robert Morris to the Honble. James Biddle Esqr. and Mr. Wm. Bell for the use and account of the Pennsylvania Property Company," [1797], Robert Morris Papers, LOC. See also Westcott, *Historic Mansions and Buildings of Philadelphia*, 367–69; Joan Church Roberts, "The Schuylkill Villas: A Revealing Look into the History of Extraordinary 18th Century Treasures in Philadelphia's Fairmount Park," 2006 Loan Exhibit, *Philadelphia Antiques Show* (Philadelphia: 2006), 124–28; Barbara Ann Chernow, "Robert Morris: Land Speculator, 1790–1801" (Ph.D. diss., Columbia University, 1974), 102–4; Rappleye, *Robert Morris*, 23–24; Oberholtzer, *Robert Morris*, 291–94; Sumner, *The Financier and the Finances of the American Revolution*, 2:227; and Roger W. Moss, *Historic Houses of Philadelphia: A Tour of the Region's Museum Homes* (Philadelphia: University of Pennsylvania Press, 1998), 59–108.

29. Manasseh Cutler, quoted in William Parker Cutler and Julia Perkins Cutler, *Life, Journals and Correspondence of Rev. Manasseh Cutler, L.L.D.* (Cincinnati: Robert Clarke and Co., 1888), 1:256–57 (first quotation); Robert Morris to Mary Morris, December 27, 1787, Collection of Papers of Robert Morris, HUNT (last quotation).

Susan Dillwyn provided a description of a Schuylkill villa, probably the Hills (or perhaps the Woodlands), in May 1789: "Not far from the ferry house and in a level with it there is a large green house fill'd with a variety of plants in a very flourishing state. The lemons and oranges in particular appear as my Uncle Jemmy says in as high perfection as in the West Indies, in their native soil & air. Behind this is a large Ball room, which opens on a lawn with borders of flowers and gravel winding walks—beyond this lawn the grounds are very uneven, but their inequalities are turn'd by proper management into additional beauties." Susan Dillwyn to [William Dillwyn], May 2, 1789, Dillwyn Manuscripts, 1770–1793, HSP.

30. Robert Morris to Mary Morris, May 13, 1789 [two letters]; Robert Morris to Mary Morris, August 28, 1789; and Robert Morris to Mary Morris, September 6, 1789; all from Collection of Papers of Robert Morris, HUNT (quotations, emphasis in the original). While Washington lived with the Morrises during the constitutional convention in 1787, he dined with them at the Hills. See entries for May, June, July, and September 1787 in Jackson and Twohig, *The Diaries of George Washington*, 5:164–72, 183–89, 246–48. For the Indians' visit in 1792, see entries for April 14 and 17, 1792, in "Journal, 1791–1801," Robert Morris Business Papers, HSP; and Robert Morris to Thomas Morris, May 12, 1792, Thomas Morris manuscripts, NYHS.

31. *National Gazette* (July 7, 1792), quoted in Waldstreicher, *In the Midst of Perpetual Fetes*, 128.

CHAPTER 3. HIS PLANS

1. Robert Morris to Mary Morris, April 26, 1788, Collection of Papers of Robert Morris, HUNT. For similar concerns about indebtedness among Morris's peers, see Terry Bouton, *Taming Democracy: "The People," the Founders, and the Troubled Ending of the American Revolution* (New York: Oxford University Press, 2007), 67–70.

2. For Morris's estimation of his "neglect of my own affairs" during this period, see Robert Morris to George Olney, September 23, 1783, and Robert Morris to Matthew Ridley, November 5, 1783, in Elizabeth M. Nuxoll and Mary A. Gallagher, eds., *The Papers of Robert Morris, 1781–1784* (Pittsburgh: University of Pittsburgh Press, 1995), 8:539 and 732. His partnerships during the 1780s included Constable, Rucker, and Company in New York; Willing, Morris, and Swanwick in Philadelphia (which reemerged out of Samuel Inglis and Company in 1783); Tench Tilghman and Company in Baltimore; Harrison, Nickolls, and Company in Virginia; and Robert Hazlehurst and Company in Charleston. See Clarence L. Ver Steeg, *Robert*

Morris, Revolutionary Financier: With an Analysis of His Earlier Career (Philadelphia: University of Pennsylvania Press, 1954), 29–36 and 187–93; "Introduction," in Nuxoll and Gallagher, *Papers of Robert Morris*, 8:xxxviii and 857–82; "Introduction," in Elizabeth M. Nuxoll and Mary A. Gallagher, eds., *The Papers of Robert Morris, 1781–1784* (Pittsburgh: University of Pittsburgh Press, 1999), 9:xlv; and Elizabeth M. Nuxoll, "Robert Morris and the Shaping of the Post-Revolutionary American Economy," unpublished paper, 9–10. For his role in the China trade, see Clarence L. Ver Steeg, "Financing and Outfitting the First United States Ship to China," *Pacific Historical Review* 22 (1953): 1–12; Philip Chadwick Foster Smith, *The Empress of China* (Philadelphia: Philadelphia Maritime Museum, 1984); and Mary A. Y. Gallagher, "Charting a New Course for the China Trade: The Late Eighteenth Century American Model," *American Neptune* 57 (1997): 201–15.

    For general treatments of Morris's late commercial activities, see Charles Rappleye, *Robert Morris: Financier of the American Revolution* (New York: Simon and Schuster, 2010); William Graham Sumner, *The Financier and the Finances of the American Revolution* (New York: Dodd, Mead, and Company, 1892); and Thomas M. Doerflinger, *A Vigorous Spirit of Enterprise: Merchants and Economic Development in Revolutionary Philadelphia* (Chapel Hill: Published for OIEAHC by the University of North Carolina Press, 1986).

3. Robert Morris to Tench Tilghman, November 4, 1784 (first quotation), and Robert Morris to Tench Tilghman, March 28, 1785 (second quotations), Robert Morris Papers, NYPL; Robert Morris to Nathaniel Green, January 2, 1786, Collection of Papers of Robert Morris, HUNT (last quotation). See Nuxoll, "Robert Morris and the Shaping of the Post-Revolutionary American Economy," 10–12; Rappleye, *Robert Morris*, 416–24, 436–37; Sumner, *The Financier and the Finances of the American Revolution*, 2:162–74; Barbara Ann Chernow, "Robert Morris: Land Speculator, 1790–1801" (Ph.D. diss., Columbia University, 1974), 28–30; Barbara A. Chernow, "Robert Morris: Genesee Land Speculator," *New York History* 58 (1977): 196–97; and Jacob M. Price, *France and the Chesapeake: A History of the French Tobacco Monopoly, 1674–1791, and of Its Relationship to the British and American Tobacco Trades* (Ann Arbor: University of Michigan Press, 1973).

4. Elizabeth M. Nuxoll, "The Financier as Senator: Robert Morris of Pennsylvania, 1789–1795," in Kenneth R. Bowling and Donald R. Kennon, eds., *Neither Separate nor Equal: Congress in the 1790s* (Athens, Oh.: Published for the United States Capitol Historical Society by Ohio University Press, 2000), 93 (first quotation); Robert Morris to Mary Morris, November 28,

1787, Collection of Papers of Robert Morris, HUNT (last quotations). See also Nuxoll, "Robert Morris and the Shaping of the Post-Revolutionary American Economy," 11; Nuxoll and Gallagher, *Papers of Robert Morris*, 9:418; Abigail Adams to Richard Cranch, May 10, 1787, in Margaret A. Hogan et al., eds., *The Adams Papers: Adams Family Correspondence* (Cambridge, Mass.: Belknap Press of Harvard University Press, 2007), 8:42–43; and entry for June 28, 1787, in Donald Jackson and Dorothy Twohig, eds., *The Diaries of George Washington* (Charlottesville: University Press of Virginia, 1979), 5:172, in which Washington relates hearing the news while dining "in a large Company" at the Morrises, "a little mal-apropos." Morris called his tobacco failures the "Tobacco Scrape." For example, see Robert Morris to Constable Rucker & Co., October 31, 1787, Robert Morris Papers, LOC.

A useful introduction to the complexities inherent in cash and credit exchanges during this time can be found in Pierre Gervais, "A Game of Claims and Expectations: Credit, Failure, and Personal Relationships Across the Atlantic" *Common-Place* 10 (April 2010), www.common-place.org /vol-10/no-03/gervais/ (accessed July 1, 2011).

5. Robert Morris to Mary Morris, December 27, 1787 (first quotation), Robert Morris to Mary Morris, September 6, 1789 (second quotation), Robert Morris to Mary Morris, June 19, 1790 (fourth quotation), all in Collection of Papers of Robert Morris, HUNT; Gouverneur Morris to Robert Morris, February 17, 1789, Gouverneur Morris Papers, LOC (third quotation); Arthur Bryan, writing in 1788, quoted in Bruce H. Mann, *Republic of Debtors: Bankruptcy in the Age of American Independence* (Cambridge, Mass.: Harvard University Press, 2002), 207 (fifth quotation); Robert Morris to Francis Hopkinson, January 21, 1788 (transcription), Box 2, Redwood Collection, MDHS (last quotation); Sumner, *The Financier and the Finances of the American Revolution*, 2:276–78.

Descriptions of Morris's merrymaking from this time can be found in Robert Morris to Gouverneur Morris, January 2, 1790, Gouverneur Morris Papers, COLU, and Robert Morris to Mary Morris, April 25, 1790, Collection of Papers of Robert Morris, HUNT.

6. A superb view into the issues surrounding eighteenth-century American land speculation can be found in Charles Royster, *The Fabulous History of the Dismal Swamp Company: A Story of George Washington's Times* (New York: Random House, 2000). Also instructive is Alan Taylor, *Liberty Men and Great Proprietors: The Revolutionary Settlement of the Maine Frontier, 1760–1820* (Chapel Hill: University of North Carolina Press, 1990), and Alan Taylor,

William Cooper's Town: Power and Persuasion on the Frontier of the Early American Republic (New York: Knopf, 1995). For background and context regarding Morris's land speculations, see Mann, *Republic of Debtors;* Bouton, *Taming Democracy;* Doerflinger, *A Vigorous Spirit of Enterprise;* Robert D. Arbuckle, *Pennsylvania Speculator and Patriot: The Entrepreneurial John Nicholson, 1757–1800* (University Park: Pennsylvania State University Press, 1975); Robert F. Jones, *"The King of the Alley": William Duer: Politician, Entrepreneur, and Speculator, 1768–1799* (Philadelphia: American Philosophical Society, 1992); and Chernow, "Robert Morris: Land Speculator."

Morris expressed an interest in land as early as the 1770s, while a partner at Willing and Morris. See [Robert Morris], *In the Account of Property* (Philadelphia [1801]), 19–20. A manuscript version of this important pamphlet is available in the Robert Morris Papers, NYPL. Morris also joined with Samuel Beall and John May in an early partnership formed for the purpose of "procuring waste or unappropriated lands in the sd state of Virginia." Quoted in Ver Steeg, *Robert Morris, Revolutionary Financier,* 35 (see also 5); Chernow, "Robert Morris: Land Speculator," 10.

7. Robert Morris to John Richard, May 20, 1790, Gouverneur Morris Papers, COLU (first quotation); Gouverneur Morris to Robert Morris, January 29, 1789, and April 10, 1789 (last quotation), in Gouverneur Morris Papers, LOC; and Nuxoll, "Robert Morris and the Shaping of the Post-Revolutionary American Economy," 13. For Robert and Gouverneur's early experiments with lands along the Saint Lawrence River, see Robert Morris to Gouverneur Morris, July 23, 1790, Gouverneur Morris Papers, COLU.

8. Robert Morris to Gouverneur Morris, August 8, 1790, Gouverneur Morris Papers, COLU (quotation); Kenneth R. Bowling and Helen E. Veit, eds., *Documentary History of the First Federal Congress of the United States of America,* vol. 9, *The Diary of William Maclay and Other Notes on Senate Debates* (Baltimore: Johns Hopkins University Press, 1988), 122–26; Robert Morris to John Richard, May 20, 1790, Gouverneur Morris Papers, COLU; Gouverneur Morris to Robert Morris, November 16, 1790, and December 30, 1791, Gouverneur Morris Papers, LOC.

Morris's initial purchase of one million acres in New York was informally known as the Phelps-Gorham purchase. An intermediary, Samuel Ogden, became involved in the proceedings on behalf of Morris. For a map of the land, see Charles F. Milliken, *A History of Ontario County, New York and Its People* (New York: Lewis Historical Publishing Co., 1911), 1:19. Two deeds from the sale are reprinted in *Report of Special Committee to Investigate the Indian Problem of the State of New York, Appointed by the Assembly of 1888* (Albany: Troy Press Company, 1889), 112–16. See also Chernow, "Robert Morris: Genesee Land Speculator," 199–204; Chernow, "Robert Morris: Land Speculator," 35–88; Sumner, *The Financier and the Finances of the American Revolution,* 2:255–62; and "Robert Morris, Senator from Pennsylvania," in William Charles DiGiacomantonio et al., eds., *Documentary History of the First Federal Congress of the United States of America,* vol. 14, *Debates in the House of Representatives: Third Session: December 1790–March 1791: Biographies of Members* (Baltimore: Johns Hopkins University Press, 1995), 768–69.

9. Robert Morris to Messrs W. & J. Willink, March 16, 1795, Robert Morris Papers, LOC (quotations). Morris also had land investments in Canada, along the Saint Lawrence River, which he was negotiating just before his large Genesee purchase. See Robert Morris to Gouverneur Morris, July 23, 1790, Gouverneur Morris Papers, COLU. See also *In the Account of Property,* 13–22. Rappleye, *Robert Morris,* 482–84, 493–97; M. Ruth Reilly Kelly, "'Rightfully Theirs and Valid in the Law': Western Pennsylvania Land Wars, 1792–1810," *Pennsylvania History* 71 (Winter 2004): 25–51; Chernow, "Robert Morris: Land Speculator," 97; Sumner, *The Financier and the Finances of the American Revolution,* 2:251–52; and James F. Vivian, "A Note on the Maryland Land Holdings of Robert Morris," *Maryland Historical Magazine* 61 (Winter 1966): 348–53. In July 1790, Gouverneur Morris itemized his own estimation of Robert Morris's major real estate holdings (before the Genesee purchase later that year) in a letter to Amsterdam investors. He calculated them to be worth a total of $740,000, "besides some very considerable tracts in the western Country." Gouverneur Morris to Messrs N. & J. Van Staphorsts & Hubbard, July 13, 1790, Gouverneur Morris Papers, LOC.

10. In the Robert Morris Papers at New York Public Library, there is an undated list of property (circa 1789) owned by Morris in the Philadelphia region, listing twenty-six separate sites, including his "dwelling House" on Market Street, the Stedman-Galloway house and lot at Sixth and Market, a lot on Eighth Street with a house leased to artist Robert Pine, a large lot on South Street, and several lots in the Northern Liberties, among others, totaling £78,492.19.4. See also *In the Account of Property,* 11–22. For an example of Morris's farming rentals, see entry for June 1, 1792, in "Journal, 1791–1801," Robert Morris Business Papers, HSP.

11. Gouverneur Morris to Robert Morris, August 31, 1790 (first quotation, emphasis in the original); September 23, 1790 (second quotation); November

29, 1790; December 31, 1790; March 30, 1791; February 14, 1792 (last quotation); April 10, 1792, and Gouverneur Morris to William Temple Franklin, February 27, 1791 (third quotation), all in Gouverneur Morris Papers, LOC. For an example of a critique of American land sales in Paris, see the 1789 engraving "Vente des deserts du Scioto, par des Anglo-americains," in the European Political Print Collection at the American Antiquarian Society, Worcester, Massachusetts. See also Cathy Matson, "Flimsy Fortunes: Americans' Old Relationship with Paper Speculation and Panic," in *Common-Place* 10 (April 2010), www.common-place.org/vol-10/no-03/matson/ (accessed July 1, 2011); Cathy Matson, "Public Vices, Private Benefit: William Duer and His Circle, 1776–1792," in William Pencak and Conrad Edick Wright, eds., *New York and the Rise of American Capitalism: Economic Development and the Social and Political History of an American State, 1780–1870* (New York: New York Historical Society, 1989); and Jones, *"The King of the Alley."*

12. François-Alexandre-Frédéric, duc de La Rochefoucauld-Liancourt, *Travels Through the United States of North America, the Country of the Iroquois, and Upper Canada, in the Years 1795, 1796, and 1797* (London: R. Phillips, 1799), 270 (first quotation). For the Delaware Works, see entry for July 6, 1792, in "Journal, 1791–1801," Robert Morris Business Papers, HSP; Robert Morris to Alexander Hamilton, December 18, 1795, and "Schedule of Property within the State of Pennsylvania conveyed by Robert Morris to the Honble. James Biddle Esqr. and Mr. Wm. Bell for the use and account of the Pennsylvania Property Company," [1797], Robert Morris Papers, LOC. See also Sumner, *The Financier and the Finances of the American Revolution*, 2:175–77; Ellis Paxson Oberholtzer, *Robert Morris: Patriot and Financier* (New York: Macmillan Company, 1903), 295–97, Nuxoll, "Robert Morris and the Shaping of the Post-Revolutionary American Economy," 12–13; Chernow, "Robert Morris: Land Speculator," 98–100; and "Robert Morris, Senator from Pennsylvania," in DiGiacomantonio et al., *Debates in the House of Representatives*, 768. For an example of goods produced at the Works, see Isaac Hazlehurst & Co. ad in *Pennsylvania Packet* (February 21, 1789). For the purchase and sale of slaves related to the works, see entries for April 5, 18, and 27, 1793, in "Journal, 1791–1801," and July 7, 1794, in "Journal, 1794–1801," all in Robert Morris Business Papers, HSP. For Morris's involvement in another Pennsylvania foundry, see Charles E. Peterson, "Morris, Foxall, and the Eagle Works: A Pioneer Steam Engine Boring Cannon," *Canal History and Technology Proceedings* 7 (March 1988):

244 NOTES TO PAGE 56

207–40, and for Morris's own thoughts on investing in the Baltimore Iron Works, see Robert Morris to Tench Tilghman, March 28, 1785, Robert Morris Papers, NYPL.

For Morris's silk-related activities, see entry for May 12, 1792, in "Journal, 1791–1801," Robert Morris Business Papers, HSP; "We are informed," [Philadelphia] *General Advertiser and Political, Commercial, and Literary Journal* (April 27, 1791).

For Morris's mining activities, see entries for July 7, 1792, December 1, 1792, June 22, 1793, August 5, 1793, November 30, 1793, and February 22, 1794, in Journal 1791–1801, and entry for December 13, 1794, in "Journal, 1794–1801," Robert Morris Business Papers, HSP. Morris also operated a stone quarry on the Schuylkill River; see Robert Morris to Henry Drinker, March 23, 1789, Henry S. Drinker Papers, HSP.

13. Jacob Cox Parsons, ed., *Extracts From the Diary of Jacob Hiltzheimer, of Philadelphia, 1765–1798* (Philadelphia: William F. Fell and Co., 1893), 171 (quotation, entry for September 14, 1791). See also entry for February 7, 1791, 166. For Morris's canal investments, see entries for April 21, June 1 and 4, August 25, and December 1, 1792; April 18, July 22, August 31, and November 30, 1793; and April 5 and September 10, 1794, in "Journal, 1791–1801," Robert Morris Business Papers, HSP. For Morris's road and bridge investments, see entries for June 8 and December 15, 1792; February 16 and November 30, 1793, in "Journal, 1791–1801," and June 14, 1794, in "Journal, 1794–1801," Robert Morris Business Papers, HSP. For his navigation company work, see "The President and Managers of the Schuylkill and Susquehanna Navigation Company . . . ," [Philadelphia] *Claypoole's Daily Advertiser* (February 24, 1792), and Doerflinger, *A Vigorous Spirit of Enterprise*, 329.

As these activities might suggest, Morris also joined organizations related to agriculture. He was a member of the Philadelphia Society for Promoting Agriculture, the Society for Promoting the Cultivation of Vines, and the Society for Promoting Maple Sugar. See entries for February 15 and May 3, 1794, in "Journal, 1791–1801," Robert Morris Business Papers, HSP, and Charles Coleman Sellers, "Portraits and Miniatures by Charles Willson Peale," *Transaction of the American Philosophical Society* 42 (1952): 36.

Morris's clublike work with improvement companies blended into his charity work, as in his leadership of the St. George's Society. He made periodic donations to a range of individuals, including "Thos. McFall a poor soldier," "Guillaume Vaillant a french man," J. Parker, John Hobart,

Alexander Hyens, "two poor women," "Count DeCockburn," "Hammet a negro," and a "Miss Cheir," the largest sum among which was $15. In May 1793, he contributed £3 toward the relief of the sufferers of a local Philadelphia fire, and the following year he donated $1,000 to victims of a fire in Boston. See entries for December 5, 1791, October 1 and 6, 1792, May 19 and June 22, 1793, and January 11 and April 5, 1794, in "Journal, 1791–1801"; and May 17, October 25, December 13, and December 31, 1794, in "Journal, 1794–1801," Robert Morris Business Papers, HSP; and [Boston] *American Apollo* (August 21, 1794): 3. The sum of these donations was dwarfed by his speculations.

14. Entry for January 14, 1792, in "Journal, 1791–1801," Robert Morris Business Papers, HSP; George G. Evans, *Illustrated History of the United States Mint* (Philadelphia: George G. Evans, 1891), 13–14. Morris's most ambitious venture into public securities involved a plan formed in the late 1780s with Gouverneur Morris, William Duer, William Constable, and Samuel Osgood to purchase the entire outstanding American debt to France (which consisted of $34 million) at half its face value, in the expectation that the debt would be more fully redeemed. This particular transaction never transpired. See E. James Ferguson, *The Power of the Purse: A History of American Public Finance* (Chapel Hill: Published for OIEAHC by the University of North Carolina Press, 1961), 264–71, and Max M. Mintz, *Gouverneur Morris and the American Revolution* (Norman: University of Oklahoma Press, 1970), 205–6 and 227–28. Beyond the pages of his journals, examples of Morris's trading and purchasing bank stocks can be found in Robert Morris to Alexander Hamilton, November 13, 1789, in Harold C. Syrett, ed., *The Papers of Alexander Hamilton* (New York: Columbia University Press, 1961), 5:513–14, and Alexander Hamilton to Brockholst Livingston, March 30, 1790, Brockholst Livingston to Alexander Hamilton, April 4, 1790, and Robert Morris to Alexander Hamilton, April 4, 1790, in Harold C. Syrett, ed., *The Papers of Alexander Hamilton* (New York: Columbia University Press, 1961), 6:329–30, 347–49. For an example of his purchase of insurance shares, see entry for June 29, 1793, in "Journal, 1791–1801," Robert Morris Business Papers, HSP. See also Bowling and Veit, *The Diary of William Maclay*, 327; Nuxoll, "Robert Morris and the Shaping of the Post-Revolutionary American Economy"; Nuxoll, "The Financier as Senator," 108; and Mann, *Republic of Debtors*, 112–27.

General background on financial speculation in the early American republic can be found in Jane Kamensky, *The Exchange Artist: A Tale of*

High-Flying Speculation and America's First Banking Collapse (New York: Viking Press, 2008); and Ferguson, *The Power of the Purse.*

15. Robert Morris to Gouverneur Morris, October 31, 1790, Gouverneur Morris Papers, LOC (first quotations); Robert Morris to Edward Tilghman, August 15, 1789, Tilghman Family Papers, MDHS (last quotation). See also Robert Morris to Walter Stewart, July 28, 1790, No. 59 in *G.51.7.4, Boston Public Library, Boston, Massachusetts.

16. Benjamin Rush to Mrs. Rush, August 12, 1791, in L. H. Butterfield, ed., *Letters of Benjamin Rush* (Princeton, N.J.: Published for the American Philosophical Society by Princeton University Press, 1951), 1:602–3 (quotation); entries for December 24, 26, and 31, 1791, and January 7, 1792, in "Journal, 1791–1801," Robert Morris Business Papers, HSP; Mann, *Republic of Debtors*, 112–14, 192–96; Robert Morris to John Nicholson and John Donaldson, April 28, 1792, Collection of Papers of Robert Morris, HUNT. See also John C. Miller, *Alexander Hamilton: Portrait in Paradox* (New York: Harper, 1959), 268–70; Doerflinger, *A Vigorous Spirit of Enterprise*, 310–14; Joseph Stancliffe Davis, "William Duer, Entrepreneur, 1744–99," in *Essays in the Earlier History of American Corporations* (Cambridge, Mass.: Harvard University Press, 1917), 1:109–345; Matson, "Public Vices, Private Benefit: William Duer and His Circle"; Jones, *"The King of the Alley,"* 168–78; Nuxoll, "The Financier as Senator," 109; and Ferguson, *Power of the Purse*, 326–30.

    Though Robert and Gouverneur Morris invested in the same bank stock and debt certificates as Duer, they believed that they were more cautious. See Gouverneur Morris to Robert Morris, September 1, 1789, Gouverneur Morris Papers, LOC, and Robert Morris to Gouverneur Morris, December 11, 1789, and August 8, 1790, Gouverneur Morris Papers, COLU.

17. Tench Tilghman & Co. dissolved upon its namesake's death in 1786. See L. G. Shreve, *Tench Tilghman: The Life and Times of Washington's Aide-de-Camp* (Centreville, Md.: Tidewater, 1982), 171–94. Constable, Rucker, and Company in New York (retitled William Constable and Company) continued until 1791, when Morris chose not to renew his share, though he subsequently conducted business with Constable. See William Constable to Robert Morris, December 14, 1792, Gouverneur Morris Papers, COLU; Nuxoll and Gallagher, *Papers of Robert Morris*, 9:329–30; and Nuxoll, "The Financier as Senator," 117. For Morris's continuing interest in the China trade, see entry for November 26, 1791, in "Journal, 1791–1801," Robert Morris Business Papers, HSP. See also Colin Jack-Hinton, "The Voyage of 'Alliance,'" *American Neptune* 25 (October 1965): 248–61. Morris would

sell his stake in Willing, Morris, and Swanwick in 1794. See Nuxoll, "The Financier as Senator," 117, and, for background, "Circular of Thomas Willing and Robert Morris," September 15, 1783, in Nuxoll and Gallagher, *Papers of Robert Morris,* 8:518. Benjamin Harrison & Co. became Harrison, Nickolls, and Company, and after Harrison's death in 1791 Morris continued a relationship with Harrison's son, Benjamin Harrison, Jr. See, for example, entries for January 12 and January 29, 1793, in "Journal, 1791–1801," Robert Morris Business Papers, HSP, and Ver Steeg, *Robert Morris,* 189–90. Robert Hazlehurst and Company continued active trading, and Morris also did a significant amount of business with Isaac Hazlehurst & Co. of Philadelphia into the 1790s. See, for example, entries for December 31, 1792, January 5, 1793, and July 1, 1794, in "Journal, 1791–1801," Robert Morris Business Papers, HSP; Robert Hazlehurst & Co. to Gouverneur Morris, January 11, 1789, Gouverneur Morris Papers, COLU.

Forrest McDonald, *We the People: The Economic Origins of the Constitution* (Chicago: University of Chicago Press, 1958), 55–58, makes some useful observations on the character of Morris's merchant activities during this period. For a different interpretation of Morris's role in trade during this period, see Gordon S. Wood, *The Radicalism of the American Revolution* (New York: Knopf, 1992), 211–12, and Gordon S. Wood, "Interests and Disinterestedness in the Making of the Constitution," in Richard Beeman, Stephen Botein, and Edward C. Carter II, eds., *Beyond Confederation: Origins of the Constitution and American National Identity* (Chapel Hill: Published for OIEAHC by the University of North Carolina Press, 1987), 96–100.

For Garrett Cottringer, see Robert Morris to Tench Tilghman, April 30, 1784, in Nuxoll and Gallagher, *Papers of Robert Morris,* 9:295–97; "Cottringer," in *Records of the American Catholic Historical Society of Philadelphia* 18 (1907): 70–74; and for an example of their working relationship, see Robert Morris to Henry Drinker, July 11, 1789, Henry S. Drinker Papers, HSP. Morris also employed James Rees as a longtime bookkeeper, from 1785 through 1797. See "Robert Morris Esq. in acct with James Rees," May 1798, Robert Morris Papers, NYPL.

18. Gouverneur Morris to Robert Morris, February 14, 1793, Gouverneur Morris Papers, LOC (first quotations); Robert Morris to Robert Morris, Jr., December 19, 1792, and Robert Morris to Thomas Morris, January 2 and January 18, 1793 (last quotation), in Collection of Papers of Robert Morris, HUNT. In his January 2 letter above, Robert wrote to Thomas, "Thus you see my Dear Son, I am put at ease, altho the sacrifice is very great," meaning

that he thought he might have sold the lands for an even higher price, "yet it is better to be at ease, as I can now do those things which may be necessary to improve my Estate" and to help his children more materially. The terms of this deal allowed the purchasers the option of withdrawing from the sale in three years, thereby turning the purchase money into a loan due. Related deeds are reprinted in *Report of Special Committee to Investigate the Indian Problem of the State of New York, Appointed by the Assembly of 1888* (Albany: Troy Press Company, 1889), 117–31. See also Chernow, "Robert Morris: Land Speculator," 53–69, and Nuxoll, "Robert Morris and the Shaping of the Post-Revolutionary American Economy," 13.

William Temple Franklin had earlier, in 1791, sold a million acres of Morris's Genesee lands to a British investment group, the Pulteney Associates, headed by William Johnstone Pulteney, earning Morris a $200,000 profit. Though it was not enough to fully right his financial ship, it probably did encourage Morris's growing faith in the potential of land sales. See Chernow, "Robert Morris: Genesee Land Speculator," 204–6, and Barbara A. Chernow, "Robert Morris and Alexander Hamilton: Two Financiers in New York," in Joseph R. Frese and Jacob Judd, eds., *Business Enterprise in Early New York* (Tarrytown, N.Y.: Sleepy Hollow Press, 1979), 77–98.

19. Entry for January 5, 1793, in "Journal, 1791–1801," Robert Morris Business Papers, HSP; Lewis Leary, "Phaeton in Philadelphia: Jean Pierre Blanchard and the First Balloon Ascension in America, 1793," *Pennsylvania Magazine of History and Biography* 67 (January 1943): 49–60.

20. W. W. Corcoran, quoted in Wilhelmus B. Bryan, "Something About L'Enfant and His Personal Affairs," *Records of the Columbia Historical Society* 2 (1899): 117 (quotation); Kenneth R. Bowling, *Peter Charles L'Enfant: Vision, Honor, and Male Friendship in the Early American Republic* (Washington, D.C.: Printed for the Friends of the George Washington University Libraries, 2002), 1–5; Scott W. Berg, *Grand Avenues: The Story of the French Visionary Who Designed Washington, D.C.* (New York: Pantheon Books, 2007), 17–48. For L'Enfant's background, see also Jules Jusserand, *With Americans of Past and Present Days* (New York: Charles Scribner's Sons, 1916); Elizabeth S. Kite, *L'Enfant and Washington, 1791–1792* (Baltimore: Johns Hopkins Press, 1929); and H. Paul Caemmerer, *The Life of Pierre Charles L'Enfant, Planner of the City Beautiful, the City of Washington* (Washington: National Republic Publishing Co., 1950).

21. Diary entry for April 6, 1782, in E. James Ferguson and John Catanzariti, eds., *The Papers of Robert Morris, 1781–1784* (Pittsburgh: University of

Pittsburgh Press, 1978), 4:522 (quotations); Oberholtzer, *Robert Morris: Patriot and Financier*, 174. L'Enfant and Morris may have met for the first time at Morris's wartime home at Manheim, Pennsylvania, where Baron von Steuben had stopped with him in early 1778. See Berg, *Grand Avenues*, 210.

22. Benjamin Rush, "The French Fête in Philadelphia in Honor of the Dauphin's Birthday," *Pennsylvania Magazine of History and Biography* 21 (1897): 257–62; Bowling, *Peter Charles L'Enfant*, 5–7; Berg, *Grand Avenues*, 48–50; William C. Stinchcombe, "Americans Celebrate the Birth of the Dauphin," in Ronald Hoffman and Peter J. Albert, eds., *Diplomacy and Revolution: The Franco-American Alliance of 1778* (Charlottesville: University Press of Virginia, 1981); and David S. Shields, *Civil Tongues and Polite Letters in British America* (Chapel Hill: Published for OIEAHC by the University of North Carolina Press, 1997), 1–10.

23. Diary entries for July 14, October 16, and November 4, 6, and 8, 1783, and Robert Morris to Alexander McDougall, November 12, 1783 (quotation), in Nuxoll and Gallagher, *Papers of Robert Morris*, 8:255, 280, 627, 646, 703–4, 737, 743, 757–58; Berg, *Grand Avenues*, 51–54; Minor Myers, Jr., *Liberty Without Anarchy: A History of the Society of the Cincinnati* (Charlottesville: University of Virginia Press, 1983), 32–34, 138, 146–50; Bowling, *Peter Charles L'Enfant*, 7–8.

24. L'Enfant, quoted in Kenneth R. Bowling, *The Creation of Washington, D.C.: The Idea and Location of the American Capital* (Fairfax, Va.: George Mason University Press, 1991), 6 (first quotations); Comte de Moustier to Comte de Montmorin, June 9, 1789, quoted Charlene Bangs Bickford et al., eds., *Documentary History of the First Federal Congress of the United States of America*, vol. 16, *Correspondence: First Session, June–August 1789* (Baltimore: Johns Hopkins University Press, 2004), 730 (second quotation); Bowling, *Peter Charles L'Enfant*, 8; Berg, *Grand Avenues*, 51–72; and Myers, *Liberty Without Anarchy*, 61, 65.

While Pennsylvania's congressional delegation plotted in 1790 to remove the federal seat from New York City to Philadelphia, they floated L'Enfant's name (in Thomas Fitzsimons's words, to be favored over Philadelphia's local builders because he was "well acquainted with the present taste in Europe") as a desirable candidate for their own federal buildings. Thomas Fitzsimons to [Miers Fisher], July 16, 1790, Miers Fisher Papers, HSP, quoted in DiGiacomantonio et al., *Debates in the House of Representatives*, xii. Surprisingly, in almost comic contrast to L'Enfant's spreading reputation, Fitzsimons also promoted L'Enfant as "a man of mild unassuming manners."

25. Pierre-Charles L'Enfant to George Washington, June 22, 1791 (last quotation), and August 19, 1791 (first and second quotations), in Mark A. Mastromarino, ed., *The Papers of George Washington: Presidential Series* (Charlottesville: University Press of Virginia, 1999), 8:287–93 and 439–48; Fiske Kimball, "The Origin of the Plan of Washington," *Architectural Review* 7 (September 1918): 41–45; Bowling, *Peter Charles L'Enfant*, 21–33; Berg, *Grand Avenues*, 117–99; Stanley Elkins and Eric McKitrick, *The Age of Federalism: The Early American Republic, 1788–1800* (New York: Oxford University Press, 1993), 169–77; and Bob Arnebeck, *Through a Fiery Trial: Building Washington, 1790–1800* (Lanham: Madison Books, 1991), 24–111. Thomas Jefferson's earliest thoughts on the federal city were informed by French designs as well, notwithstanding his aversion to powerful American cities. Along with his grid design for the Potomac project, he proposed squares to be set aside for public parks, a large president's house and garden, streets one hundred feet wide, and regulations on construction activity to elevate a uniform vision.

26. Pierre L'Enfant to George Washington, February 27, 1792, and George Washington to Pierre L'Enfant, February 28, 1792 (quotation), in Mark A. Mastromarino and Jack D. Warren, eds. *The Papers of George Washington: Presidential Series* (Charlottesville: University Press of Virginia, 2000), 9:603–6; Bowling, *Peter Charles L'Enfant*, 31–34; Berg, *Grand Avenues*, 188–99.

27. Roberdeau, quoted by Abraham Faw, in Arnebeck, *Through a Fiery Trial*, 90 (quotation); George Washington to David Stuart, March 8, 1792, in Robert F. Haggard and Mark A. Mastromarino, eds., *The Papers of George Washington: Presidential Series* (Charlottesville: University Press of Virginia, 2002), 10:62–67. Bowling, *Peter Charles L'Enfant*, 37.

28. Berg, *Grand Avenues*, 198–99, 208; Bowling, *Peter Charles L'Enfant*, 37–38; Jacob E. Cooke, "Tench Coxe, Alexander Hamilton, and the Encouragement of American Manufactures," *William and Mary Quarterly* 32 (1975): 369–92; and Joseph Stancliffe Davis, "The 'S.U.M.': The First New Jersey Business Corporation," in *Essays in the Earlier History of American Corporations* (Cambridge, Mass.: Harvard University Press, 1917), 1:349–522. The shared manager was Samuel Ogden. For Ogden's role as shareholder and overseer at Morris's Delaware Works, see, for example, Gouverneur Morris to Samuel Ogden, August 25, 1789, Gouverneur Morris Papers, LOC, and entry for July 6, 1792, in "Journal, 1791–1801," Robert Morris Business Papers, HSP.

29. "Draft Minutes of a Meeting of a Committee of the Directors of the Society for Establishing Useful Manufactures," August 1, 1792, and Alexander Hamilton to the Governor and Directors of the Society for Establishing Useful Manufactures, August 16, 1792 (quotation), in Harold C. Syrett, ed., *The Papers of Alexander Hamilton* (New York: Columbia University Press, 1967), 12:140–42, 216–18; Bowling, *Peter Charles L'Enfant*, 37–38; Caemmerer, *The Life of Pierre Charles L'Enfant*, 249–54.

    Roberdeau had left his post at the federal city, L'Enfant explained to Hamilton, "from a regard for me." "I need not mention to you my attachment to him and the consideration which lead [*sic*] me to retain him near me," he wrote. Pierre Charles L'Enfant to Alexander Hamilton, August 21, 1792, in Syrett, *Papers of Alexander Hamilton*, 12:262–63.

30. Peter Colt to Alexander Hamilton, February 28, 1793 (first quotation); Nicholas Low to Alexander Hamilton, March 4, 1793 (second quotation); Pierre Charles L'Enfant to Alexander Hamilton, March 26, 1793 (third quotation); Peter Colt to Alexander Hamilton, May 7, 1793 (last quotations), in Harold C Syrett, ed., *The Papers of Alexander Hamilton* (New York: Columbia University Press, 1969), 14:170–71, 189, 248–49, 419–21. See also Elisha Boudinot to Alexander Hamilton, March 26, 1793, in ibid., 245–46; and Nicholas Low to Alexander Hamilton, June 27, 1793, and Pierre Charles L'Enfant to Alexander Hamilton, October 16, 1793, in Harold C. Syrett, ed., *The Papers of Alexander Hamilton* (New York: Columbia University Press, 1969), 15:30, 363–5. Evidence that L'Enfant could be found "at Robert Morris's" in Philadelphia by June appears in Isaac Roberdeau to Major L'Enfant, June 18, 1793, James Dudley Morgan collection of Digges-L'Enfant-Morgan Papers, LOC. See also Davis, "The 'S.U.M.,'" 458–68; Caemmerer, *The Life of Pierre Charles L'Enfant*, 254; Bowling, *Peter Charles L'Enfant*, 37–38.

31. P. Charles L'Enfant to John Kean, March 19, 1793, Etting Collection, HSP, written from New York City, states that L'Enfant had recently been in Philadelphia and that he would return there in about three weeks. Likewise, David Burnes mentioned seeing L'Enfant in the city sometime that winter. See David Burnes to Commissioners of the District of Columbia, April 8, 1793, Letters Received, vol. 3, M371, reel 9, National Archives and Records Administration, Washington, D.C.

    No letter or diary entry survives to reveal exactly how Robert Morris first engaged L'Enfant for his new residence. John F. Watson, Philadelphia's early annalist who drew much of his source material from hearsay, recorded four decades later that a "gentleman was present at R. Morris' table when L'Enfent [*sic*] was there, and first broached the scheme of building him a grand house for 60,000 dollars." The scenario is realistic. Watson continued: "Mr. Morris said he could sell out his lots and houses on High street for 80,000 dollars, and so the thing was begun." John F. Watson, *Annals of Philadelphia and Pennsylvania, in the Olden Time; Being a Collection of Memoirs, Anecdotes, and Incidents of the City and its Inhabitants, and of the Earliest Settlements of the Inland Part of Pennsylvania, From the Days of the Founders* (Philadelphia: Penington and Hunt, 1844), 1:409. This story of L'Enfant's proposal over dinner did not appear in the earlier 1830 issue of Watson's work; but it would be repeated in Thompson Westcott, *The Historic Mansions and Buildings of Philadelphia With Some Notice of Their Owners and Occupants* (Philadelphia: Porter and Coates, 1877), 360–61, and frequently thereafter. One contemporary did record a comparable quote: James Kent, visiting Philadelphia from New York in December 1793, viewed the construction site and asserted that Morris's house "is estimated to cost £50,000, sterling." James Kent, "Journal of a Trip to Washington, D.C., December 5, 1793 to January 3, 1794," James Kent Papers, reel 1, volume 1, LOC. Purchases of oysters, venison, and claret appear in Morris's account books from this time; see entries for November and December 1792 in "Journal, 1791–1801," Robert Morris Business Papers, HSP.

Morris also indicated later that L'Enfant had given him an initial estimate for the total cost. See Robert Morris to Major C. L'Enfant, September 25, 1795, Robert Morris Papers, LOC, in which Morris writes that a single stone contractor "alone has received from me a sum equal to what you told me in the outset the whole Building would cost."

Some art historians have found that in 1791, L'Enfant had had a hand in designing the Philadelphia house of John Nicholson, Morris's partner in land speculations. See Fiske Kimball, "Pierre Charles L'Enfant," in Dumas Malone, ed., *Dictionary of American Biography* (New York: Charles Scribner's Sons, 1933), 6:165–69. None of Morris's correspondence with Nicholson mentions the commission.

32. Robert Morris to Major [Peter Charles] L'Enfant, May 9, 1793, Morgan collection of Digges-L'Enfant-Morgan Papers, LOC. There is some undated scribble at the bottom of this page, apparently written later by L'Enfant during negotiations over payment, which reads in part: "Remark on the above. This note pursuant to previous Invitation determined my leaving the Business of the [town factory] at Paterson. And took me way from an

Employement worth Stg 1500 [c] yearly of salary [beside] a much larger sum . . . by his friend Collo Ogle." Deborah Logan to Mary Norris, March 25, 1793, in the Maria Dickinson Logan Family Papers, HSP, makes it clear that Morris had engaged L'Enfant by mid-March 1793. "The thing was begun" is Watson's language—see previous note.

CHAPTER 4. HIS HOUSE

1. Carole Shammas, "The Housing Stock of the Early United States: Refinement Meets Migration," *William and Mary Quarterly* 64 (July 2007): 7. This percentage includes the housing of Indians and slaves within the borders of the United States. The highest percentage of such untaxed houses appeared in frontier or southern locales.

2. Billy G. Smith, *The "Lower Sort": Philadelphia's Laboring People, 1750–1800* (Ithaca, N.Y.: Cornell University Press, 1990), 7–39, 150–75; Donna J. Rilling, *Making Houses, Crafting Capitalism: Builders in Philadelphia, 1790–1850* (Philadelphia: University of Pennsylvania Press, 2001), 10–13.

A general study of Philadelphia housing can be found in George B. Tatum, *Penn's Great Town: 250 Years of Philadelphia Architecture Illustrated in Prints and Drawings* (Philadelphia: University of Pennsylvania Press, 1961). For the context of Philadelphia houses in the broader Atlantic world, see Bernard L. Herman, *Town House: Architecture and Material Life in the Early American City, 1780–1830* (Chapel Hill: Published for OIEAHC by the University of North Carolina Press, 2005).

3. Kenneth Roberts and Anna M. Roberts, trans. and eds., *Moreau de St. Méry's American Journey, 1793–1798* (Garden City, N.Y.: Doubleday and Co., 1947), 261–64 (first quotation); Thomas Condie and Richard Folwell, *History of the Pestilence, Commonly Called Yellow Fever, Which Almost Desolated Philadelphia, in the Months of August, September & October, 1798* (Philadelphia: R. Folwell, [1799]), 6–8 (second quotations); Grant Miles Simon, "Houses and Early Life in Philadelphia," *Transactions of the American Philosophical Society* 43 (1953): 286–87; Benjamin Rush, quoted in Smith, *The "Lower Sort,"* 162 (last quotation); Barbara G. Carson and Kym S. Rice, *Ambitious Appetites: Dining Behavior and Patterns of Consumption in Federal Washington* (Washington, D.C.: American Institute of Architects Press, 1990), 30–31. In 1798, Benjamin Henry Latrobe visited Philadelphia and agreed that "it is true that there are narrow and often very filthy Alleys which intersect the interior of the squares bounded by the principal streets

and in which the air may stagnate. The back Yards of most of the houses, are also depositories of filth to a degree which is surprising." Entry for April 29, 1798, in Edward C. Carter II, ed., *The Virginia Journals of Benjamin Henry Latrobe, 1795–1798* (New Haven, Conn.: Published for the Maryland Historical Society by Yale University Press, 1977), 2:379. See also *Dunlap and Claypoole's American Daily Advertiser* (February 25, 1796) and *Gazette of the United States* (March 23, 1796). For similar trends in Boston, see Robert Blair St. George, *Conversing by Signs: Poetics of Implication in Colonial New England Culture* (Chapel Hill: University of North Carolina Press, 1998), 231–42. More generally, see Richard L. Bushman, *The Refinement of America: Persons, Houses, Cities* (New York: Knopf, 1992).

4. David Montagu Erskine to his father, January 1, 1799, Letterbook of David Montagu Erskine, 1798–1799, Small Special Collections Library, University of Virginia, Charlottesville, Virginia (quotation). William Drayton, visiting Philadelphia from Charleston, South Carolina, in 1786, described this row house type in detail, calling it the "General Style of Houses in Philadelphia"; quoted in Herman, *Town House*, 3–4. James Kent, visiting from New York in 1793, observed that the city's "houses are generally plain 3 story brick Buildings." James Kent, "Journal of a Trip to Washington, D.C., December 5, 1793 to January 3, 1794," James Kent Papers, reel 1, volume 1, LOC. These houses sheltered an average of six people. See William John Murtagh, "The Philadelphia Row House," *Journal of the Society of Architectural Historians* 16 (December 1957): 8–13; Dell Upton, *Another City: Urban Life and Urban Spaces in the New American Republic* (New Haven: Yale University Press, 2008), 3–5, 22–27; Thomas M. Doerflinger, *A Vigorous Spirit of Enterprise: Merchants and Economic Development in Revolutionary Philadelphia* (Chapel Hill: Published for OIEAHC by the University of North Carolina Press, 1986), 21–36; Simon, "Houses and Early Life in Philadelphia"; Tatum, *Penn's Great Town*, 24, 33–34; George B. Tatum, *Philadelphia Georgian: The City House of Samuel Powel and Some of Its Eighteenth-Century Neighbors* (Middletown, Conn.: Wesleyan University Press, 1976); Roger W. Moss, *Historic Houses of Philadelphia* (Philadelphia: University of Pennsylvania Press, 1998), 22–45; Karie Diethorn with John Bacon, "Domestic Work Portrayed: Philadelphia's Restored Bishop William White House—A Case Study," in Gail Lee Dubrow and Jennifer B. Goodman, eds., *Restoring Women's History Through Historic Preservation* (Baltimore: Johns Hopkins University Press, 2003), 96–110; and Kenneth R. Bowling, "The Federal Government and the Republican Court Move to Philadelphia,

November 1790–March 1791," in Kenneth R. Bowling and Donald R. Kennon, eds., *Neither Separate nor Equal: Congress in the 1790s* (Athens, Oh.: Published for the United States Capitol Historical Society by Ohio University Press, 2000), 3–33. Given this housing stock, Stuart M. Blumin calculated that the median living space for artisan families in Philadelphia in 1798 was only 648 square feet, while storekeepers, grocers, and other "middling folk" enjoyed only 900 square feet on average. Many of these residences also included workshops. Blumin, *The Emergence of the Middle Class: Social Experience in the American City, 1760–1900* (New York: Cambridge University Press, 1989), 42–58. A useful first-person account of entering these houses is found in Julian Ursyn Niemcewicz, *Under Their Vine and Fig Tree: Travels through America in 1797–1799, 1805 with Some Further Account of Life in New Jersey*, trans., ed., and with an introduction and notes by Metchie J. E. Budka (Elizabeth, N.J.: Grassmann Publishing Co., 1965), 36.

5. John F. Watson, *Annals of Philadelphia, Being a Collection of Memoirs, Anecdotes, & Incidents of the City and Its Inhabitants From the Days of the Pilgrim Founders* (Philadelphia: Carey and Hart, 1830), 351–52, 355.

6. Memorandum of Agreement between John Dickinson and Robert Morris, October 9, 1790, Logan Papers, vol. 12:51, HSP (quotations); Tobias Lear to George Washington, November 4, 1790, in Mark A. Mastromarino, ed., *The Papers of George Washington: Presidential Series* (Charlottesville: University Press of Virginia, 1996), 6:622; Philadelphia City Council Minute Book (1789–1793), Collection 1411, September 9, 1790, HSP. Dickinson's memorandum suggests that he had proposed a sale of this lot earlier, as it mentions that these terms would be "at the sum I have before mentioned." The relative height of the block's land comes from Watson, *Annals of Philadelphia*, 355: "Its original elevation was 12 to 15 feet above the present level of the adjacent streets."

For the geography of Philadelphia in the early 1790s, see James Hardie, *The Philadelphia Directory and Register* (Philadelphia: Dobson, 1793); Roberts and Roberts, *Moreau de St. Méry's American Journey*, 260–61; and Mary M. Schweitzer, "The Spatial Organization of Federalist Philadelphia, 1790," *Journal of Interdisciplinary History* 24 (Summer 1993): 31–57.

7. Morris's property involved in the swap was his "Estate in Brandywine hundred," located in northern Delaware. Memorandum of Agreement between Dickinson and Morris, October 9, 1790; Robert Morris to John Dickinson, October 10, 1790, Logan Papers, vol. 12:51, HSP (quotation). See also entry for March 9, 1793, in "Journal, 1791–1801," Robert Morris Business

Papers, HSP; Watson, *Annals of Philadelphia*, 355; Thompson Westcott, *The Historic Mansions and Buildings of Philadelphia, With Some Notice of Their Owners and Occupants* (Philadelphia: Porter and Coates, 1877), 363. Morris received title for Dickinson's property March 7, 1791. See Philadelphia Deed book D, City Archives, Philadelphia, Pennsylvania.

The merchant who had owned the small strip on Morris's block was Samuel Mickle. The strip owned by his estate measured 49½ feet on Chestnut and 255 feet on Seventh Street, and Morris's 1791 deed lists the owner as Peter Ricks. For Mickle, see John W. Jordan, *Colonial and Revolutionary Families of Philadelphia* (New York: Lewis Pub. Co., 1911), 1:318–19.

8. "Report of the Committee of Aug. 9th & 23d for the Accommodation of the President," October 20, 1790, Etting Collection, Independence Hall, Catalogued items, HSP (quotation); "Executive Minutes of Governor Thomas Mifflin," October 8, 1791, and October 11, 1792 [1791], *Pennsylvania Archives*, 9th series, part 1, (1931), 1:239–42; Jacob Cox Parsons, ed., *Extracts From the Diary of Jacob Hiltzheimer, of Philadelphia, 1765–1798* (Philadelphia: William F. Fell and Co., 1893), entries for October 8 and 12, 1791, 172. The state of Pennsylvania initially appropriated £17,000 for the project. See Damie Stillman, "Six Houses for the President," *Pennsylvania Magazine of History and Biography* 129 (October 2005): 419–23; Dennis C. Kurjack, "The 'President's House' in Philadelphia," *Pennsylvania History* 20 (1953): 380–86; and Tatum, *Penn's Great Town*, 45–46.

In March 1792, one resident observed that "Philadelphia does in reality increase very fast particularly toward the state House. Great numbers of Houses tis said are to be built this summer and materials and wages of workmen are greatly increased in price." Susan Dillwyn to William Dillwyn, March 24, 1792, Dillwyn Manuscripts, HSP.

9. Parsons, *Extracts From the Diary of Jacob Hiltzheimer*, 174–78; entry for July 2, 1792, in "Journal, 1791–1801," Robert Morris Business Papers, HSP; Gouverneur Morris to Robert Morris, June 25, 1792, Gouverneur Morris Papers, LOC. For the alterations and additions made to the Stedman-Galloway House in mid-1792, see entries from June 1792 through April 1793, in "Journal, 1791–1801," Robert Morris Business Papers, HSP.

10. Entries from April through September 1792, in "Journal, 1791–1801," Robert Morris Business Papers, HSP.

11. Entry for March 19, 1793, in "Journal, 1791–1801," Robert Morris Business Papers, HSP (first quotation); Robert Morris to Thomas Morris, January 2, 1793, Collection of Papers of Robert Morris, HUNT (second quotation);

Hardie, *The Philadelphia Directory* (1793); *Dunlap's Advertiser* (June 28, 1793) (last quotation). This notice, by Edward Pole, appeared only a few months after Morris's house construction began, and Pole advertised that his Walnut Street lots were "near to the new Building now erecting for the Residence of the President of the United States, as well as those on Chesnut street for the residence of Mr. Morris, Mr. Fitzsimons, and Doctor Rusten." Given the nearby public buildings and notable residences, one visitor in December 1793 called this neighborhood the "Court End of the town." See Kent, "Journal of a Trip to Washington, D.C." Morris's lot was valued at £3,000 in the tax ledger for 1792 and 1793. Tax Assessor's Ledger, South Ward, 1792 and 1793, Philadelphia City Archives. For Oeller's Hotel, see Peter Thompson, *Rum Punch and Revolution: Taverngoing and Public Life in Eighteenth-Century Philadelphia* (Philadelphia: University of Pennsylvania Press, 1999), 190–99; for the New Theatre on Chestnut Street, see Heather S. Nathans, *Early American Theatre from the Revolution to Thomas Jefferson: Into the Hands of the People* (New York: Cambridge University Press, 2003), 64–70, and D. Dodge Thompson, "The Public Work of William Rush: A Case Study in the Origins of American Sculpture," in *William Rush, American Sculptor* (Philadelphia: Pennsylvania Academy of the Fine Arts, 1982), 31–35.

12. Deborah Logan to Mary Norris, March 25, 1793, Maria Dickinson Logan Family Papers, Box 2, HSP. Logan's reference to "140 feet front" would prove to be roughly correct in the actual construction (estimated at 120 feet). Logan's letter refers to "H. Hill," which I am interpreting as Henry Hill, who with Logan's husband George and Robert Morris was a member of the Philadelphia Society for Promoting Agriculture at the time. See Simon Baatz, *"Venerate the Plough": A History of the Philadelphia Society for Promoting Agriculture, 1785–1985* (Philadelphia: PSPA, 1985). Further, Hill had a country home near the Hills and participated in the city's Dancing Assembly. See Amy H. Henderson, "A Family Affair: The Design and Decoration of 321 South Fourth Street," in John Styles and Amanda Vickery, ed., *Gender, Taste and Material Culture in Britain and America in the Long Eighteenth Century* (New Haven: Published for Yale Center for British Art and Paul Mellon Centre for British Art by Yale University Press, 2006), 267–91, and Amy Hudson Henderson, "Furnishing the Republican Court: Building and Decorating Philadelphia Homes, 1790–1800" (Ph.D. diss., University of Delaware, 2008), 84, 88–90. For a report that the house would be 160 feet, see Bob Arnebeck, *Through a Fiery Trial: Building Washington, 1790–1800* (Lanham, Md.: Madison Books, 1991), 168.

13. Pierre-Charles L'Enfant to George Washington, Report on the Plan for the Intended City, June 22, 1791, in Mark A. Mastromarino, ed., *The Papers of George Washington: Presidential Series* (Charlottesville: University Press of Virginia, 1999), 8:287–93 (quotations); William Seale, *The President's House: A History* (Washington, D.C.: White House Historical Association with the cooperation of the National Geographic Society, 1986), 1:17–20, 23; Russell L. Mahan, "Political Architecture: The Building of the President's House," in Robert P. Watson, ed., *Life in the White House: A Social History of the First Family and the President's House* (Albany: State University of New York Press, 2004), 39; Stillman, "Six Houses for the President," 424–27; Bates Lowry, *Building a National Image: Architectural Drawings for the American Democracy, 1789–1912* (Washington, D.C.: National Building Museum, 1985). L'Enfant used the term again in his August 1791 letter to Washington. See Pierre-Charles L'Enfant to George Washington, August 19, 1791, in Mastromarino, *Papers of George Washington: Presidential Series,* 8:439–48. Other observers, including Congressman William Loughton Smith and the district's commissioners themselves, occasionally used the term "palace" as a name for the President's House. See Arnebeck, *Through a Fiery Trial,* 50.

14. David Stuart to George Washington, February 26, 1792, in Mark A. Mastromarino and Jack D. Warren, eds., *The Papers of George Washington: Presidential Series* (Charlottesville: University Press of Virginia, 2000), 9:596–602 (quotation); Kenneth R. Bowling, *Peter Charles L'Enfant: Vision, Honor, and Male Friendship in the Early American Republic* (Washington, D.C.: Printed for the Friends of the George Washington University Libraries, 2002), 32–33. Stuart's objections also probably had a financial component, as the expansive grounds would take up land that might otherwise have been sold for badly needed funds. Washington, deeply involved in L'Enfant's plan, responded to Stuart's criticism with practical compromise but agreed in principle with L'Enfant's long view of the house's design. See George Washington to David Stuart, March 8, 1792, in Robert F. Haggard and Mark A. Mastromarino, eds., *The Papers of George Washington: Presidential Series* (Charlottesville: University Press of Virginia, 2002), 10:62–67; Rubil Morales-Vázquez, "George Washington, the President's House, and the Projection of Executive Power," *Washington History* 16 (Spring/Summer 2004): 36–53; and Jeffrey F. Meyer, *Myths in Stone: Religious Dimensions of Washington, D.C.* (Berkeley and Los Angeles: University of California Press, 2001), 115–17. Still, the city commissioners used the term "president's palace" when referring to the building. See Isaac Rob-

erdeau to Major L'Enfant, January 11, 1792, James Dudley Morgan collection of Digges-L'Enfant-Morgan Papers, LOC, and Wilhelmus Bogart
Bryan, *A History of the National Capital from Its Foundation Through the Period of the Adoption of the Organic Act* (New York: Macmillan Company,
1914), 1:149–50, 192, 195, 204.

15. Entries for March 9, March 19, April 18, May 4, and May 11, 1793, in "Journal, 1791–1801," Robert Morris Business Papers, HSP. On April 18, Morris
made his first remittance in L'Enfant's name for supplies. The work on the
President's House in Philadelphia stalled on May 3, 1793, when money ran
out. It would not be resumed until 1795, after another state appropriation.
See Parsons, *Extracts from the Diary of Jacob Hiltzheimer*, 185, 191; Stillman,
"Six Houses for the President," 420.

16. Entries for May through August 1793 in "Journal, 1791–1801," Robert
Morris Business Papers, HSP. For Wallace's background, see Hardie, *The
Philadelphia Directory* (1793), 150; Jesse Lee, *A Short History of the Method-
ists, in the United States of America* (Baltimore: Magill and Clime, 1810),
238; Abel Stevens, *The Women of Methodism: Its Three Foundresses, Susanna
Wesley, the Countess of Huntingdon, and Barbara Heck* (New York: Carlton
and Porter, 1866), 219; and Tobias Lear to George Washington, November
4, November 7, and November 14, 1790, in Mastromarino, *Papers of George
Washington: Presidential Series*, 6:622–25, 636–39, 655–58. For the pay of
masons and laborers, see "Agreement for Executing the Marble Work of
the Bank of Pennsylvania," [February 26, 1799] in John C. Van Horne and
Lee W. Formwalt, eds., *The Correspondence and Miscellaneous Papers of Benjamin Henry Latrobe* (New Haven: Published for the Maryland Historical
Society by Yale University Press, 1984), 1:128–36; and Rilling, *Making
Houses, Crafting Capitalism*, 139 and passim.

17. Samuel Blodget, Jr., to Commissioners of the District of Columbia, July 27,
1793, Letters Received, vol. 3, M371, reel 9, National Archives and Records
Administration, Washington, D.C. (emphasis in the original), and Arnebeck, *Through a Fiery Trial*, 168.

18. Isaac Roberdeau to Major L'Enfant, March 21, 23, and 28, July 26, and September 8 and 17, 1792, Morgan collection of Digges-L'Enfant-Morgan Papers, LOC; Roberdeau Buchanon, *Genealogy of the Roberdeau Family,
Including a Biography of General Daniel Roberdeau . . .* (Washington, D.C.:
Pearson, 1876), 104–22; *An Historical Account of the Rise, Progress and
Present State of the Canal Navigation in Pennsylvania* (Philadelphia: Zacha-
riah Poulson, 1795), 58–59. Roberdeau had lived with his aunt Elizabeth

Roberdeau in Philadelphia prior to his marriage to Susan Blair. Bob Arnebeck suggests that Roberdeau and L'Enfant may have had a romantic/sexual
relationship. See Bob Arnebeck, " 'The Nature of the Man': L'Enfant's
Sexuality and Its Relevance to the Planning of Washington," http://www
.starbacks.ca/bobarnebeck/PCL.html (accessed January 6, 2012); and
Arnebeck, "To Tease and Torment: Two Presidents Confront Suspicions
of Sodomy," at http://bobarnebeck.com/LEnfant.htm (accessed July 27,
2010). Bowling's careful account is agnostic on the question of L'Enfant's
sexuality, though he does explore the nature of his emotional relationships
with men. Bowling, *Peter Charles L'Enfant*, 50–52. L'Enfant's sexuality
seems never to have been a factor in his relations with Morris.

19. L'Enfant, Account dated 1804 (quotation), and P. C. L'Enfant to David
Stewart and Daniel Carroll, March 11 and 14, 1792, Morgan collection of
Digges-L'Enfant-Morgan Papers, LOC; Bowling, *Peter Charles L'Enfant*,
20, 30, 33; Scott W. Berg, *Grand Avenues: The Story of the French Visionary
Who Designed Washington, D.C.* (New York: Pantheon Books, 2007),
196–97; Bryan, *A History of the National Capital*, 1:179–80. L'Enfant did
receive £225 plus expenses during the year he worked at Washington. See
also Pierre Charles L'Enfant to Alexander Hamilton, October 16, 1793, in
Harold C. Syrett, ed., *The Papers of Alexander Hamilton* (New York: Columbia University Press, 1969), 15:363–65; P. Charles L'Enfant to John
Kean, March 19, 1793, Etting Collection, HSP. For mention of drawings,
now lost, and Mary's involvement, see entry for April 26, 1798, in Carter,
The Virginia Journals of Benjamin Henry Latrobe, 2:376.

20. Comte de Moré, quoted in François Furstenberg, "U.S. and French Atlan-
tic Connections: The Case of French Émigrés in Philadelphia, c. 1789–
1803," 7, at www.librarycompany.org (accessed January 6, 2012); Frances
Sergeant Childs, *French Refugee Life in the United States, 1790–1800: An
American Chapter of the French Revolution* (Baltimore: Johns Hopkins Uni-
versity Press, 1940), 103; and Roberts and Roberts, *Moreau de St. Méry's
American Journey*, 265. See also Susan Branson, *These Fiery Frenchified
Dames: Women and Political Culture in Early National Philadelphia* (Phila-
delphia: University of Pennsylvania, 2001), 55–70; Ashli White, *Encounter-
ing Revolution: Haiti and the Making of the Early Republic* (Baltimore: Johns
Hopkins University Press, 2010); François Furstenberg, *When the United
States Spoke French: Five Refugees Who Shaped a Nation* (New York: Penguin,
2014); and Gary B. Nash, *Forging Freedom: The Formation of Philadelphia's*

Black Community, 1720–1840 (Cambridge, Mass.: Harvard University Press, 1988). At the national level, L'Enfant was not the only noted French architect; Stephen Hallet worked at the federal city on the Potomac at the time, and the engineer James Blois soon joined him there. See Seale, *The President's House,* 1:27, and Arnebeck, *Through a Fiery Trial,* 62, 126, 133, 206, 209.

21. Parsons, *Extracts from the Diary of Jacob Hiltzheimer,* 190–91; Charles Marion Thomas, *American Neutrality in 1793: A Study in Cabinet Government* (New York: AMS Press, Inc., 1967), 21–52 and 137–42; John D. Gordon III, *"United States v. Joseph Ravara:* 'Presumptuous Evidence,' 'Too Many Lawyers,' and a Federal Common Law Crime," in Maeva Marcus, ed., *Origins of the Federal Judiciary: Essays on the Judiciary Act of 1789* (New York: Oxford University Press, 1992), 110. More generally, see Stanley Elkins and Eric McKitrick, *The Age of Federalism: The Early American Republic, 1788–1800* (New York: Oxford University Press, 1993), 303–73; Eugene Perry Link, *Democratic Republican Societies, 1790–1800* (1940); David Waldstreicher, *In the Midst of Perpetual Fetes: The Making of American Nationalism, 1776–1820* (Chapel Hill: Published for OIEAHC by the University of North Carolina Press, 1997), 126–41; Simon P. Newman, *Parades and the Politics of the Street: Festive Culture in the Early American Republic* (Philadelphia: University of Pennsylvania Press, 1997), 134–47; and Robert C. Alberts, *The Golden Voyage: The Life and Times of William Bingham, 1752–1804* (Boston: Houghton-Mifflin, 1969).

22. Edmond Charles Genet to Thomas Jefferson, September 18, 1793, in John Catanzariti, ed., *The Papers of Thomas Jefferson* (Princeton, N.J.: Princeton University Press, 1997), 27:126–34; extract of a letter from Genet to Jefferson, 1797, printed in Geo. Clinton Genet, *Washington, Jefferson, and "Citizen" Genet, 1793* (New York, 1899), 24–25. Harry Ammon, *The Genet Mission* (New York: W. W. Norton and Co., 1973), 55–59; Thomas, *American Neutrality,* 84–86; and Thomas Jefferson, "Notes of Cabinet Meeting and Conversations with Edmond Charles Genet," July 5, 1793, in John Catanzariti, ed., *The Papers of Thomas Jefferson* (Princeton, N.J.: Princeton University Press, 1995), 26:437–39.

23. *National Gazette* (May 22, 1793) (first quotation), *General Advertiser* (July 6, 1793), *General Advertiser* (July 10, 1793) (last quotations).

24. Thomas Jefferson, "Notes of Cabinet Meeting on Edmond Charles Genet," August 2, 1793 (first quotation), and "Notes of Cabinet Meeting on Edmond

Charles Genet," July 23, 1793 (second quotations), in Catanzariti, *Papers of Thomas Jefferson*, 26:601–3 and 553–56; "Helvidius" Number 1, [August 24,] 1793, in Thomas A. Mason, Robert A. Rutland, and Jeanne K. Sisson, eds., *The Papers of James Madison* (Charlottesville: University Press of Virginia, 1985), 15:66–74 (last quotations, emphasis in the original); Ron Chernow, *Alexander Hamilton* (New York: Penguin, 2004), 441–44; Elkins and McKitrick, *The Age of Federalism*, 359–65; and Alexander De Conde, *Entangling Alliance: Politics & Diplomacy Under George Washington* (Durham, N.C.: Duke University Press, 1958).

Much later, John Adams recalled "the terrorism excited by Genet, in 1793, when ten thousand people in the streets of Philadelphia, day after day, threatened to drag Washington out of his house, and effect a revolution in the government, or compel it to declare war in favor of the French revolution and against England"; quoted in Newman, *Parades and the Politics of the Street*, 134.

25. H. E. Scudder, ed., *Recollections of Samuel Breck With Passages From His Note-Books (1771–1862)* (Philadelphia: Potter and Coates, 1877), 194 (first quotations); Mathew Carey, *A Short Account of the Malignant Fever, Lately Prevalent in Philadelphia*, 4th ed. (Philadelphia: Mathew Carey, 1794), 32 (last quotation); Parsons, *Extracts from the Diary of Jacob Hiltzheimer*, 194; J. H. Powell, *Bring Out Your Dead: The Great Plague of Yellow Fever in Philadelphia in 1793* (Philadelphia: University of Pennsylvania Press, 1949); and Eve Kornfeld, "Crisis in the Capital: The Cultural Significance of Philadelphia's Great Yellow Fever Epidemic," *Pennsylvania History* 51 (July 1984): 189–205.

26. Entries for November 30 and December 16, 1793, in "Journal, 1791–1801," Robert Morris Business Papers, HSP; Robert Morris to Thomas Morris, November 24, 1793, Collection of Papers of Robert Morris, HUNT; Powell, *Bring Out Your Dead*, 46 and 230; Robert Morris to P. Charles L'Enfant, October 3, 1793, Society Miscellaneous Collection, small, Robert Morris, letters, HSP (quotations). Throughout the rest of the 1790s, L'Enfant frequently spent a few winter months in New York City, even in the absence of yellow fever outbreaks. See L'Enfant, Account dated 1804, Morgan collection of Digges-L'Enfant-Morgan Papers, LOC.

27. Robert Morris to P. Charles L'Enfant, October 3, 1793, Society Miscellaneous Collection, small, Robert Morris, letters, HSP; Memorandum dated October 26, 1793, Robert Morris Papers, LOC; *Independent Gazetteer* (October 26, 1793).

28. Robert Morris to Le Roy & Bayard, November 9, 1793, and Robert Morris to Thomas Morris, November 24, 1793, Collection of Papers of Robert Morris, HUNT; Robert Morris to Thomas Morris, November 15, 1793, NYHS; Carey, *A Short Account of the Malignant Fever,* 9–12 (quotations) and 116–17; Kornfeld, "Crisis in the Capital"; J. Thomas Scharf and Thompson Westcott, *History of Philadelphia, 1609–1884* (Philadelphia: L. H. Everts and Co., 1884), 3:2355–56.

29. J. Henry C. Helmuth, *A Short Account of the Yellow Fever in Philadelphia, for the Reflecting Christian* (Philadelphia: Jones, Hoff and Derrick, 1794), 10, 21 (first quotations); *National Gazette* (July 17, 1793) (second quotations); Thomas Learning to Thomas Bradford, October 16, 1793, Bradford Family Collection, HSP (last quotation). Thanks to Kenneth Cohen for this reference.

30. Entries for November 30, December 8, December 16, and December 28, 1793, in "Journal, 1791–1801," Robert Morris Business Papers, HSP.

CHAPTER 5. HIS ARCHITECT

1. James Lowell to John Jay, March 18, 1785 (first quotation), William Tudor to Rufus King, March 22, 1785 (second and last quotation), memorandum from John Jay, March 2, 1785 (third quotation), printed in *The Diplomatic Correspondence of the United States of America, From the Signing of the Definitive Treaty of Peace, 10th September 1783, to the Adoption of the Constitution, March 4, 1789* (Washington, D.C.: Blair and Rives, 1837), 3:795–808; Florence Anderson, "Richard Soderstrom: The First Swedish Consul in Boston," in Adolph B. Benson, ed., *American Swedish Historical Foundation: Yearbook 1958* (Philadelphia: Chancellor Press, 1958), 4–5.

2. Robert Morris to James Carey, January 30, 1795, Robert Morris Papers, LOC (quotation). For Robert Morris's early familiarity with the Soderstrom brothers as traders, see Daniel Parker to Robert Morris, February 10, 1784, in Elizabeth M. Nuxoll and Mary A. Gallagher, eds., *The Papers of Robert Morris, 1781–1784* (Pittsburgh: University of Pittsburgh Press, 1999), 9:98–99. For an example of Morris's advances and payments to Soderstrom, see Robert Morris to Tench Tilghman, March 28, 1785, Robert Morris Papers, NYPL; entries throughout "Journal, 1791–1801," Robert Morris Business Papers, HSP, including December 31, 1791, April 3, 1792, July 14, 1792, and February 2, 1793; and also Ledger, 1794–1801, Robert Morris Business Papers, HSP, folio 55. For the ship *Soderstrom,* see Le Couteulx & Co. to Gouverneur Morris, August 30, 1791, Gouverneur Morris

Papers, COLU. For Soderstrom's actions as Morris's agent, see Robert Morris to Thomas Davis, December 16, 1792, Ch C 4.13, Boston Public Library, Boston, Massachusetts, and "Resolve on the Petition of Robert Morris, Esq. by His Agent Richard Soderstrom, Esq. Respecting Two Bonds," February 5, 1793, in *Acts and Laws of the Commonwealth of Massachusetts* (Boston: Thomas Adams, 1895), 224–25. In 1793, Morris also seems to have attempted to aid Richard Soderstrom's attempts to bring his brother Carl to America, as when he reimbursed a partner for forty pounds sterling paid for that purpose on July 19, 1793. See entry for March 28, 1796, in "Journal, 1791–1801," Robert Morris Business Papers, HSP.

3. L'Enfant, Account dated 1804, James Dudley Morgan collection of Digges-L'Enfant-Morgan Papers, LOC; Kenneth R. Bowling, *Peter Charles L'Enfant: Vision, Honor, and Male Friendship in the Early American Republic* (Washington, D.C.: Printed for the Friends of the George Washington University Libraries, 2002), 42–45; Scott W. Berg, *Grand Avenues: The Story of the French Visionary Who Designed Washington, D.C.* (New York: Pantheon Books, 2007), 214. In 1793, Soderstrom was advising L'Enfant on the purchase of shares in the Bank of the United States. See P. Charles L'Enfant to John Kean, March 19, 1793, Etting Collection, HSP.

4. Robert Morris to P. Charles L'Enfant, October 3, 1793, Society Miscellaneous Collection, small, Robert Morris letters, HSP (quotation); Memorandum dated October 26, 1793, Robert Morris Papers, LOC. For an example of Soderstrom's other activities in Philadelphia that year, see Richard Soderstrom to Edmond Charles Genet, July 6, 1793, reprinted in Maeva Marcus, ed., *The Documentary History of the Supreme Court of the United States, 1789–1800* (New York: Columbia University Press, 1998), 6:313. Before L'Enfant quit the federal city project in early 1792, he may have discussed with Soderstrom the possibility that Sweden build an embassy in Washington, D.C. See Bowling, *Peter Charles L'Enfant*, 31, 42.

5. L'Enfant, Account dated 1804, Morgan collection of Digges-L'Enfant-Morgan Papers, LOC (quotations); James Hardie, *The Philadelphia Directory and Register*, 2d ed. (Philadelphia: Jacob Johnson and Co., 1794), 144. Soderstrom is listed as the "consul general from Sweden," though his position beyond the northern states had not yet been confirmed. Soderstrom's early land speculations are mentioned in Robert F. Jones, *"The King of the Alley": William Duer: Politician, Entrepreneur, and Speculator, 1768–1799* (Philadelphia: American Philosophical Society, 1992), 152. See also Anderson, "Richard Soderstrom," 3–9.

As apparent from Morris's 1793 letter above, Soderstrom had at least one son. J. Thomas Scharf and Thompson Westcott, *History of Philadelphia, 1609–1884* (Philadelphia: Everts and Co., 1884), 2:923, declare that Soderstrom married a Philadelphia woman and had children with her, but the date of this marriage is unclear. L'Enfant's extensive accounting notes make no mention of Soderstrom's family. For an interpretation of L'Enfant and Soderstrom's relationship as one involving romantic love and sex, see Bob Arnebeck, "To Tease and Torment: Two Presidents Confront Suspicions of Sodomy," at http://bobarnebeck.com/LEnfant.htm (accessed July 27, 2010). Arnebeck cites John Trumbull's papers to say that "Friends like the artist John Trumbull thought of the two as a pair." For a more cautious exploration of the two men's relationship, see Bowling, *Peter Charles L'Enfant.* For background, see Thomas A. Foster, ed., *Long Before Stonewall: Histories of Same-Sex Sexuality in Early America* (New York: New York University Press, 2007), and Richard Godbeer, *The Overflowing of Friendship: Love Between Men and the Creation of the American Republic* (Baltimore: Johns Hopkins University Press, 2009).

6. Entries for January 11, March 15 and 22, and April 5, 1794 in "Journal, 1791–1801," Robert Morris Business Papers, HSP; Joseph Jackson, *Market Street, Philadelphia: The Most Historic Highway in America, Its Merchants and Its Story* (Philadelphia: Joseph Jackson, 1918), 151; Jacob Cox Parsons, ed., *Extracts from the Diary of Jacob Hiltzheimer, of Philadelphia, 1765–1798* (Philadelphia: William F. Fell and Co., 1893), 177; and entry for Sproul in Sandra L. Tatman and Roger W. Moss, *Biographical Dictionary of Philadelphia Architects, 1700–1930* (Boston: G.K. Hall, 1985), 745.

7. Burton Wallace to Major L'enfaunt, February 6, [1794 or 1795], Morgan collection of Digges-L'Enfant-Morgan Papers, LOC (quotations). This letter is filed in the folder for February 1792, but the top right of the paper is missing, where the year is written. I have not been able to determine an exact year based on the letter's internal evidence (digging a water well, finishing lath in the Basement), but the letter was certainly written later than 1792. L'Enfant was in Philadelphia during late February 1794 (thus obviating the need for a letter to him in New York), so it was likely written in 1795. For John Sproul, see James F. O'Gorman, *Drawing Toward Building: Philadelphia Architectural Graphics, 1732–1986* (Philadelphia: Published for the Pennsylvania Academy of Fine Arts by the University of Pennsylvania Press, 1986), 43; *The Carpenters' Company of the City and County of Philadelphia: Instituted 1724* (Philadelphia: H. C. Coates, 1887), 88; *Reminiscences of*

Carpenters' Hall, in the City of Philadelphia, and Extracts from the Ancient Minutes of the Proceedings of the Carpenters' Company of the City and County of Philadelphia (Philadelphia: Crissy and Markley, 1858); and Hardie, *Philadelphia Directory* (1794), 146. For some reason, Sproul was listed as a "B[lack?]Smith" in the city tax ledger for 1791. See Tax Assessor's Ledger, South Ward, 1791, City Archives, Philadelphia, Pennsylvania.

8. The suggestion that L'Enfant played a role in the design of the New Theatre, also known as the Chestnut Street Theater, comes from Richard D. Stine, "The Philadelphia Theatre 1682–1829; Its Growth as a Cultural Institution" (Ph.D. diss., University of Pennsylvania, 1951), and James D. Kornwolf, *Architecture and Town Planning in Colonial North America* (Baltimore: Johns Hopkins University Press, 2002), 3:1421. For the theater itself, see Heather S. Nathans, *Early American Theatre from the Revolution to Thomas Jefferson: Into the Hands of the People* (New York: Cambridge University Press, 2003), 64–68, 72–73, and George B. Tatum, *Penn's Great Town: 250 Years of Philadelphia Architecture* (Philadelphia: University of Pennsylvania Press, 1961), 61, 169.

9. John O'Keeffe, *The Castle of Andalusia; A Comic Opera, in Three Acts,* reprinted in Mrs. Inchbald, *The British Theatre; or, A Collection of Plays, which are acted at The Theatres Royal, Drury-Lane, Covent Garden, and Haymarket* (London: Longman, Hurst, Rees, and Orme, 1808), vol. 22 (first quotation); *General Advertiser* (April 14, 1794) (last quotations). For the opening night program, see *General Advertiser* (February 17, 1794). Morris's role in the theater can be seen in Nathans, *Early American Theatre,* 64–68, 72–73, and in the entries for April 22, June 15, and July 13, 1793, and January 11 and February 15, 1794, in "Journal, 1791–1801," Robert Morris Business Papers, HSP. See also Thomas Clark Pollock, *The Philadelphia Theatre in the Eighteenth Century* (Philadelphia: University of Pennsylvania Press, 1933), 53–55; Scharf and Westcott, *History of Philadelphia,* 2:970, 1076; and George O. Seilhamer, *History of the American Theatre: New Foundations* (Philadelphia: Globe Printing House, 1891), 151.

10. James Hardie, *Philadelphia Directory and Register,* 2d ed. (Philadelphia: Jacob Johnson and Co., 1794), 89 (first quotation); Deborah Logan to John F. Watson, in "Letters & Communications addressed to John F. Watson on the subject of his Annals of Philadelphia, and Respecting the primitive manners & customs, and the early Historical incidents of Philadelphia and the adjacent Country," vol. 1, HSP (last quotation); Jeffery M. Dorwart, *Fort Mifflin of Philadelphia: An Illustrated History* (Philadelphia: University of Pennsylvania Press, 1998), 70–73.

11. Parsons, *Extracts from the Diary of Jacob Hiltzheimer,* 206–7; Tench Coxe to Alexander Hamilton, June 30, 1794 (first quotations), and Tench Coxe to Henry Knox, July 9, 1794 (last quotations), in Harold C. Syrett, ed., *The Papers of Alexander Hamilton* (New York: Columbia University Press, 1972), 16:538–40; Bowling, *Peter Charles L'Enfant,* 41–42.

12. J. Hiltzheimer to Charles L'Enfant, September 11, 1794, in Morgan collection of Digges-L'Enfant-Morgan Papers, LOC; Parsons, *Extracts from the Diary of Jacob Hiltzheimer,* 207; Logan to Watson, in "Letters & Communications addressed to John F. Watson," vol. 1, HSP; Pierre Charles L'Enfant to Alexander Hamilton, September 15, 1794, in Harold C. Syrett, ed., *The Papers of Alexander Hamilton* (New York: Columbia University Press, 1972), 17:236 (quotations). Earlier that summer, L'Enfant had called on the assistance of Tench Francis, Philadelphia's port agent and a War Department contact, to help clear the "maneuvering" involving supplies of stone and logs which had served to "delay and frustrate the accomplishment of" work on the project. P. L'Enfant to Tench Francis, [circa July 1794], Morgan collection of Digges-L'Enfant-Morgan Papers, LOC.

13. Logan to Watson, in "Letters & Communications addressed to John F. Watson," vol. 1, HSP (first quotations); entries for December 20 and 31, 1792, in "Journal, 1791–1801," Robert Morris Business Papers, HSP; Henry Wansey, *The Journal of an Excursion to the United States of North America, in the Summer of 1794* (Salisbury: J. Easton, 1796), 132 (last quotation); "Dancing Assembly of Philadelphia," *Pennsylvania Magazine of History and Biography* 21 (1897): 122–23; and O'Gorman, *Drawing Toward Building,* 42–43. Curiously, Logan added that the unfinished Dancing Hall "is now the African Church," but the two church buildings erected in the 1790s for black congregations—St. Thomas and Bethel—were constructed and acquired under different circumstances. Perhaps the building was moved. Joshua Francis Fisher corroborated L'Enfant's connection with the Dancing Assembly's commission; he asserted that "Major L'Enfant was also employed to build the Hall for the City Dancing Assembly. A sum was raised which was estimated sufficient, but it was all used up before the building had risen many feet above the surface of the ground, kitchens, wine-vaults and ice-house being all that was to show. The undertaking was abandoned & never renewed." But Fisher added that the Assembly's "lot on 5th Street was next South of St. Thomas African Church, and was for a long time covered by a shell of a building, perhaps the superstructure to Major L'Enfant's cellars." He stated that his uncle was a treasurer of the Assembly's

building fund. See Joshua Francis Fisher, "A Section of the Memoirs of Joshua Francis Fisher, Philadelphia Social Scene from the Time of the Hamiltons to the Early Part of the Nineteenth Century," Cadwalader Collection, Series 9, Joshua Francis Fisher Papers, HSP.

It is unclear exactly when (and even if) L'Enfant refurbished the Assembly's room at Oeller's, but if he did, it must have been between 1792 and 1794. Historians who attribute his hand there include Fiske Kimball, "Pierre Charles L'Enfant," in *Dictionary of American Biography,* edited by Dumas Malone (New York: Charles Scribner's Sons, 1933), 6:165–69 and H. Paul Caemmerer, *The Life of Pierre Charles L'Enfant, Planner of the City Beautiful, the City of Washington* (Washington, D.C.: National Republic, 1950), 264.

14. John Bach McMaster, *The Life and Times of Stephen Girard: Mariner and Merchant* (Philadelphia: J. B. Lippincott Company, 1918), 1:278–79 (quotation); Roger Kennedy, *Orders from France: The Americans and the French in a Revolutionary World, 1780–1820* (New York: Knopf, 1989), 99.

15. Robert G. Stewart, *Robert Edge Pine: A British Portrait Painter in America* (Washington, D.C.: Smithsonian Institution Press, 1979), 13, 15, 71 (quotations); entries for July 17, 1792, July 22, 1793, and February 7, 1795, in "Journal, 1791–1801," Robert Morris Business Papers, HSP. For Morris's hand in early coinage, see John Catanzariti, ed., *The Papers of Robert Morris, 1781–1784* (Pittsburgh: University of Pittsburgh Press, 1988), 7:737–43, and for his involvement with coin design as senator, see Elizabeth M. Nuxoll, "The Financier as Senator: Robert Morris of Pennsylvania, 1789–1795," in Kenneth R. Bowling and Donald R. Kennon, eds., *Neither Separate nor Equal: Congress in the 1790s* (Athens, Oh.: Published for the United States Capitol Historical Society by Ohio University Press, 2000), 109. For Morris's involvement with the national flag, see Marla R. Miller, *Betsy Ross and the Making of America* (New York: Henry Holt and Co., 2010). In 1793, the Morrises worked with noted artist John Trumbull, commissioning two portraits from him. See entry for June 29, 1793, in "Journal, 1791–1801," Robert Morris Business Papers, HSP.

16. Robert Morris to George Washington, June 15, 1784, in Nuxoll and Gallagher, *Papers of Robert Morris,* 9:394–95 (first quotations); Robert Morris to Mary Morris, and Robert Morris to Thomas Morris, January 9, 1788, and January 18, 1793, respectively, Collection of Papers of Robert Morris, HUNT (second and last quotations).

17. Robert Morris to C. P. L'Enfant, September 24, 1794, Robert Morris Papers, LOC (quotation). After visits to Washington, D.C., in 1796, Morris

would state plainly that "Major L'Enfant deserves high credit for his Plan of the city" and that "in my opinion the Commissrs aught never to have parted with his services." Robert Morris to John Miller, October 5, 1796, Robert Morris Papers, LOC. For his subscription to the *Columbia Magazine*, see entry for January 14, 1792, in "Journal, 1791–1801," Robert Morris Business Papers, HSP.

18. Berg, *Grand Avenues*, 105–12; Cynthia R. Field, Isabelle Gournay, and Thomas P. Somma, eds., *Paris on the Potomac: The French Influence on the Architecture and Art of Washington, D.C.* (Athens, Oh.: Ohio University Press, 2007); Ron Katz, ed., *French America: French Architecture from Colonialization to the Birth of a Nation* (New York: Published for the French Heritage Society, 2004).

19. *Cassell's French-English, English-French Dictionary* (New York: Macmillan, 1981), 405. Michel Gallet, *Paris Domestic Architecture of the 18th Century* (London: Barrie and Jenkins, 1972); Wend von Kalnein and Michael Levey, *Art and Architecture of the Eighteenth Century in France*, translation of part two by J. R. Foster (Harmondsworth, Middlesex: Penguin Books, 1972); Kornwolf, *Architecture and Town Planning in Colonial North America*, 1:185–99.

In 1864, Philadelphian Joshua Francis Fisher observed this connection, stating that Morris's "house was in the style of a French Château, or rather private Hôtel of the largest class." Joshua Francis Fisher, "A Section of the Memoirs of Joshua Francis Fisher."

20. The building is now the Musée Rodin. Jean Aubert, who is assigned primary design credit for the Hôtel Biron, was trained as a draftsman under Jules Hardouin-Mansart. Ange-Jacques Gabriel, the more prominent of the pair, also trained under Mansart and was premier architect to Louis XV. See Jacques-François Blondel, *Architecture Française* (Paris: C. A. Jombert, 1752), 2:205–7; J. Vacquier, *Ancien Hôtel du Maine et de Biron en Dernier Lieu Établissement des Dames du Sacré-Cœur* (Paris: Contet, 1909); Gallet, *Paris Domestic Architecture*, 40; Wend von Kalnein, *Architecture in France in the Eighteenth Century* (New Haven: Yale University Press, 1995), 53; Kalnein and Levey, *Art and Architecture of the Eighteenth Century in France*, 245–46; Fiske Kimball, *The Creation of the Rococo* (New York: Norton and Co., 1943), 78, 98, 131, 136, 148; and Andrew Ayers, *The Architecture of Paris: An Architectural Guide* (Stuttgart; London: Edition Axel Menges, 2004), 146–47.

Fiske Kimball initially proposed the connection between the Folly and the Hôtel Biron, specifically in the "end 'pavilions' with curved faces" on each of the buildings. See Fiske Kimball, *Domestic Architecture of the American*

Colonies and of the Early Republic (New York: Charles Scribner's Sons, 1922), 169–70 (quotation); Kimball, "Pierre Charles L'Enfant," *Dictionary of American Biography,* 6:168. James Kornwolf proposed that L'Enfant's plan for Morris's house be traced back to the primary precedent in France for an H plan, the Château de Madrid, near Paris, begun in 1527, with its narrow loggia connecting two larger, square pavilions. Kornwolf also noted the relation between the curvilinear features of Morris's house and the feel of the French Baroque at the Château de Vaux-le-Vicomte, near Melun, built between 1657 and 1661. See Kornwolf, *Architecture and Town Planning in Colonial North America,* 1:186, 194–96 and 3:1461–62.

   L'Enfant's willingness to adapt Parisian architecture to Philadelphia generally is demonstrated in a 1787 letter to William Temple Franklin, in which he outlines his vision for an unknown (probably unbuilt) Philadelphia commission for the cosmopolitan young man: "The outside of the building I propose to surround with small shops under cover of a gallery the effect of which you are to be better juge [*sic*] than anyone here having seen something similar in the _____ that surround the comedie francaise at Paris or that surround the palais _____ garden." P. C. L'Enfant to W. T. Franklin, January 29, 1787, American Philosophical Society, reprinted in Caemmerer, *The Life of Pierre Charles L'Enfant,* 264–65.

21. "Odier & Bousquet, Brothers," *Philadelphia Gazette* (January 6, 1794) (quotation); Andrew J. Brunk, "'To Fix the Taste of Our Country Properly': The French Style in Philadelphia Interiors, 1788–1800" (M.A. thesis, University of Delaware, 2000); David McCullough, *John Adams* (New York: Simon and Schuster, 2001), 302–32; Howard C. Rice, Jr., *Thomas Jefferson's Paris* (Princeton, N.J.: Princeton University Press, 1976), 8–9, 121–22; Field, Gournay, and Somma, *Paris on the Potomac.*

22. Robert Mills, quoted in Kennedy, *Orders from France,* 429–52 (first quotation, on p. 443); "List of Baggage Shipped by Jefferson from France" memorandum, in Julian P. Boyd, ed., *The Papers of Thomas Jefferson* (Princeton, N.J.: Princeton University Press, 1958), 15:375–77; "Charlottesville-Monticello-Mr. Jefferson-University of Va," *Niles National Register* 56 (July 6, 1839), 302 (last quotation); Susan R. Stein, *The Worlds of Thomas Jefferson at Monticello* (New York: H.N. Abrams; Thomas Jefferson Memorial Foundation, 1993), 152–54; Marc Leepson, *Saving Monticello: The Levy Family's Epic Quest to Rescue the House That Jefferson Built* (New York: Free Press, 2001), 9–29; *Thomas Jefferson's Monticello* (Chapel Hill: University of North Carolina Press for the Thomas Jefferson Foundation, 2002), 1–33.

For an examination of Monticello as political metaphor, see Dell Upton, *Architecture in the United States* (New York: Oxford University Press, 1998), 20–56, and Duncan Faherty, *Remodeling the Nation: The Architecture of American Identity, 1776–1858* (Durham, N.H.: University of New Hampshire Press, 2007), 24–36. Jan Cohn, in *The Palace or the Poorhouse: The American House as a Cultural Symbol* (East Lansing: Michigan State University Press, 1979), voices a common judgment that Jefferson "was the first [American] to pioneer in building his home in accordance with a unique model" (p. 34), which we find is not correct.

Jefferson had corresponded with L'Enfant on April 10, 1791, regarding the President's House in Washington, D.C., when he recommended "the Galerie du Louvre, the Gardes meubles, and two fronts of the Hotel de Salm," as examples of "the celebrated fronts of Modern buildings which have already received the approbation of all good judges" and which would serve as good models. Jefferson also proposed to circulate copies of illustrations obtained in Europe of "a dozen or two of the handsomest fronts of private buildings" to Georgetown residents, to help "decide the taste of the new town." Thomas Jefferson to Pierre Charles L'Enfant, April 10, 1791, and Thomas Jefferson to George Washington, April 10, 1791, in Julian P. Boyd, ed., *The Papers of Thomas Jefferson* (Princeton, N.J.: Princeton University Press, 1982), 20:86–88. See also Damie Stillman, "Six Houses for the President," *Pennsylvania Magazine of History and Biography* 129 (October 2005): 424.

23. Robert Morris to Thomas Morris, December 15, 1793, Thomas Morris manuscripts, NYHS; William Morris to Mary Morris, February 25, 1794 (first quotations), and William Morris to Mary Morris, June 16, 1794 (last quotations), Collection of Papers of Robert Morris, HUNT; entry for December 16, 1793, in "Journal, 1791 1801," Robert Morris Business Papers, HSP. In his June letter, William added that "the only fault I found with my voyage was that it was not sufficiently boisterous." It seems that immediately prior to this trip, William had worked a short stint at the office of Matthew Carey. See Tax Assessor's Ledger, Middle Ward, 1794, Philadelphia City Archives. For Robert's description of William, see Robert Morris to Samuel Bean, June 1, 1795, Robert Morris Papers, LOC.

24. Robert Morris to Thomas Morris, March 30, 1794, Collection of Papers of Robert Morris, HUNT. In New York, Thomas considered joining the army in the event of war, an idea to which his father gave his reluctant support.

25. John Jay to Sarah Jay, April 9, 1794, quoted in Landa M. Freeman, Louise V. North, and Janet M. Wedge, eds., *Selected Letters of John Jay and Sarah*

Livingston Jay (Jefferson, N.C.: McFarland and Co., 2004), 219 (quotation); Richard Norton Smith, *Patriarch: George Washington and the New American Nation* (Boston and New York: Houghton Mifflin Company, 1993), 202; Syrett, *Papers of Alexander Hamilton,* 16:262; and Stanley Elkins and Eric McKitrick, *The Age of Federalism: The Early American Republic, 1788–1800* (New York: Oxford University Press, 1993), 375–96.

26. Angelica Church to Elizabeth Hamilton, July 30, 1794, printed in Allan McLane Hamilton, *The Intimate Life of Alexander Hamilton* (New York: Charles Scribner's Sons, 1910), 259–60 (first quotation); Robert Gilmor, "Memorandums made in a Tour to the Eastern States in the Year 1797," reprinted in *Bulletin, Showing Titles of Books Added to the Boston Public Library with Bibliographical Notes, Etc.* 11 (April 1892): 85 (last quotation); Fiske Kimball, *Mr. Samuel McIntire, Carver: The Architect of Salem* (Portland, Maine: Southworth-Anthoensen Press, 1940), 88; "Palace," *Oxford English Dictionary* online; Gwyn Headley, *Architectural Follies in America* (New York: John Wiley and Sons, Inc., 1996), 60. Prior to the American Revolution, the term "palace" had appeared as one of derision in New England; for example, in 1761, Anglicans in Cambridge, Massachusetts, made plans for a large home which local dissenters then ridiculed as the "bishop's palace." See Jon Butler, *Awash in a Sea of Faith: Christianizing the American People* (Cambridge, Mass.: Harvard University Press, 1990), 197.

27. Robert Morris to Laurent Concler, June 15, 1795, facsimile in Society Small Collection, Robert Morris section, HSP (quotations). See also Gouverneur Morris to Robert Morris, January 24, 1794, Gouverneur Morris Papers, LOC; Robert Morris to Thomas Morris, March 28, 1794, Collection of Papers of Robert Morris, HUNT; Robert Morris to Sylvanus Bourne, June 27, 1794, Society Small Collection, Robert Morris section, HSP; John Jay to Alexander Hamilton, September 11, 1794, in Syrett, *Papers of Alexander Hamilton,* 17:221–23.

28. Robert Morris to Laurent Concler, June 15, 1795, facsimile in Society Small Collection, Robert Morris section, HSP (first quotations) and Robert Morris to Patrick Colquhoun, December 22, 1794, Robert Morris Papers, LOC (last quotation); *Independent Gazetteer* (November 19, 1794). For Robert Morris, Jr.'s, position at the Delaware Works, see Robert Morris to Charles Croxall, February 24, 1795, Robert Morris Papers, LOC.

29. John F. Watson, *Annals of Philadelphia, Being a Collection of Memoirs, Anecdotes, & Incidents of the City and Its Inhabitants From the Days of the Pilgrim Founders* (Philadelphia: Carey and Hart, 1830), 355 (first quotation); James

Kent, "Journal of a trip to Washington, D.C., December 5, 1793 to January 3, 1794," James Kent Papers, reel 1, volume 1, LOC (last quotation, emphasis in the original); entries for May through August 1794, in "Journal, 1794–1801," Robert Morris Business Papers, HSP. Kent confirmed earlier observations by Samuel Blodget, who in 1793 stated that the house's walls were intended to be five feet thick. See Samuel Blodget to commissioners of the District of Columbia, July 7 and July 17, 1793, quoted in Arnebeck, *Through a Fiery Trial,* 168. The Chestnut Street property's tax valuation went up in 1794 from £3,000 to £3,500, with the new notation "Robert Morris's Est. Lotts & Cellars." Tax Assessor's Ledger, South Ward, 1794, Philadelphia City Archives. Watson's friend Deborah Logan recalled that Morris spent "20 000 in the construction of the vaults." See Logan to Watson, in "Letters & Communications addressed to John F. Watson," vol. 1, HSP. In 1887, the *American Architect and Building News* reported that workmen then digging a cellar at 723 Sansom Street, in the center of what was Morris's block, "came upon the massive foundations" of Morris's house. The report stated that "the cellars were divided into two stories" with "broad six-foot foundations." "Robert Morris's Folly," *American Architect and Building News* 22 (October 8, 1887): 176. Belowground servant spaces and even kitchens were not uncommon in the era, as demonstrated at Jefferson's Monticello and in town houses throughout the North Atlantic rim. See Bernard L. Herman, *Town House: Architecture and Material Life in the Early American City, 1780–1830* (Chapel Hill: Published for OIEAHC by the University of North Carolina Press, 2005), 135–46.

30. Entries throughout 1794 in "Journal, 1794–1801," Robert Morris Business Papers, HSP.

31. Gouverneur Morris to Robert Morris, August 14 (first quotation) and October 2, 1794 (last quotations), Gouverneur Morris Papers, LOC.

32. Gouverneur Morris to Robert Morris, December 28, 1794, Gouverneur Morris Papers, LOC; Robert Morris to Josiah Watson, January 27, 1795, Robert Morris Papers, LOC; entries for January 11, February 15, and June 16, 1794, in "Journal, 1791–1801," Robert Morris Business Papers, HSP; entries for April through November 1794 in "Journal, 1794–1801," Robert Morris Business Papers, HSP; William Morris to Mary Morris, December 6, 1794, Collection of Papers of Robert Morris, HUNT; Alexander Hamilton to Elizabeth Hamilton, July 31, 1794, in Syrett, *Papers of Alexander Hamilton,* 16:627–28.

33. Gouverneur Morris to Robert Morris, December 28, 1794, Gouverneur Morris Papers, LOC.

34. Timothy Pickering, quoted in *Pennsylvania Archives* (Philadelphia and Harrisburg, Penn.: Joseph Severns and State Printers), 12:411 (quotation); entries for May 17, October 25, and December 13, 1794, in "Journal, 1794–1801," Robert Morris Business Papers, HSP; Parsons, *Extracts From the Diary of Jacob Hiltzheimer,* 208; Promissory note from Robert Morris to P. L'Enfant, October 22, 1794, James Dudley Morgan collection, LOC; Bowling, *Peter Charles L'Enfant,* 42; and Dorwart, *Fort Mifflin of Philadelphia,* 71–75.

CHAPTER 6. HIS FOLLY

1. "The Folly of Pride," *The Philadelphia Minerva* 1 (March 21, 1795), 2. Earlier, in 1788, Philadelphian Peter Markoe had attacked William Bingham and the Federalists directly in his satirical poem "The Times," which included such lines as: "Tho' to thy mansion wits and fops repair, / To game, to feast, to saunter, and to stare— / Thine eyes amid the crowd, who fawn and bend, / View many a parasite, but not one friend." His poem also targeted the "villainy" of Bingham's wartime acquisition of wealth and anticipated his downfall. See Peter Markoe, *The Times, A Poem* (Philadelphia: Prichard and Hall, 1788).

2. "To the Printers of the American Daily Advertiser" [Philadelphia: 1795], Printed Ephemera Collection, Portfolio 148, Folder 27, LOC (first quotation); "Foreign Miscellany" *Federal Mirror* [Concord, New Hampshire] 3 (June 26, 1795) (last quotations). The American newspapers used an English translation of the French letters that was more charged than the translation Morris used when he published them in his broadside response. To highlight the effect on American readers, I have used the American newspapers' translation. See also, for example, "London. March 13," *Daily Advertiser* [New York City] (June 8, 1795); "State of Georgia, County of Greene &c.," *Hampshire Gazette* [Northampton, Massachusetts] (June 24, 1795). Morris often refers to Fauche as Fauches, as in his broadside and in a letter to his son William on April 26, 1795, Robert Morris Papers, LOC. The "tippling house" keeper Fauche was a major in the Georgia militia. See Harold C. Syrett, ed., *The Papers of Alexander Hamilton* (New York: Columbia University Press, 1973), 18:366. Fauche and Fauchet's letters were also published in British newspapers.

3. "To the Printers of the American Daily Advertiser"; *Dunlap's American Daily Advertiser* (June 15, 1795); *American Minerva; an Evening Advertiser*

[New York City] (June 19, 1795). See also *Observations on the North-American Land-Company, Lately Instituted in Philadelphia* (London: Galabin, 1796), 83–96. Morris's strategy also included placing his rebuttals in Parisian and British newspapers. See Robert Morris to John Richard, April 26, 1795, Robert Morris to John B. Church, June 7, 1795, and Robert Morris to William Temple Franklin, June 17, 1795, Robert Morris Papers, LOC. For an example of a purchaser who, at this time, had difficulty taking up Morris on his offer to repurchase sales from unsatisfied parties, see Robert Morris to Le Roy, April 6, 1795, Robert Morris Papers, LOC. Morris seems to have meant it, though, as he reiterated the general offer in a private letter to his son William, then in France; see Robert Morris to William W. Morris, April 26, 1795, Robert Morris Papers, LOC.

4. In another example of his affability, or his salesmanship, he even insisted that "This unprovoked and unexpected Attack will produce good instead of Evil as it affords an oppy of laying before the Public Proofs of the good quality of the Lands of the Certainty of Title, and of the Cautions I used previous to the purchase in regard to those points, which I could not otherwise have introduced into the public View." Robert Morris to John B. Church, June 7, 1795, Robert Morris Papers, LOC.

5. Entries throughout 1793 and early 1794, in "Journal, 1791–1801," and entries for 1794 and early 1795, in "Journal, 1794–1801," Robert Morris Business Papers, HSP.

   By way of explanation for this behavior, again, William Sumner's conclusions are just: "The habit of dealing with large sums on paper when he was public Financier, the glory of giving credit to the United States by his personal endorsement, the discovery that he could with facility circulate his personal notes as currency, and the prestige which he had enjoyed, were enough to turn the head of any man. They led him to that saddest of all human delusions . . . namely, that although other men are fools, one's self is wise." William Graham Sumner, *The Financier and the Finances of the American Revolution* (New York: Dodd, Mead, and Company, 1892), 2:278.

6. Gouverneur Morris to Robert Morris, February 26, May 26, and September 8, 1793, Gouverneur Morris Papers, LOC; Oliver Wolcott, Jr., to Alexander Hamilton, January 4, 1794, in Harold C. Syrett, ed., *The Papers of Alexander Hamilton* (New York: Columbia University Press, 1969), 15:618–19; and John Nicholson to Robert Morris, July 12, 1793, John Nicholson Letter Books, HSP. See also Bourdieu, Chollet, and Bourdieu to Talleyrand de Périgord, August 6, 1794, and "Introduction," in Hans Huth and

Wilma J. Pugh, eds., "Talleyrand in America as a Financial Promoter, 1794–1796," vol. 2, *Annual Report of the American Historical Association For the Year 1941* (1942), 12, 67; Thompson Westcott, *The Historic Mansions and Buildings of Philadelphia, With Some Notice of Their Owners and Occupants* (Philadelphia: Porter and Coates, 1877), 364; Sumner, *The Financier and Finances of the American Revolution*, 2:278.

7. James Kent, "Journal of a trip to Washington, D.C., December 5, 1793 to January 3, 1794," James Kent Papers, reel 1, volume 1, LOC (first quotations); Bob Arnebeck, *Through a Fiery Trial: Building Washington, 1790–1800* (Lanham: Madison Books, 1991), 182; Gouverneur Morris to Robert Morris, July 9, 1793, Gouverneur Morris Papers, LOC (last quotation). After a week in Philadelphia, Kent stated flatly that Morris "has more men under his Patronage & moneyed Influence than any other man in the Union." Kent concluded his observations on Morris by joking that "had he lived during the free Period of Athenian Liberty, he would have had the Honor of the Ostracism." For a similar observation, see Huth and Pugh, "Talleyrand in America as a Financial Promoter," 25, 28–29. For an example of Morris's continued involvement in securities, see Robert Morris to James Dunlop, February 7, 1795, Robert Morris Papers, LOC. For the Morris family's trips to the Delaware Works, see entries for 1794 in "Journal, 1791–1801," Robert Morris Business Papers, HSP. For Morris's canal leadership, see *Dunlap's American Daily Advertiser* (January 7, 1794) and *Stephens's Philadelphia Directory, For 1796; or, Alphabetical Arrangement: Containing the Names, Occupations, and Places of Abode of the Citizens* (Philadelphia: W. Woodward for Thomas Stephens, 1796), 53. For his participation in canal and bridge company activity on the Potomac River, see Robert D. Arbuckle, *Pennsylvania Speculator and Patriot: The Entrepreneurial John Nicholson, 1757–1800* (University Park: Pennsylvania State University Press, 1975), 129. For his mercantile activity and the sale of his ships, see entries for July 1, 1794, and June 25, 1796, in "Journal, 1791–1801," and entry for June 5, 1800, in "Journal, 1794–1801," Robert Morris Business Papers, HSP. He kept his barque *Cesar* to ship flour, as in entries for July 19, July 28, and August 26, 1794, in "Journal, 1794–1801," and he kept his brig *Superb,* as in entry for August 4, 1794, in "Journal, 1794–1801." For another example of his use of his ships for trading during this time, see Robert Morris to Josiah Watson, January 27, 1795, Robert Morris Papers, LOC. For Morris's partnerships, see Nuxoll, "The Financier as Senator," 117 and Chapter 3 above.

8. "At a meeting of the Subscribers to the new Dancing Assembly," October 24, 1792, in oversize "City Dancing Assembly of Philadelphia" folio, AM.3075, HSP; Robert Morris to the President of Pennsylvania (John Dickinson), November 9, 1782, in John Catanzariti, ed., *The Papers of Robert Morris, 1781–1784* (Pittsburgh: University of Pittsburgh Press, 1988), 7:29–38; Charles Rappleye, *Robert Morris: Financier of the American Revolution* (New York: Simon and Schuster, 2010), 392, 496. For John Nicholson's background generally, see Arbuckle, *Pennsylvania Speculator and Patriot*, 1–12.

   While trying to sort through these details, I humbly recall Harold C. Syrett's sobering, expert opinion, offered forty years ago, that "no scholar has had the termerity [*sic*], let alone the ability, to undertake a full-length study analyzing all of Morris's incredibly complex land speculations and his prolonged, as well as spectacular, descent into bankruptcy." Syrett, *Papers of Alexander Hamilton*, 18:359.

9. Arbuckle, *Pennsylvania Speculator and Patriot*, 39, 43–44, 54, 67–68, 151 (Nicholson quoted on 44), and Robert Morris to John Nicholson and John Donaldson, April 28, 1792, Collection of Papers of Robert Morris, HUNT; entries for June 30, 1792, and September 19, 1795, in "Journal 1791–1801," Robert Morris Business Papers, HSP. Nicholson and Morris also ventured into mining operations early: in 1792 they helped form the Lehigh Coal Company near Bethlehem, Pennsylvania. For another view of Nicholson and the origins of his connection to Morris, see Eliza Cope Harrison, ed., *Philadelphia Merchant: The Diary of Thomas P. Cope, 1800–1851* (South Bend, Ind.: Gateway Editions, 1978), 50–51.

10. *Plan of Association of the Pennsylvania Population Company* (n.p., 1792) (quotation); R. Nelson Hale, "The Pennsylvania Population Company," *Pennsylvania History* 16 (April 1949): 122–30; Arbuckle, *Pennsylvania Speculator and Patriot*, 75–92; Rappleye, *Robert Morris*, 497; Barbara Ann Chernow, "Robert Morris: Land Speculator, 1790–1801," (Ph.D. diss., Columbia University, 1974), 104–7; Barbara A. Chernow, "Robert Morris and Alexander Hamilton: Two Financiers in New York," in Joseph R. Frese and Jacob Judd, eds., *Business Enterprise in Early New York* (Tarrytown, N.Y.: Sleepy Hollow Press, 1979), 84; and Elizabeth K. Henderson, "The Northwestern Lands of Pennsylvania, 1790–1812," *Pennsylvania Magazine of History and Biography* 40 (1936): 130–60. For an early, private purchase by the two, involving 9,200 acres of Pennsylvania land, see Robert Morris to John Nicholson, March 6, 1793, Society Small Collection, Robert Morris section, HSP.

11. The two initial French promoters of the Asylum Company were Antoine Omer Talon and Louis Marie, Vicomte de Noailles. See *Plan of Association of the Asylum Company. As Established April 22d. 1794 and Improved April 25th 1795* (Philadelphia: Aitken and Son, 1795); Arbuckle, *Pennsylvania Speculator and Patriot*, 92–99; J. W. Ingham, *A Short History of Asylum, Pennsylvania, Founded in 1793 by the French Exiles in America* (Towanda, Pa.: Towanda Printing Company, 1916), 30–32; Elsie Murray, *Azilum: French Refugee Colony of 1793* (Athens, Pa.: Tioga Point Museum, 1940); Alexander D. Gibson, "The Story of Azilum," *The French Review* 17 (December 1943): 92–98; Chernow, "Robert Morris: Land Speculator," 109–15; Roger G. Kennedy, *Orders from France: The Americans and the French in a Revolutionary World, 1780–1820* (New York: Knopf, 1989), 93; and Norman B. Wilkinson, "A French Asylum on the Susquehanna River," *Historic Pennsylvania Leaflet No. 11* (Harrisburg: Pennsylvania Historical and Museum Commission, 1991).

12. George Washington to the Commissioners for the District of Columbia, August 20, 1793, in Theodore J. Crackel, ed., *The Papers of George Washington: Presidential Series* (Charlottesville: University of Virginia Press, 2007), 13:508–9; Gouverneur Morris to Robert Morris, September 8, 1793, Gouverneur Morris Papers, LOC; [Robert Morris,] *In the Account of Property* (Philadelphia [1801]), 7–11; Allen C. Clark, *Greenleaf and Law in the Federal City* (Washington, D.C.: W. F. Roberts, 1901); Bob Arnebeck, "Tracking the Speculators: Greenleaf and Nicholson in the Federal City," *Washington History* 3 (Spring/Summer 1991): 112–25; Arnebeck, *Through a Fiery Trial*, 176–95; Stanley Elkins and Eric McKitrick, *The Age of Federalism: The Early American Republic, 1788–1800* (New York: Oxford University Press, 1993), 176–79; Chernow, "Robert Morris, Land Speculator," 92–97, 104–38, 175; Bruce H. Mann, *Republic of Debtors: Bankruptcy in the Age of American Independence* (Cambridge, Mass.: Harvard University Press, 2002), 199–201; Sumner, *The Financier and the Finances of the American Revolution*, 2:246–47, 262–65; Arbuckle, *Pennsylvania Speculator and Patriot*, 114–38 and 165–84; and Charles Royster, *The Fabulous History of the Dismal Swamp Company: A Story of George Washington's Times* (New York: Borzoi Books, 1999), 356–60, 372–77, and 382–90. Morris invented and promoted two subscriber schemes in late 1793 and early 1794 to help propel the trio's federal city purchases and finance house construction there.

Nicholson had made initial purchases of squares in the federal city in early 1793, prior to his engagement with Greenleaf. See Arnebeck, *Through a Fiery Trial*, 147. Morris seems to have had financial dealings with Greenleaf as early as January 1793. See Samuel Blodget to Commissioners of the District of Columbia, January 4, 1793, Letters Received, vol. 2, M371, reel 9, National Archives, Washington, D.C.

13. Rappleye, *Robert Morris,* 496 (quotation); Arbuckle, *Pennsylvania Speculator and Patriot,* 47–58; Hale, "The Pennsylvania Population Company"; Sumner, *The Financier and the Finances of the American Revolution,* 2:263.

14. Greenleaf covered the other two partners' portion of the first installment due the city commissioners for their purchases in May 1794. In turn, Morris and Nicholson floated Greenleaf for one year in the land purchases he had bought into with them. In the summer of 1794, strains appeared in Morris and Nicholson's relationship with Greenleaf, as the latter was incurring construction expenses in the federal city, and the plan for their Amsterdam loan was encountering obstacles. Prior to the sale to Law, Morris attempted to enlist the help of Gouverneur, still in France, in selling the Washington lots, but Gouverneur protested that "an Idea had spread itself all over that this Business of the Washington Lotts was a speculation in the nature of Stock jobbing." Gouverneur Morris to Robert Morris, December 28, 1794, Gouverneur Morris Papers, LOC. Law signed his intention to purchase the lots on December 3, 1794, amounting to a total price of $133,000, with the ongoing requirement to build brick houses on a proportion of the lots. Law and Duncanson retained a right to reject their purchase within eighteen months. See Robert Morris to William Constable, April 3, 1795, Robert Morris to James Greenleaf, January 6, February 23, April 3, April 24, and May 27, 1795, and February 26, 1796, and Robert Morris to John Swanwick, January 12, 1795, Robert Morris Papers, LOC; and *In the Account of Property,* 7–11. See also Chernow, "Robert Morris, Land Speculator," 129–69; Mann, *Republic of Debtors,* 199–201; Arbuckle, *Pennsylvania Speculator and Patriot,* 114–38; Arnebeck, "Tracking the Speculators"; and Arnebeck, *Through a Fiery Trial,* 240–80, 293–95.

15. *Plan of Association of the North American Land Company* (Philadelphia: Aitken and Son, 1795), 3 (quotation). The partners forbade themselves from selling shares for less than $100 each, and the total number of shares was thirty thousand. The company's three trustees, settled upon after initial selections including Thomas Willing backed out, were Frederick Muhlenberg, Matthew Clarkson, and Jared Ingersoll. For Morris's explanation of how the company's operations would work, and his view of its unique advantages, see Robert Morris to W. & J. Willink, March 16, 1795, Robert Morris to Bird Savage & Bird, March 20, 1795, and Robert Morris to

William Temple Franklin, April 22, 1795, Robert Morris Papers, LOC. His letters that season reveal that he was basing his faith in land on his earlier Genesee sales and even on the original example of William Penn in Pennsylvania. See also Chernow, "Robert Morris, Land Speculator," 170–98; Katharine M. Beals, "The Land Speculations of a Great Patriot," *Bulletin of the Business Historical Society* 3 (1929): 1–9; and Arbuckle, *Pennsylvania Speculator and Patriot*, 165–84.

16. For the Asylum Company transaction, see Robert Morris to John Nicholson, April 23, 1795, Robert Morris Papers, LOC. Morris initially considered selling his and Nicholson's interest in the Washington lots to Greenleaf, rather than the other way around, but decided that "it was more likely that the Lotts would command money to pay our Debts than Mr. G's paper." See Robert Morris to William Constable, July 27, 1795, Robert Morris Papers, LOC; deed from James Greenleaf to Robert Morris and John Nicholson, May 13, 1796, in pursuance of an agreement made by the parties the 10 July 1795, "Robert Morris Papers," Reed and Forde Collection, HSP; Arbuckle, *Pennsylvania Speculator and Patriot*, 90, 100, 165–84; Mann, *Republic of Debtors*, 200–201; Thomas M. Doerflinger, *A Vigorous Spirit of Enterprise: Merchants and Economic Development in Revolutionary Philadelphia* (Chapel Hill: Published for OIEAHC by the University of North Carolina Press, 1986), 323–29.

An example of mortgage violations during this time appears in Morris's Genesee dealings. In 1794, Morris was overdue on a $50,000 loan from Pulteney Associates, one of his Genesee clients in London, the principal of which had been secured on an unsold Genesee tract known as the Morris Reserve. To make payments on this and other loans, Morris began selling these same mortgaged Reserve lands to other purchasers. This outraged his creditors; in 1795, Pulteney Associates went to court to freeze Morris's sales. See Robert Morris to Benjamin Walker, July 30, 1795, Robert Morris Papers, LOC; Robert Morris to Thomas Morris, March 6, 1796, Collection of Papers of Robert Morris, HUNT; Robert Morris to Alexander Hamilton, April 27, 1796, in Harold C. Syrett, ed., *The Papers of Alexander Hamilton* (New York: Columbia University Press, 1974), 20:141–45; Chernow, "Robert Morris: Land Speculator," 56, 69–72; and Rappleye, *Robert Morris*, 495. Morris expressed embarrassment as this situation unfolded and sought to correct it. See Robert Morris to Samuel Ogden, January 8, 1796, Robert Morris Papers, LOC.

17. Robert Morris to Andrew Craigie, February 24, 1795 (first quotations), Robert Morris to James Smith, Jr., January 10, 1795 (second quotations), Robert Morris to Sharpe Delaney, March 30, 1795 (third quotations), Robert Morris to Thomas Russell, March 18, 1795, and Robert Morris to William Constable, April 3, 1795 (last quotation), all from Robert Morris Papers, LOC.

For other choice examples of Morris's attempted salesmanship, see Robert Morris to Wilhem and Jan Willinks, March 8, 1795, and Robert Morris to John B. Church, May 28, 1795, Robert Morris Papers, LOC. Morris assured John Parish in Europe that "this is not visionary. This is certain as fate." Robert Morris to Parish & Co., May 13, 1795, Robert Morris Papers, LOC. At one point, he described "my own personal Security" to one creditor's agent in 1795 as "perhaps more sufficient than any other Individual in America, notwithstanding what you may hear from the idle Bablers of the day." Robert Morris to Benjamin Walker, July 30, 1795, Robert Morris Papers, LOC.

For Morris's anticipation of peace in Europe, see Robert Morris to Josiah Watson, January 27, 1795, Robert Morris Papers, LOC. Elizabeth Nuxoll concluded that Morris "ultimately gambled on peace—and that constituted a fatal mistake. Renewed war in Europe and French occupation of Holland in 1795 cut off the capital Morris needed for his land schemes and inhibited passage of the migrants needed for settlement—and war lasted too long for him to have any chance to turn his fortunes around as he had done many times before." Elizabeth M. Nuxoll, "Robert Morris and the Shaping of the Post-Revolutionary American Economy," unpublished paper, 28. See also Elizabeth M. Nuxoll, "The Financier as Senator: Robert Morris of Pennsylvania, 1789–1795," in Kenneth R. Bowling and Donald R. Kennon, eds., *Neither Separate nor Equal: Congress in the 1790s* (Athens, Oh.: Published for the United States Capitol Historical Society by Ohio University Press, 2000), 110.

18. Entry for February 24, 1795, in Duc de La Rochefoucauld-Liancourt, *Journal de voyage en Amérique et d'un séjour a Philadelphie, 1 Octobre 1794–18 Avril 1795*, introduction and notes by Jean Marchand (Baltimore: Johns Hopkins Press, 1940), 102–3 (quotation) (thanks to François Furstenberg for this reference); George C. Mason, *The Life and Works of Gilbert Stuart* (New York: Charles Scribner's Sons, 1879), 225; Eleanor Pearson DeLorme, "Gilbert Stuart: Portrait of an Artist," *Winterthur Portfolio* 14 (Winter 1979): 339–60. For the porcelain orders, see Robert Morris to James Chalmers, March 17, 1795, and Robert Morris to J. Richard, April 11, 1795, Robert Morris Papers,

LOC. In October, Mary would place an order through her daughter traveling abroad for "a Suit of Lace in London." Robert Morris to James Marshall, October 17, 1795, Robert Morris Papers, LOC.

John Adams indicated that little had changed at the Morris home, despite the bad news. After dining there in January 1795, he described "a company of venerable old rakes of us, threescore years of age . . . , smoking cigars, drinking Burgundy and Madeira, and talking politics till almost eleven o'clock." John Adams to Abigail Adams, January 29, 1795, in Charles Francis Adams, ed., *Letters of John Adams, Addressed to His Wife* (Boston: Little and Brown, 1841), 2:175–77.

19. *Gazette of the United States and Daily Evening Advertiser* (January 29, 1795) (first quotation) and *Philadelphia Gazette & Universal Daily Advertiser* (January 29, 1795); Robert Morris to Wilhem and Jan Willinks, March 8, 1795, Robert Morris Papers, LOC (last quotation). For an example of Morris discussing retirement from the Senate earlier, see Thomas Jefferson to James Madison, June 9, 1793, in John Catanzariti, ed., *The Papers of Thomas Jefferson* (Princeton: Princeton University Press, 1995), 26:239–42. For Morris and the navy, see Henry Knox to Alexander Hamilton, April 21, 1794, in Harold C. Syrett, ed., *The Papers of Alexander Hamilton* (New York: Columbia University Press, 1972), 16:304–8 and Nuxoll, "The Financier as Senator." For Hamilton's departure, see entry for February 28, 1795, in "Journal, 1794–1801," Robert Morris Business Papers, HSP; and Alexander Hamilton to Robert Morris, March 18, 1795, in Syrett, *Papers of Alexander Hamilton*, 18:295–301.

Pennsylvania's legislature appointed William Bingham to Morris's seat in the senate, while President Washington replaced Hamilton, returning to New York, with Oliver Wolcott, Jr., previously a treasury official. Morris's last day in the Senate was March 4. That year, a congressional committee found that Morris and his partners owed $93,312 from his position on the Secret Committee during the Revolutionary War. Morris rejected their calculations. See editorial note in Robert Morris, "Memorial to the President, Senate, and House of Representatives," February 8, 1790, in Elizabeth M. Nuxoll and Mary A. Gallagher, eds., *The Papers of Robert Morris, 1781–1784* (Pittsburgh: University of Pittsburgh Press, 1999), 9:633–36; *In the Account of Property*, 29–30; Nuxoll, "The Financier as Senator," 122–23; and Rappleye, *Robert Morris*, 503.

20. Robert Morris to Edward Tilghman, December 27, 1794, Robert Morris to George Hammond, March 23, 1795 (quotation), and Robert Morris to

[P. C.] L'Enfant, September 24, 1795, Robert Morris Papers, LOC; entries for February 12, 1795, and May 30, 1797, in "Journal, 1794–1801," Robert Morris Business Papers, HSP. Morris agreed to pay Bell $1,000 per year in rent while his family continued living in the house. For Bell, see James Hardie, *The Philadelphia Directory and Register,* 2d ed. (Philadelphia: Jacob Johnson and Co., 1794), 10. Robert Kidd bought another piece of the lot, with thirty feet fronting Market Street, for $8,000.

21. March 18, 1795, indenture between Robert and Mary Morris and Andrew Kennedy, reprinted in *Address of Nathaniel Burt, February 12, 1875, on the Washington Mansion in Philadelphia* (Philadelphia: James A. Moore, 1875), 31–32. Morris negotiated to remove certain unique elements in the house; Kennedy agreed to let go of two large mirrors then hanging on the walls, the hall stove, and the marble and wooden baths with their hot water boilers. See also Damie Stillman, "Six Houses for the President," *Pennsylvania Magazine of History and Biography* 129 (October 2005): 419–23. Morris told his creditors abroad that he had sold these properties for "a great price." See Robert Morris to Wilhem and Jan Willink, April 2, 1795, Robert Morris Papers, LOC.

22. Entries for January through March 1795 in "Journal, 1794–1801," Robert Morris Business Papers, HSP. For praise of the stone's quality, see entry for March 1, 1795, in Duc de La Rochefoucauld-Liancourt, *Journal de voyage en Amérique,* 104. For L'Enfant's enthusiasm for stone at the federal city, see Arnebeck, *Through a Fiery Trial,* 81, and William Seale, *The President's House: A History* (Washington, D.C.: White House Historical Association with the cooperation of the National Geographic Society, 1986), 1:24.

23. Entries for January through March 1795 in "Journal, 1794–1801," Robert Morris Business Papers, HSP; entry for April 17, 1795, in Rochefoucauld-Liancourt, *Journal de voyage en Amérique,* 120–21. Morris placed an additional order for more window glass through his son William, who was in Paris. See Robert Morris to William Morris, March 17, 1795, Robert Morris Papers, LOC.

24. Entries for January through September 1795 in "Journal, 1794–1801," Robert Morris Business Papers, HSP. Proviny was also spelled Provini or Provine elsewhere. He does not appear in Philadelphia's city directories for 1794, 1795, or 1796. For Proviny's work in the city of Washington, see entry for April 1794, "Proceedings of the Commissioners for the District of Columbia, 1791–1795," Records of the District of Columbia Commissioners and of the Offices Concerned with Public Buildings, 1791–1867, M371,

microfilm reel 1, National Archives, Washington, D.C., and Virgil E. Mc-
Mahan, *The Artists of Washington, D.C., 1796–1996: An Illustrated Guide*
(Washington, D.C.: Artists of Washington, 1995). For the context of Phila-
delphia interior craftsmanship, see Morrison H. Heckscher and Leslie
Greene Bowman, *American Rococo, 1750–1775: Elegance in Ornament* (New
York: Metropolitan Museum of Art and Los Angeles County Museum of
Art, Distributed by Harry N. Abrams, 1992), and George B. Tatum, *Phila-
delphia Georgian: The City House of Samuel Powel and Some of Its Eighteenth-
Century Neighbors* (Middletown, Conn.: Wesleyan University Press, 1976).

25. Entries for June and July 1795 and February 1796, in "Journal, 1794–1801,"
Robert Morris Business Papers, HSP. The first time the Jardellas showed
up in the Philadelphia directories was in 1802. See James Robinson, *The
Philadelphia Directory, City and County Register, for 1802* (Philadelphia:
Woodward, 1802), 10, 129. For William Bingham's use of Coade stone,
see Robert C. Alberts, *The Golden Voyage: The Life and Times of William
Bingham, 1752–1804* (Boston: Houghton-Mifflin, 1969), 158, and Amy
Hudson Henderson, "Furnishing the Republican Court: Building and
Decorating Philadelphia Homes, 1790–1800" (Ph.D. diss., University of
Delaware, 2008), 94–97.

Most researchers have posited only one Jardella, calling him by the first
name of Giuseppe. Morris's account books and the city directories refer to
the two as "Andrew" and "Joseph." Of the two, Joseph seems to have done
most of the work for Morris. For authors asserting that Giuseppe was
brought from Italy on behalf of Morris, see J. Thomas Scharf and Thompson Westcott, *History of Philadelphia: 1609–1884* (Philadelphia: Everts and
Co., 1884), 2:1066–67; "A Pair of French Girandoles," *Bulletin of the Pennsylvania Museum* 18 (April 1923): 6; and Susan James-Gadzinski and Mary
Mullen Cunningham, *American Sculpture in the Museum of American Art of
the Pennsylvania Academy of the Fine Arts* (Seattle and London: Museum of
American Art of the Pennsylvania Academy of the Fine Arts in association
with the University of Washington Press, 1997), 6–7. In contrast, Richard
N. Juliani has suggested that Jardella arrived in Philadelphia in 1792 and
first began working for other local stonecutters, such as James Traquair.
See Richard N. Juliani, *Building Little Italy: Philadelphia's Italians Before
Mass Migration* (University Park: Pennsylvania State University Press,
1998), 89. That the Jardellas executed the surviving sculpted reliefs, and that
they did so on-site, is a long-standing supposition. The pieces are not signed.
After the house was torn down, William Birch and Joshua Francis Fisher

stated their beliefs that these reliefs were sculpted in Italy. See Chapter 7 and Chapter 8, below. The Jardellas had been preceded in America by an Italian sculptor, Giuseppe Ceracchi, whose proposal to create a huge monument commemorating Washington and the American Revolution, to be placed in the federal city, was not taken up. See Thomas Jefferson to Robert R. Livingston, March 6, 1792, in Charles T. Cullen, ed., *The Papers of Thomas Jefferson* (Princeton, N.J.: Princeton University Press, 1990), 23:229–30.

An additional figure began working on the site that spring—John Paterson, a "Steam Engineer," who was working on a "Steam Engine" that seems not to have been directly related to the house. See entries for February 21 and March 25, 1795, and July 30, 1797, in "Journal, 1794–1801," Robert Morris Business Papers, HSP; and Robert Morris to John Nicholson, March 28, 1795, and Robert Morris to David Ramsay, December 7, 1795, Robert Morris Papers, LOC. See also Jacob Cox Parsons, ed., *Extracts From the Diary of Jacob Hiltzheimer, of Philadelphia, 1765–1798* (Philadelphia: William F. Fell and Co., 1893), 221, and *In the Account of Property*, 23.

26. For Rickett's circus, see Edmund Hogan, *The Prospect of Philadelphia, and Check on the Next Directory, Part 1* (Philadelphia: Bailey, 1795), 141, and Heather S. Nathans, *Early American Theatre from the Revolution to Thomas Jefferson: Into the Hands of the People* (New York: Cambridge University Press, 2003), 102. The lot advertisement comes from *Philadelphia Gazette & Universal Daily Advertiser* (February 21, 1795) (quotation). For the gardens, see *Philadelphia Gazette* (July 2, 1795). The size of Morris's gardens would be roughly equivalent to those of the statehouse. See Anna Coxe Toogood, "Philadelphia as the Nation's Capital, 1790–1800" in Bowling and Kennon, eds., *Neither Separate nor Equal*, 52–53.

Morris bought additional property facing his Chestnut Street block just north on Seventh Street in 1795. See entries for November 2, 1795, and June 13, 1798, in "Journal, 1794–1801," Robert Morris Business Papers, HSP. Humphrey Marshall erected a house on this lot in 1796 after swapping it for Tennessee lands. Also at this time, the city passed a law requiring all new constructions in the city center to be built of brick. See Kenneth Roberts and Anna M. Roberts, trans. and eds., *Moreau de St. Méry's American Journey, 1793–1798* (Garden City, N.Y.: Doubleday and Co., 1947), 261.

27. Parsons, *Extracts From the Diary of Jacob Hiltzheimer*, 214 (first quotation), 220–21; Isaac Weld, Jr., *Travels Through the States of North America, and the Provinces of Upper and Lower Canada, During the Years 1795, 1796, and 1797*, 2d ed. (London: Stockdale, 1799), 1:8–9 (second quotations); and

Moreau de St. Méry, in Roberts, *Moreau de St. Méry's American Journey*, 363 (last quotations). Hiltzheimer recorded visiting the site again in September and November 1795.

28. "Interesting Travels in America. Translated from the German of Bulow . . . Chapter XXXIII," *The Port-Folio* 2 (August 21, 1802), 257 (first quotation), and Edward Fisher to Benjamin Rush, April 15, 1795, Correspondence of Benjamin Rush, vol. F, HSP (last quotation).

29. For the royal clock, see Moreau de St. Méry, in Roberts, *Moreau de St. Méry's American Journey*, 336, and entry for June 5, 1795, in Elaine Forman Crane, *The Diary of Elizabeth Drinker* (Boston: Northeastern University Press, 1991), 1:689. It was "a very curious Clock and Organ," Drinker observed, "that did belong to the Queen of France." Said to have originally cost one thousand guineas, it "plays twenty different tunes, stands on two large fluited mahogany pillars guilt," and was bought in France "by Govr. Morris, for Robt. Morris of this City, for 500 pounds, as we were inform'd." The repairman was Herbert Droze. See entry for July 6, 1795, in "Journal, 1794–1801," Robert Morris Business Papers, HSP, and Henderson, "Furnishing the Republican Court," 181–82. For tales of a royal Gobelin tapestry purchased by Gouverneur for the Morrises and handed down by Philadelphians over generations, see "Historical Relic," *Philadelphia Inquirer* (November 16, 1876).

30. Entry for July 21, 1795, in "Journal, 1794–1801," Robert Morris Business Papers, HSP; Robert Morris to Gilbert Robertson & Munro, July 17, 1705, Robert Morris to L'Enfant, September 24, 1795 (first quotation), Robert Morris Papers, LOC; note for five shares of the North American Land Company, March 24, 1795, in the James Dudley Morgan collection of Digges-L'Enfant-Morgan Papers, LOC. For Morris's business affairs with Soderstrom, see Robert Morris to James Carey, January 30, 1795, Robert Morris to Thomas Russell, March 23, 1795, and Robert Morris to Richard Soderstrom, March 24, 1795, in Robert Morris Papers, LOC.

31. Robert Morris to P. C. L'Enfant, September 24, 1795, Robert Morris Papers, LOC; entry for May 12, 1795, in "Journal, 1794–1801," Robert Morris Business Papers, HSP.

32. Robert Morris to P. C. L'Enfant, September 24, 1795, Robert Morris Papers, LOC.

33. Robert Morris to P. C. L'Enfant, September 25, 1795, Robert Morris Papers, LOC.

34. Robert Morris to Patrick Colquhoun, December 22, 1794, Robert Morris Papers, LOC.

35. For Morris's patience and optimism toward the administration's approach, see Robert Morris to Thomas Jefferson, June 1, 1795, Robert Morris Papers, LOC. See also Elkins and McKitrick, *The Age of Federalism*, 396–414; and Jerald A. Combs, *The Jay Treaty: Political Battleground of the Founding Fathers* (Berkeley and Los Angeles: University of California Press, 1970).

36. Combs, *The Jay Treaty*, 177 (quotation).

37. Parsons, *Extracts From the Diary of Jacob Hiltzheimer*, 215; Len Travers, *Celebrating the Fourth: Independence Day and the Rites of Nationalism in the Early Republic* (Amherst, Mass.: University of Massachusetts Press, 1997), 96–99; David Waldstreicher, *In the Midst of Perpetual Fetes: The Making of American Nationalism, 1776–1820* (Chapel Hill: Published for OIEAHC by the University of North Carolina Press, 1997), 138–39.

38. Oliver Wolcott, Jr., to George Washington, July 26, 1795 (first quotations), and Oliver Wolcott, Jr., to Mrs. Oliver Wolcott, Jr., July 26, 1795, in George Gibbs, *Memoirs of the Administrations of Washington and John Adams, edited from the Papers of Oliver Wolcott, Secretary of the Treasury* (New York: Van Norden, 1846), 1:217–18. See also Combs, *The Jay Treaty*, 161–63, and Alberts, *The Golden Voyage*, 258–60. In May, Benjamin Franklin Bache had organized a related rally to protest a new law banning new wooden buildings in central Philadelphia. Bache saw the act as unconstitutional and "oppressive to the mechanic and poor man." See *General Advertiser* (May 7, 1795), and Toogood, "Philadelphia as the Nation's Capital," 43.

39. Robert Morris to Thomas Jefferson, June 1, 1795, Robert Morris to William Morris, June 28, 1795 (quotations), and Robert Morris to Charles Croxall, June 4 and August 25, 1795, Robert Morris Papers, LOC. Morris had leased the Hills to William Crouch. See Robert Morris to William Crouch, November 29, 1796, Robert Morris Papers, LOC, and Parsons, *Extracts From the Diary of Jacob Hiltzheimer*, 153.

40. Robert Morris to William Morris, June 28, 1795 (first quotations), and Robert Morris to James Marshall, July 27, 1795 (last quotation), Robert Morris Papers, LOC. See Nuxoll, "The Financier as Senator," 110–13.

41. Combs, *The Jay Treaty*, 164–70.

42. Entry for "folly" in the *Oxford English Dictionary* online; Robert Morris to Tench Tilghman, February 22, 1785, Robert Morris Papers, NYPL (first quotation); Robert Morris to Gouverneur Morris, January 3, 1790,

Gouverneur Morris Papers, COLU (second quotation); Robert Morris to Mary Morris, March 4, 1790, Collection of Papers of Robert Morris, HUNT (third quotation); Robert Morris to Laurent Concler, June 15, 1795, facsimile in Society Small Collection, Robert Morris section, HSP (fourth quotation); Robert Morris to Benjamin Harrison, Jr., July 1, 1795, Robert Morris Papers, LOC (last quotation); *The Age of Folly: A Poem* (London: W. Clarke, [1797]); Frederick Reynolds, *Folly as it Flies, A Comedy, in Five Acts* (Charleston, S.C.: Young, 1802); and "The Folly of Pride," *The Philadelphia Minerva* (March 21, 1795).

43. Barbara Jones, *Follies & Grottoes* (London: Robert MacLehose and Co. Ltd., 1953). Of this type, Jones observed, "Follies come from money and security and peace; usually poor men do not build them, while only the calm of a settled life promotes enough malaise to breed a folly," a description that applies to the beleaguered Morris only in regard to his wealth (1). However, her observation of these structures that "follies are personal in a way that great architecture never is," is relevant (3). See also Gwyn Headley and Wim Meulenkamp, *Follies: A National Trust Guide* (London: Cape, 1986), xxi–xxiii, and, for a pattern book example, Charles Over, *Ornamental Architecture in the Gothic, Chinese, and Modern Taste: Being Above Fifty Intire New Designs of Plans, Sections, Elevations, &c. (many of which may be executed with roots of trees) for Gardens, Parks, Forests, Woods, Canals, &c. . . .* (London: Printed for Robert Sayer, 1758).

44. The *Oxford English Dictionary* traces the origins of such a usage, as "a popular name for any costly structure considered to have shown folly in the builder," from 1654. See entry for "folly" in the *Oxford English Dictionary* online. For Bladen's Folly, see Victor Hugo Paltsits, ed., *Journal of Benjamin Mifflin: The Record of a Tour from Philadelphia to Delaware and Maryland, July 26 to August 14, 1762* (New York: New York Public Library, 1935), 11 (quotation); for a 1771 poem mentioning Bladen's Folly, see Philip Randall Voorhees, in *1789–1889: Commemoration of the One Hundredth Anniversary of St. John's College* (Baltimore: Boyle and Son, 1890), 81–82; *"The Georgian Period" Being Measured Drawings of Colonial Work* (Boston: American Architect and Building News Co., 1900), part 7, 60–61; Gwyn Headley, *Architectural Follies in America* (New York: John Wiley and Sons, Inc., 1996), 49–50; and Clay Lancaster, *Architectural Follies in America, or Hammer, Saw-tooth & Nail* (Rutland, Vt.: Charles E. Tuttle Company, 1960), 45. Mary Morris had once gestured to this meaning when she wrote her mother

during the Revolutionary War from their family's inland rental, "at this once famous place . . . where, perhaps, we may yet trace some vestages of the late owner's folly." Mary Morris, in 1777, quoted in Charles Henry Hart, "Mary White—Mrs. Robert Morris," *Pennsylvania Magazine of History and Biography* 2 (1878): 161.

45. Lancaster, *Architectural Follies in America*, 14–16. For Smith's Folly, see the 1762 journal of a visitor from New York, in "Notes and Queries," *Pennsylvania Magazine of History and Biography* 10 (1886), 115, and J. H. Powell, *Bring Out Your Dead: The Great Plague of Yellow Fever in Philadelphia in 1793* (Philadelphia: University of Pennsylvania Press, 1949), 109. Cooke's Folly was torn down around 1838. It is unclear exactly when the title "Cooke's Folly" was first applied to the building. See W[illiam]. Birch & Son, *The City of Philadelphia, in the State of Pennsylvania North America; As it Appeared in the Year 1800* (Philadelphia: W. Birch, 1800), plate 8; Scharf and Westcott, *History of Philadelphia*, 1:487; James D. Kornwolf, *Architecture and Town Planning in Colonial North America* (Baltimore: Johns Hopkins University Press, 2002), 3:1423–24; Stuart M. Blumin, *The Emergence of the Middle Class: Social Experience in the American City* (New York: Cambridge University Press, 1989), 23; Dell Upton, *Another City: Urban Life and Urban Spaces in the New American Republic* (New Haven: Yale University Press, 2008), 28; and George B. Tatum, *Penn's Great Town: 250 Years of Philadelphia Architecture Illustrated in Prints and Drawings* (Philadelphia: University of Pennsylvania Press, 1961), 43. Downriver from Philadelphia, in Chester, Pennsylvania, prior to the American Revolution, Francis Richardson had built a series of ineffective, expensive wharves along the Delaware River which residents had called "Richardson's Folly." See Paltsits, *Journal of Benjamin Mifflin*, 7. Another eighteenth-century example appeared in Petersburg, Virginia, where, in 1763, Peter Jones built a house that would be called "Folly Castle." See Headley, *Architectural Follies in America*, 40.

46. Jones, *Follies & Grottoes*, 4–5 (quotation). The type or usage of the term generally seems to have increased in the nineteenth century. See Lancaster, *Architectural Follies in America*, and Headley, *Architectural Follies in America*.

47. Robert Morris to Thomas Russell, July 28, 1795, Robert Morris Papers, LOC. A few months later, Morris acknowledged, "I now perceive that all is vanity." Robert Morris to William Constable, September 22, 1795, Robert Morris Papers, LOC.

CHAPTER 7. HIS ENTREATIES

1. Robert Morris to Thomas Morris, March 26, 1796, Collection of Papers of Robert Morris, HUNT. The Dutch had retained £37,500 sterling from the purchase money until Morris extinguished the Indian title; their earlier advances were also contingent on this event taking place. See [Thomas Morris] to Judge [James] Kent, 1847, James Kent Papers, reel 5, LOC and Barbara Ann Chernow, "Robert Morris: Land Speculator, 1790–1801," (Ph.D. diss., Columbia University, 1974), 62–79.

2. Thomas Morris, "Personal Memoir," 1852, vol. 15, O'Rielly Collection, NYHS; Alan Taylor, "The Divided Ground:" *Journal of the Early Republic* 22 (Spring 2002): 55–75; Alan Taylor, *The Divided Ground: Indians, Settlers, and the Northern Borderland of the American Revolution* (New York: Knopf, 2006), 309–17; Thomas S. Abler, *Cornplanter: Chief Warrior of the Allegany Senecas* (Syracuse, N.Y.: Syracuse University Press, 2007), 58–96.

3. Morris, "Personal Memoir" (first quotation); Robert Morris to Anthony Wayne, March 27, 1795, Robert Morris Papers, LOC (last quotation); Abler, *Cornplanter,* 97–120.

4. Red Jacket, quoted in Norman B. Wilkinson, "Robert Morris and the Treaty of Big Tree," *Mississippi Valley Historical Review* 40 (September 1953): 257 (first quotation, emphasis in the original); Morris, "Personal Memoir" (last quotation, emphasis in the original); Robert Morris to Thomas Morris, June 7, 1796, Collection of Papers of Robert Morris, HUNT; Granville Ganter, ed., *The Collected Speeches of Sagoyewatha, or Red Jacket* (Syracuse, N.Y.: Syracuse University Press, 2006), 79–81; Abler, *Cornplanter,* 116; and Christopher Densmore, *Red Jacket: Iroquois Diplomat and Orator* (Syracuse, N.Y.: Syracuse University Press, 1999), 36–37, 46–49.

5. John Nicholson to Robert Morris, July 1, 1795, John Nicholson Letter Books, vol. 2, HSP (first quotation, emphasis in the original). For his attempts to offset these European debts with recovered assets from London's John Warder & Co., see, for example, Robert Morris to Bird Savage & Bird, May 22 and July 18, 1795, Robert Morris Papers, LOC. For the loan due Church, see introductory note to Robert Morris to Alexander Hamilton, June 7, 1795, in Harold C. Syrett, ed., *The Papers of Alexander Hamilton* (New York: Columbia University Press, 1973), 18:359–65, Robert Morris to Alexander Hamilton, December 18, 1795, and Robert Morris to John B. Church, May 17, 1796, Robert Morris Papers, LOC; entry for June 8, 1793, in "Journal, 1791–1801," Robert Morris Business Papers, HSP; and [Robert Morris,] *In the Account of Property* (Philadelphia [1801]), 3. For the debt to

Bourdieu Chollet & Bourdieu, see Ledger, 1794–1801, folio 22, Robert Morris Business Papers, HSP; Wilhem and Jan Willink, Nicholaas and Jacob Van Staphorst, and Nicholas Hubbard to Alexander Hamilton, July 1, 1793, in Harold C. Syrett, ed., *The Papers of Alexander Hamilton* (New York: Columbia University Press, 1969), 15:47–49; Robert Morris to Bourdieu Chollet & Bourdieu, March 20, April 3, April 25, September 14, and October 7, 1795, and January 1, 1796, Robert Morris Papers, LOC; Robert Morris to William Constable, November 22, 1795, and Robert Morris to James Dunlop, February 3, 1796, Robert Morris Papers, LOC; entry for June 23, 1795, in Melanie Randolph Miller, ed., *The Diaries of Gouverneur Morris: European Travels, 1794–1798* (Charlottesville: University of Virginia Press, 2011), 104; *In the Account of Property*, 38; Bourdieu, Chollet, and Bourdieu to Talleyrand Périgord, August 6, 1794, and "Introduction," in Hans Huth and Wilma J. Pugh, eds., "Talleyrand in America as a Financial Promoter, 1794–1796," vol. 2, *Annual Report of the American Historical Association For the Year 1941* (1942), 12, 67–68. For the debt to J. H. Cazenove Nephew & Co., made in connection with John Nicholson, see Robert Morris to John Pasley, March 18, 1795, and Robert Morris to J. Henry Cazenove Nephew & Co., September 22 and October 7, 1795, Robert Morris Papers, LOC; John Nicholson to Cazenoves, June 5, 1795, John Nicholson Letter Books, vol. 2, HSP; Ledger, 1794–1801, folio 12, Robert Morris Business Papers, HSP; and *In the Account of Property*, 37. For the debt to Bird Savage & Bird, see, for example, Robert Morris to Bird Savage & Bird, December 31, 1795, Robert Morris Papers, LOC. For the debt to Pulteney Associates, see Robert Morris to Richard Harrison, October 28, 1795, Robert Morris Papers, LOC; Robert Morris to Thomas Morris, March 6, 1796, Collection of Papers of Robert Morris, HUNT; introductory note to Robert Morris to Alexander Hamilton, April 27, 1796, in Harold C. Syrett, ed., *The Papers of Alexander Hamilton* (New York: Columbia University Press, 1974), 20:141–45; and *In the Account of Property*, 2–3. For the status of overdue payments on his longstanding debts to the Le Couteulx, see Gouverneur Morris to Robert Morris, September 1, 1791, Gouverneur Morris Papers, LOC, and Robert Morris to J. B. Le Couteulx, April 6, 1795, Robert Morris Papers, LOC. For the debt to the Willinks, see Ledger, 1794–1801, folios 80 and 149, Robert Morris Business Papers, HSP, and *In the Account of Property*, 3, 11, 48. Generally, see Chernow, "Robert Morris: Land Speculator," and William Graham Sumner, *The Financier and the Finances of the American Revolution* (New York: Dodd, Mead, and Company, 1892), 2:279–86.

6. For his debts to the banks, see Ledger, 1794–1801, folios 8, 9, and 10, and 80, Robert Morris Business Papers, HSP, and *In the Account of Property*, 36, 37, and 47. For his debt to the Insurance Company of North America, see Robert Morris to James Marshall, October 12, 1795, Robert Morris Papers, LOC; Ledger, 1794–1801, folios 36 and 163, Robert Morris Business Papers, HSP; and *In the Account of Property*, 58. He also owed £22,500 Pennsylvania currency to the Insurance Company of Pennsylvania, for a loan dating to 1794. See Robert Morris to the Insurance Company of the State of Pennsylvania, October 30, 1794, in Society Small Collection, Robert Morris section, HSP. For the private debts above, see Ledger, 1794–1801, folios 17, 21, 52, 74, 123, and 275, Robert Morris Business Papers, HSP; *In the Account of Property*; Robert Morris to General Stewart, June 5, 1795, Robert Morris to Standish Forde, June 22, 1795, and Robert Morris to Thomas Fitzsimons, February 22, 1796, Robert Morris Papers, LOC; and the Reed and Forde Papers, HSP. In December 1796, Ball loaned Morris $30,000 and Ball with Standish Forde loaned him an additional $20,000. See Emmett William Gans, *A Pennsylvania Pioneer: Biographical Sketch with Report of the Executive Committee of the Ball Estate Association* (Mansfield, Ohio: Kuhl, 1900), 12, 32, 47, 71, and 74. I am a descendant of James Yard. Morris therefore owes my family money, though, as we have seen, this is not a singular claim. For Morris's debts to his daughter, see Ledger, 1794–1801, folio 19, Robert Morris Business Papers, HSP, and *In the Account of Property*, 37. For his debts to Bishop White, see the work of William Pencak. For Greenleaf's notes, see Robert D. Arbuckle, *Pennsylvania Speculator and Patriot: The Entrepreneurial John Nicholson, 1757–1800* (University Park: Pennsylvania State University Press, 1975), 137. For all of Morris's proven claims, see Case of Robert Morris, No. 42, BA1800-PA, microfilm 993, reel 7, Records of the U.S. District Court of the Eastern District of Pennsylvania, Bankruptcy Act of 1800, Record Group 21, National Archives Mid-Atlantic Region, Philadelphia, Pennsylvania.

7. Robert Morris to Thomas Russell, September 18, 1795, Robert Morris Papers, LOC (quotation). For Morris's concern regarding overdue payment to the commissioners, see Robert Morris to William Cranch, July 24, 1795, Collection of Papers of Robert Morris, HUNT; Robert Morris to George Washington, September 21 and December 7, 1795, Robert Morris to the Commissioners of the Federal City, November 2, 1795, and Robert Morris to Alexander White, May 9, 1796, Robert Morris Papers, LOC. For the deal to buy out Greenleaf, and Morris's thoughts regarding it, see "Memo-

randum of an Agreement between J. Greenleaf & R. Morris & J. Nicholson Relative to the Quantity of Lots in the Federal City," May 13, 1796, Robert Morris Papers, NYPL; Robert Morris to William Constable, July 27, 1795, Robert Morris Papers, LOC. Morris and Nicholson's credit to Greenleaf, for $681,904, would be partially offset by $300,000 Greenleaf still owed to the North American Land Company affair. For samples of Nicholson and Morris's early construction efforts in the federal city and of the workers' discontent, see John Nicholson and Robert Morris to William Lovering, August 17, 1795, and John Nicholson to Lewis Deblois, November 17 and November 18, 1795, in John Nicholson Letter Books, vols. 2 and 3, HSP; Arbuckle, *Pennsylvania Speculator and Patriot,* 120–37; Bruce H. Mann, *Republic of Debtors: Bankruptcy in the Age of American Independence* (Cambridge, Mass.: Harvard University Press, 2002), 200–2; Bob Arnebeck, *Through a Fiery Trial: Building Washington, 1790–1800* (Lanham: Madison Books, 1991), 303–5; Bob Arnebeck, "Tracking the Speculators: Greenleaf and Nicholson in the Federal City," *Washington History* 3 (Spring/Summer 1991): 112–25; Allen C. Clark, *Greenleaf and Law in the Federal City* (Washington, D.C.: W. F. Roberts, 1901), 134–44, 151–67; Chernow, "Robert Morris: Land Speculator," 138–69. On July 15, 1796, after Morris and Nicholson missed that year's deadline, the district commissioners exclaimed to them that, for their own part, there was "a certain point beyond which forbearance becomes folly and total dereliction of public trust," quoted in Arnebeck, *Through a Fiery Trial,* 384.

8. Robert Morris to James Smith, May 23, 1796, Robert Morris Papers, LOC (first quotation); Robert Morris to John Nicholson, August 29, 1796, Robert Morris Papers, LOC (last quotation). For the suits of Lymondton, Gullen, and others in early 1796, see box 4, Ball Estate, Dupuy Papers, HSP. James Dunlop threatened a suit in January 1796. See Robert Morris to James Dunlop, January 14, 1796, Robert Morris Papers, LOC. George Lauman and Benjamin West brought suit in early 1796. See Robert Morris to Alexander Wilcocks, May 12, 1796, Robert Morris Papers, LOC. For the Bank of Pennsylvania suit, see Robert Morris to President & Directors of the Bank of Pennsylvania, May 6, 1796, Robert Morris Papers, LOC, and Jasper Yeates, *Reports of Cases Adjudged in the Supreme Court of Pennsylvania: With Some Select Cases at Nisi Prius, and in the Circuit Courts* (Philadelphia: Campbell, 1871), 4:456–61. In June, Morris faced a chancery claim filed against him in Delaware. See Robert Morris to Isaac Hazlehurst, June 6, 1796, Robert Morris Papers, LOC. For the federal commissioners' actions,

see Robert Morris to Commissioners of the City Washington, August 8, 1796, Robert Morris Papers, LOC. For other suits into the fall of 1796, see Robert Morris to John Nicholson, November 22, 1796, Robert Morris Papers, LOC, and Society Small Collection, Robert Morris section, HSP. Morris had been warding off suits as early as April 1795. See Robert Morris to the President & Directors of the Bank of North America, April 16, 1795, and Robert Morris to Lloyd & Sparks, June 12, 1795, Robert Morris Papers, LOC. Robert Arbuckle found that as of August 31, 1796, there were sixty-one cases brought against John Nicholson. See Arbuckle, *Pennsylvania Speculator and Patriot*, 120 and 193. More suits against Morris from this period can be found in the Case of Robert Morris, Records of the U.S. District Court of the Eastern District of Pennsylvania, National Archives. For legal representation, Morris employed Edward Tilghman, James Gibson, Alexander Wilcocks, Joseph Karrick, and John Marshall, among others.

9. Benjamin Rush, December 1796, in George W. Corner, *The Autobiography of Benjamin Rush: His "Travels Through Life" Together with His Commonplace Book for 1789–1813* (Princeton, N.J.: Princeton University Press for the American Philosophical Society, 1948), 236–37 (quotation). Chauncey Goodrich, also in Philadelphia that December, observed that "this place furnishes indication of great depravity; bankruptcies are frequently happening. Mr. Morris is greatly embarrassed." See Chauncey Goodrich to Oliver Wolcott, Sr., December 13, 1796, in George Gibbs, ed., *Memoirs of the Administrations of Washington and John Adams, edited from the Papers of Oliver Wolcott, Secretary of the Treasury* (New York: Burt Franklin, 1971), 1:410; Arbuckle, *Pennsylvania Speculator and Patriot*, 196. For attitudes toward speculators during this time, see Mann, *Republic of Debtors*, 198–205.

10. Gouverneur Morris to Samuel Ogden, February 2 (first quotation) and June 1 (last quotation), 1796, and Gouverneur Morris to Robert Morris, December 7, 1795, Gouverneur Morris Papers, LOC; Robert Morris to James Marshall, September 24, 1795, and Robert Morris to Sylvanus Bourne, October 8, 1795, Robert Morris Papers, LOC; John Nicholson and Robert Morris to James Marshall, October 14 and October 16, 1795, John Nicholson Letter Books, vol. 3, HSP; *In the Account of Property*, 60–61; Robert Morris to William Temple Franklin, September 14, November 14, and November 16, 1795, Robert Morris Papers, LOC; Arbuckle, *Pennsylvania Speculator and Patriot*, 119, 131. Other important salesmen for Morris and Nicholson included Enoch Edwards, Joseph Barnes, and James Tate.

Robert also looked to European firms to arrange for sales of hundreds of shares of the Bank of the United States upon which he had his hand. See Robert Morris to Bourdieu Chollet & Bourdieu, March 17, 1795; Robert Morris to Wilhem and Jan Willink, April 2, 1795; and Robert Morris to Bird Savage & Bird, April 4, 1795, Robert Morris Papers, LOC.

11. George Washington to Robert Morris, September 14, 1795, in John C. Fitzpatrick, ed., *The Writings of George Washington from the Original Manuscript Sources, 1745–1799* (Washington, D.C.: United States Government Printing Office, 1940), 34:303–5 (quotations). For the darkening of George Washington's view toward the commissioners' deal with Morris and his partners, see George Washington to Daniel Carroll, January 7, 1795, General Correspondence, George Washington Papers, LOC, and George Washington to Edmund Randolph, July 22, 1795, in Fitzpatrick, *The Writings of George Washington*, 34:243–46.

12. Robert Morris to George Washington, September 21, 1795, Robert Morris Papers, LOC (first quotations, emphasis in the original); George Washington to Commissioners, July 1, 1796, in John C. Fitzpatrick, ed., *The Writings of George Washington from the Original Manuscript Sources, 1745–1799* (Washington, D.C.: United States Government Printing Office, 1940), 35:111–12 (last quotations). In May 1796, Morris could write to a Madeira wine merchant: "I have lately tasted the two pipes of Wine shipped by you from Venus Captn Mason on my accot. . . . And I have the pleasure to acknowledge that they deserve the Character given of them in that letter," so he placed another order. See Robert Morris to John Ayres, May 23, 1796, Robert Morris Papers, LOC.

13. Robert Morris to Thomas Jefferson, March 2, 1801, in Barbara B. Oberg, ed., *The Papers of Thomas Jefferson* (Princeton: Princeton University Press, 2006), 33:121–22 (first quotation); Robert Morris to Thomas Morris, August 24, 1796, Collection of Papers of Robert Morris, HUNT (second quotation); Robert Morris to Mary Morris, September 7, 1796, Collection of Papers of Robert Morris, HUNT (last quotation). For Garrett Cottringer's work, see Robert Morris to Mary Morris, October 5, 1796, Collection of Papers of Robert Morris, HUNT; John Nicholson to Garrett Cottringer, March 20, March 24, March 25, and July 1, 1796, in John Nicholson Letter Books, vols. 1 and 2, HSP. For Morris's servants, see entries for February, October, and November 1795 and February, April, June, July, and September 1796 in "Journal, 1794–1801," Robert Morris Business Papers, HSP. Robert Morris, Jr., married Anne Shoemaker of Philadelphia; see *Philadelphia*

Minerva (May 14, 1796) for the wedding announcement. For examples of
Mary's visits to Morrisville, see Robert Morris to Robert Morris Jr., June 9,
1796, and Robert Morris to Thomas Law, July 4, 1796, Robert Morris Papers,
LOC.

14. Robert Morris to Major L'Enfant, December 19, 1795, Robert Morris Pa-
    pers, LOC (quotation). For Morris's draft on Willing for $500, see entries
    for May and November 1795, in "Journal, 1794–1801," Robert Morris Busi-
    ness Papers, HSP. For drafts to and from Soderstrom, see Ledger, 1794–
    1801, folio 55, Robert Morris Business Papers, HSP, and Robert Morris to
    Richard Soderstrom, April 28, 1795, Robert Morris Papers, LOC. For
    Constable, see Robert Morris to William Constable, July 30, October 1,
    and November 22, 1795, Robert Morris Papers, LOC. For Cazenove and
    Talleyrand, see Edwin R. Baldridge, Jr., "Talleyrand's Visit to Pennsyl-
    vania, 1794–1796," *Pennsylvania History* 36 (April 1969): 145–60 and "In-
    troduction," in Huth and Pugh, "Talleyrand in America as a Financial
    Promoter," vol. 2, *Annual Report of the American Historical Association For
    the Year 1941*, 22.

15. *In the Account of Property*, 64–65 (quotation); John Nicholson to Ashbel
    Greene, November 17, 1795, John Nicholson Letter Books, vol. 3, HSP;
    and Arbuckle, *Pennsylvania Speculator and Patriot*, 188.

16. For Morris's operation of the Delaware Works, see Robert Morris to Alex-
    ander Hamilton, December 17, 1795, Robert Morris Papers, LOC. Nichol-
    son also opened a store in the federal city, and owned part of an iron furnace
    there. See Arnebeck, *Through a Fiery Trial*, 211, 247, 295, and Arbuckle,
    Pennsylvania Speculator and Patriot, 126, 159. For the pair's shipments of
    flour, see Robert Morris to Jean Joseph Fauchet, March 5, 1795, Robert
    Morris Papers, LOC, and John Nicholson to Robert Morris, April 22, 1795,
    in John Nicholson Letter Books, vol. 1, HSP. For Morris's arrangements to
    import English dry goods to Philadelphia, see Robert Morris to James Mar-
    shall, November 22, 1795, in Robert Morris Papers, LOC. In summer 1796,
    a man inquired about a job with the defunct firm of Willing & Morris; Mor-
    ris told him that "I have retired from all Mercantile Pursuits." Robert Mor-
    ris to William Furse, August 5, 1796, Robert Morris Papers, LOC.

17. As early as July 1795, Nicholson observed to Morris that "I am again com-
    pelled to resort to the old mode of raising money by notes." See John Nich-
    olson to Robert Morris, July 17, 1795, John Nicholson Letter Books, vol. 2,
    HSP. Citations for the above, and others from the time, include John Nich-
    olson to Garrett Cottringer, July 1, 1795 (first quotation); Robert Morris to

John Nicholson, August 24, 1795 (second quotation); John Nicholson to Robert Morris, September 17, 1795 (third quotation); Robert Morris to William Cranch, October 9, 1795, showing the pair concocting notes for $13,739.20; Robert Morris to John Nicholson, November 12, 1795, showing $2,495 in paper; John Nicholson to Robert Morris, December 2, 1795 (fourth quotation); Robert Morris to John Nicholson, January 8, 1796; John Nicholson to Robert Morris, March 1, 1796 (fifth quotation); Robert Morris to John Nicholson, August 12, 1796 (sixth quotation); all from John Nicholson Letter Books, HSP, and Robert Morris Papers, LOC. One account with Charles Young dated February 25, 1797, shows Nicholson and Morris signing $1,320,000 to each other in 1795 for bills payable in three years. See Agreement between Charles Young and Robert Morris and John Nicholson, February 25, 1797, Collection of Papers of Robert Morris, HUNT. In the Robert Morris Business Papers at HSP, there is a "Bill book" that recorded these promissory notes between Nicholson and Morris. Entries date from May 1794 to July 1796 and involve millions of dollars (perhaps totaling $4 million), with most notes drawn from $1,000 to $8,000, but some up to $40,000 at a time. Most were payable three years from their issuing date. For what it was worth, Morris was uncomfortable with this practice. In 1799, while in debtors' prison, Morris told Nicholson, "You remember I am sure how I used to grumble and growl at the issueing our notes." See Robert Morris to John Nicholson, April 27, 1799, Robert Morris Papers, NYPL. See also Case of Robert Morris, Records of the U.S. District Court of the Eastern District of Pennsylvania, National Archives; and Howard Swiggett, *The Forgotten Leaders of the Revolution* (Garden City, N.Y.: Doubleday and Company, Inc., 1955), 145–54.

18. *Gazette of the United States* (April 12, 1796) (first quotation); Robert Morris to John Nicholson, November 27, 1796, Robert Morris Papers, LOC (last quotation). See also the advertisement for Freeman's auction house in the *Aurora General Advertiser* (April 26, 1797). William Graham Sumner reports M & Ns as trading at 3.6 cents on the dollar in February 1797. See Sumner, *The Financier and the Finances of the American Revolution*, 2:282–83; and also Arbuckle, *Pennsylvania Speculator and Patriot*, 187–91; Mann, *Republic of Debtors*, 200–4, 325; and Arnebeck, *Through a Fiery Trial*, 392.

19. John Nicholson to Robert Morris, November 16, 1796, John Nicholson Letter Books, vol. 4, HSP (first quotation); Robert Morris to John Nicholson, November 20, 1796 (second quotation, emphasis in the original), Robert Morris to John Nicholson, December 4, 1796 (third quotation), Robert

Morris to James Marshall, July 4, 1796 (fourth quotation), all in Robert
Morris Papers, LOC. For Morris's interest in Shakespeare during this time,
see entries for September, October, and December 1795, and February,
June, and July 1796 in "Journal, 1794–1801," Robert Morris Business Pa-
pers, HSP. For his club participation with the St. George's Society, see
entry for May 30, 1796. For a rare example of a jab between Morris and
Nicholson, see John Nicholson to Robert Morris, January 1797, cited in
Arbuckle, *Pennsylvania Speculator and Patriot*, 127–28.

20. Robert Morris to Mary Morris, September 7 (first quotation) and October
    19, 1796, Robert Morris to Thomas Morris, October 23, 1796 (second quo-
    tation), Collection of Papers of Robert Morris, HUNT; Lewis Deblois,
    quoted in Arbuckle, *Pennsylvania Speculator and Patriot*, 125 (third quota-
    tion); "Washington, Sept. 28," *Philadelphia Gazette & Universal Daily
    Advertiser* (October 6, 1796); Arnebeck, *Through a Fiery Trial*, 327–29,
    339–40, 346–47, 388–405. In October, the pair also toasted a handful of
    new sales in the city.

    The North American Land Company had been publicly attacked in
    Europe and America in late 1795 as chicanery. Morris came to its defense,
    attributing attacks on it to envy and political grudges. See Robert Morris to
    Bourdieu Chollet & Bourdieu, October 7, 1795, and Robert Morris to John
    Pasley, October 8, 1795, Robert Morris Papers, LOC. But by January 1797,
    Morris proposed dissolving the company, though Nicholson did not approve.
    See also Chernow, "Robert Morris: Land Speculator," 170–98; Swiggett,
    The Forgotten Leaders of the Revolution, 148.

21. Robert Morris to James Chalmers, October 30, 1796, Robert Morris Pa-
    pers, NYPL (first quotation); Robert Morris to John Nicholson, November
    20, 1796, Robert Morris Papers, LOC (last quotations).

22. [James Thomson Callender,] *The American Annual Register, or Historical
    Memoirs of the United States, for the Year 1796* (Philadelphia: Bioren and
    Madan, 1797), 279 (first quotation); entry for January 4, 1796, in Thomas
    Lee Shippen diary, vol. 3, Shippen Family Papers, LOC (second quotation);
    Joseph Farington quoting Frank Philips of Manchester in his diary, in James
    Greig, ed., *The Farington Diary by Joseph Farington, R.A.*, 3d ed. (New
    York: George H. Doran Company, 1923), 1:168 (third quotations) (thanks to
    Charles Brownell for this reference); William H. Safford, ed., *The Blenner-
    hassett Papers, Embodying the Private Journal of Harman Blennerhassett, and
    the Hitherto Unpublished Correspondence of Burr, Alston, Comfort Tyler, De-
    vereaux, Dayton, Adair, Miro, Emmett, Theodosia Burr Alston, Mrs. Blenner-*

hassett, and Others, Their Contemporaries . . . and a Memoir of Blennerhassett (Cincinnati: Moore, Wilstach and Baldwin, 1864), 35 (last quotations).

23. *The Debates and Proceedings in the Congress of the United States . . . , Fourth Congress, First Session* (Washington, D.C.: Gales and Seaton, 1855), 366–67 (first quotations); Isaac Weld, Jr., *Travels Through the States of North America, and the Provinces of Upper and Lower Canada, During the Years 1795, 1796, and 1797,* 2d ed. (London: Stockdale, 1799), 1:84 (third quotation); Arnebeck, *Through a Fiery Trial,* 331, 352, 378, 592 (last quotations).

24. Robert Morris to John Thompson, October 28, 1796, Robert Morris Papers, LOC; John F. Watson, *Annals of Philadelphia, Being a Collection of Memoirs, Anecdotes, & Incidents of the City and Its Inhabitants From the Days of the Pilgrim Founders* (Philadelphia: Carey and Hart, 1830), 356 (first quotation); "A Short Account of Philadelphia," in *Stephens's Philadelphia Directory, For 1796; or, Alphabetical Arrangement: Containing the Names, Occupations, and Places of Abode of the Citizens* (Philadelphia: W. Woodward for Thomas Stephens, 1796), 1 (last quotation).

25. Jacob Cox Parsons, ed., *Extracts From the Diary of Jacob Hiltzheimer, of Philadelphia, 1765–1798* (Philadelphia: William F. Fell and Co., 1893), 228 (first quotation). Morris made an early payment for a slate contract in August 1795, but he waited until the following year to try and complete it. See Robert Morris to William Cranch, May 22, 1796, Robert Morris to William Lovering, May 30, 1796, Robert Morris to William Cranch, July 4, 1796, Robert Morris to William and James Constable, August 20, 1796, Robert Morris to William Cranch, August 31, 1796, Robert Morris Papers, LOC, and entries for August 1795 and February, March, April, July, August, and November 1796 in "Journal, 1794–1801," Robert Morris Business Papers, HSP. The entry for October 8, 1796, states that Morris also ordered slate up from Washington. Morris had briefly considered using sheet iron for the roof. See Robert Morris to Robert Morris, Jr., June 9, 1796, Robert Morris Papers, LOC. See also James Kent, "Journal of a trip to Washington, D.C., December 5, 1793 to January 3, 1794," James Kent Papers, reel 1, volume 1, LOC; and George B. Tatum, *Penn's Great Town: 250 Years of Philadelphia Architecture Illustrated in Prints and Drawings* (Philadelphia: University of Pennsylvania Press, 1961), 45.

26. Tax Assessor's Ledger, South Ward, 1796, City Archives, Philadelphia, Pennsylvania. For the development of the site's gardens and walkways, see *Claypoole's Daily Advertiser* (February 16, 1797) and entry for January 25, 1796, in "Journal, 1794–1801," Robert Morris Business Papers, HSP. For

reference to the outbuildings, see *Philadelphia Gazette* (June 8, 1796). For the street wall, see Robert Morris to M. Clarkson, August 17, 1796, Robert Morris Papers, LOC.

Morris was still unable to buy the lone strip of property on the northeast corner of his own block. In 1796, the strip was owned by Elizabeth Fox, widowed granddaughter of the lot's earlier owner, Samuel Mickle. See Tax Assessor's Ledger, South Ward, 1796, Philadelphia City Archives, and *Stephens's Philadelphia Directory, For 1796*, 64.

27. Robert Morris to Burton Wallace, June 27, 1796 (first quotation), Robert Morris to John Miller, October 5, 1796 (last quotations), Robert Morris Papers, LOC; entry for April 11, 1796, in "Journal, 1794–1801," Robert Morris Business Papers, HSP, which records one of the last payments made to Wallace; and *In the Account of Property*, 39. New payments would be made to "Cromwell & Gln" for bricklayers' wages (presumably John Cromwell) beginning March 14, 1796. Morris's last payment to John Sproul was on October 19, 1795. The first entry for Crozier, a member of the Carpenters' Company, in the Journal appears on November 23, 1795. Sproul died shortly thereafter, and Morris remained indebted to his estate for $273.59. See notice by Jonathan Penrose, in *Aurora General Advertiser* (November 13, 1797); and entries for Crozier and Sproul in Sandra L. Tatman and Roger W. Moss, *Biographical Dictionary of Philadelphia Architects, 1700–1930* (Boston: G. K. Hall, 1985), 175 and 745. Morris had advanced money to a New Jersey lumber dealer on Sproul's order in fall 1795, but the dealer delayed the delivery and work stalled. So Sproul's exit may have involved the carpenter's sense of foreboding. See Robert Morris to Benjamin Barton, October 31 and November 25, 1795, and Robert Morris to Charles Croxall, November 28, 1795, Robert Morris Papers, LOC.

28. For lumber, see Robert Morris to Gilbert Robertson & Munro, April 18 and May 23, 1796, Robert Morris Papers, LOC. For James Traquair, see entry for April 2, 1796, in "Journal, 1794–1801," Robert Morris Business Papers, HSP, and William Seale, *The President's House: A History* (Washington, D.C.: White House Historical Association with the cooperation of the National Geographic Society, 1986), 1:52–53. For the glaziers' work, see entry for March 14, 1796. For the carpenters' work, see entry for August 4, 1796. For Beauvais, see entries for August 22, October 8, and December 31, 1796. For Callegan, see entry for January 7, 1797. For liquor, see entries for August 18, 1798, and June 27, 1801.

29. Peter Colt to Alexander Hamilton, in Harold C. Syrett, ed., *The Papers of Alexander Hamilton* (New York: Columbia University Press, 1969), 14:419–21 (first quotation); Robert Morris to Major L'Enfant, August 15, 1796 (second quotations), and Robert Morris to Major L'Enfant, August 16, 1796 (last quotation), Robert Morris Papers, LOC.

30. Robert Morris to John Nicholson, December 22, 1796, Robert Morris Papers, LOC (first quotation); Robert Morris to John Nicholson, November 27, 1796, Gratz collection, HSP; *In the Account of Property*, 11. Morris paid Crozier and Proviny as late as July 30, 1797, but this seems to have been on accounts due. For this and Jardella's departure, see entry for July 30, 1797, in "Journal, 1794–1801," Robert Morris Business Papers, HSP. Andrew Jardella would be listed in the city directory 1802 as a marble carver. "Joseph Jardally" is also listed as a carver. See James Robinson, *The Philadelphia Directory, City and County Register, for 1802* (Philadelphia: Woodward, 1802), 10, 129. For Proviny's new shop, see Cornelius William Stafford, *The Philadelphia Directory for 1798* (Philadelphia: William W. Woodward, 1798), 115.

31. Robert Morris to Gustavus Scott, May 10, 1797, Robert Morris Papers, LOC. The massive, stone-fronted Bank of the United States, finished in 1800, also cost $110,000. See Tatum, *Penn's Great Town*, 40. In 1800, Thomas Cope also recorded the use of the term "folly" in connection to Morris's affairs. See Eliza Cope Harrison, ed., *Philadelphia Merchant: The Diary of Thomas P. Cope, 1800–1851* (South Bend, Ind.: Gateway Editions, 1978), 37.

32. Robert Morris to Major L'Enfant, May 15, 1797 (first quotations), Robert Morris to P. C. L'Enfant, July 20, 1797, and Account dated 1804, all in James Dudley Morgan collection of Digges-L'Enfant-Morgan Papers, LOC; *In the Account of Property*, 11 (last quotation).

33. William Birch, *The Life of William Birch, Enamel Painter, Written By Himself* (manuscript from HSP, on Microfilm 188 at Winterthur Library). See also Martin P. Snyder, "William Birch: His Philadelphia Views," *Pennsylvania Magazine of History and Biography* 73 (July 1949): 271–315; Wendy Bellion, *Citizen Spectator: Art, Illusion, and Visual Perception in Early National America* (Chapel Hill: Published for OIEAHC by the University of North Carolina Press, 2011), 113–71; Emily T. Cooperman and Lea Carson Sherk, *William Birch: Picturing the American Scene* (Philadelphia: University of Pennsylvania Press, 2010); and Anne-Marie Tyler Schaaf, "Representing the City in 1800: William Birch's Views of Philadelphia" (M.A. thesis, University of Delaware, 1991).

34. Birch, *The Life of William Birch* (quotation); Schaaf, "Representing the City," 79; W[illiam]. Birch & Son, *The City of Philadelphia, in the State of Pennsylvania North America; As it Appeared in the Year 1800* (Philadelphia: W. Birch, 1800).

35. Tatum, *Penn's Great Town*, 45.

36. Ibid.; Damie Stillman, "City Living, Federal Style," in Catherine E. Hutchins, ed., *Everyday Life in the Early Republic* (Winterthur, Del.: Winterthur Museum, 1994), 137–74.

37. Birch, *The Life of William Birch;* William Russell Birch and W. Barker, *The City of Philadelphia, in the State of Pennsylvania, North America; as it Appeared in the Year 1800* 2d ed. ([Philadelphia]: W. Birch, 1804); Snyder, "William Birch," 282–84; Schaaf, "Representing the City," 33–34; and Tatum, *Penn's Great Town*, 61. In his memoir above, Birch stated his belief that the sculpted reliefs "were executed in Italy at great expence for" Morris and did not mention the Jardellas.

38. Indenture between Robert Morris and Thomas Fitzsimons and inventory, May 19, 1797, Thomas Fitzsimons Papers, McAllister Collection, HSP. The inventory does *not* state that it includes the entire household's goods; rather, the indenture is intended to satisfy $20,000 Morris then owed to Fitzsimons. The dining rooms seem to be omitted. There is no mention of anything on the "2d floor" [today's third floor] beyond three small items in the entry.

   Morris paid $1,020 annually to William Bell for rent on the Stedman-Galloway House. His last rental payment was through May 31, 1797. See entries for June 1 and July 30, 1797, in "Journal, 1794–1801," Robert Morris Business Papers, HSP.

39. For Mary's primacy in decorating, see Robert Morris to Gustavus Scott, January 29, [1797], Robert Morris Papers, LOC, and Fisher, "A Section of the Memoirs of Joshua Francis Fisher." For these issues generally, see Bernard L. Herman, *Town House: Architecture and Material Life in the Early American City, 1780–1830* (Chapel Hill: Published for OIEAHC by the University of North Carolina Press, 2005), 55–76, and Amy Hudson Henderson, "Furnishing the Republican Court: Building and Decorating Philadelphia Homes, 1790–1800" (Ph.D. diss., University of Delaware, 2008).

40. The girandoles are in the collection of the Philadelphia Museum of Art, Philadelphia, Pennsylvania, accession numbers 1923-5-1a,b. See Philadelphia Museum of Art catalogue and collections database, as well as "A Pair of French Girandoles," *Bulletin of the Pennsylvania Museum* 18 (April 1923): 6–9. An inlaid mahogany desk made in Philadelphia circa 1790 with a Mor-

ris provenance is also in the museum's collection; see accession number 1977-32-1. See also Esther Singleton, *The Furniture of Our Forefathers,* part 6 (New York: Doubleday, Page and Company, 1901), facing 458, 472, 484.

41. Indenture between Morris and Fitzsimons and inventory, May 19, 1797. Morris had received a shipment of carpeting from France, presumably intended for the house, in August 1795. See Robert Morris to James Constable, August 31, 1795, Robert Morris Papers, LOC.

42. The "Leda and the Swan" chimneypiece is currently installed at Lemon Hill Mansion, Fairmount Park, Philadelphia. Oral tradition, including a communication to me from Joyce Jones, House Director of Lemon Hill for the Colonial Dames of America, on June 11, 2010, ties this piece to Morris's Folly. An unsigned inventory of the furnishings in Lemon Hill dated 1982, located in the Martha Crary Halpern Research Papers at the Philadelphia Museum of Art Archives, states only: "c. 1790 Carrara marble imported from Italy, 'Leda and the Swan,' hand carved," without provenance. The earliest mention of the "Leda and the Swan" piece at Lemon Hill is in a press release circa 1925 found in the Fiske Kimball Records, Box 195, Folder 9, Philadelphia Museum of Art Archives. See also Fiske Kimball, "Golden Age of American Collecting," unfinished mss, Fiske Kimball Papers, Series 7, Writing and Research, Subseries 1, Memoirs, Box 159, Folder 35, Philadelphia Museum of Art Archives.

The "Apollo and the Muses" chimneypiece is currently installed at the Historical Society of Pennsylvania, curated as part of the collection of the Philadelphia History Museum at the Atwater Kent, object number HSP.X-154. A letter in the object file, dated June 12, 1900, from R. J. Dutton of Burlington to John W. Jordan, states that the piece was "supposed to have been imported from Italy for the Mansion which Robert Morris (the Financier of the Revolution) partially erected, but was unable to Complete." Dutton's letter also mentions a legend circulating that this chimneypiece was given to the Morrises by the General Marquis de Lafayette upon the latter's hearing that they were erecting a mansion. See also Henderson, "Furnishing the Republican Court," 239–40.

43. Inventory of the Mansion House, completed in 1805, reprinted in Robert C. Alberts, *The Golden Voyage: The Life and Times of William Bingham, 1752–1804* (Boston: Houghton-Mifflin, 1969), Appendix 4 (quotations); Julian Ursyn Niemcewicz, *Under Their Vine and Fig Tree: Travels Through America in 1797–1799, 1805 with Some Further Account of Life in New Jersey,* trans., ed., and with an introduction and notes by Metchie J. E. Budka (Elizabeth,

N.J.: Grassmann Publishing Co., 1965), 36; and Henderson, "Furnishing the Republican Court," 97–106, 217–77.

44. Susanna Dillwyn, quoted in Henderson, "Furnishing the Republican Court," 218 (first quotation); Niemcewicz, *Under Their Vine and Fig Tree,* 36–37 (second quotations). Leading political opponents, such as James Madison, Thomas Mifflin, John Swanwick, and Pierce Butler, all resident in Philadelphia, kept up the attacks on Federalist pretensions even while partaking in the same refined lifestyles.

45. Robert Morris to Thomas Fitzsimons, August 23, 1797, Robert Morris Papers, LOC (quotation). For the Morrises' move, see Robert Morris to David Allison, August 11, 1797, Robert Morris Papers, LOC; and entry for July 30, 1797, in "Journal, 1794–1801," Robert Morris Business Papers, HSP. The Philadelphia city directory for 1798 finds the Morris residence located "next door to the corner of eighth in Chesnut Street." See Stafford, *The Philadelphia Directory for 1798,* 163. This house sat between Thomas Fitzsimons's house and Philemon Dickinson's house. The 1797 directory gives only the address of Robert Morris's counting house (at 227 High Street), not his residence. See Cornelius William Stafford, *The Philadelphia Directory for 1797* (Philadelphia: William W. Woodward, 1797), 132.

46. See Mann, *Republic of Debtors,* particularly 24–26 and 51–52, and Norman B. Wilkinson, *Land Policy and Speculation in Pennsylvania, 1779–1800* (New York: Arno Press, 1979). The colony of Pennsylvania had passed an insolvency statute in 1730, which provided a mechanism for the release of debtors, but it restricted it to those imprisoned prior to that year. Another was passed after the Revolution, in 1785, for debtors whose debts exceeded £150, which was renewed in 1794. It required the debtor to assign away all of his property to effect a discharge. See *Laws of the Commonwealth of Pennsylvania* (Philadelphia: John Bioren, 1810), 3:61–62, 125–26; "Greenleaf v. Banks," in Maeva Marcus, ed., *The Documentary History of the Supreme Court of the United States, 1789–1800* (New York: Columbia University Press, 2007), 8:369–88; and Thomas M. Doerflinger, *A Vigorous Spirit of Enterprise: Merchants and Economic Development in Revolutionary Philadelphia* (Chapel Hill: Published for OIEAHC by the University of North Carolina Press, 1986), 142.

47. Robert Morris to John Nicholson, November 20, 1796 (first quotation), and December 28, 1796 (second quotation), Robert Morris to Alexander Wilcocks and James Gibson, May 26, 1797 (last quotations), Robert Morris Papers, LOC. For rumors of Nicholson's flight, see Chauncey Goodrich to Oliver Wolcott, Senior, December 13, 1796, reprinted in Gibbs, *Memoirs of*

the Administrations of Washington and John Adams, 1:410. For rumors of
Morris's flight, see Gouverneur Morris to John Parish, March 4, 1797, Gouverneur Morris Papers, LOC; entry for April 4, 1797, in Miller, *The Diaries
of Gouverneur Morris,* 454; and Mann, *Republic of Debtors,* 202. For the Pennsylvania Property Company, see *Plan of Association of the Pennsylvania Property Company, established March 1797* (Philadelphia: Aitken, 1797), and
Arbuckle, *Pennsylvania Speculator and Patriot,* 186. The company offered
10,000 shares. Bishop William White ended up with 144 of its worthless
shares, issued at $100 each. John Nicholson's parallel Pennsylvania Land
Company would fail likewise. For Allison, see Robert Morris to David Allison, August 11, 1797, Robert Morris Papers, LOC, and entry for July 30,
1797, in "Journal, 1794–1801," Robert Morris Business Papers, HSP.

48. Robert Morris to Gustavus Scott, January 29, [1797], Robert Morris Papers, LOC (first quotations); Harrison Gray Otis, in Samuel Eliot Morison,
The Life and Letters of Harrison Gray Otis, Federalist, 1765–1848 (Boston
and New York: Houghton Mifflin Company, 1913), 1:133; John Marshall to
Mary W. Marshall, July 3 (second quotations) and July 14, 1797 (fourth
quotation), in William C. Stinchcombe and Charles T. Cullen, eds., *The
Papers of John Marshall* (Chapel Hill: University of North Carolina Press,
1979), 3:94–95 and 101–2; William Bingham to Rufus King, quoted in Alberts, *The Golden Voyage,* 318 (third quotation).

49. "An Alarm," Philadelphia *Aurora General Advertiser* (October 29, 1796)
(first quotation). For Washington's farewell banquet, see William Spohn
Baker, *Washington after the Revolution 1784–1799* (Philadelphia: J. B. Lippincott Company, 1898), 343; Rufus Wilmot Griswold, *The Republican
Court, or American Society in the Days of Washington,* rev. ed. (New York:
D. Appleton and Company, 1856), 362–63. No evidence survives confirm-
ing that Mary Morris was in attendance, but other ladies were there, and it
is my assumption that Mary joined the party. For the lustre, see George
Washington to Bartholomew Dandridge, April 3, 1797, and George Wash-
ington to Mrs. [Mary] Morris, May 1, 1797 (second quotation), George
Washington Papers, Series 2 Letterbooks, LOC; Mary Morris to George
Washington, May 9, 1797, George Washington Papers, Series 4 General
Correspondence, LOC (third quotations).

50. *Porcupine's Gazette and United States Daily Advertiser* (April 1, 1797) (quotations, emphasis in the original); *Aurora General Advertiser* (October 6,
1796). For Morris's disapproval of the newspaper war, see Robert Morris
to James Marshall, November 1, 1796, Robert Morris Papers, LOC, and

306 NOTES TO PAGE 157

Robert Morris to John Nicholson, January 6, 1797, Collection of Papers of Robert Morris, HUNT; Arnebeck, *Through a Fiery Trial*, 397–98. James Greenleaf had been hunted by sheriffs for imprisonment as early as October 1795. See John Nicholson to James Greenleaf, October 1, 1795, in John Nicholson Letter Books, vol. 3, HSP.

For the Aggregate Fund—composed of Henry Pratt, Thomas W. Francis, John Miller, Jr., John Ashley, and Jacob Baker—see Robert Morris and John Nicholson to Pratt, Francis, Miller, Ashley, and Baker, April 17, May 15 and 16, June 12 and 15, 1797, Robert Morris Papers, NYPL; John Nicholson and Robert Morris to Trustees of the Aggregate Fund, July 17, 1797, in John Nicholson Letter Books, vol. 7, HSP; and also Arbuckle, *Pennsylvania Speculator and Patriot*, 135–36; Arnebeck, *Through a Fiery Trial*, 444; and Chernow, "Robert Morris: Land Speculator," 162–67. Morris's initial proposal to these trustees was prompted by public auctions of the falling M & N notes. His contract with the new Aggregate Fund offered to reimburse via lot sales $720,000 of Greenleaf's debts plus those of Morris and Nicholson conveyed by the trustees.

In July 1797, one of Morris's major creditors, John Church, recently arrived in America from England, filed suit against him in a New York chancery court. See Syrett, *Papers of Alexander Hamilton*, 18:359–66. Morris also learned in 1797 that Talleyrand, who had been in Pennsylvania the previous year and had agreed to purchase 106,875 acres from the financier, reversed his decision. See Robert Morris to M. Talleyrand-Perigord, January 18, 1797, Robert Morris Papers, LOC; Edwin R. Baldridge, Jr., "Talleyrand's Visit to Pennsylvania, 1794–1796," *Pennsylvania History* 36 (April 1969): 145–60; and Arbuckle, *Pennsylvania Speculator and Patriot*, 105.

51. Thomas Morris, "Personal Memoir," 1852; Introductory note for Alexander Hamilton to Herman LeRoy, William Bayard, and James McEvers, December 16, 1796, in Syrett, *Papers of Alexander Hamilton*, 20:447–48. By 1797, the Holland Land Company had advanced Morris £9,000 from the withheld sum to enable the negotiations.

52. Thomas Morris, "Personal Memoir," 1852; Robert Morris to Thomas Morris, November 23, 1796, Robert Morris Papers, LOC; Robert Morris to Thomas Morris, March 11, 1797 (first quotations), and Robert Morris to Thomas Morris, March 6, 1797 (last quotation), Collection of Papers of Robert Morris, HUNT. Robert Morris had tried to get a commissioner appointed since 1796: see Robert Morris to Thomas Morris, June 7, July 31, August 24, and August 29, 1796, Collection of Papers of Robert Morris, HUNT. Washington nomi-

nated Isaac Smith as commissioner, but Smith declined, to be replaced by Jeremiah Wadsworth. See Abler, *Cornplanter*, 120–23.

53. Thomas Morris to Robert Morris, May 29, 1797 (quotations), and Robert Morris to Thomas Morris, July 20, 1797, Thomas Morris manuscripts, NYHS; Thomas Morris, "Personal Memoir," 1852; Robert Morris to Thomas Morris, June 30, 1797, Collection of Papers of Robert Morris, HUNT; Wilkinson, "Treaty of Big Tree," 262–63. Thomas's May 29 letter above tells his version of what happened when he confronted Red Jacket about the earlier "great Eater" remark: Red Jacket "appeared to be very much mortified at having called you the big Eater[.] he said that there were so many large men in the United States that if he had called you the big man that the Indians would have been at a loss to know whom he meant, but having dined with you at the Green House [the Hills] out of Town they observed you eat very heartily and he knew that they would know whom he meant when he called you the 'big eater.'"

54. Undated speech in Thomas Morris manuscripts, NYHS, and also Collection of Papers of Robert Morris, HUNT (first quotation). For the food, drink, and gifts, see Thomas Morris to Robert Morris, September 9, 1796, and Robert Morris to Thomas Morris, July 6, 1797, Thomas Morris manuscripts, NYHS; entry for April 1, 1797, "Journal, 1794–1801," Robert Morris Business Papers, HSP. Thomas thought his father's attendance at the treaty advisable. See also Thomas Morris, "Personal Memoir," 1852; and Wilkinson, "Treaty of Big Tree," 264–65. Morris's directives to his son and Williamson are found in Robert Morris to Thomas Morris and Charles Williamson, August 1, 1797, Collection of Papers of Robert Morris, HUNT; and Robert Morris to Thomas Morris, July 20 (last quotation) and July 29, 1797, Thomas Morris manuscripts, NYHS. Williamson declined to serve in the treaty negotiations. See Thomas Morris, "Personal Memoir," 1852.

55. Robert Morris to Gustavus Scott, July 29, 1797 (first quotation), Robert Morris to Robert Morris, Jr., April 30, 1797, Robert Morris Papers, LOC (second quotation). For the practice of keeping close, see Mann, *Republic of Debtors*, 28. For Greenleaf's seizure, see Robert Morris and John Nicholson to the Trustees of the Aggregate Fund, July 13, 1797, Robert Morris Papers, NYPL. For Nicholson's movements, see Robert Morris to John Nicholson, August 31, 1797, Robert Morris Papers, LOC. Lawyers instructed Nicholson to stay at his own house—see Robert Morris to John Nicholson, September 2, 1797, and Robert Morris to Théophile Cazenove, September 6, 1797, Robert Morris Papers, LOC. For an example of their usage of the

terms "Castle Defiance" for the Hills and "Castle Defense" for Nicholson's Chalkley Hall, see Robert Morris to John Nicholson, August 31 and November 20, 1797, Robert Morris Papers, LOC. For brief background on Chalkley Hall, see Arbuckle, *Pennsylvania Speculator and Patriot*, 194, and Harold Donaldson Eberlein and Horace Mather Lippincott, *The Colonial Homes of Philadelphia and Its Neighbourhood* (Philadelphia: J. B. Lippincott Co., 1912), 325–33.

56. Robert Morris to James Marshall, October 12, 1795 (first quotation), Robert Morris to William Crouch, November 29, 1796, Robert Morris to Thomas Fitzsimons, August 18, 1797 (last quotation), Robert Morris to Robert Morris, Jr., August 21, 1797, Robert Morris to Thomas Morris, August 29, 1797, and Robert Morris to John Nicholson, September 6, 1797 (second quotation), Robert Morris Papers, LOC; Robert Morris to Thomas Morris, September 18, 1797, Thomas Morris manuscripts, NYHS. In October 1794, Morris had mortgaged the Hills to the Insurance Company of Pennsylvania in exchange for funds due for repayment the following year. See *In the Account of Property*, 12; "Robert Morris Esq. in a/c with Insurance Co. of the state of Penna," 1796–1799, Reed and Forde Papers, HSP; and Jasper Yeates, *Reports of Cases Adjudged in the Supreme Court of Pennsylvania: With Some Select Cases at Nisi Prius, and in the Circuit Courts* (Philadelphia: John Bioren, 1818), 4:456–61. For its inventory and arrangement, see "Proposals by R. Morris," February 16, 1797, and contract between Robert Morris and Standish Forde, dated January 26, 1798, Reed and Forde Papers, HSP, and "A Schedule of Property within the State of Pennsylvania, Conveyed by Robert Morris, to the Hon. James Biddle, Esq. and Mr. William Bell, in Trust for the Use and Account of The Pennsylvania Property Company," *Plan of Association of the Pennsylvania Property Company*, 17–18, which estimated the estate's value at $150,000. For David Landreth, see entries for April 24 and December 7, 1795, and June 6, 1796, in "Journal, 1794–1801," Robert Morris Business Papers, HSP. For visitors' reports of the Hills, see Kenneth Roberts and Anna M. Roberts, trans. and eds., *Moreau de St. Méry's American Journey, 1793–1798* (Garden City, N.Y.: Doubleday and Co., 1947), 231, and Parsons, *Extracts From the Diary of Jacob Hiltzheimer*, 243. For the yellow fever that season, see Anna Coxe Toogood, "Philadelphia as the Nation's Capital, 1790–1800" in Kenneth R. Bowling and Donald R. Kennon, eds., *Neither Separate nor Equal: Congress in the 1790s* (Athens, Oh.: Published for the United States Capitol Historical Society by Ohio University Press, 2000), 53–54.

57. Thomas Morris, "Personal Memoir," 1852; contract between Robert Morris and the Seneca nation of Indians, September 15, 1797, reprinted in *Report of Special Committee to Investigate the Indian Problem of the State of New York, Appointed by the Assembly of 1888* (Albany: Troy Press Company, 1889), 131–34; William L. Stone, *The Life and Times of Red-Jacket, or Sa-Go-Ye-Wat-Ha; Being the Sequel to the History of the Six Nations* (New York: Wiley and Putnam, 1841), 147–62; Anthony F. C. Wallace and Sheila C. Steen, *The Decline and Rebirth of the Seneca* (New York: Knopf, 1970), 181–83; Taylor, *The Divided Ground*, 313–17, 325; Densmore, *Red Jacket*, 50–54; and Abler, *Cornplanter*, 120–34. The Seneca reservations set aside by the contract came to about 311 square miles total.

58. Robert Morris to Thomas Morris, September 29, 1797, Thomas Morris manuscripts, NYHS (quotation, emphasis in the original); Robert Morris to Jeremiah Wadsworth, October 5, 1797, Robert Morris Papers, LOC.

59. Robert Morris to John Nicholson, September 7, 1797, Robert Morris Papers, NYPL (quotation). For the advertised sale, see Robert Morris to John Nicholson, September 6, 1797, Robert Morris Papers, LOC.

60. These phrases are drawn, in sequence, from Robert Morris to John Nicholson, September 6, 1797, Robert Morris Papers, LOC; Robert Morris to Major L'Enfant, October 18, 1797, James Dudley Morgan collection of Digges-L'Enfant-Morgan Papers, LOC; Robert Morris to John Nicholson, October 25, 1797, Dreer Collection, Robert Morris letters, HSP; Robert Morris to John Nicholson, December 6, 1797, No. 1, and Robert Morris to William Sansom, December 8, 1797, Robert Morris Papers, LOC; and Robert Morris to John Nicholson, December 21, 1797, Dreer Collection, Robert Morris letters, HSP.

In contrast, that September, local resident Elizabeth Hewson wrote to her brother that "I think [Morris] should be in jail. He deserves to be there if ever any man did." Hewson, quoted in Charles Rappleye, *Robert Morris: Financier of the American Revolution* (New York: Simon and Schuster, 2010), 508.

61. Robert Morris to John Nicholson, December 30, 1797, No. 4, Robert Morris Papers, LOC (first quotation); Robert Morris to James Rees, January 3, [1798], Robert Morris Papers, NYPL (second quotation); Robert Morris to John Nicholson, January 22, 1798, No. 2, Dreer Collection, Robert Morris letters, HSP (last quotation). See also Mann, *Republic of Debtors*, 28–29, and Swiggett, *The Forgotten Leaders of the Revolution*, 151–54.

62. Robert Morris to George Eddy, December 29, 1797, Robert Morris Papers, LOC.

63. Robert Morris to John Nicholson, February 5, 1798, No. 2 (first quotation), and February 8, 1798, No. 1 (last quotations, emphasis in the original), Dreer Collection, Robert Morris letters, HSP; Robert Morris to John Nicholson, February 2, 1798, No. 4, Marion S. Carson Collection, LOC; Robert Morris to John Nicholson, February 5, 1798, No. 3, Robert Morris Papers, LOC (second quotation).

    Previous scholars have found warrants for his arrest, from Blair McClenachan and others, dating as early as December 30, 1797. See Benson J. Lossing, "The Arrest of Robert Morris," *The American Historical Record* 2 (1873): 229, and Sumner, *The Financier and the Finances of the American Revolution,* 2:287.

64. Robert Morris to John Nicholson, February 14, No. 2, and February 15 (first quotation), 1798, and Robert Morris to Mary Morris [February 14, 1798], Robert Morris Papers, LOC; Harrison Gray Otis, cited in Morison, *The Life and Letters of Harrison Gray Otis,* 1:133 (last quotations). The official notice of imprisonment was signed by J. Rolph on February 16, 1798, and is archived in the Society Small Collection, Robert Morris section, HSP. That same month, courts in New York were advertising for the arrest of Morris there. See "The People of the State of New York," *Time Piece* (February 5, 1798).

CHAPTER 8. HIS RUINS

1. Robert Morris to John Nicholson, December 9 and December 11, No. 2, 1797, Robert Morris Papers, LOC. See also "Sheriff's Sale," *Philadelphia Gazette & Universal Daily Advertiser* (November 30 and December 11, 1797), and the *Aurora General Advertiser* (November 23, 1797).

2. William Sansom to John Dickinson, January 16, 1798, Gratz Collection, HSP (quotations). Robert Morris to William Sansom, December 8, 1797; Robert Morris to Jonathan Penrose, December 9, 1797; Robert Morris to Joseph Ball and Messrs Reede & Forde, December 9, 1797; and Robert Morris to James McEvers, January 1, 1798, Robert Morris Papers, LOC. For background on William Sansom, see Elva Tooker, *Nathan Trotter: Philadelphia Merchant, 1787–1853* (Cambridge, Mass.: Harvard University Press, 1955), 8–9, 39–40. Earlier, Sansom had advertised a house for sale in the northeast area of the city, around Arch Street, and signaled his interest in developing that area, in *Porcupine's Gazette and United States Daily Advertiser* (April 1, 1797). John Nicholson owed Sansom even more than Morris did. See John Nicholson to Robert Morris, March 19, 1795, and John

Nicholson to William Sansom, March 23, 1795, John Nicholson Letter Books, vol. 1, HSP; Robert Morris to William Sansom, October 31, 1796, Robert Morris Papers, LOC; and accounts between William Sansom and John Nicholson/Robert Morris, August 1, 1800 (dating back to November 1794), in box 5, Ball Estate, Dupuy Papers, HSP. For Ball, see Robert Morris to John Nicholson, November 29, 1797, No. 2, Dreer Collection, Series 1, HSP; Louis Richards, "A Sketch of some of the Descendants of Owen Richards, who Emigrated to Pennsylvania Previous to 1718," *Pennsylvania Magazine of History and Biography* 6 (1882): 76, and Emmett William Gans, *A Pennsylvania Pioneer: Biographical Sketch with Report of the Executive Committee of the Ball Estate Association* (Mansfield, Ohio: Kuhl, 1900), 10–15, 47. For Reed & Forde, see Arthur P. Whitaker, "Reed and Forde: Merchant Adventurers of Philadelphia," *Pennsylvania Magazine of History and Biography* 61 (1937): 237–62, and Thomas M. Doerflinger, *A Vigorous Spirit of Enterprise: Merchants and Economic Development in Revolutionary Philadelphia* (Chapel Hill: Published for OIEAHC by the University of North Carolina Press, 1986), 294–95. Reed & Forde had served as agents for Morris's goods as early as January 1796. See Robert Morris to Reed & Forde, January 25, 1796, Robert Morris Papers, LOC. For the Insurance Company of North America, see "A Short Account of Philadelphia," in *Stephens's Philadelphia Directory, For 1796; or, Alphabetical Arrangement: Containing the Names, Occupations, and Places of Abode of the Citizens* (Philadelphia: W. Woodward for Thomas Stephens, 1796), 28–32. Standish Forde was also a director of the Insurance Company of North America.

In October 1797, Morris had dealt briefly with officials interested in renting his Chestnut Street construction for the federal government's use until the relocation to the Potomac in 1800. He noted at the time that he needed an advance on the rent "to finish the roof in such way as to secure the building and otherwise to make it fit for their purposes." The deal fell through, probably because of the risk of Morris's losing control of the property before the end of the lease. No mention was made of its intended function. See Robert Morris to Théophile Cazenove, October 9, 1797, Robert Morris Papers, LOC.

3. Robert Morris to John Nicholson, December 11[?], 1797, No. 2, Robert Morris Papers, LOC (quotation); deed of January 26, 1798, between Robert Morris and Standish Forde, Reed and Forde Papers, Robert Morris section, HSP. At the time of its sale, the Chestnut Street property was still subject to its original mortgage owed to John Dickinson of £7,000 Pennsylvania currency,

or approximately $19,000 (the principal only—Morris had been making interest payments on that principal). See entries for May 3, 1794, and April 2, 1796, in "Journal, 1794–1801," Robert Morris Business Papers, HSP, and Robert Morris to John Dickinson, December 20, 1797, Robert Morris Papers, LOC. For Bingham's comment, see Edward Channing, *A History of the United States* (New York: Macmillan Company, 1917), 4:112. See also Thompson Westcott, *The Historic Mansions and Buildings of Philadelphia With Some Notice of Their Owners and Occupants* (Philadelphia: Porter and Coates, 1877), 366, and Barbara Ann Chernow, "Robert Morris: Land Speculator, 1790–1801" (Ph.D. diss., Columbia University, 1974), 213.

For Rick's lot, See "Sheriff's Sale," *Philadelphia Gazette & Universal Daily Advertiser* (November 30, 1797). In 1864, Philadelphian Joshua Francis Fisher stated of this corner sliver that "no price could tempt Mr. George Fox to sell" it to Robert Morris. Joshua Francis Fisher, "A Section of the Memoirs of Joshua Francis Fisher, Philadelphia Social Scene from the Time of the Hamiltons to the Early Part of the Nineteenth Century," Cadwalader Collection, Series 9, Joshua Francis Fisher Papers, HSP.

For the $30,000 mortgage on the Hills contracted in 1794 with Morris's other property Trout Spring, see Robert Morris to Jonathan Penrose, December 9, 1797, Robert Morris to Thomas Fitzsimons, January 21[?], 1798, and Robert Morris to Nicklin & Griffith, February 5, 1798, Robert Morris Papers, LOC; [Robert Morris,] *In the Account of Property* (Philadelphia [1801]), 12; and "Robert Morris Esq. in a/c with Insurance Co. of the state of Penna," 1796–1799, Reed and Forde Papers, HSP. For Ball and Forde's purchase of the Hills, for a sale price of $6,800, see proceedings of April 8, 1799, Reed and Forde Papers, and Jasper Yeates, *Reports of Cases Adjudged in the Supreme Court of Pennsylvania: With Some Select Cases at Nisi Prius, and in the Circuit Courts* (Philadelphia: Campbell, 1871), 4:456–61.

4. Robert Morris to John Nicholson, December 11[?], 1797, No. 2, Robert Morris to Théophile Cazenove, December 27, 1797, and Robert Morris to Thomas Fitzsimons, December 27, 1797, Robert Morris Papers, LOC. Morris's Amsterdam contact in America was Théophile Cazenove.

5. Robert Morris to James McEvers, January 1, 1798 (first quotations), Robert Morris to Thomas Fitzsimons, December 29, 1797, Robert Morris Papers, LOC. In the ensuing confusion, Morris would continue to vacillate between this understanding and a hope that the properties could be saved. On January 25, 1798, he told Nicholson that "I understood I had conveyed to Le Roy & Bayard the House & lot" in a custodial transaction earlier that

month, but an ensuing sheriff's sale of the property's movables confused him in this regard. See Robert Morris to John Nicholson, January 25, 1798, No. 3, Robert Morris Papers, LOC.

6. Robert Morris to John Nicholson, January 21, No. 1 (first quotation), and January 25, 1798, No. 3 (last quotations), Robert Morris Papers, LOC; Deed of January 26, 1798, between Robert Morris and Standish Forde, Reed and Forde Papers, Robert Morris section, HSP. The movables of the Chestnut Street lot were advertised for sale the first week of February. It is unclear whether this was at the behest of Sansom or the sheriff. See Robert Morris to William Sansom, February 7, 1798, Robert Morris Papers, LOC.

7. Robert Morris to John Nicholson, February 2, 1798, No. 4 (first quote), Robert Morris to Charles Morris February 3, 1798 (second quote), Robert Morris to Théophile Cazenove, February 3 and March 2, 1798, Robert Morris to Nicklin & Griffith, February 5, 1798, Robert Morris to William Sansom, February 5, 1798, and Robert Morris to Thomas Fitzsimons, February 6, 1798, Robert Morris Papers, LOC; *In the Account of Property*, 11.

8. Robert Morris to John Nicholson, March 25, 1798, Gratz collection, HSP (quotations). The President's House in Philadelphia was eventually bought by the University of Pennsylvania in 1800. See George E. Thomas and David B. Brownlee, *Building America's First University: An Historical and Architectural Guide to the University of Pennsylvania* (Philadelphia: University of Pennsylvania Press, 2000), 38–41. Viewing it in early 1799, a British visitor judged that the President's House "now stands in a conspicuous situation, half in ruins, a great staring, red brick building, a monument of American extravagance & folly." David Montagu Erskine to his father, January 1, 1799, Letterbook of David Montagu Erskine, 1798–1799, Small Special Collections Library, University of Virginia, Charlottesville, Virginia. For George Street, see John Hills and John Cooke, *This Plan of the City of Philadelphia and it's [sic] Environs . . .* (Philadelphia: John Hills, 1797; London: John and Josiah Boydell, 1798); Robert I. Alotta, *Street Names of Philadelphia* (Philadelphia: Temple University Press, 1975), 125; and Westcott, *Historic Mansions and Buildings of Philadelphia*, 366. See also John Adems Paxton, *(The Stranger's Guide): An Alphabetical List of All the Wards, Streets, Roads . . . Wharves, Ship yards, Public Buildings, &c. in the City and Suburbs of Philadelphia, with References for Finding their Situations on an Alphabetical Plan* ([Philadelphia]: Edward Parker, [c1810]), 46.

The tax assessor's ledger for 1798 shows entries for "William Sansom's Est. vacant Lot 99 feet front & 236 feet on 7th St. to Geo Street—$1826" and "William Sansom's Est. New House formerly R. Morris's Lot 396 feet on Walnut Street & 255 feet deep & 347 feet on Chesnut Street Extending same Depth 15000." Tax Assessor's Ledger, South Ward, 1798, pp. 12–13, Philadelphia City Archives, Philadelphia, Pennsylvania.

9. Benjamin Henry Latrobe, Virginia Journals, entry for April 26, 1798, MDHS (quotation). See also Edward C. Carter II, ed., *The Papers of Benjamin Henry Latrobe,* microfiche edition (Clifton, N.J.: Published for the Maryland Historical Society by James T. White and Co., 1976); Edward C. Carter II, ed., *The Virginia Journals of Benjamin Henry Latrobe, 1795–1798* (New Haven: Published for the Maryland Historical Society by Yale University Press, 1977); and Talbot Hamlin, *Benjamin Henry Latrobe* (New York: Oxford University Press, 1955), 128–32.

10. Latrobe in Carter, *The Virginia Journals of Benjamin Henry Latrobe,* 1:79–80 (quotations); Charles E. Brownell and Jeffrey A. Cohen, eds., *The Architectural Drawings of Benjamin Henry Latrobe* (New Haven: Published for the Maryland Historical Society and the American Philosophical Society by Yale University Press, 1994), 84; "Design of the House of Captain William Pennock in the Main Street, Norfolk," [September 8, 1799,] in John C. Van Horne and Lee W. Formwalt, eds., *The Correspondence and Miscellaneous Papers of Benjamin Henry Latrobe* (New Haven: Published for the Maryland Historical Society by Yale University Press, 1984), 1:147–49; Bernard L. Herman, *Town House: Architecture and Material Life in the Early American City, 1780–1830* (Chapel Hill: Published for OIEAHC by the University of North Carolina Press, 2005), 51–54; [Charles H. Simmons], *Simmons's Norfolk Directory, Containing the Notes, Occupations, and Places of Abode of the Inhabitants, Arranged in Alphabetical Order* (Norfolk: Augustus C. Jordan, 1801), 26–27.

11. Latrobe, Virginia Journals, April 26, 1798.

12. Ibid.

13. Ibid. (emphasis in the original), and James D. Kornwolf, *Architecture and Town Planning in Colonial North America* (Baltimore: Johns Hopkins University Press, 2002), 3:1461–62. In comparison, the Hôtel Biron featured nine public rooms on its ground floor, with a grand staircase on one side of the entry vestibule. For Jefferson's Monticello, which the Virginian began to reconstruct in 1796, three years after the start of Morris's mansion, see Dell Upton, *Architecture in the United States* (New York: Oxford University Press, 1998), 17–56; Ron Katz, *French America: French Architecture from Colonialization to the Birth of a Nation* (New York: Published for the French

Heritage Society, 2004), 192, 197, 204–6. Jefferson's letters make no reference to Morris's mansion.

As I differ from Kornwolf's proposed details of the Folly's interior, I prefer not to suggest specific, unknowable features of the plan. For an alternative approach, see Jane Kamensky's excellent *The Exchange Artist: A Tale of High-Flying Speculation and America's First Banking Collapse* (New York: Viking, 2008).

14. Latrobe, Virginia Journals, April 26, 1798 (emphasis in the original). Earlier, for Federal Hall in New York City, L'Enfant had invented designs for the capitals of the building's pilasters, drawing together an assemblage of foliage, drapery, and a patriotic star with rays. See J. J. Jusserand, *With Americans of Past and Present Days* (New York: Charles Scribner's Sons, 1916), 155–56.

15. Ibid. (first quotations); *Porcupine's Gazette* (April 3, 1798) (last quotations, emphasis in the original); Hamlin, *Benjamin Henry Latrobe*, 129–30. For the surface flatness and Palladian elements common in Federal era architecture, see George B. Tatum, *Penn's Great Town: 250 Years of Philadelphia Architecture Illustrated in Prints and Drawings* (Philadelphia: University of Pennsylvania Press, 1961), 40–43; William H. Pierson, Jr., *American Buildings and Their Architects*, vol. 1, *The Colonial and Neoclassical Styles* (Garden City, N.Y.: Doubleday, 1970); and Damie Stillman, "City Living, Federal Style," in Catherine E. Hutchins, ed., *Everyday Life in the Early Republic* (Winterthur, Del.: Winterthur Museum, 1994), 137–74. Latrobe's judgment of L'Enfant's abilities did not soften over time. At Washington, D.C., he declared that everything in that city "was badly planned and conducted. L'Enfant's plan has in its contrivance every thing that could prevent the growth of the city." He named it all "this *Gigantic Abortion.*" Latrobe to Philip Mazzei, May 29, 1806, in Van Horne and Formwalt, *The Correspondence and Miscellaneous Papers of Benjamin Henry Latrobe*, 2:225–31.

16. Julian Ursyn Niemcewicz, *Under Their Vine and Fig Tree: Travels Through America in 1797–1799, 1805 with Some Further Account of Life in New Jersey*, trans., ed., and with an introduction and notes by Metchie J. E. Budka (Elizabeth, N.J.: Grassmann Publishing Co., 1965), 37–38.

17. L. M., "On American Palaces," *Monthly Magazine, and American Review* 3 (October 1800): 241 (quotation). This author does not explicitly identify the building here, but the author mentions the Morrises' old Masters-Penn House in Philadelphia just prior to this reference. For Morris's early sale of the building's materials, see entry for October 9, 1797, in "Journal, 1794–1801," Robert Morris Business Papers, HSP. For the sheriff's actions, see

Robert Morris to John Baker, March 7, 1798, Robert Morris Papers, LOC. For evidence that the building was still intact in September 1798, see "Serious Disturbance at the Gaol," *Gazette of the United States, and Philadelphia Daily Advertiser* (September 19, 1798). The 1799 city directory still references "Morris's building" on Chestnut Street. See Cornelius William Stafford, *The Philadelphia Directory, for 1799* (Philadelphia: Woodward, 1799), 53.

18. Robert Morris to John Nicholson, February 28, 1798, Robert Morris Papers, LOC (first quotation); Joseph Ball and Reed & Forde to William Sansom, November 21, 1799, and Joseph Ball to Reed & Forde, December 10, 1799, Reed and Forde Papers, Robert Morris section, HSP; Fisher, "A Section of the Memoirs of Joshua Francis Fisher" (last quotation). Tantalizingly, Fisher stated that "I am told that even lately when a block of marble was removed from the front of one of these houses [near Morris's block], fragments of a sculptured frieze, turned inside, indicated the source from which it came."

    Thomas Billington became involved in the lot in 1799. A Mr. Kid and Mr. Allen were also involved that year. See Joseph Ball to Reed & Forde, December 10, 1799, Reed and Forde Papers, Robert Morris section, HSP. For the dismantling of the Folly, see Articles of Agreement between Patrick Dougherty and John Reed & Standish Forde, February 26, 1800, Reed and Forde Papers. For the purchases of Traquair, Miller, Sansom, Latrobe, and others, see list dated March 1–April 19, 1800, Reed and Forde Papers. See also Abraham Ritter, *Philadelphia and Her Merchants, As Constituted Fifty @ Seventy Years Ago, Illustrated by Diagrams of the River Front, and Portraits of Some of Its Prominent Occupants* (Philadelphia: Published by the author, 1860), 199–200. Latrobe would also employ many of Morris's same stoneworkers for the Bank of Pennsylvania, including James Traquair, John Miller, and John Bennet. See "Agreement for Executing the Marble Work of the Bank of Pennsylvania" [February 26, 1799], in Van Horne and Formwalt, *The Correspondence and Miscellaneous Papers of Benjamin Henry Latrobe*, 1:128–36.

19. Charles Dempsey, *Inventing the Renaissance Putto* (Chapel Hill: University of North Carolina Press, 2001), xiv, 1–61. For French overdoor traditions, see Katie Scott, *The Rococo Interior: Decoration and Social Spaces in Early Eighteenth-Century Paris* (New Haven: Yale University Press, 1995). The Metropolitan Museum of Art in New York City has a number of European overdoors in its collections which show similarities to these reliefs.

20. J. Thomas Scharf and Thompson Westcott, *History of Philadelphia, 1609–1884* (Philadelphia: L. H. Everts and Co., 1884), 2:1066–67; Susan James-

Gadzinski and Mary Mullen Cunningham, *American Sculpture in the Museum of American Art of the Pennsylvania Academy of the Fine Arts* (Seattle and London: Museum of American Art of the Pennsylvania Academy of the Fine Arts in association with the University of Washington Press, 1997), 6–7. The full-size wooden sculptures were "Comedy" and "Tragedy," executed by William Rush. See D. Dodge Thompson, "The Public Work of William Rush: A Case Study in the Origins of American Sculpture," in *William Rush, American Sculptor* (Philadelphia: Pennsylvania Academy of the Fine Arts, 1982), 33. See also Amy Hudson Henderson, "Furnishing the Republican Court: Building and Decorating Philadelphia Homes, 1790–1800" (Ph.D. diss., University of Delaware, 2008), 104. The reliefs had been cut into lunettes during the refurbishment of the Chestnut Street Theater after a fire in 1820. This theater was demolished in 1856. See Tatum, *Penn's Great Town*, 169.

   On the back of the images of "Music" and "Drama" held by the Historical Society of Pennsylvania, a note by architect H. Louis Duhring states that the sculptures were taken to W. Struther's marble yard upon the demolition of the theater and were purchased there by the Rev. Dr. E. T. Benson of 2014 DeLancey St. [Place?]. Duhring stated that they were installed in a sunroom there, where they still reside. See Society Photo Collection, Robert Morris Residence, HSP.

21. William Birch, *The Life of William Birch, Enamel Painter, Written By Himself* (manuscript from HSP, on Microfilm 188 at Winterthur Library) (first quotation); James-Gadzinski and Cunningham, *American Sculpture in the Museum of American Art of the Pennsylvania Academy of the Fine Arts*, 6–7; *"The Georgian Period": Being Measured Drawings of Colonial Work* (Boston: American Architect and Building News, 1902), part 9, 23–24; John T. Faris, *Old Roads Out of Philadelphia* (Philadelphia: Lippincott, 1917), 185–86 (which includes an image of the relief on "Angel House"); Fiske Kimball, *Domestic Architecture of the American Colonies and of the Early Republic* (New York: Charles Scribner's Sons, 1922), 289; Francis Burke Brandt, Henry Volkmar Gummere, and Corn Exchange National Bank, *Byways and Boulevards in and About Historic Philadelphia* (Philadelphia: Corn Exchange National Bank, 1925), 132 (which also includes an image of the relief on "Angel House"); Thomas H. Keels, *Forgotten Philadelphia: Lost Architecture of the Quaker City* (Philadelphia: Temple University Press, 2007), 68; undated newspaper clipping, written by "M. H. W.," in Campbell Collection, vol. 12, HSP; J. Alexis Shriver, "Permanence or Change?

The History of Old Olney Again Brings Up an Unsettled Question," *Baltimore Sun* (May 27, 1928) (last quotation). See also Gertrude Louise Johnson Stephens and Maurine Collins Schmitz, *Children of Mt. Soma: Baltimore (Now in Harford) County, Maryland* (Franklin, N.C.: Genealogy Pub. Service, 1992), 952.

22. For the piece at the William Gibbes House, see the photograph titled "64 South Battery, Gibbes, William House, Charleston, Charleston County, South Carolina," by Frances Benjamin Johnston, 1937, call number LC-J7-SC- 1275 [P&P], Prints and Photographs Division, Library of Congress, Washington, D.C.; and for background on this house, see Martha A. Zierden and Jeanne A. Calhoun, "An Archaeological Interpretation of Elite Townhouse Sites in Charleston, South Carolina, 1770–1850," *Southeastern Archaeology* 9 (Winter 1990): 79–92; and Jonathan H. Poston, *The Buildings of Charleston: A Guide to the City's Architecture* (Columbia: University of South Carolina Press, 1997), 277–78. I thank Lisa Randle for informing me of this piece. For the piece at Magnolia Plantation, see *"The Georgian Period,"* part 11, plate 20; Henry A. M. Smith, "The Ashley River: Its Seats and Settlements," *South Carolina and Historical Magazine* 20 (April 1919): 95–97; Kimball, *Domestic Architecture of the American Colonies,* 289; Robert Molloy, *Charleston: A Gracious Heritage* (New York: D. Appleton Century Company, 1947), 22; James-Gadzinski and Cunningham, *American Sculpture in the Museum of American Art of the Pennsylvania Academy of the Fine Arts,* 7; and www.magnoliaplantation.com (accessed December 17, 2013). For Morris's earlier correspondence with the Draytons, see Robert Morris to John Drayton, May 28, 1795, Robert Morris Papers, LOC. In 1886, an earthquake damaged the relief at Magnolia Plantation, indicating that it had been installed by then.

23. Abraham Ritter, *Philadelphia and Her Merchants,* 199–200, states that Traquair decorated his Philadelphia house and stone-yard with relics from the Folly. Further, *"The Georgian Period,"* part 9, 23–24, asserted that Traquair owned another house and yard outside Philadelphia in Conshohocken (presumably the "Angel House"), behind which were kept the surviving capitals from the Folly. For Fisher's observations, see "A Section of the Memoirs of Joshua Francis Fisher" (quotation). For the journalist's observations, see Westcott, *Historic Mansions and Buildings of Philadelphia,* 360. Of these floral tablets, Westcott added that "they were long supposed to have been of marble, but from the falling off of some of the ornaments in

later times it is probable that they were of stucco or some artificial stone." James Mease and Thomas Porter made mention of another Jardella curiosity which may have been sculpted for the Folly. In 1831, they stated that pedestrians took note of "the two dogs carved in stone, by the celebrated Jardella, lately deceased," displayed at the front of Peter Fritz's stonecutting operation at 226 Race Street. See James Mease and Thomas Porter, *Picture of Philadelphia* (Philadelphia: Robert DeSilver, 1831), 2:118. George Tatum, in *Penn's Great Town*, 40, noted that a French sculptor, Claudius F. Le Grand, active in Philadelphia from 1785 to 1801 and responsible for carved details on the new Bank of the United States building (1797), was also situated at Tenth and Market Streets. Curiously, none of Morris's account books mention Le Grand.

24. For the "Leda and the Swan" chimneypiece, see note in Chapter 7, above. For the "Apollo and the Muses" chimneypiece, see object file for HSP.X-154, the Philadelphia History Museum at the Atwater Kent, Philadelphia, Pennsylvania. R. J. Dutton of Burlington stated that Boudinot had installed the piece in his back parlor at Burlington and that it was moved to Memorial Hall in Fairmount Park before being transferred to the Historical Society of Pennsylvania in the 1880s. See R. J. Dutton to John W. Jordan, June 12, 1900, in HSP.X-154 file above. For both pieces, see Henderson, "Furnishing the Republican Court." For the cherry doors and Maris's Folly, see Hannah Coryell Anderson, " 'Cintra,' " *American Magazine of Art* 8 (June 1917): 310, and Roy Ziegler, *New Hope, Pennsylvania: River Town Passages* (Bloomington, Ind.: iUniverse, 2008), 35–37.

25. For Fitzsimons's 1798 sales of Morris's furniture, see Robert Morris to John Nicholson, July 5, 1798, Dreer Collection, HSP; Robert Morris to Charles Young, December 5, 1798, Society Miscellaneous Collection, Robert Morris letters, HSP. For the 1799 auction, see "Sale of Furniture," *Claypoole's American Daily Advertiser* (May 13, 1799), which announces the sale of "a variety of Household Furniture, Great part of which is of the most elegant kind." For the offer of chairs to Jefferson, see Robert Morris to Thomas Jefferson, January 29, 1802, and Thomas Fitzsimons to Robert Morris, January 18, 1802, quoted in Barbara B. Oberg, ed., *The Papers of Thomas Jefferson* (Princeton: Princeton University Press, 2009), 36:449 (quotations). For the tapestry chair, see "Historical Relic," *Philadelphia Inquirer* (November 16, 1876). Three cut glass bowls—small, round, and colorless, probably used as either fingerbowls or wine glass coolers—and three silver

serving spoons—with script M's on their handle fronts—are held in the collections of the Winterthur Museum, Winterthur, Delaware, with a tradition of ownership attributed to the Morrises. The items were donated to Winterthur by Duncan I. Selfridge and his wife in the 1950s and 1960s.

26. Robert Blair St. George, *Conversing by Signs: Poetics of Implication in Colonial New England Culture* (Chapel Hill: University of North Carolina Press, 1998), 231–42; Thomas McCormick, *Ruins as Architecture, Architecture as Ruins* (Dublin, N.H.: William L. Bauhan, 1999); and Paul Zucker, *Fascination of Decay: Ruins: Relic, Symbol, Ornament* (Ridgewood, N.J.: Gregg, 1968).

27. *In the Account of Property,* 12; Robert Morris to Standish Forde, July 26, 1798, Reed and Forde Papers, Robert Morris section, HSP; Robert Morris to John Nicholson, January 2, 1799, Dreer collection, HSP.

28. Robert Morris to John Nicholson, February 12, 1799, Robert Morris Papers, LOC; *Claypoole's American Daily Advertiser* (March 3, 1799); sheriff's summons to William Crouch and attached note, April 8, 1799, and also "Account between Robert Morris, Esq. and Insurance Company of the State of Pennsylvania," 1796–1799, Reed and Forde Papers, Robert Morris section, HSP; Westcott, *Historic Mansions and Buildings of Philadelphia,* 376; *Lemon Hill in its connection with the efforts of our citizens and councils to obtain a private park: Philadelphia, June 1856* (Philadelphia: Crissy and Markley, 1856), 5, 8 (quotations); Fisher, "A Section of the Memoirs of Joshua Francis Fisher"; Tatum, *Penn's Great Town,* figure 29; and [Joan Church Roberts], "The Schuylkill Villas: A Revealing Look into the History of Extraordinary 18th Century Treasures in Philadelphia's Fairmount Park," 2006 Loan Exhibit, 124–27. In 1801, Pratt bought all of Morris's plants in the greenhouse for $750. See entry for July 27, 1801, in "Journal, 1794–1801," Robert Morris Business Papers, HSP. For construction of Lemon Hill, see Martha Crary Halpern, "Henry Pratt's Account for Lemon Hill," *Antiques & Fine Art Magazine* (June 2005); the Martha Crary Halpern Research Papers at the Philadelphia Museum of Art Archives; and Virginia N. Naude, "Lemon Hill Revisited," *Antiques* (April 1966): 578–79. Henry Pratt sold Lemon Hill in 1836 to Knowles Taylor.

29. *In the Account of Property,* 13–14 (first quotation); Robert Morris to Alexander Hamilton, December 18, 1795, Robert Morris Papers, LOC; W. W. H. Davis, *The History of Bucks County, Pennsylvania, From the Discovery of the Delaware to the Present Time* (Doylestown, Penn.: Democrat Book and Job Office, 1876), 657–63; *Plan of Association of the Pennsylvania Property Company, established March 1797* (Philadelphia: Aitken, 1797) (last quotation).

For Morris's role in the sale, see Robert Morris to the President and Directors of the Insurance Company of North America, March 1, 1798, Robert Morris Papers, LOC. Robert Morris, Jr., moved into 256 High Street in 1799. See Stafford, *The Philadelphia Directory, for 1799*, 101.

30. Louis Le Guen to Alexander Hamilton, July 13, 1799, in Harold C. Syrett, ed., *The Papers of Alexander Hamilton* (New York: Columbia University Press, 1976), 23:263–65; and Davis, *The History of Bucks County, Pennsylvania*, 659–60.

31. *In the Account of Property*, 8.

32. Latrobe, quoted in Hamlin, *Benjamin Henry Latrobe*, 152 (quotation). The tax ledger for 1798 lists William Sansom owning a vacant lot 99 feet front by 236 feet on Seventh Street to George Street. He is also listed as the owner of "New House formerly R. Morris's Lot," 396 feet on Walnut Street by 255 feet deep, and 347 feet on Chestnut Street extending the same depth. See Tax Assessor's Ledger, South Ward, 1798, Philadelphia City Archives. The tax ledger for 1799 lists William Sansom as owner of "1 Lot . . . [with] unfinishd Building formerly Robert Morris's together with 11 Three Story B. Houses Shingling in & 2 others Just began on Walnut Street," valued at $16,150. Joseph Ball and Reed & Forde are still listed as owning "part of the Lott formerly R. Morris." One Philadelphia resident confirmed that "Mr Sansom & others have built I believe 23 houses on the back of the lot where Mr. Morris had built his large house" by December 1799. See Stephen Moylan to James Madison, December 11, 1799, in David B. Mattern, ed., *The Papers of James Madison* (Charlottesville: University Press of Virginia, 1991), 17:292. The map of Philadelphia in W[illiam]. Birch & Son, *The City of Philadelphia, in the State of Pennsylvania North America; As it Appeared in the Year 1800* (Philadelphia: W. Birch, 1800) shows the bottom half of Morris's block already filled in, presumably with Latrobe's row houses, with the Morris House still represented on the map. Today, 707 Walnut Street is the most substantial remnant of the original construction.

33. Residents of the Carstairs houses are found using the Sansom Street addresses listed in James Robinson, *The Philadelphia Directory for 1804* (Philadelphia: Robinson, 1804). Thomas Cope moved into 191 Walnut Street, in the Latrobe-designed row. See entry for June 11, 1801, in Eliza Cope Harrison, ed., *Philadelphia Merchant: The Diary of Thomas P. Cope, 1800–1851* (South Bend, Ind.: Gateway Editions, 1978), 63 (quotation). For general discussion of Sansom's house developments, see Hsin-Yi Ho, "A Proposal for Preserving and Restoring the Streetscape of Jewelers' Row" (M.S.

thesis, University of Pennsylvania, 2004), 6–9; Dell Upton, *Another City: Urban Life and Urban Spaces in the New American Republic* (New Haven: Yale University Press, 2008), 3; Tatum, *Penn's Great Town*, 47–48 and 164; William John Murtagh, "The Philadelphia Row House," *Journal of the Society of Architectural Historians* 16 (December 1957): 10; John Andrew Gallery, *Philadelphia Architecture: A Guide to the City* (Cambridge, Mass: M.I.T. Press, 1984), 32; "Thomas Carstairs," in James C. Massey, *Two Centuries of Philadelphia Architectural Drawings* (Philadelphia: Philadelphia Museum of Art and the Society of Architectural Historians, 1964); Richard J. Webster, *Philadelphia Preserved: Catalog of the Historic American Building Survey* (Philadelphia: Temple University Press, 1976), 53; Kornwolf, *Architecture and Town Planning*, 3:1564–65; Russell Frank Weigley, Nicholas B. Wainwright, and Edwin Wolf, *Philadelphia: A 300 Year History* (New York: Norton, 1982), 251–52; and Donna J. Rilling, *Making Houses, Crafting Capitalism: Builders in Philadelphia, 1790–1850* (Philadelphia: University of Pennsylvania Press, 2001), 79. Sansom also restricted the height of outbuildings between the Latrobe row and the Carstairs row to ten feet. Today, 700, 730, and 732 Sansom Street appear to be the closest surviving properties of the original plan.

34. "Plan of 5 Lotts of ground on Eighth Street and 6 Lotts on Chesnut Street to be disposed of at Public vendue," May 11, 1801, Reed and Forde Papers, Robert Morris section, HSP; James Robinson, *The Philadelphia Directory for 1806* (Philadelphia: Robinson, 1806). The name "Morris Street" was used as early as 1862. See Samuel L. Smedley, *Smedley's Atlas of the City of Philadelphia* (Philadelphia: J.B. Lippincott, 1862), although the name seems to have continued shifting later, to Bennett and later Ionic Street. See Ho, "A Proposal for Preserving and Restoring the Streetscape of Jewelers' Row," 138–43, and also Westcott, *Historic Mansions and Buildings of Philadelphia*, 366. This northwest corner of the block had been the site of the edifice itself. See materials in the Reed and Forde Papers, and P. C. Varlé, "To the Citizens of Philadelphia This New Plan of the City and its Environs is Respectfully Dedicated" ([Philadelphia,] 1802).

35. Stephen Moylan to James Madison, December 11, 1799, in Mattern, *Papers of James Madison*, 17:292 (first quotation); Robinson, *The Philadelphia Directory for 1804*, 8 (second quotations); James Mease, *The Picture of Philadelphia, Giving An Account of its Origin, Increase and Improvements in Arts, Sciences, Manufactures, Commerce and Revenue* (Philadelphia: B. and T. Kite, 1811), 21 (third quotations); Charles William Janson, *The Stranger in America* (London: James Cundee, 1807), 183 (last quotation).

36. John F. Watson, *Annals of Philadelphia, Being a Collection of Memoirs, Anecdotes, & Incidents of the City and its Inhabitants From the Days of the Pilgrim Founders* (Philadelphia: Carey and Hart, 1830); Benjamin Dorr, *A Memoir of John Fanning Watson, the Annalist of Philadelphia and New York* (Philadelphia: Collins, 1861); and Deborah Dependahl Waters, "Philadelphia's Boswell: John Fanning Watson," *Pennsylvania Magazine of History and Biography* 98 (January 1974): 3–52.

37. Watson, *Annals of Philadelphia*, 355–56 and 424.

38. "Robert Morris' Mansion," *Atkinson's Casket* 7 (February 1832): 72; *Life of Robert Morris, the Great Financier; with an Engraving and Description of the Celebrated House, Partly Erected in Chesnut Street, Between Seventh and Eighth, South Side* (Philadelphia: Desilver, 1841); Martin P. Snyder, "William Birch: His Philadelphia Views," *Pennsylvania Magazine of History and Biography* 73 (July 1949): 292. In 1833, William Sullivan recalled the story, stating that Morris "had laid the foundation of a palace in the square . . . with the intention of making the whole of that space his residence." See William Sullivan and John T. S. Sullivan, *The Public Men of the Revolution* (Philadelphia: Carey and Hart, 1847), 141. In 1835, a Philadelphian remembered the stir caused by the first appearance of commercial shops on Chesnut Street's residential blocks where Morris's Folly, "a princely palace," once stood. See *Blackbeard: A Page from the Colonial History of Philadelphia* (New York: Harper and Brothers, 1835), 2:67. In 1853, the *Philadelphia Inquirer* reprinted the view and retold the story in three columns. See "Philadelphia in Olden Times. No. IV: Morris' Mansion," in *Philadelphia Inquirer* (April 20, 1853), newspaper clipping in C. A. Poulson Scrapbooks, Library Company of Philadelphia, Philadelphia, Pennsylvania. Although this writer acknowledged the construction as "ill-starred" and spoke of Morris's "wild architectural dreams," he or she concluded that "Mr. Morris, although not infallible, was a great and good man" due to his patriotism and that "Philadelphians especially should revere and cherish his memory." Likewise in 1853, *Gleason's Pictorial Drawing Room Companion* 5 (August 6, 1853), 84–85, printed an image of Morris and a view based on the Birch print, along with the financier's life story. In 1864, Joshua Francis Fisher heaped scorn on the Folly, calling it a "palace" and stating that its sculpture was "all imported from Italy." He likewise charged L'Enfant with his culpability for being "skilled in the art of seductive estimates." See Fisher, "A Section of the Memoirs of Joshua Francis Fisher." Watson's version was reprinted nearly verbatim in response

to a reader's query in "Notes and Queries," *Potter's American Monthly* 14 (February 1880): 149.

Joseph Delaplaine, working prior to Watson, gave a sympathetic biography of Morris and blamed his fall on his sacrificing his own private interests for the "safety of the commonwealth." He did not mention the Chestnut Street mansion. See Joseph Delaplaine, *Delaplaine's Repository of the Lives and Portraits of Distinguished American Characters* (Philadelphia: [Delaplaine], 1815–1818), 3:141–48.

39. Westcott, *Historic Mansions and Buildings of Philadelphia*, 351–80 (first quotations); J. Thomas Scharf and Thompson Westcott, *History of Philadelphia: 1609–1884* (Philadelphia: Everts and Co., 1884); Ellis Paxon Oberholtzer, "A Great Philadelphian: Robert Morris," *Pennsylvania Magazine of History and Biography* 28 (1904): 273–74 (last quotation). Rufus Wilmot Griswold's *The Republican Court, or American Society in the Days of Washington*, rev. ed. (New York: D. Appleton and Company, 1856), a work contemporary with Westcott's, dealing with similar themes, had only this to say about the Folly, in a footnote on 109: L'Enfant "designed a magnificent residence for Robert Morris, in Philadelphia, in which, before it was half finished, the great financier sunk all his fortune."

L'Enfant's skills were widely praised after the period of Westcott's writing. For example, in "Pierre Charles L'Enfant," *The American Architect and Building News* 10 (October 22, 1881): 192–94, reprinted from the *New York Tribune*, the author held that L'Enfant was responsible for designing "the most ambitious house which had then been put up in any city of the country—that of Robert Morris, the financier. It gives the first instance ever seen on the Western Continent of Mansard roofs, which a century afterwards became so common here. The building was never finished, the estimates being too large, and the owner's money too irregularly forthcoming."

In the early twentieth century, *"The Georgian Period,"* part 9, 23–24, lamented the loss of Morris's house and described it as "lordly." Later in the century, the story of the Folly was retold in Tatum, *Penn's Great Town*, 44–45. More recently, Gordon Wood used the Folly to demonstrate Morris's strivings to be a "disinterested aristocrat." See Gordon Wood, *The Radicalism of the American Revolution* (New York: Knopf, 1992), 212. And Carroll Smith-Rosenberg mentioned it briefly to illustrate how Morris "overreached himself" and "failed to perform gentility in a convincing manner." See Carroll Smith-Rosenberg, *This Violent Empire: The Birth of an American National Identity* (Chapel Hill: Published for the OIEAHC by the University of North Carolina Press, 2010), 354–55.

40. Robert Ellis Thompson, "Lessons of Social Science in the Streets of Philadelphia," *Penn Monthly* 11 (December 1880), 929, reported: "The block of buildings on the south side of Chestnut street, between Seventh and Eighth streets, is erected on the site of a magnificent mansion, which was never finished. Those who have occasion to dig down into the yards of these houses, sometimes come upon the remains of the vast foundation walls of what was long known as 'Morris's Folly.' "

CHAPTER 9. HIS RELEASE

1. Robert Morris to John Nicholson, April 9, 1798, Dreer Collection, Robert Morris letters, HSP (quotation). For the Walnut Street Prison and Prune Street debtors' apartment (originally designed in 1785 as a workhouse), see Robert J. Turnbull, *A Visit to the Philadelphia Prison: Being an Accurate and Particular Account of the Wise and Humane Administration Adopted in Every Part of that Building; . . . with Observations on the Impolicy and Injustice of Capital Punishments. In a Letter to a Friend* (Philadelphia: Budd and Bartram, 1796); Negley K. Teeters, *They Were in Prison: A History of the Pennsylvania Prison Society, 1787–1937, Formerly the Philadelphia Society for Alleviating the Miseries of Public Prisons* (Chicago: John C. Winston Co., 1937); Negley K. Teeters, *The Cradle of the Penitentiary: The Walnut Street Jail at Philadelphia, 1773–1835* ([Philadelphia,] 1955); George B. Tatum, *Penn's Great Town: 250 Years of Philadelphia Architecture Illustrated in Prints and Drawings* (Philadelphia: University of Pennsylvania Press, 1961), 37–38; and Bruce H. Mann, *Republic of Debtors: Bankruptcy in the Age of American Independence* (Cambridge, Mass.: Harvard University Press, 2002), 87–100.

2. Robert Morris to John Nicholson, February 20, 1798, No. 1 (first quotations), February 23, 1798, No. 1, and February 28, 1798 (last quotation), and Robert Morris to Théophile Cazenove, February 26, 1798, Robert Morris Papers, LOC; entry for September 1, 1798, in "Journal, 1794–1801," Robert Morris Business Papers, HSP; Robert Morris to John Nicholson, February 21, 1798, No. 1, Dreer Collection, Robert Morris letters, HSP; Robert Morris to Charles Young, February 23, 1798, Society Small Collection, Robert Morris section, HSP. Morris's monthly rental included board. See also Mann, *Republic of Debtors*, 100, and Charles Rappleye, *Robert Morris: Financier of the American Revolution* (New York: Simon and Schuster, 2010), 508–10.

326 NOTES TO PAGES 193–94

3. Robert Morris to John Nicholson, January 31, 1798, Robert Morris Papers, LOC (quotation). For the location of Greenleaf's room, see Robert Morris to William Cranch, February 26, 1798, Robert Morris Papers, LOC. According to William B. Wood, *Personal Recollections of the Stage, Embracing Notices of Actors, Authors, and Auditors, During a Period of Forty Years* (Philadelphia: Henry Carey Baird, 1855), 37–40, in the outdoor yards, Greenleaf "had the privilege of forming a very small circle, and indulging himself with a rapid ride, on a fine horse, each morning" at the time Morris went for his walks. Morris earlier had a hand in ensuring Greenleaf remained in prison. Greenleaf had attached the financier's assets in Europe, damaged his relationships with major creditors there, sued Morris and Nicholson repeatedly, scared off potential purchasers of their lands, and "in short he has injured [Nicholson] and me in every way he could think of." See Robert Morris to John Nicholson, October 18, 1797, No. 3, Robert Morris Papers, LOC; Bob Arnebeck, *Through a Fiery Trial: Building Washington, 1790–1800* (Lanham: Madison Books, 1991), 455; and Mann, *Republic of Debtors*, 204.

   For Bingham's troubles, see Ethel E. Rasmusson, "Democratic Environment—Aristocratic Aspiration," *Pennsylvania Magazine of History and Biography* 90 (April 1966): 179–80, and Robert C. Alberts, *The Golden Voyage: The Life and Times of William Bingham, 1752–1804* (Boston: Houghton-Mifflin, 1969), 320–23. For the activities of Morris's sons, see for example Robert Morris to James Rees, February 28, 1798, Robert Morris Papers, NYPL; Robert Morris to Théophile Cazenove, March 2, 1798, Robert Morris Papers, LOC; and Robert Morris to William Morris, April 25, 1798, Tilghman Family Papers, MDHS. In early 1798, Abigail Adams observed that "as many as two Hundred Heads of Families and persons formerly in good circumstances are now in confinement." See Abigail Adams to Mary Cranch, February [1–5], 1798, in Stuart Mitchell, ed., *The New Letters of Abigail Adams, 1788–1801* (Boston: Houghton Mifflin Company, 1947), 129.

4. Robert Morris to Thomas Morris, February 24, 1798, Collection of Papers of Robert Morris, HUNT (quotation); [Robert Morris,] *In the Account of Property* (Philadelphia [1801]), 1. For Morris's rejection of the option of suicide, see Robert Morris to John Nicholson, April 30, 1799, Dreer Collection, Robert Morris letters, HSP.

5. Wood, *Personal Recollections of the Stage*, 37–40 (quotations, emphasis in the original); Robert Morris to John Nicholson, March 7, 1798, No. 1, Robert Morris Papers, LOC; Robert Morris to John Nicholson, April 9, 1798, Dreer Collection, Robert Morris letters, HSP. In 1847, Redwood Fisher

claimed that "the mechanics of Philadelphia repeatedly made him offers of pecuniary relief, assigning as a reason, that since in his days of prosperity he had always aided to advance their interests, and showed himself their friend, it was right that in the hour of his adversity they should do whatever they could to alleviate his misfortunes"; Morris "gracefully declined the proffered aid." See Redwood Fisher, "Revolutionary Reminiscences Connected with the Life of Robert Morris, Esq., the Financier," *The American Review: A Whig Journal of Politics, Literature, Art, and Science* 6 (July 1847): 79.

6. Entry for February 19, 1798, in Elaine Forman Crane, ed., *The Diary of Elizabeth Drinker* (Boston: Northeastern University Press, 1991), 2:1005 (first quotation); Harrison Gray Otis to Mrs. Otis, February 16 [1798], in Samuel Eliot Morison, *The Life and Letters of Harrison Gray Otis, Federalist, 1765–1848* (Boston and New York: Houghton Mifflin Company, 1913), 1:139 (second quotations). Toby Ditz alerts us to the gendered sensitivities of men who lost their fortunes during this era. See Toby L. Ditz, "Shipwrecked; or, Masculinity Imperiled: Mercantile Representations of Failure and the Gendered Self in Eighteenth-Century Philadelphia," *Journal of American History* 81 (June 1994): 51–80.

7. Abigail Adams to Mary Cranch, February 21, 1798, in Mitchell, *The New Letters of Abigail Adams,* 134–35.

8. See entry for September 1, 1798, in "Journal, 1794–1801," Robert Morris Business Papers, HSP. Their landlord for the rental house on Chestnut Street near Eighth Street was Edward Shippen. For Mary's distress regarding the furniture auction, see Robert Morris to John Nicholson, July 5, 1798, Dreer Collection, Robert Morris letters, HSP.

9. Robert Morris to John Nicholson, August 15, 1798, No. 1, Robert Morris Papers, LOC (quotation); Thomas Condie and Richard Folwell, *History of the Pestilence, Commonly Called Yellow Fever, Which Almost Desolated Philadelphia, in the Months of August, September & October, 1798* (Philadelphia: R. Folwell, [1799]).

10. George Washington to Robert Morris, August 19, 1798, in W. W. Abbot, ed., *The Papers of George Washington: Retirement Series* (Charlottesville: University Press of Virginia, 1998), 2:535. For Cottringer's movements, see Robert Morris to Garrett Cottringer, September 4, 1798, Society Small Collection, Robert Morris section, HSP. For Greenleaf's release, see Robert Morris to John Nicholson, March 31, 1798, No. 3, Dreer Collection, Robert Morris letters, HSP; Abigail Adams to Mary Cranch, February [1–5], April 13, and May 7, 1798, in Mitchell, The *New Letters of Abigail Adams,*

129, 155, 169; and Allen C. Clark, *Greenleaf and Law in the Federal City* (Washington, D.C.: W. F. Roberts, 1901), 171–72. For William's initial sickness, see Robert Morris to John Nicholson, September 7, 1798, Dreer Collection, Robert Morris letters, HSP, and William W. Morris to John Nicholson, September 8, 1798, John Nicholson Papers in the Pennsylvania State Archives, microfilm reel 13, Harrisburg, Pennsylvania. For the fever hitting the jail, see "Serious Disturbance at the Gaol," *Gazette of the United States, and Philadelphia Daily Advertiser* (September 19, 1798) (which reported of the prisoners that "the females have been removed to Morris's building"); Condie and Folwell, *History of the Pestilence,* 75–76, 86, 90, 93 (quotation) (which reported the male and female prisoners being removed); and Mann, *Republic of Debtors,* 98.

11. Robert Morris to John Nicholson, September 25, 1798, Dreer Collection, Robert Morris letters (first quotation), and Robert Morris to John Nicholson, September 20, 1798, Conarroe Papers (second quotation), HSP; William W. Morris to John Nicholson, October 2 and October 4, 1798, John Nicholson Papers in the Pennsylvania State Archives, microfilm reel 13. Morris's plight during this time is recorded in letters in the Dreer and Canarroe collections cited above, as well as in the Gratz Collection at the HSP, the Collection of Papers of Robert Morris at HUNT, the Robert Morris Papers at NYPL, and in Box 18 of the Robert Morris Papers at LOC. Morris, along with several other inmates, seems to have been given the opportunity to relocate to a prison at Norristown, Pennsylvania, but he declined, probably to remain near his family. For background on medical treatments, see J. H. Powell, *Bring Out Your Dead: The Great Plague of Yellow Fever in Philadelphia in 1793* (Philadelphia: University of Pennsylvania Press, 1949).

12. Robert Morris to John Nicholson, October 9, 1798, Gratz Collection, HSP; Robert Morris to Thomas Morris, October 10, 1798, Collection of Papers of Robert Morris, HUNT (first quotation); Robert Morris to John Nicholson, October 10, 1798, No. 2, Dreer Collection, Robert Morris letters, HSP (second quotations); Daniel Brodhead to Henry Banks, October 11 and 12, 1798, Ball Family Papers, HSP; and Robert Morris to John Nicholson, October 15, 1798, Conarroe Papers, HSP.

13. Robert Morris to John Nicholson, October 15 (first quotations), and October 18, 1798, No. 1 and No. 2, Dreer Collection, Robert Morris letters, and Robert Morris to John Nicholson, October 16, 1798 (second quotation), Conarroe Papers, HSP; Robert Morris to Maria Morris, October 20, and

Robert Morris to Thomas Morris, November 11, 1798, Collection of Papers of Robert Morris, HUNT; Robert Morris to Philip S. Physick, October 22, 1798, MSS Correspondence of Benjamin Rush, HSP; Condie and Folwell, *History of the Pestilence*, 95. Morris's companion Henry Banks deliberated breaking out; see Daniel Brodhead to Henry Banks, October 19, 1798, Ball Family Papers, HSP.

14. Thaddeus Brown, *An Address in Christian Love, to the Inhabitants of Philadelphia; on the Awful Dispensation of the Yellow Fever, in 1798* (Philadelphia: R. Aitken, 1798), 29, 42 (first quotations); Robert Morris to Charles Young, November 6, 1798, Society Small Collection, Robert Morris section, HSP (last quotation).

15. Robert Morris to John Nicholson, Monday, November 12, 1798, Conarroe Papers, HSP.

16. Robert Morris to John Nicholson, November 14, 1798, Dreer Collection, Robert Morris letters, HSP; Donald Jackson and Dorothy Twohig, eds., *The Diaries of George Washington* (Charlottesville: University Press of Virginia, 1979), 6:326. Morris had invited Nicholson to meet Washington at the jail, but the former did not venture there. For the men's pledge, see Martha Washington to Eliza Powell, December 17, 1797, quoted in Anne Hollingsworth Wharton, *Martha Washington* (New York: Charles Scribner's Sons, 1897), 271–73.

17. George and Martha Washington to Mary Morris, September 21, 1799, quoted in Charles Henry Hart, *Mary White—Mrs. Robert Morris* (Philadelphia, 1878). For Washington's passing, see François Furstenburg, *In the Name of the Father: Washington's Legacy, Slavery, and the Making of a Nation* (New York: Penguin, 2006), and David Waldstreicher, *In the Midst of Perpetual Fetes: The Making of American Nationalism, 1776–1820* (Chapel Hill: Published for OIEAHC by the University of North Carolina Press, 1997).

18. James Hardie, *The Philadelphia Directory and Register*, 2d ed. (Philadelphia: Jacob Johnson and Co., 1794), 89 (quotation); L'Enfant, Account dated 1804, and Robert Morris to Major L'Enfant, May 15, July 20, and October 18, 1797, and May 16, 1802, all in James Dudley Morgan collection of Digges-L'Enfant-Morgan Papers, LOC; Kenneth R. Bowling, *Peter Charles L'Enfant: Vision, Honor, and Male Friendship in the Early American Republic* (Washington, D.C.: Printed for the Friends of the George Washington University Libraries, 2002), 41, 46; W. W. Abbot and Edward G. Lengel, eds., *The Papers of George Washington: Retirement Series* (Charlottesville: University Press of Virginia, 1999), 3:360.

19. Pierre Charles L'Enfant to Alexander Hamilton, July 1, 1798, in Harold C. Syrett, ed., *The Papers of Alexander Hamilton* (New York: Columbia University Press, 1974), 21:523–24 (quotation); Bowling, *Peter Charles L'Enfant*, 45–46; Arnebeck, *Through a Fiery Trial*, 564–66, 604.

20. *In the Account of Property*, 43; Thomas Morris, quoted in Robert Morris to Major L'Enfant, January 14, 1801 (first quotation), Thomas Morris to Robert Morris, January 20, 1801, Robert Morris to Major L'Enfant, January 22, 1801 (second quotation), Thomas Morris to L'Enfant, January 24, 1801, Robert Morris to Major L'Enfant, January 25, February 3, and February 27, 1801, and May 16, 1802 (last quotation), and [A. V. Rawls] to Major L'Enfant, January 13, 1823, and September 24, 1825, all in James Dudley Morgan collection of Digges-L'Enfant-Morgan Papers, LOC; Bowling, *Peter Charles L'Enfant*, 48–49.

21. L'Enfant, account dated 1804, James Dudley Morgan collection of Digges-L'Enfant-Morgan Papers, LOC; Bowling, *Peter Charles L'Enfant*, 42–45, 48–50.

22. Entry for August 12, 1806, in Edward C. Carter II, John C. Van Horne, and Lee W. Formwalt, eds., *The Journals of Benjamin Henry Latrobe, 1799–1820, from Philadelphia to New Orleans* (New Haven: Published for the Maryland Historical Society by Yale University Press, 1980), 3:71–72 (quotations); Scott W. Berg, *Grand Avenues: The Story of the French Visionary Who Designed Washington, D.C.* (New York: Pantheon Books, 2007), 227, 237; Bowling, *Peter Charles L'Enfant*, 50.

23. Syrett, *Papers of Alexander Hamilton*, 21:524; Bowling, *Peter Charles L'Enfant*, 54–55, 60; "Pierre Charles L'Enfant," *The American Architect and Building News* 10 (October 22, 1881): 192–94. In 1810, Congress granted L'Enfant $666.67 with interest from March 1, 1792.

24. Digges, quoted in Bowling, *Peter Charles L'Enfant*, 61–63.

25. "Pierre Charles L'Enfant," 194 (quotation); Fiske Kimball, "Pierre Charles L'Enfant," in Dumas Malone, ed., *Dictionary of American Biography* (New York: Charles Scribner's Sons, 1933), 6:165–69; Berg, *Grand Avenues*, 222–43; Bowling, *Peter Charles L'Enfant*, 64. One obituary was published in Washington's *National Intelligencer* (June 25, 1825). Toward the end of the century, interest in L'Enfant's role in the federal city would be renewed, culminating in a rededication to executing the "L'Enfant plan" in the early twentieth century.

26. Robert Morris to Charles Young, November 6, 1798 (second quotation), and November 26, 1798, Society Small Collection, Robert Morris section,

HSP; Robert Morris to John Nicholson, April 22, 1799, ChE.9.23, Boston Public Library, Boston, Massachusetts (first and fourth quotations); Robert Morris to John Nicholson, April 30, 1799, Dreer Collection, Robert Morris letters, HSP (third and last quotations). Letters from Morris describing his continued financial scrambling during this time can be found in the Tilghman Family Papers at the MDHS, the Robert Morris Papers at the NYPL, and the Dreer, Gratz, and Society Small collections at the HSP. Working closely with Nicholson, he corresponded most often on the Washington lots, the Genesee lands, and the North American Land Company.

27. *In the Account of Property,* 64–65 (first quotation); Robert Morris to John Nicholson, June 13, 1798, No. 3, Robert Morris Papers, NYPL; "Died," *Poulson's American Daily Advertiser* (December 8, 1800) (last quotations). See also Robert D. Arbuckle, *Pennsylvania Speculator and Patriot: The Entrepreneurial John Nicholson, 1757–1800* (University Park: Pennsylvania State University Press, 1975), 199–201, and Arnebeck, *Through a Fiery Trial,* 493, 526. Arbuckle calculates Nicholson's debts at over $12 million. It is not certain that Morris authored the obituary. It is signed "A Friend of the Deceased."

28. Gouverneur Morris to Robert Morris, December 26, 1798, Gouverneur Morris Papers, LOC; Anne Cary Morris, ed., *The Diary and Letters of Gouverneur Morris* (New York: Charles Scribner's Sons, 1888), 2:378 (first quotation); Robert Morris to John Nicholson, April 27, 1799, Robert Morris Papers, NYPL; Robert Morris to John Nicholson, April 24, 1799, Dreer Collection, Robert Morris letters, HSP (last quotations); Gouverneur Morris to Robert Morris, Jr., June 4, 1799, and Gouverneur Morris to Robert Morris, June 29, 1800, Gouverneur Morris Papers, LOC. For another visit from Gouverneur to Robert's prison, in 1801, see Morris, *The Diary and Letters of Gouverneur Morris,* 2:406. See also James J. Kirschke, *Gouverneur Morris: Author, Statesman, and Man of the World* (New York: St. Martin's, 2005), 248–59.

Later in 1799, Abigail Adams confirmed Gouverneur's view of Mary Morris. In Abigail Adams to Mary Cranch, December 11, 1799, in Mitchell, *The New Letters of Abigail Adams,* 220, Abigail wrote of her visit to Mary Morris's home: "She received me with all that dignity of manners for which she more than any Lady I ever saw, is distinguished. I calld rather at an improper hour, (having been detaind from going sooner by visitors). She was in a small neat Room and at dinner with her daughter & youngest son, who is with a merchant, and on whose account she said, she always dinned at one oclock, but instead of refusing herself, she rose and met me at the door. Her feelings were evidently strongly excited. She endeavoured to smile away the Melancholy which was evident upon her whole countenance, and enterd into conversation. When I left her, I requested her to come and take Tea with me. I took her by the Hand. She said she did not visit, but she would not refuse herself the pleasure of comeing some day when I was alone. She then turnd from me, and the tears burst forth. I most sincerely felt for her."

29. Mann, *Republic of Debtors*, 166–220; S. Laurence Shaiman, "The History of Imprisonment for Debt and Insolvency Laws in Pennsylvania as They Evolved from the Common Law," *American Journal of Legal History* 4 (1960): 205–25. The state of Pennsylvania had enacted a bankruptcy law in 1785, targeting commercial debtors, but it expired in 1793.

30. Morris's thoughts on engaging the state insolvency law, and his attempts to find alternate routes out of prison, can be found in Robert Morris to John Nicholson, November 22 and December 10, 1798, and Robert Morris to James Gibson, June 14, 1799, Society Small Collection, Robert Morris section, HSP; Robert Morris to John Nicholson, February 12, 1799, Robert Morris Papers, LOC; Robert Morris to John Nicholson, April 22, 1799, Ch.E.9.23, Boston Public Library; Robert Morris to John Nicholson, April 27, 1799, Robert Morris Papers, NYPL.

31. Robert Morris to Thomas Morris, March 23 (first quotation), July 29 (second quotation), August 27 (last quotations), and October 1, 1801, Collection of Papers of Robert Morris, HUNT. The bankruptcy petition against Morris was filed July 28, 1801. Morris's judge was Richard Peters of the District Court of the United States for Pennsylvania, and the three commissioners appointed to his case were John Hallowell, Joseph Hopkinson, and Thomas Cumpston. See Case of Robert Morris, No. 42, BA1800-PA, microfilm 993, reel 7, Records of the U.S. District Court of the Eastern District of Pennsylvania, Bankruptcy Act of 1800, Record Group 21, National Archives Mid-Atlantic Region, Philadelphia, Pennsylvania. The mechanisms involved in these proceedings are outlined in Mann, *Republic of Debtors*, 221–53. See also Barbara Ann Chernow, "Robert Morris: Land Speculator, 1790–1801" (Ph.D. diss., Columbia University, 1974), 219.

32. Robert Morris to Thomas Morris, December 5, 1801, Collection of Papers of Robert Morris, HUNT (quotation); Cornelius William Stafford, *The Philadelphia Directory for 1801* (Philadelphia: Woodward, 1801), 69, and James Robinson, *The Philadelphia Directory, City and County Register for 1802* (Philadelphia: Woodward, [1802]), 176; *In the Account of Property*, 23–

24; *Record of Pennsylvania Marriages, Prior to 1810* (Harrisburg, Pa.: Hart, 1880), 1:183; Robert Morris to Maria Morris, June 26, 1799, Society Small Collection, Robert Morris section, HSP; Gouverneur Morris to Robert Morris, November 10, 1801, Gouverneur Morris Papers, LOC. Garrett Cottringer remained on hand, himself in straitened circumstances as a result of his employer.

33. Alberts, *The Golden Voyage*, 411–29, 440, 467–73, and Julian Ursyn Niemcewicz, *Under Their Vine and Fig Tree: Travels Through America in 1797–1799, 1805 with Some Further Account of Life in New Jersey*, trans., ed., and with an introduction and notes by Metchie J. E. Budka (Elizabeth, N.J.: Grassmann Publishing Co., 1965), 277.

34. *In the Account of Property*, 1 (quotation); Case of Robert Morris, No. 42, BA1800-PA, microfilm 993, reel 7, National Archives; Robert Morris to Thomas Morris, December 5, 1801, Collection of Papers of Robert Morris, HUNT; "Notice in the case of Robert Morris, a Bankrupt," newspaper clipping in Gratz Collection, HSP. Box 1 of the Robert Morris Business Papers at the Historical Society of Pennsylvania contains handwritten drafts of materials created for Morris's bankruptcy proceedings. In his *Account*, Morris acknowledged that the issuing of M & N notes "is the blameable part of our conduct." See also Mann, *Republic of Debtors*, 253; and William Graham Sumner, *The Financier and the Finances of the American Revolution* (New York: Dodd, Mead, and Company, 1892), 2:293–305. Litigation involving Morris's creditors continued to 1880.

35. Thomas Jefferson to James Madison, March 12, 1801, in Barbara B. Oberg, ed., *The Papers of Thomas Jefferson* (Princeton: Princeton University Press, 2006), 33:255–56 (first quotation); Morris, *The Diary and Letters of Gouverneur Morris*, 2:378 (second quotation); Eliza Cope Harrison, ed., *Philadelphia Merchant: The Diary of Thomas P. Cope, 1800–1851* (South Bend, Ind.: Gateway Editions, 1978), 37 (third quotation); Thompson Westcott, *The Historic Mansions and Buildings of Philadelphia With Some Notice of Their Owners and Occupants* (Philadelphia: Porter and Coates, 1877), 356; Joshua Francis Fisher, "A Section of the Memoirs of Joshua Francis Fisher, Philadelphia Social Scene from the Time of the Hamiltons to the Early Part of the Nineteenth Century," Cadwalader Collection, Series 9, Joshua Francis Fisher Papers, HSP (fourth quotations); Daniel Brodhead to Henry Banks, October 11, 1798, Ball Family Papers, HSP (last quotation); Elizabeth Elliot to Rebecca Gore, August 30, 1798, in Eugene Devereux, ed., *Chronicles of the Plumsted Family, with Some Family Letters, Compiled and Arranged*

with Notes (Philadelphia, 1887), 167–68. See also H. E. Scudder, ed., *Recollections of Samuel Breck With Passages From His Note-Books (1771–1862)* (London: Sampson, Low, Marston, Searle, and Rivington, 1877), 204; and Charles Brockden Brown, *Arthur Mervyn; Or, Memoirs of the Year 1793*, ed. and with an introduction and notes by Philip Barnard and Stephen Shapiro (Indianapolis, Ind.: Hackett Publishing Company, 2008), 174.

36. Morris, *The Diary and Letters of Gouverneur Morris*, 2:432 (first quotations); Gouverneur Morris to Robert Morris, April 7, 1800, Gouverneur Morris Papers, LOC; Robert Morris to Thomas Morris, January 9 and April 19, 1802, March 20, 1803 (last quotation), and Robert Morris to Mary Morris, January 24 and 31 (second quotation), 1802, Collection of Papers of Robert Morris, HUNT; Gouverneur Morris to Alexander Hamilton, August 31, 1802, in Harold C. Syrett, ed., *The Papers of Alexander Hamilton* (New York: Columbia University Press, 1979), 26:42–43; Indenture dated September 4, 1802, between James Donatianus Le Ray de Chaumont of the first Part, Gouverneur Morris of the second part, and Alexander Hamilton of the third part, Gouverneur Morris Papers, Columbia University. See also Rasmusson, "Democratic Environment—Aristocratic Aspiration," 180, for the Morrises at this time.

    In the 1802 Philadelphia directory, the Morrises are still listed on South Eighth Street. See Robinson, *The Philadelphia Directory, City and County Register for 1802*, 176. They are not listed in the 1803 or 1804 directories. In 1805, they are listed at 2 South Twelfth Street in James Robinson, *The Philadelphia Directory for 1805* (Philadelphia: Robinson, 1805). See also Castner Scrapbooks, vol. 6, p. 69, and vol. 36, p. 15, Free Library of Philadelphia, Philadelphia, Pennsylvania. Another image of this house, drawn in the early twentieth century by Frank H. Taylor, was included in Taylor's "Old Philadelphia" series issued from 1915 to 1925, under the title "Where Robert Morris Closed His Eventful Life."

37. Robert Morris to Thomas Morris, January 9, 1802, and April 27, September 22, and December 20 (quotation, emphasis in the original), 1803, Collection of Papers of Robert Morris, HUNT.

38. Will of Robert Morris, June 13, 1804, proved May 25, 1806. Copies found in Society Small Collection, Robert Morris section, HSP, and Robert Morris Papers, LOC (first quotations); Robert Morris to Thomas Morris, January 31, 1805, Collection of Papers of Robert Morris, HUNT (last quotation).

39. "Yesterday being the 23d of April," *United States Gazette* (April 24, 1806); Robert Morris, Jr., to Charles Croxall, May 9, 1806, Croxall-Morris family

papers, LOC; "Died," *United States Gazette* (May 9, 1806) (quotation). The same obituary was reprinted in the Philadelphia *Aurora* and *Poulson's American Daily Advertiser* the following day. Elizabeth Drinker recorded Morris's passing in her diary on May 10, 1806. See Crane, *Diary of Elizabeth Drinker*, 3:1927. Mary Morris died on January 16, 1827, in Philadelphia and was buried next to her husband in the family vault. See Charles Henry Hart, "Mary White—Mrs. Robert Morris," *Pennsylvania Magazine of History and Biography* 2 (1878): 157–84.

40. "Oration on the Love of Wealth," June 1805, Gouverneur Morris Papers, COLU (quotations); Kirschke, *Gouverneur Morris*, 259. On August 15, 1805, in an article titled "Columbia College Commencement," *Poulson's American Daily Advertiser* praised an oration delivered a week earlier by J. H. Bibby, a student participating in the commencement ceremonies, on the subject of luxury. It seems that Gouverneur took Bibby's oration into account when preparing his own a short time later, as he wrote on the draft of his oration that it had been "anticipated by a senior student." See also the Trenton *Miscellany* (August 12, 1805). Thanks to an anonymous reader for these additional references. There is no direct evidence (only implied) that Gouverneur actually delivered this oration.

   Gouverneur personally engaged with the question of wealth throughout his life; while he lived comfortably on his family's New York estate, he also consistently cautioned that "our Country and government do not require and hardly forgive immense Property." See Gouverneur Morris to Samuel Ogden, July 12, 1792, Gouverneur Morris Papers, LOC.

   Useful for further reflection on these issues are Jennifer Nedelsky, *Private Property and the Limits of American Constitutionalism* (Chicago: University of Chicago Press, 1990); Jan Cohn, *The Palace or the Poorhouse: the American House as a Cultural Symbol* (East Lansing: Michigan State University Press, 1979); Wayne Andrews, *Architecture, Ambition, and Americans: A Social History of American Architecture*, rev. ed. (New York: Free Press, 1978); and Richard L. Bushman, *The Refinement of America: Persons, Houses, Cities* (New York: Knopf, 1992). See also *Citizen Kane*, directed by Orson Welles, RKO Radio Pictures, 1941, and *The Queen of Versailles*, directed by Lauren Greenfield, Magnolia Pictures, 2012.

Acknowledgments

This project seemed so easy and fortuitous at the outset. I had already written a bit about Morris's house while in graduate school, and I thought returning to this story after my first book came out in 2006 would be timely and interesting. I planned to spend two or three years writing five chapters to make a brisk book, and then I would move on. But, as I should have foreseen, the plot thickened. A global financial crisis hit in 2008, while my own publishing plans changed. As I grew more enmeshed in Morris's story and my own follies, a number of generous, knowledgeable colleagues helped me finish.

Foremost, I would like to thank Bernard Herman. He spurred the project from the beginning and did his best to nurture it toward something meaningful. Likewise, James West Davidson spent a significant amount of time and energy with me on the initial material, helping bring it to life. And, as always, I remain deeply indebted to Christine Leigh Heyrman, who read the manuscript, offered her singular sagacity, and cheered me along each time I needed it.

Many others contributed. Marion Nelson read the entire work with a smile and a sharp eye—I can't thank her enough for her encouragement throughout the project. Brent Tarter, Catherine Ingrassia, and Sarah Meacham offered close readings of portions of the manuscript and helped me make progress at key points. My other reading group colleagues in Richmond were likewise a great source of support and advice. Additionally, for expert suggestions, research help, and selfless favors, I thank Bob Arnebeck, Scott Berg, Kenneth Bowling, Charles Brownell, Gretchen Buggeln, Kenneth Cohen, François Furstenberg, Timothy Gilfoyle, Amy Henderson, Woody Holton, Ami Howard, Jane Kamensky, Edward Lawler, Bruce Mann, Cathy Matson, Douglas Mooney, Rob Morris, Louis Nelson, Elizabeth Nuxoll,

Mark Rubenstein, and Charles Rappleye. None are responsible for errors that remain.

Further support came from a research grant from the Winterthur Library, allowing me to take advantage of its skillful, cheerful staff, which includes Rosemary Krill, Emily Guthrie, and Jeanne Solensky. Other institutions that made this work possible include the Library of Virginia (particularly David Grabarek); the James Branch Cabell Library of Virginia Commonwealth University (particularly Ray Bonis); the Library Company of Philadelphia (particularly Nicole Joniec); the Historical Society of Pennsylvania (particularly Tamara Gaskell, David Haugaard, Sarah Heim, and Hillary Kativa); the Philadelphia History Museum at the Atwater Kent (particularly Jeffrey Ray); the Free Library of Philadelphia (particularly Karen Lightner); the Philadelphia City Archives; the Philadelphia Historical Commission (particularly Jonathan Farnham); the Philadelphia Museum of Art and its archives (particularly Susan Anderson); Independence National Historical Park; the Pennsylvania Academy of the Fine Arts; the Manuscript Division of the Library of Congress (particularly Jennifer Brathovde, Jeffrey M. Flannery, and Lewis Wyman); Magnolia Plantation and Gardens (particularly Lisa Randle and Preston Cooley); the Huntington Library; the New York Public Library; the New-York Historical Society; the University of Rochester's Rare Books division at the Rush Rhees Library; the Rare Book and Manuscript Library at Columbia University; the Maryland Historical Society; the American Antiquarian Society; and the Boston Public Library.

At Virginia Commonwealth University, the College of Humanities and Sciences provided valuable resources for research and writing time. I thank my department chairs, Bernard Moitt and John Kneebone, for helping nurture this project along.

At Yale University Press, Christopher Rogers and Christina Tucker came through at the right time, every time, with all I needed. Their support and flexibility rescued the folly. Jeffrey Schier and other members of the staff showed admirable care and expertise to improve the final manuscript. Additionally, three anonymous reviewers made indispensable observations and suggestions.

When I was in Philadelphia doing research, Patrick, Marianne, and Jordan Fugeman offered support of every kind, and the project would have been much poorer without them. Finally, I thank my family, including Bella, Finn, and especially Andrea, to whom I will always happily owe so much.

Index

Page numbers in *italics* refer to illustrations.

339

Louis (cook), 134, 151
Louis XIII, king of France, 171, 174
Louis XIV, king of France, 93
Louis XV, king of France, 60
Louis XVI, king of France, 60, 78
Lymondton, Alexander, 132

Maclay, William, 10, 12, 16
Madison, James, 16, 17, 26, 52, 78, 80, 201, 207, 304 n. 44
Maine, Hôtel du. *See* Hôtel Biron
M & N notes, 136, 137, 203, 204, 206
Mansion House. *See* Bingham Mansion
Marie Antoinette, Queen, 108–9, 119
Maris, William, 181
Marshall, Humphrey, 285 n. 26
Marshall, James, 123, 133, 137
Marshall, John, 123, 155, 293–94 n. 8
Maryland, 53, 55
Massachusetts, 15, 53
Masters-Penn House, *28*, 29, 42, 76, 79; ice house at, 91; as presidential residence, 39, 44, 70, 74; sale of, 115; size of, 27, 28, 39
May, John, 240–41 n. 6
McClenachan, Blair, 133, 203
McGee, Robert, 206
Meade, George, 133
Mease, James, 318–19 n. 23
Miami Indians, 129
Mickle, Samuel, 299–300 n. 26
Mifflin, Thomas, 72, 88, 109, 133, 304 n. 44
Miller, Alexander, 185
Miller, John, 86, 101, 116, 119, 141, 171, 175
Miller, John, Jr., 305–6 n. 50
Mills, Robert, 97
Moffatt, Robert, 66–67, 68
Monroe, James, 101, 121, 201
Monticello, 97, 170–71, 273 n. 29
Montor, James, 52
Moore, Anna, 185
Moré, Comte de, 78
Moreau, Jean Victor Maria, 184
Morris, Charles (son), 39, 40, 102, 159, 166, 193, 197, 205
Morris, Esther ("Hetty"), 39, 40, 102, 123, 131, 205, 208
Morris, Gouverneur, 23, *24*, 41, 52–53, 99, 119, 125, 149, 181, 245 n. 14; delivers

"Oration on the Love of Wealth," 209–12, 335 n. 40; as diplomatic envoy, 45, 52, 101, 108; fiscal prudence of, 54–55, 102–3, 106, 109, 133; kindness of, 203; luxury goods imported by, 102; Nicholson mistrusted by, 110; Robert Morris's bequest to, 208; Robert Morris viewed by, 206, 207; winding up of affairs urged by, 58–59, 103, 104–5, 106
Morris, Henry (son), 39, 40, 102, 158, 197, 205
Morris, Maria (daughter), 14, 102, 158, 194; birth of, 39; father's bequest to, 208; marriage of, 205; playfulness of, 40; prison visits by, 40, 195, 197, 198; Washington family and, 4, 9, 198
Morris, Mary. *See* Croxall, Mary ("Polly")
Morris, Mary (White) (wife), 4, 9, 14, 18, 29, *32*, 39, 41–42, 51, 55, 78, 80, 87, 100, 102, 104, 123, 134, 163, 182, 194–95, 197, 198, 203, 204, 207; Binghams envied by, 33; country estate viewed by, 46; depictions of, 113, *114;* during epidemic, 81, 196; furnishings of, 147, 149–53; as grandmother, 205; household employees of, 43–45, 151; husband's bequest to, 208–9; as mother, 38–41; political instincts of, 16–17, 22, 32–33, 38, 40; social life of, 31, 33, 40, 41–43, 147, 155, 194; upbringing of, 21; at Washington's retirement, 156; Washington's view of, 45; as widow, 209
Morris, Robert: as agent of marine, 23; architectural acumen of, 90–92, 117; as artistic patron, 87–88, 89, 90; attacks on, 17–19, 47–48, 104–6, 138–40; bankruptcy of, 204, 206; construction abandoned by, 143, 147; country estate of, 45–47, 54, 76, 90, 102, 123, 154, 158, 159, *160*, 165–66, 180, 182, 190; death of, 209; depictions of, *5, 18, 19, 24, 58, 91*, 113, *114;* Dickinson's proposal to, 69–72; dissolution of estate of, 164–91; early years of, 20; during epidemic, 81; failure feared by, 126–27; as father, 38–41; as Federalist, 14, 57, 123; financial improprieties imputed to, 22, 24–25, 56–57, 107; foreign intervention opposed by, 98; French Revolution and, 79–80; furnishings of, 147, 149–53; geniality of, 19, 43, 47, 155, 194; Gouverneur Morris's